CHORAL MUSIC IN THE
TWENTIETH CENTURY

CHORAL MUSIC IN THE
TWENTIETH CENTURY

Nick Strimple

Amadeus Press

Originally published in hardcover by Amadeus Press in 2002

Paperback edition published in 2005 by

AMADEUS PRESS, LLC
512 Newark Pompton Turnpike
Pompton Plains, New Jersey 07444, USA

For sales, please contact

NORTH AMERICA

AMADEUS PRESS, LLC
c/o Hal Leonard Corp.
7777 West Bluemound Road
Milwaukee, Wisconsin 53213, USA
Phone: 800-637-2852
Fax: 414-774-3259

UNITED KINGDOM AND EUROPE

ROUNDHOUSE PUBLISHING LTD.
Millstone, Limers Lane
Northam, North Devon EX39 2RG, UK
Phone: 01237-474474
Fax: 01237-474774
E-mail: roundhouse.group@ukgateway.net

E-mail: orders@amadeuspress.com
Website: www.amadeuspress.com

Printed in the United States of America

The Library of Congress has cataloged the hardcover edition as follows:

Strimple, Nick.
        Choral music in the twentieth century / Nick Strimple.
            p.   cm.
        Includes bibliographical references (p.   ) and index.
        ISBN 1-57467-074-3
        1. Choral music—20ᵗʰ century—History and criticism. I. Title.

    ML1506.S77 2002
    782.5'09'04—dc21

                                                        2002018680

Cover: Nick Strimple conducts a performance in Salzburg's Universitätskirche (Kollegienkirche) by the Oratorio Society of New York, the Choral Society of Southern California, and the European Symposium Orchestra, 18 July 1982. Photo by Ralph Crawford.

In memory of my teachers

Charles C. Hirt

and

Marcel Couraud

CONTENTS

ACKNOWLEDGMENTS

I wish to thank the following people, without whose help this book could not have been completed:

Michael Isaacson, Albert McNeil, Alexander Ruggieri, Gilbert Seeley, and James H. Vail, who read the manuscript, or portions of it, and made many valuable corrections and suggestions;

Barbara Schoenberg, Lawrence Schoenberg, Randol Schoenberg, and Paul F. Cummins, who granted special permission to reprint the words of Arnold Schoenberg, Eric Zeisl, and Herbert Zipper;

So Ming Chuen Allison in Hong Kong, Adelpha Jane Diaz in the Philippines, Marcela Pulido in Colombia, and Nadine Breuer and Haesook Park in Los Angeles, who provided much valuable information, as did the Music Information Centers of many countries;

The Arnold Schoenberg Institute in Vienna, the State Jewish Museum in Prague, Jan Hanuš, and Charles C. Hirt, for providing manuscript materials;

Mimi Hiller and Dale Jergenson, who prepared the examples and illustrations, and Ruth Ballenger, who prepared the works lists and index.

Special thanks go to my editor, Mindy Seale, and my family, friends, and colleagues, who demonstrated wisdom and patience beyond measure.

Nick Strimple
Los Angeles, California

～ 1

A BRIEF OVERVIEW

Although some of the twentieth century's greatest works of art were choral, perceptions of choral music varied widely during the century, generating debates over its function, both in sacred and secular contexts, as well as its continued viability in terms of modern composition. For Leoš Janáček, at the beginning of the century, choral music was a natural extension of what he called "the music of Truth" (Střelcova 1994), the vocal folk music that he felt provided the only sufficient means of expressing profound humanistic and cultural ideas. But to critic Josef Woodard, reviewing a concert for the *Los Angeles Times* (26 January 1999), choral music had become only "an esoteric, if vital, tributary in the music world." In between, choral music educated children, promoted political agendas, enhanced worship, expanded experiences, created pleasing diversions, and provided hope for people in circumstances of extreme duress, as it has done in every other century.

CULMINATIONS AND NEW BEGINNINGS (1900–1932)

By 1900 the last great composers of the previous era were in the final stages of maturity. Most, like Sir Edward Elgar, Horatio Parker, Max Reger, Camille Saint-Saëns, and Richard Strauss, happily continued in their accustomed styles, while others, such as Claude Debussy, Charles Ives, Leoš Janáček, and Gustav Mahler, gave clear indications that a new age was dawning.

During the first three decades composers were profoundly affected by nationalism, technological advances, social instability, and the previously inconceivable ravages of World War I. The influence of religious institutions declined as knowledge of the human psyche increased. Social justice beckoned. Nineteenth-century romantic impulses seemed delusory or immoral and no longer had impact. Many young composers were attracted to the new ideals of impressionism or expressionism, while others sought their own language through the study of folk music, jazz, and pre-nineteenth-century music.

In France, Claude Debussy's impressionism influenced other composers and served as an exceptionally compatible ingredient in the development of Russian and Latin American music. Young composers from the United States also flocked to the music school at Fontainebleau to study with Nadia Boulanger, breaking the stylistic grip of older, German-trained composers at home. More attracted to French neoclassicism than impressionism, they returned to the United States with a solid technique, a very free approach to style, and in many cases an active interest in American folk music.

The choral medium was ideally suited to the incorporation of folk elements, and in some countries, such as Bulgaria, Latvia, and Denmark, the folk music revival in the first third of the century helped establish a vital choral tradition outside the church through interest in new choral arrangements of folk songs. Folk music study was not always confined to a composer's native region, and Indonesian, Balinese, Middle Eastern, South American, African, and Romanian elements exercised disproportionate influence throughout the century. South Americans and Palestinian Jews (soon to be called Israelis) organized choirs based on European models and used composition techniques learned in European conservatories to fuse indigenous elements into new national styles. Chinese, Japanese, Greek, and other composers adapted native scales to European structures and harmonies. In the United States, folk song arrangements provided a readily available and necessary secular component for choral music education in public schools. For composers such as Béla Bartók, Aaron Copland, Janáček, Darius Milhaud, and Ralph Vaughan Williams, folk music was a catalyst in the full realization of their genius.

Some sought a new vitality through reexamination of artistic roots separate from folk music. In France this resulted in the vilification of everything German and the glorification of technology and popular society, as exemplified by the group known as Les Six. In Germany the result was a renewed appreciation of Bach and certain of his predecessors, especially Heinrich Schütz. In Italy and other places there was renewed interest in Gregorian chant and Renaissance polyphony.

Many European composers were intrigued by the natural expressiveness of jazz—its syncopated rhythms, sensuous harmonies, and improvisational elasticity—and embraced it as a pure art form long before their American colleagues. It became indelibly fused with German cabaret style in the early twenties, and by 1933 several choral pieces had been written in jazz style, including the jazz oratorio *HMS Royal Oak* by Ervín Schulhoff and works by Emil Burian, Constant Lambert, and Kurt Weill.

In Vienna, Gustav Mahler propelled nineteenth-century aesthetics into uncharted waters with large symphonic canvases composed in an extravagantly personal and probing style well suited to psychoanalysis. Taking over from him, Arnold Schoenberg started a revolution by moving the emotionally supercharged and highly chromatic style of expressionism beyond the bounds of tonality, eventually codifying a composition system in which the twelve notes of the chromatic scale were equal and there was no functional harmonic hierarchy.

A young Russian named Igor Stravinsky started a revolution of his own by synthesizing impressionism, folk influences, elements of jazz, and polyphonic techniques of older composers, with his own highly original rhythmic, harmonic, and structural sensibilities.

By 1926, nearly a decade since the end of World War I, the aesthetic forces that would control the musical destiny of the century were in place: folk music, jazz, Bach (and his predecessors), Debussy, Mahler, Schoenberg, Stravinsky, and in the United States a one-man-band named Charles Ives. The world had six more years for these elements to settle before another terribly black force materialized.

WORLD WAR II: PRELUDE, HOLOCAUST, AND AFTERMATH (1933–1965)

In January 1933 Adolf Hitler became chancellor of Germany and immediately instituted profoundly terrifying social change. The first concentration camps were opened. Jazz was prohibited and other foreign art forms discouraged. Numerous artists, writers, and composers were declared unfit and their work dismissed as *Entartete künst* ("degenerate art"). Many people left Europe. Those who stayed in Germany and were not dyed-in-the-wool Nazis were forced into positions of compromise with the regime in order to survive. This was especially unfortunate for German Protestant composers, many of whom claimed, after the war, to have cooperated as little as possible with the government. However, in reality they had been trapped—some by ambition, some by pursuance of artistic agenda, but all by a tenet of Lutheran Orthodoxy laid down by the great reformer himself during the peasant revolt of 1525, which stipulated unswerving allegiance to civic authority no matter how unjust it might be.

In 1935 the Nuremberg Laws were passed, effectively removing Jews from participation in German society. Vaughan Williams and Hanns Eisler wrote prophetic choral works (respectively, *Dona nobis pacem* and *Deutsche Sinfonie*) as the world marched irrevocably toward war.

By 1937 reform of German church music was in full swing, perceived romantic excesses that had been in vogue since the late nineteenth century now replaced by a neobaroque style that would produce some of the twentieth century's finest choral music. Outside the church, Carl Orff polished his new "primitive" style, creating *Carmina burana*, the century's most popular large-scale choral work, while other German composers wrote overtly patriotic pieces.

On 29 September 1938, France, Italy, and Great Britain acquiesced to German demands concerning Czechoslovakia. Fewer than six weeks later, synagogues and Jewish shops were destroyed all over Germany. The following March, Germany annexed Czechoslovakia. These outrages were commemorated in moving choral works by Michael Tippett (*A Child of Our Time*) and Bohuslav Martinů (*Field Mass*).

World War II began in September 1939. Throughout the war, composers felt compelled to write all kinds of choral pieces. Sergei Prokofiev made a cantata from his score for the patriotic (or propagandistic) film *Alexander Nevsky*; Benjamin Britten wrote *The Ballad of Little Barnard and Lady Musgrave* as an entertainment for prisoners of war; Randall Thompson composed *The Testament of Freedom* as a patriotic gesture; Francis Poulenc's *Figure humaine* and Luigi Dallapiccola's *Canti di prigionia* were created as odes to freedom; Richard Strauss, sensing the end, wrote the moving *An den Baum Daphne*; Gideon Klein, William Hilsley, and others composed for choirs formed in various Nazi concentration camps. In Japan, Kiyoshi Nobutoki composed the inflammatory cantata *Along the Coast, Conquer the East*; Chinese composer Hsien Hsing-hai composed the inspirational *Yellow River Cantata*; and courageous Dutch, British, and Australian women formed an outstanding chorus in a prisoner-of-war camp much to the chagrined admiration of their Japanese captors.

At war's conclusion many younger composers came to terms with devastation and uncertainty by developing extremely objective styles, often based on Anton Webern's particularly acute serialism and increasingly utilizing electronically generated sounds. For some, choral music had little credibility, either because the sound was too sensuous or because the learning curve tended to be too slow for choruses newly exposed to avant-garde music. Other composers, among them Benjamin Britten, Jan Hanuš, Hans Werner Henze, Paul Hindemith, Dmitri Kabelevsky, György Ligeti, Frank Martin, Darius Milhaud, Dmitri Shostokovich, and Bernd Alois Zimmermann, produced commemorative or proactive political works to purge the conscience, ease the memory, and warn the future.

In countries not directly affected by World War II, avant-garde procedures were often embraced simply because of the new creative opportunities afforded. In South America especially, composers such as Alberto Ginastera, Gilberto Mendes, and Juan Orrego-Salas quietly assimilated serial and other new techniques into their nationalistic and impressionistic synthesis.

Many North American composers of choral music, confronted by prevailingly conservative tastes, became generally preoccupied with practical performance considerations and remained aloof from compositional experiments. Others eventually turned from choral music altogether in order to pursue more personally fulfilling aesthetic agendas. In Canada, parallel development of composition schools in the French neoclassic and English cathedral styles continued, while in the United States an alarming phenomenon emerged. Though all major composers espoused the importance of music education—Roy Harris, for example, gave speeches about grass roots music in schools, Aaron Copland wrote books to enlighten listeners, and Leonard Bernstein conducted young people's concerts—it was becoming obvious that most composers had no interest at all in education below the advanced high school or collegiate level. With the exception of a small group that included Henry Cowell, David Diamond (who wrote one piece for children), and Normand Lockwood, no important American composer felt the need to personally contribute to the repertoire for children. Simultaneously, the same composers, while continuing to set religious texts for concert works, developed a studied disinterest in liturgical music. The resulting absence of functional church music by major composers is inadvertently well illustrated in Robert Stevenson's chapter on American music in Friedrich Blume's *Protestant Church Music* (1974, 689–690), in which only large concert works on sacred texts are discussed. Most incongruous among the examples is *In the Beginning*, written by Aaron Copland, a Jew, for a secular contemporary music symposium at Harvard University. While some other countries witnessed a similar decline in production of liturgical music, the professional American composers' appalling abdication of responsibility in regard to children's repertoire is unique. The consequences were also typically American. Educators, church musicians, and other amateur composers rapidly filled the resulting vacuum, specialty publishing firms proliferated, and in the most blatant tradition of American commercialism, choral music in the United States was largely divided into three distinct markets: concert, educational, and church. Interconnected with these categories and yet standing apart from them, African American composers polished the art of the spiritual, and Jewish composers created a lively and varied repertoire for synagogue worship.

THE POSTMODERN WORLD (1966–2000)

In general, European composers born around the beginning of World War II were not initially interested in choral music. Some younger postwar composers considered the sensuousness of the human voice to be inappropriate in an era dominated by the threat of nuclear holocaust. Further, the aesthetic imperatives of John Cage (1912–1992) and Karlheinz Stockhausen (b. 1928) pointed toward a predominantly instrumental musical future. The direction of new music changed dramatically, however, with the premiere of Krzysztof Penderecki's *Saint Luke Passion* in 1966. Composers young and old were

thereafter filled with new confidence in the expressive potential of choral sing-
ing. Ensembles such as those conducted by Marcel Couraud—the Soloists of
LORT (French Radio) and later the Group Vocal du France—as well as the
John Aldis Choir in England, the Eric Ericson Chamber Choir in Sweden, the
Schoenberg Choir in Vienna, the University of the Philippines Madrigal
Singers, and the University of Southern California Chamber Singers, reinforced this optimism by demonstrating a previously unheard of technical
capacity. In Maurice Fleuret's words (1972, 20), "Music since Webern has
grown progressively more flexible. Chance elements have been used to expand
closed structures. Electronic modulation of sounds has coupled with *musique
concrete*. Mixed media and collage have put about a facile humanism. Expressionism and romanticism are back in force."

Marcel Couraud, c. 1977. Courtesy of Marcel Couraud.

Avant-garde elements became common in choral music throughout the
world from 1966 to 1976. Advanced techniques were most conducive for the
development of national styles, especially in Scandinavia, the Philippines, and
Israel. In Canada, R. Murray Schafer demonstrated that avant-garde music
could be a potent tool in music education.

At the same time, jazz was beginning to be taken much more seriously in
the United States, as were spirituals and other works by black composers.

Duke Ellington and Dave Brubeck created the first important American jazz works for chorus. Separately, vocal jazz ensembles and jazz choirs were formed (in Europe as well), not to champion the new works of Ellington and Brubeck, or the older works of Schulhoff or Lambert, but rather to perform choral arrangements of jazz standards. (Paradoxically, the large-scale jazz works of Brubeck, Ellington, Lambert, Nils Lindberg, Schulhoff, and others usually require the chorus to sing "classically" while the "jazz" is handled by instruments and vocal soloists.) After the Vietnam War, popular culture began to have a new and significant effect on American educational and religious systems. Music derived from popular styles became commonplace in churches, and show choirs developed in schools. The show choir phenomenon exerted an ever increasing influence on ensemble development in the United States, but, like the jazz choir movement, produced no significant original repertoire of its own, relying instead on choral arrangements of popular songs.

Throughout the century, choral music tended to be more conservative than its instrumental counterparts. Folk elements continued to dominate choral music throughout the Pacific Rim, the Middle East, and Latin America, and everywhere a panoply of advanced techniques mingled freely with more conservative tonal elements. During the last quarter of the century some composers, such as Osvaldo Golijov, Sofia Gubaidulina, and Tan Dun, embraced a paneclectic style to create remarkably stimulating and individualistic works. Older masters, such as Olivier Messiaen and Krzysztof Penderecki, synthesized their earlier styles into great tonal edifices. A few, like Hans Werner Henze, continued to write rather traditional dodecaphonic fare. Numerous younger composers, unaffected by the early and midcentury aversion to nineteenth-century romanticism, and newly acquainted with the delights of Frank Martin, Francis Poulenc, Randall Thompson, and Ralph Vaughan Williams, wrote unabashedly old-fashioned music. Several paid homage to the Renaissance motet. Morten Lauridsen honored the French cabaret song. William Hawley devised a faux-nineteenth-century style so generic as to be confused with Felix Mendelssohn, Camille Saint-Saëns, or Sir Arthur Sullivan. Minimalists explored the continued potency of unadorned triads. Thus, as the new millennium dawned, many composers were more inclined to glance over their shoulders than to gaze into the future.

✍ 2

AUSTRIA AND GERMANY

At the turn of the century, Gustav Mahler (1860–1911) had already composed his first great symphonies incorporating chorus: No. 2 (*Resurrection*) and No. 3. By 1906, when he composed the Eighth Symphony ("Symphony of a Thousand") for seven soloists, mixed chorus, children's chorus, and very large orchestra, concertgoers on both sides of the Atlantic were familiar with his expansive, psychologically probing style. Even so, few were prepared for the new work, which combined a medieval Latin text with the final scene of Goethe's *Faust*, and at the end of the century critics were still struggling to come to grips with it. From its highly successful premiere in Munich in 1910 (by most accounts, the pinnacle of Mahler's career) through the third quarter of the century, it was either intensely hated or loved almost without reservation. A journalist for *Chronik der Stadt München*, for example, remarked when reviewing the premiere that "the success of the evening was extraordinary, as befitted the participation in it of the whole musical world. The final scene left an unforgettable impression" (Blaukopf 1976, 267). Yet two days later a reviewer for *Münchener Neueste Nachrichten* stated flatly that he had "never been able to rouse either admiration or even a trace of sympathy for this sort of music" (Blaukopf 1976, 268). As late as 1978, Egon Gartenberg (322) would write that "regardless of how kind or cruel history's judgment will be, Mahler's Eighth Symphony unquestionably represents the end of one development that began with Beethoven's *Eroica*—with respect to the enlargement of sonorities and form—and of another that began with Beethoven's Ninth—with respect to inclusion of the human voice into the symphonic structure." This reflects the widely held view, still orthodox in 1978, that Mahler constituted a summation of nineteenth-century aesthetics—a view inadvertently promoted by Mahler himself, who considered the Eighth Symphony the culmination of his middle period.

The notion of Mahler as only the fulfillment of a stylistic era is misleading, however, in that it does not acknowledge the impact that he exerted on composition throughout the twentieth century. Certainly, various techniques asso-

16

ciated with Beethoven were fulfilled in Mahler; and since his tonal language was essentially diatonic and remained firmly planted in the major-minor system, the truly original aspects of his vision were not immediately apparent to listeners like the aforementioned critic of the *Münchener Neueste Nachrichten*. Furthermore, since he did not surround himself with compositional disciples, as did Schoenberg, no official Mahlerian school of composition developed. By 1999, though, it had become clear that the century's numerous symphonies with voice or chorus were more indebted to Mahler's models than to Beethoven, and that many important composers, including Luciano Berio, Leonard Bernstein, Benjamin Britten, Alfredo Casella, Jan Hanuš, Alfred Schnittke, Anton Webern, and Alexander Zemlinsky, were otherwise profoundly influenced by him.

By the last decade of the century, too, critics had adopted a more balanced approach, perceiving Mahler's greatness but with warts attached. In this generally receptive climate, the Eighth Symphony still elicited astonishing remarks. Discussing letters Mahler sent to his wife concerning Goethe's text, the highly respected commentator Michael Kennedy (1991, 151) claimed to find a kind of antisemitism in the composer's humanistic mysticism, which he praised with an apparently straight face:

> Could there be more eloquent testimony to the extraordinary breadth of Mahler's human sympathy and to the power of the mysticism which impelled his creative activity, a mysticism with roots far deeper than the Catholicism superficially implicit in some of Goethe's text and deeper too than any atavistic Judaism? Indeed Mahler is an exemplar of Bryan Magee's assertion, in his splendid *Aspects of Wagner* (London, 1968), that "it is only Jews who have escaped from their religious and intellectual tradition who have achieved greatness." So much for the impulse behind the Eighth Symphony.

Rudolf Louis, writing for *Die Deutsche Musik der Gegenwart* in 1909, complained that Mahler "speaks musical German, but with an accent, with an inflection, and above all, with the gestures of an eastern, all too eastern Jew. So, even to those whom it does not offend directly, it cannot possibly communicate anything" (Slonimsky 2000, 121). Decades later, the Nazi musicologist Karl Blessinger (1939), continuing these sentiments, sought to insult Mahler by referring to his "rabbinical mind." Kennedy's comment may have been intended to counter this view, but it is still flagrantly antisemitic.

Like Beethoven's *Missa solemnis*, the Eighth Symphony looks both backward and forward. For instance, the diatonic and somewhat four-square nature of the thematic material is closer in spirit to Mahler's early symphonies than to the Eighth's immediate predecessors (the Sixth and Seventh Symphonies); and the contrapuntal skill exhibited in the first movement's gigantic double fugue recalls several masters from a previous age. Still, an astute contemporary observed new tendencies. In a letter to Mahler, Bruno Walter wrote, "[In the Fifth through Eighth Symphonies] you are less and less inclined explicitly to harmonize your melodies. Instead, you develop several melodic lines that seem completely independent and hence achieve a purely horizontal texture. Their vertical meeting results in harmonic progressions that are as economical as possible and yet as full as necessary. In that way you arrive at an extremely complicated polyphonic style, whose necessary artistic contrast could only be provided by occasional, very simple harmony" (Floros 1993, 242).

The Eighth points toward other new territory as well. There is no preexisting model for its two-movement structure. While there may be broad organizational precedents for the movements if considered individually, there is no model for the ways in which Mahler interfaces material from the first movement to the next. There is no precedent for the psychological and theological complexities inherent in the choice of texts, and—outside Mahler's own works, at least—its resulting cathartic impact on the listener.

Max Bruch (1838–1920) remained firmly planted in the nineteenth century to the very end of his long life. His immediately attractive style, unconcerned with progressive tendencies, was international in the sense that it often incorporated folk music from other countries. His contemporaries regarded him primarily as a master of choral composition, especially in large forms, but his oratorios, such as the massive *Moses* (1896), and other works fell quickly into disuse after his death, eventually to be revived during the last decade of the twentieth century. His last twenty years saw the completion of nine large works with orchestra and two sets of partsongs, including *Damajanti*, Opus 78 (1903), a cantata on an anonymous Indian poem; *Österkantate*, Opus 81 (1908) for soprano, chorus, and orchestra; *Sechs Lieder*, Opus 86 (1911) for mixed chorus; and *Trauerfeier für Mignon*, Opus 93 (1919) for soloists, double chorus, organ, and orchestra.

Max Reger (1873–1916) was influenced by German romanticism in general and by Wagner and Bach in particular. For him, harmony and counterpoint were equal. This translated in his music as frequent, sometimes sudden, and occasionally awkward modulations within a complex contrapuntal fabric. Although he was Catholic, his abiding love of Lutheran chorales is apparent in his *Four Chorale Cantatas* (1903) and the somewhat more homophonic nature of the late partsongs and motets. An appreciation of Brahms can be seen in his works for alto solo: *Weihegesang* (1908), with mixed chorus and winds, and *Die Weihe der Nacht*, Opus 119 (1911), with male chorus and orchestra. Other interesting late works are *Die Nonnen*, Opus 112 (1909) for chorus and orchestra, *Acht geistliche Gesänge*, Opus 138 (1914) for mixed chorus, and the deeply spiritual pieces of *Zwei Gesänge*, Opus 144 (1915): "Der Einsiedler" and "Requiem."

Georg Schumann (1866–1952), an important choral conductor and teacher, served as music director of the Danzig Gesängverein and Bremen Philharmonic Orchestra and Chorus before being named director of the Berlin Singakademie. He held the last position for fifty years, influencing succeeding generations of conductors and composers. Early in the century his major works were considered important representatives of German style. The oratorio *Ruth*, Opus 50 (1909), for instance, was impressive enough to warrant performances outside Germany, specifically at England's Sheffield Festival in 1911 and by the New York Oratorio Society in 1913. But his works are mostly forgotten now, with only a few of his smaller pieces, like *Three Chorale Motets*, Opus 75, written in a fully blossomed late-nineteenth-century style, still being occasionally performed. The small piece *How Great Are Thy Wonders*, edited by Paul Christiansen, found an extended life as an anthem in the United States.

Hans Pfitzner (1869–1949) was an ultranationalist Wagnerite, totally devoted to nineteenth-century concepts of German art and willing to defend those concepts in print, as demonstrated in "The New Aesthetic and Musical Impotency" (1919), an essay in which he attacked Busoni, Schoenberg, and other modernists. Of his several choral compositions, all but one date from after 1900, and all are secular, with texts chosen from a wide variety of authors (all German, except for Michelangelo, including Richard Dehmel, Joseph von Eichendorff, Goethe, and Heinrich von Kleist). Perhaps the most representative is the cantata *Von deutscher Seele* (1922), a heartfelt, if not to say self-indulgent, expression of the intricacies and profundities of the German spirit. It is perhaps no surprise that after a successful premiere in Berlin it failed to win an audience beyond the Rhine.

The choral music of Richard Strauss (1864–1949) is now virtually unknown, with the exception perhaps of *Deutsche Motet* (1913). However, much of this music is as excellent as his operas and symphonic works. Most of the choral pieces were written early in the new century, before Strauss turned his attention to the Nazi regime, which he initially viewed as a potential ally in the reform of German opera but which, before long, left him quite disillusioned. In November 1933 he accepted Goebbels's invitation to become president of the Reich's Music Chamber, and served in that capacity until the middle of 1935, when he was ousted because of his continued support of his Jewish librettist Stefan Zweig. Even though his music was popular throughout German society and frequently performed, Strauss was personally snubbed by the governmental hierarchy, and following the infamous Kristallnacht of 1938, his family was hounded by the Gestapo because his daughter-in-law was Jewish.

Like Pfitzner, Strauss's style matured before the turn of the century, although his was much less narrowly nationalistic. Thereafter, he did not concern himself with the vicissitudes of modern trends. The enormous cantata *Taillefer* (1902–03), a romanticized ballad about the Battle of Hastings, represents Strauss at his most expansive. There are numerous smaller settings for male voices, including *Six Folk Songs* (1905), *Cantata* (1914), the wonderfully entertaining *Die Göttin im Putzzimmer* (The Goddess in the Boudoir, 1935), and some occasional pieces with orchestra. Two are masterpieces: *Deutsche Motette* (1913) for soloists and sixteen-part mixed chorus, often considered the most difficult of all tonal choral works, and *An den Baum Daphne* (1943) for double mixed chorus and boys' choir, his last choral piece, written as an epilogue to the opera *Daphne*. *Deutsche Motette*, which explores the extremes of vocal range and effectively contrasts antiphonal and polyphonic effects in a highly chromatic and contrapuntal fabric, requires performers of the utmost professionalism. *An den Baum Daphne* imaginatively recycles themes from *Daphne* to create a different commentary on the opera's final scene. It was designed for the Vienna State Opera Chorus, but circumstances toward the end of the war prevented performance, and it was not premiered until 1947.

Arnold Mendelssohn (1855–1933), Heinrich Kaminski (1886–1946), and Kurt Thomas (1904–1973) made valuable contributions to Protestant choral music during the first four decades of the century.

Arnold Mendelssohn was distinguished as a teacher (Paul Hindemith was one of his pupils), a choral scholar who edited works of Heinrich Schütz and Hans Leo Hassler, and an early advocate of a return to post-reformation ideals in liturgical music, an idea that would be taken up with lasting effect by Hugo Distler, Ernst Pepping, and others. In addition to several cantatas for chorus, organ, and orchestra, his works include *Deutsche Messe* (1923) for eight-part mixed chorus and the fourteen liturgical motets of *Geistliche Chormusik* (1926).

Heinrich Kaminski was a member of the Old Catholic church, a small denomination begun in 1871 by Kaminski's father and other German and Swiss academics who could not accept the Vatican's pronouncement, in 1870, that the pope was infallible when speaking *ex cathedra*. He therefore stood somewhat apart from the various musical factions already operating among German Protestants. His style derived initially from Bach and Brahms, with late romantic harmonies supporting tightly controlled, multilayered counterpoint. His later pieces, however, are marked by ever increasing harmonic austerity. Kaminski's music is encompassed by profound and unique mysticism, quite unlike that of his contemporaries, but similar to the more recent aesthetic of Georges Migot, Arvo Pärt, or John Tavener. Among his best compositions are *Psalm 130* (1912) for mixed chorus, *Magnificat* (1925) for

soprano, offstage chamber chorus, viola, and orchestra, and the unaccompanied *Messe deutsch* (1934), an astounding three-movement contemplation of
the words *Kyrieleis*, *Christe eleison*, and *Gloria patri*. This last piece emerged
as though from the depths of Kaminski's soul, having virtually nothing in
common with traditional Lutheran vernacular or chorale cantus-firmus
Masses.

Kurt Thomas, a student of Mendelssohn, lived and worked well into the
second half of the century, but his primary impact as a composer occurred
between 1925 and 1935. During that period he produced Latin Mass in A
(1925) for double chorus and soloists, and the double chorus *Psalm 137*
(1925), both generating considerable public interest in newly perceived possibilities for unaccompanied choral writing. His chorale cantata *Jerusalem, du
hochgebaute Stadt* (1928–29) for soloists, chorus, organ, and orchestra, as
well as several smaller choral pieces, helped pave the way for the following
decade's church music reformers by focusing attention on post-reformation
forms. When Thomas was named conductor of the choir at the Leipzig Institute of Church Music in 1928, his immense talent as a choral conductor manifested itself. Although he continued to compose, his most important contributions thereafter were in the realm of choral development, culminating
in the famous *Lehrbuch der Chorleitung* (Handbook of Choral Directing,
1935–48).

Arnold Schoenberg and the Second Viennese School

Arnold Schoenberg (1874–1951) is surely among the most influential composers in history. When the old compositional system no longer provided
adequate options for him, the development of the twelve-tone system became
not only necessary but inevitable. Thereafter, he was often viewed as intoler-
ant of other techniques, a view aided in part by his own comments. Hyper-
sensitive to criticism and driven by a heightened sense of justice and integrity,
Schoenberg never minced words. For example, in the preface to *Three Satires*
(1925) he listed his "targets" as "all those who seek their personal salvation
by taking the middle course [sometimes translated as "all those who seek
refuge in mediocrity"] . . . [and] those who pretend to strive *back to*. . . . Folk-
lorists are my target as well, who apply a technique, which only suits a complicated way of thinking, to the naturally primitive ideas of folk music. . . .
Finally all . . . *ists* in whom I can see only mannerists" (Nono 1988, 25).
Though Schoenberg was clearly very uncompromising, the real targets of his
writings seem to be artists who are not true to themselves. Even when his student Hanns Eisler abandoned him to seek a style compatible with leftist philosophy, Schoenberg's letters clearly indicate more displeasure with Eisler's
handling of the schism than with his differing viewpoint. To a student express-

ing disdain for Shostokovich, Schoenberg snapped, "Never let me hear you speak of Shostokovich in that way! He is a composer born" (Raksin 1989, 5).

Schoenberg spent his life being true to himself and his art. It is good to know, therefore, that he was a friend, admirer, and tennis buddy of George Gershwin, and also, according to his student David Raksin (1989, 1), that he was quite proud of Raksin's success as a composer of film and popular music. It is also worth remembering that he never repudiated his early compositions and that well into his maturity he composed several folk song settings and other pieces that do not use the twelve-tone system. In a 1923 letter to Werner Reinhart, Schoenberg wrote, "For the present, it matters more to me if people understand my older works. . . . They are the natural forerunners of my later works, and only those who understand and comprehend these will be able to acquire a broader understanding of the later works that goes beyond the fashionable bare-minimum. . . . I do not attach so much importance to being a musical bogey-man as to being a natural continuer of properly understood good old tradition!" (Stein 1987, 100).

Whether or not Schoenberg was writing in twelve-tone technique, the most outstanding characteristic of his music is an unrelenting emotional intensity. He understood, too, that sentimentality is often confused with emotion. Time and again he argued against—and complained about—sentimentality in music. In a note he wrote to himself sometime after moving to Los Angeles in 1934 (Nono 1988, 125), Schoenberg discussed the emotions that dominate his own music:

> My music's supposedly not emotional: Of course it is not, "Oh darling. I love you so much." There are also other kinds of love, for instance Alberich's, Monostaten's, Don Juan's. But also Petrarca's (not expecting early reward). There are also different kinds of emotion. There is jealousy, hatred, enthusiasm. There is love of ideals, of virtues, of one's country, town, or village, and its inhabitants. There is not only joy, there is also sadness, mourning, pity, and envy. There is also anger. There is contempt, pride, devotion, madness, fear, panic, courage, admiration. Love of justice, of honesty, of good manners. Love of good food and drinks and of the beauty of nature; of animals, flowers, and exotic stones!

Schoenberg's first choral work, *Gurrelieder* (1900–01), is a setting of Robert Franz Arnold's German translation of an epic Danish poem by Jens Peter Jacobson (1847–1885). Pressed by other responsibilities, Schoenberg did not complete the orchestration until 1911, and *Gurrelieder* did not premiere until 1913 in Vienna's Singverein. This first performance ended with an ovation that lasted for over fifteen minutes. Schoenberg, however, while acknowledging the praise of the performers, refused to acknowledge the audience, feeling that these same people had not properly appreciated his more recent work. While this incident has come to represent Schoenberg's supposed intractability, *Gurrelieder* itself has come to represent a great valedictory of nineteenth-century German procedures. This view is difficult to defend, though, when one considers that German romanticism continued to thrive after 1901, in the hands of Mahler, Zemlinsky, Pfitzner, and Richard Strauss. *Gurrelieder* is perhaps better understood as Schoenberg's first great experiment, utilizing the methods and resources then at hand. For example, tonalities are expanded in impressionistic ways; the melodrama of part three is the direct predecessor of *Pierrot lunaire*; and the huge orchestra's winds are divided into sets of four so that each individual tone color can produce a complete chord. Further, the male voices in one section are divided into three four-part choirs of considerable contrapuntal complexity, each doubled by a different family of orchestral instruments. The effect, while tremendous, requires an inordinately large number of singers. Schoenberg would never again resort to this kind of extravagance.

In 1950 Schoenberg provided a practical performance instruction for *Gurrelieder* that is of particular interest, since it surely pertains to his other choral works as well: "ONE THING IS VERY IMPORTANT [Schoenberg's capitals]: Make the performance in ENGLISH, not in German. People do not understand German, neither here [United States], nor in Australia, England, Canada, and in many other places. There is an excellent translation. . . . There is no reason why it should be given in German" (Stein 1987, 282). This reflects a still-flourishing Continental view that music should be performed in the language of the listeners, since singers should be trained well enough to make the text intelligible. Rather than considering the value of foreign languages to performers in educational situations, or remaining absolutely true to a composer's original text underlay, foreign language performance is considered a kind of faux sophistication, which further widens what Paul Hindemith called a "gulf between producers and consumers" of music (Blom 1954, 4:288). In any case, it is clear that Schoenberg wanted audiences to understand the texts. He was fond of *Gurrelieder* throughout his life. In 1949 he wrote about the "merits in expression and color that counterbalance the deficiencies. Especially in peculiarities of construction of phrases and in their relation to a fast-moving harmony, much can be seen that at least in my music has become important. I am not ashamed when people call me a romanticist. If making music is not romantic, what else can it be?" (Nono 1988, 115).

His next choral work, *Friede auf Erden*, Opus 13 (Peace on Earth, 1906) had almost become standard repertoire for the world's better choirs by the end of the century, with excellent performances occurring rather frequently. However, the comments Schoenberg made to Hermann Scherchen in 1923

(Stein 1987, 96) not only reveal his practicality but also clearly indicate that choruses in the century's early decades were not really prepared to sing modern music, even when the works were tonal: "My chorus *Peace on Earth* is an illusion for mixed choir, an illusion, as I know today. For when I composed it in 1906 I believed that pure harmony was conceivable. . . . Since then I have had to learn to yield and have learned that *Peace on Earth* is only possible if the harmony is closely safeguarded, in a word, not left unaccompanied."

It is somewhat surprising then that Schoenberg's first twelve-tone choruses—*Four Partsongs*, Opus 27 (1925) and *Three Satires*, Opus 28—are mostly unaccompanied. The apparent contradiction, however, may be explained by the completely different nature of the compositions. *Peace on Earth* relies heavily on rich vertical sonorities that are difficult to tune, while *Four Partsongs* and *Three Satires* are conceived linearly and can be effectively performed as vocal quartets. *Four Partsongs* is not as striking as *Three Satires*, but the last movement, in which violin, clarinet, cello, and mandolin weave an elaborate tapestry around rather static vocal lines, is an interesting, accessible, and quite beautiful introduction to twelve-tone technique.

Shortly after composing Opuses 27 and 28, Schoenberg set *Three German Folk Songs* (1929), to be followed much later by *Three Folk Songs*, Opus 49 (1948). Unabashedly tonal, these pieces range from rather simple, straightforward settings to complicated constructs in which the folk tune serves only as a basis for contrapuntal exercise. In the middle of these extremes is an undisputed jewel from *Three German Folk Songs*, "Schein uns, du liebe Sonne." In this setting each voice sings part of the melody in turn, while an ever changing contrapuntal web—created from small motives inherent in the tune—is spun around it. Miraculously, the character of the theme is never lost, and the intensely understated opening of verse three is absolutely riveting.

Arnold Schoenberg: "Schein uns, du liebe Sonne," measures 35–40.

In November 1941 Schoenberg wrote to Paul Dessau concerning *Kol nidre*, Opus 39 (1938) for speaker, mixed chorus, and chamber orchestra, written for Rabbi Jacob Sonderling:

> At my request the text of the traditional Kol nidre was altered, but the introduction was an idea of Dr. Sonderling's. When I first saw the traditional text I was horrified by the traditional view that all the obligations that have been assumed during the year are supposed to be cancelled on the Day of Atonement. Since this view is truly immoral, I consider it false. It is diametrically opposed to the lofty morality of all the Jewish commandments. From the very first moment I was convinced (as later proved correct, when I read that the Kol nidre originated in Spain) that it merely meant that all who had either voluntarily or under pressure made believe to accept the Christian faith (and who were therefore to be excluded from the Jewish community) might, on this Day of Atonement, be reconciled with their God, and that all oaths (vows) were cancelled. (Stein 1987, 212)

In earlier writings Schoenberg commented that this seemed to him "the very idea of atonement" (Nono 1988, 94). He explained to Dessau that as he created his melody out of various traditional versions he "chose the phrases that a number of versions had in common and put them into a reasonable order . . . vitriolizing out the cello-sentimentality of the Bruchs, etc., and giving this DECREE the dignity of . . . an *edict* [Schoenberg's emphases]." In conclusion he added, "I am very glad you like the piece. . . . It is a pity that people . . . decline to adopt the piece for use in the synagogue, on ritual and musical grounds. I believe it must be tremendously effective both in the synagogue and in the concert hall."

The primary objections to synagogue use were removed in 1992, when Leonard Stein, following Schoenberg's suggestion, finally completed an organ transcription of the orchestration. Schoenberg was correct in thinking *Kol nidre* a powerful work. It is puzzling, in fact, that "Schoenberg's shocker," as one critic referred to it (*Los Angeles Times*, 30 May 1992), is not more widely performed, considering that it is not twelve-tone (but in fact quite tonal), the choral writing not difficult, and the orchestra not large.

In 1944 the popular Hollywood composer and arranger Nathaniel Shilkret (1895–1989) commissioned several leading composers, including Schoenberg, to participate in an attempt to set the entire Bible. The enormous project got only as far as Genesis and includes the following works, in addition to a piece by Shilkret himself: the textless "Genesis Prelude" by Schoenberg, "Adam and Eve" by Alexandre Tansman, "Cain and Abel" by Darius Milhaud, "Noah's Ark" by Mario Castelnuovo-Tedesco, "The Covenant" by Ernst Toch, and "Babel" by Igor Stravinsky. The resulting *Genesis Suite* was performed and subsequently recorded privately, at Shilkret's expense, in Los

Angeles in 1945. Schoenberg entitled his contribution with an eye to independent performance. Even so, "Genesis Prelude" (1945) for chorus and orchestra has remained essentially unknown, although it contains much to recommend it. In program notes for the Los Angeles Philharmonic in 1981, Eric Salzman (1981, 30) commented that "a prelude to Creation is traditionally supposed to represent Chaos but the basic conception underlying Schoenberg's version might be described as creative, complex, resolved order." Thoroughly twelve-tone, it is laid out as a large prelude and double fugue. A particularly interesting aspect of the serial writing is Schoenberg's creation of new tone rows by combining the original and inversion forms of each hexachord. Since the result is new material created from existing matter, this might be considered a dodecaphonic representation of the Creation narrative.

Schoenberg's musical reaction to the Holocaust, *A Survivor from Warsaw*, Opus 46 (1947) for speaker, male chorus, and orchestra, is one of his most accessible twelve-tone works (if one can use the term *accessible* in regard to anything relating to the deaths of millions of people). The directness of the music is so appropriate to the subject matter and text that listeners are simply drawn into it without having time to consider the compositional technique. The unison male chorus sings only once, coming in at the end of the piece with *Shema Yisroel* (Hear, O Israel, the Lord Our God Is One), which had a special meaning for Schoenberg:

> I think the *Shema Yisroel* is the *Glaubensbekenntnis*, the confession of the Jew. It is our thinking of the one, eternal God who is invisible, who forbids imitations. . . . The miracle is, to me, that all these people who might have forgotten, for years, that they are Jews, suddenly facing death, remember who they are. And this seems to me a great thing. (Nono 1988, 105)

The choral writing is rhythmically complex, though not particularly difficult, and the dramatically effective men's entrance is well timed. Good performances of this little masterpiece are overpowering.

Other choral works include the oratorio fragment *Die Jacobsleiter* (1917) and the three of Opus 50: *Dreimal tausend Jahre* (1949); *Psalm 130* (1950), his last completed composition; and *Moderner Psalm*, left incomplete.

Anton Webern (1883–1945) and Alban Berg (1885–1935), two of Schoenberg's students, who along with him were the primary composers of the Second Viennese School, produced only a small amount of choral music.

Anton Webern developed the most extremely concentrated and uncompromising serial technique of all Schoenberg's pupils. He also had the most profound impact on the next generation of composers in Europe and the Americas. Webern's years of experience as a choral conductor in Vienna (1926–34) inform his choral works, even though the later serial pieces are

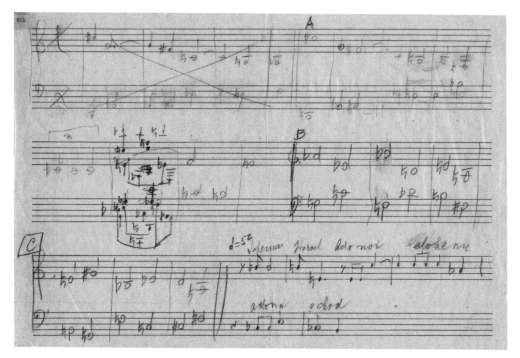

Manuscript page of Arnold Schoenberg's *A Survivor from Warsaw*. Courtesy of the Arnold Schoenberg Center.

quite difficult. The very early *Entflieht auf leichten Kähnen*, Opus 2 (1908) is a strict double canon written in a lushly chromatic post-romantic style. The constantly evolving tonalities resolve beautifully into a final G major chord. *Two Songs*, Opus 19 (1926) for mixed chorus, on texts by Goethe, is especially interesting for its imaginative chamber ensemble accompaniment: violin, two clarinets, celesta, and guitar. The choral-orchestral works *Das Augenlicht*, Opus 26 (1935) for mixed chorus and orchestra, Cantata No. 1, Opus 29 (1938–39) for soprano, mixed chorus, and orchestra, and Cantata No. 2 (1941–43) for soprano and bass soloists, mixed chorus, and orchestra are all on texts by Hildegard Jone. Dominated by canonic writing, they are examples of Webern's most mature serialism. His abiding admiration of Mahler—in this case, the ambiguous formal structures of Mahler's late works—is reflected in the last movement of Cantata No. 1, which Webern characterized as a simultaneous four-voice fugue, scherzo, and set of variations. A third cantata, also on text by Jone, was left incomplete at the composer's death.

Alban Berg left only two small pieces. The early *Die Nachtigall* for four SATB choruses clearly indicates that Berg was well versed in the post-romantic style of early-twentieth-century Vienna, and that the use of timbres at the extreme limits of vocal range, which would become prominent in the work of later serialists, already held interest for him. The four-voice canon *An das Frankfurter Opernhaus* (1930) is simply an exercise in counterpoint.

Among others active before 1933 was Karl Marx (1897–1985), who studied at the Munich Academy of Music. In 1928, a few years after graduating, he became director of the Munich Bach Society Chorus. During World War II he taught in Graz, moving to a similar position in Stuttgart after the war. Primarily a vocal composer, Marx produced a very large number of choral works notable for their solid craftsmanship, polyphonic finesse, and practical understanding of the voice. His works include at least fifteen partsong cycles, beginning with *Drei gemischten Chöre*, Opus 1 (1925), on texts by Rainer Maria Rilke, and other unaccompanied pieces on secular and sacred texts, as well as several larger works including two on texts by Friedrich Hölderlin: *Und endet doch alles mit Frieden* (1953) for soloists, mixed chorus, and orchestra, and *Versöhnender* (1973) for mixed chorus and strings.

In addition to his absorption of Schoenberg's principles, Ernst Krenek (1900–1991) was also influenced by jazz and Renaissance polyphony. Igor Stravinsky described Krenek as "an intellectual and a composer, a difficult combination to manage, and he is profoundly religious, which goes nicely with the composer side, less nicely with the other thing" (Stravinsky and Craft 1963). Krenek himself alluded to this conflict in brief comments on composing and listening, which appeared in a biographical catalogue entitled *Ernst Krenek*, published in New York by Broadcast Music International (BMI) in 1968:

> Music may be appreciated on different levels, separately or simultaneously: as a vital force that affects us immediately, at the core of our being; as a symbolism that through traditional associations suggests emotional qualities; as an artful combination of sound materials that fascinates our intellect. In a great work of music these elements are integrated, and the listener will enjoy such a work to the fullest extent if he is mentally equipped for such a three-fold integrating perception. Aesthetic study will go very far in explaining the artistic perfection of a great work. Psychological investigation may reveal just what musical factors cause the particular emotional reactions to such a work. It is the element of vitality that seems to defy analysis. We only know that it must be present, for without it neither the subjective soulfulness nor the intricate construction will suffice to arouse our sustained attention. One may call this mysterious element "inspiration," which is substituting one unknown quantity for another. The only control that a composer has over the factor of inspiration is that he must not release any musical thoughts of which he is not absolutely sure that they completely satisfy his inner vision. In other words, he must like what he has written to

such an extent that even after thorough search of his conscience he would not consider changing a single note. If he does that, he has done all that is humanly possible. Whether the criteria by which his nature compels him to decide what he likes are the right ones in order to endow his work with greatness and vitality, is a matter of divine grace.

This intellectual-inspirational dichotomy is obvious in Krenek's music and plays out in surprising ways. For example, the intensely chromatic motet *O Holy Ghost* (1964) for unaccompanied mixed chorus leaves the impression of a purely emotional outburst, while the uncompromising neo-Renaissance diatonicism of *Psalmverse zur Kommunion* (1955), also for unaccompanied mixed chorus, strikes the listener as a much more intellectual work, even though it stands sonically in stark contrast to the popular conception of Krenek's music.

Ernst Krenek: final measures of *O Holy Ghost*.

Ernst Krenek: final measures of *Psalmverse zur Kommunion*.

Perhaps Krenek's most important work based on serial procedures is the exceptionally difficult *The Lamentations of Jeremiah the Prophet*, Opus 93 (1941–42) for unaccompanied mixed chorus, which had considerable influence on Stravinsky's *Threni: id est Lamentationes Jeremiae prophetae*. (Krenek details the specific serial procedures in Lang 1960, 72–94; discusses its medieval roots in Hines 1963, 24; and comments on the impetus for its composition in Town and Schrock 1991, 6–7.) Among his numerous other choral compositions are *Three Madrigals and Three Motets*, Opus 174 (1960) for children's choir, *The Santa Fe Timetable*, Opus 102 (1945) for mixed chorus, and the oratorio *Opus sine nomine*, Opus 238 (1980–88) for mixed chorus and large orchestra.

Like Krenek, Paul Hindemith (1895–1963) was eventually forced out of Germany by the Nazis. However, his style was far removed from that of Krenek and other serialists. Early on he repudiated not only Schoenberg's system but also his ideas concerning emotional and psychological expression through music, preferring to develop an uncompromisingly objective view of tonality and counterpoint that was often harsh and dry. In 1927 his concern that composers were separating themselves from their audience forced him to reevaluate his aesthetic principles.

By the time of his first big choral work, the oratorio *Das Unaufhörliche* (The One Perpetual, 1931), Hindemith had loosened up enough to produce a more warmly compelling musical effect. Even so, the oratorio is still a remarkably intellectual reaction to the Weimar Republic's volatile political situation. The libretto, greatly influenced by Goethe, views creative acts by poets and others as transformation, or "perpetual," and virtually everything else—including love, history, religion, and technology—as resistance to it.

Hindemith's complete conversion to a more accessible style, obvious by 1934, was brought about through his involvement with amateurs. His idea, similar to Benjamin Britten's (see chapter 4), was to provide opportunities and compositions for children, parents, teachers, townspeople—in short, everybody—to share in the experience of music making. Being a teacher, it was natural for him to become involved with the musical undertakings of the *Jugendbewegung* (Youth Activities Organization), for which he wrote a series of pieces. Unfortunately, a term that became attached to this—*Gebrauchsmusik*—does not exactly fit the concept, as Hindemith (1952) himself explained:

> In a discussion with German choral conductors, I pointed out the danger of an esoteric isolationism in music by using the term *Gebrauchsmusik*. Apart from the ugliness of the word—in German it is as hideous as its English equivalents workaday music, music for use, utility music, and similar verbal beauties—nobody found anything remarkable in it . . . and when, years after, I first came to [the United States], I felt

like the sorcerer's apprentice who had become the victim of his own conjurations: the slogan *Gebrauchsmusik* hit me wherever I went, it had grown to be as abundant, useless, and disturbing as thousands of dandelions in a lawn.

Hindemith much preferred the term *Sing- und Spielmusik* (Sing- and Play-music), though terminology aside, he produced some interesting and effective music to promulgate the concept that music should be for everybody. Two works in this vein are cantatas. The first, saddled with an ungainly title, is *Admonition to Youth to Apply Itself to Music* (sometimes simply translated as *Advice to Youth*, 1932) for children's choir, speaker, and string orchestra, with ad libitum vocal soloist, winds, and percussion. It is part of the last set of *Sing- und Spielmusik*, composed before the Nazis took control and prohibited Hindemith's further participation with the *Jugendbewegung*. The second work is actually a collection of three smaller cantatas, all calling for audience participation and known collectively as *Ite, angeli veloces*. The individual cantatas include *Cantique de l'espérance* (1952), which was written for the 1953 UNESCO Convention, *Chant de triomphe du roi David* (1955), and *Custos quid de nocte* (1955).

Hindemith settled in the United States in 1939, where he produced his best-known choral works: *Six Chansons* (1939), on texts by Rainer Maria Rilke, *When Lilacs Last in the Dooryard Bloom'd: Requiem for Those We Love* (1946), and *Apparebit repentina dies* (1947).

Six Chansons provides basic examples of Hindemith's mature style. Tonalities are clear-cut, with many open sonorities and important cadences on major triads. As implied by the title, the forms are simple and straightforward. Here Hindemith demonstrates his melodic and accompanimental abilities, as opposed to the complex contrapuntal techniques showcased in other works.

Like numerous other composers, Hindemith was quite attracted to the poetry of Walt Whitman. When World War II ended, preceded closely by the death of Franklin Delano Roosevelt, Hindemith turned to Whitman for an appropriate commemorative text. The resulting piece, *When Lilacs Last in the Dooryard Bloom'd* for mezzo and bass soloists, mixed chorus, and orchestra, is unlike any other Requiem, not only by virtue of its secular text (after all, Frederick Delius had done the same thing), but also by intent. It is not a prayer for eternal peace; it does not sanctify the memory of an individual; it is not a political statement; it does not call on humanity to do better next time. It is simply a deeply felt appreciation of the sacrifice made by those who died in the war. One suspects, too, that Hindemith had in his mind as he composed the names of a few old German friends, as well as the myriad of Allied soldiers and President Roosevelt. Following a somber orchestral prelude, the lengthy

poem is presented in a connected and well-balanced series of solos and choruses. The sun comes out about halfway through in a wonderful double fugue
celebrating virtually everything in "this land." Thereafter, the work gradually
takes on an unremitting sense of resignation. An understated ending, in which
both soloists and chorus take part, is effective. One only wishes afterward
that the sun had reappeared just once, however briefly, during the last twelve
minutes or so. Robert Shaw referred to the "grey-brown" character of the
piece (Mussulman 1996, 66), an impression that is created entirely by the
intensity of the emotional sameness following the great fugue of affirmation.

A brilliantly caustic view of Judgment Day, *Apparebit repentina dies* sets
an early medieval text that predates the famous "Dies irae" sequence by several centuries. The text itself is quite interesting, being an extremely early
example of a poetic form in which each stanza begins with the next letter of
the alphabet. Just a glimpse reveals Hindemith's mastery of technique: the
tone is set immediately by a dramatic introductory motive followed by an
equally dramatic instrumental fugato of some length, and the chorus enters in
a declamatory style soon accompanied by an expansion of the introductory
motive. Eventually the chorus weaves its own contrapuntal web over a repeat
of the opening instrumental fugato. Later the supplications of repentant
dead—soon, possibly, to be damned—are given to women's voices; the soloistic duel role of narrator-Christ is given to tutti basses. The brass throughout
lend a weighty sense of severity to the proceedings.

Later works include *Twelve German Madrigals* (1958) and Mass (1963),
both for unaccompanied mixed chorus, in which can be found the same
wealth of contrapuntal procedures and reliance on sonorities of open fourths
and fifths. Mass, Hindemith's last completed composition, is somewhat more
chromatic than his other choral works.

Kurt Weill (1900–1950) was one of several composers in the twentieth
century—among them George Gershwin, Leonard Bernstein, and Malcolm
Williamson—who attempted to straddle the genres of popular musical theater and serious concert music. In 1926, after study with Engelbert Humper-
dinck, Feruccio Busoni, and Philipp Jarnach, Weill began incorporating jazz
elements into his work, creating, in David Drew's words (Sadie 1980), "a
new concept of style: unity is no longer sought through the culturally
approved hegemony of any one idiom, but through a (more or less) intensely
personal view of a multiplicity of idioms, with particular emphasis on those
which are for one reason or another discredited or taboo." It was a concept
in opposition to the stylistic ideals envisioned by both Pfitzner and Schoenberg. Coming before this stylistic cataclysm, Weill's earliest extant choral
piece, *Recordare*, Opus 11 (1923), is generally considered to be the major
work of his formative years. Thereafter, he produced the cantatas *Das Berliner Requiem* (1928) and *Der Lindberghflug* (1929) for radio performance,

the unaccompanied *Die Legende vom toten Soldaten* (1929), and the choral ballet *Die sieben Todsünden der Kleinbürger* (1933), all on librettos by Bertolt Brecht, as well as the moving and curiously little-known *Kiddush* (1946) for cantor, mixed chorus, and organ. The chorus also plays a prominent role in several of Weill's other stage works, particularly *Happy End* (1929), *Der Jasager* (1930), and *Die Burgschaft* (1932).

Others active at this time include Alexander Zemlinsky (1872–1942), Ernst Toch (1887–1964), and Eric Zeisl (1905–1959), all of whom immigrated to America just ahead of the Holocaust, and Egon Wellesz (1885–1974), who settled in England after the Nazi Anschluss in Austria.

Alexander Zemlinsky was held in very high esteem by his brother-in-law Arnold Schoenberg even though he was never inclined toward serial procedures. In 1949 Schoenberg said, "I owe almost everything I know about composing and its problems to Alexander Zemlinsky. I always thought he was a great composer, and I still think so. Perhaps his time will come sooner than one thinks" (Gulke 1987). A good introduction to Zemlinsky's music is *Psalm 13*, Opus 24 (1935), an effective essay on human values, faith, and traditional Austrian choral techniques. It quotes two of Zemlinsky's other choral pieces, *Psalm 83* (1900) and *Psalm 23* (1910), but the directness of expression is otherwise untypical of his earlier, more florid style.

Ernst Toch became famous among choral conductors with his entertaining and clever partsongs for speaking chorus, *The Geographical Fugue* (1930) and *Valse* (1961), written before he left Germany. More than mere novelties, these pieces are carefully laid out along classical lines. *The Geographical Fugue*, for instance, contains the basic elements of a textbook fugue, except that the subject's answer cannot appear in the dominant since the parts are spoken on indeterminate pitches. Among numerous other choral works the most outstanding example is perhaps the fine Passover cantata *Cantata of the Bitter Herbs*, Opus 65 (1938) for mixed chorus and orchestra.

Before the Nazis gained power, Eric Zeisl had a bright future in Vienna. He won the Austrian State Prize in 1934, and his numerous songs and other works were frequently performed. After the Anschluss in 1938, however, he was forced to emigrate, eventually settling in Los Angeles where he continued to compose. Although he only met Arnold Schoenberg on one occasion, their destinies were forever joined when Zeisl's daughter married Schoenberg's son. Unlike Schoenberg, Zeisl was quite comfortable remaining on the tonal side of the Viennese musical fence with fellow émigrés to Hollywood Erich Wolfgang Korngold and Max Steiner. Zeisl's best-known choral work is a setting of Psalm 92, which he called *Requiem ebraico* (1944–45). It was written immediately after he learned of the deaths of his father and other relatives in a Nazi concentration camp. The first performance, in the spring of 1945, was broadcast live during an interfaith forum at Hollywood First Methodist

Arnold Schoenberg and Alexander Zemlinsky in Prague, 1917. Courtesy of the Arnold Schoenberg Center.

Church. In a letter to his publisher later that year Zeisl eloquently defended his surprising combination of text and title:

> There is very much in the Ninety-second Psalm that suits the occasion, which brought out this particular music from me. I know that it is prominently the power of custom that wants to see in *Tov l'hodos* a festival sabbothsong [sic] but I could just as well argue that it would be bordering the ridiculous when at the present time the Jews would sing a festive song. With a heart full of tears they nevertheless hold on to God and do not cease to thank Him and do not cease to hope. This is the message and the consolation which I found in the Ninety-second Psalm. I can safely say that in the course of ages the Jews have had much more occasion to see things that way, there have been very little occasions for festive moods, countless for mourning, yet the Ninety-second Psalm has been sung every Sabbath.

Musically, *Requiem ebraico* combines Mahlerian Viennese sensibilities with melodic elements common to Jewish modes. The rather melancholy opening progresses inexorably, in one continuous movement, to the immense life-affirming fugue that ends the work. Other choral pieces by Zeisl include the lovely *Harlem Nightsong* (1930), on text by Langston Hughes, *Spruchkantate* (Cantata of Verses, 1935) for mixed chorus and orchestra, and *From the Book of Psalms* (1953) for tenor, male chorus, and small orchestra.

Egon Wellesz was not only a fine composer but also the world's leading Byzantine music scholar. Although he studied under Schoenberg, his music reveals a strongly independent character, no less impressed by Anton Bruckner than by modern trends. Wellesz wrote much music for the Catholic church, the best of which is the finely wrought Mass in F Minor (1934) for mixed chorus and organ. He also contributed a few secular pieces: *Fünf kleine Männerchöre* (1932), on texts by August Derleth; *Quant' è bella giovinessa* (1940), a frottola for female chorus; and *To Sleep* (1965) for mixed chorus, on text by John Keats.

AUSTRIAN AND GERMAN COMPOSERS DURING THE NAZI ERA

In 1937 Carl Orff (1895–1982) was catapulted into fame by the success of *Carmina burana*. Originally staged as a ballet with chorus but most frequently performed as a concert work, *Carmina burana* became one of the most popular twentieth-century works of any kind. Almost devoid of expressive subtlety, the music is painted in broad strokes of primary colors. Counterpoint is nonexistent; harmonies consist of major or minor triads with occasional added notes for spice, and a single riveting instance of bitonality; the chorus sings only in unison, parallel thirds, or triads; structures are reduced to song forms, usually strophic; rhythms, often derived from Bavarian folk dances, are uncomplicated and propulsive. The huge orchestra is overloaded with percussion. The text, a collection of secular medieval poems found at a monastery in Benediktbeuern, Bavaria, celebrates the coming of spring in rather hedonistic ways. It flirts with indecency, and to quote Kenneth Clark (1969) out of context, "like all forms of indecency, it's irresistible." Orff retained the style created for *Carmina burana*, known as primitivism, for all of his succeeding works and with ever diminishing effect.

A year after completing *Carmina burana*, Orff participated in Nazi efforts to obliterate Mendelssohn from German history by composing substitute music for *A Midsummer Night's Dream*. Thereafter, he went under contract with the Gauleiter (regional leader) of Vienna for various ongoing musical services and was given exemption from military service. He also tried, unsuccessfully, to sell the Nazis on his Orff-Schulwerk, an extremely effective music education curriculum whose time had not yet come. Orff may have been genuinely apolitical, but his music, though quite popular, pushed the Nazis' conceptual envelope. Constantly watched for some breech in officially sanctioned artistic etiquette, Orff was also on guard because of his partially Jewish ancestry. His collaboration with the regime was therefore probably the result of a desire to survive rather than to achieve personal advantage or to advance some high-minded artistic agenda, unlike certain Protestant composers, such as Johann Nepomuk David and Hugo Distler.

Orff's international reputation after the war was aided greatly by the increasing acceptance of Orff-Schulwerk. Developed prior to 1933, it lay dormant until 1948 when West German Radio realized its potential. Since then its combination of choral singing and unique percussion instruments has made it at least as popular as the Kodály Method for the training of young children.

In 1953 Orff created a full concert-length work, *Trionfi*, by combining *Carmina burana* with two other works: the scenic cantata *Catulli carmina* (1943) for mixed chorus, percussion, and four pianos, and the incredibly tasteless *Trionfo di Afrodite* (1953) for soloists, chorus, and orchestra. The latter work combines somewhat innovative choral writing with an exceptionally graphic wedding night bedroom scene in which the tenor and soprano soloists wail at the uppermost extremes of their ranges. Other works include settings of Schiller poems, *Nänie und Dithyrambe* (1956) and *Die Sänger der Vorwelt* (1956) for mixed chorus, and *Stücke* (1969) for speaking chorus.

Johann Nepomuk David (1895–1977), Ernst Pepping (1901–1981), Wolfgang Fortner (1907–1987), and Hugo Distler (1908–1942) occupy central positions in German choral music from about 1937. After the war the dissemination of their work was aided by apologists who presented them as unwilling victims of Hitler's regime, persecuted for their devotion to the church, and with the exception of Distler, ultimately saved by hiding in its bosom. Their artistic accomplishments are beyond dispute, but their personal integrity has been tarnished somewhat by recently uncovered evidence showing their cooperation with the Nazis to have been more willing, extensive, and profitable than previously thought. Michael H. Kater (1997, 164) summarized their situation:

> They were sufficiently close to the regime to hold teaching positions at institutions of higher learning that enjoyed official protection. Their music, sacred or profane, was also performed publicly throughout the Third Reich and, for the most part, applauded. The regime accorded them its respect by nominating them for generous prizes, at the level of the Reich Music Chamber, in 1942. Moreover, toward the end of the war, David and Pepping were placed on a most-favored-artist list, which meant preferential treatment such as being shielded from military conscription. When Distler committed suicide in 1942, the regime-beholden *Zeitscrift für Musik* called him "a strong talent" and deplored his loss, and the Hitler Youth Thomaner-Chor of Leipzig sang his hymns in his memory.

Johann Nepomuk David was an Austrian elementary school teacher, choirmaster, and organist who rose to the directorship of the Leipzig Conservatory by the middle of the war. Following critically successful performances at the 1937 Protestant Church Music Festival in Berlin—an event produced by the musical reformers in the confessional branch of the Lutheran Church, with the full support of the government's Reich Music Chamber—David's compositions became widely known, one being approved for use at Nazi celebrations. A work for chorus and trombones, performed in Leipzig under the composer's direction, was based on a slogan of the Führer's. (This piece, incidentally, is omitted from David's composition list in Sadie 1980). Michael Kater (1997, 166) made a pointed observation on David's popularity:

> In retrospect, it is difficult not to be overwhelmed by the official reception of his works in the supervised press. Review after review, one more positive than the next, identified him as one of the most respected composers of the Nazi cultural establishment, no matter how much these works may have revolved around religious subjects. Therefore, David's complaint to Carl Orff in 1943 that he felt neglected shows either a man of great naïveté or an artist with an enormous ego.

After 1945 David served with distinction as professor of composition at the Salzburg Mozarteum and later at the Stuttgart Hochschule für Musik. He had stopped composing sacred music early in the war, not returning to those forms until 1948. Traces of Gregorian chant, Bach, Bruckner, Stravinsky, and Hindemith can be felt in David's music, which is characterized primarily by reliance on quartal harmony and complete devotion to all manner of contrapuntal techniques. His church music, written for both Roman Catholic and Lutheran liturgies, is particularly effective. Outstanding works include the unaccompanied *Victimae pascali laudes* (1948), the two sets of *Evangelien-motteten* (1958, 1971), Mass (1968), and the cantata *Komm, Heiliger Geist* (1972) for double chorus and orchestra.

Throughout his career, Ernst Pepping relied on baroque models. Initially his works were extremely severe and laced with uncompromising dissonance, but coincidental with Hitler's rise to power, the natural progression of his development smoothed out the early astringency. The new cultural guardians, therefore, began to hear his music as pleasingly modern—without being *too* modern. They noted his abilities as a teacher and also his participation in the 1937 Church Music Festival; and in return for composing music that fell easily on national socialist ears, the Nazis—well aware of Pepping's ties to the increasingly treasonous Confessional Church—simply left him alone. After 1938, in addition to two symphonies (successfully premiered by Karl Boehm and Wilhelm Furtwängler), Pepping composed the cantata *Das Jahr* (1940), which reflected the annual festival cycle devised by the Nazis, as well as other works commissioned for various political ceremonies. *Deutsche Messe "Kyrie Gott Vater in Ewigkeit"* (1938) for six-part mixed chorus, the first work in this string of compromises, is still performed. There was, of course, a strong tradition of German Masses based on appropriate Lutheran liturgical tunes, so the lineage of this attractive vernacular setting would not be suspect except for the timing of its composition, which was just after the 1937 Church Music Festival, a time when "Deutsche" in any title indicated adherence to the party line. It is perhaps significant that except for some little Christmas songs written at the same time Pepping, like David, composed no more sacred music until after the war, when he brought forth the unaccompanied eight-part *Missa dona nobis pacem* (1948), which may in fact have been a personal plea. Other works include *Drei Evangelien-Motetten* (1937–38), *Passionsbericht des Matthäus* (1950), and *Te Deum* (1956) for soloists, mixed chorus, and orchestra. Also of interest is the relatively early *Deutsche Choralmesse* (1931), which is not a Mass at all but a series of chorale motets corresponding to the Ordinary. In concept, therefore, *Deutsche Choralmesse* is related to Schubert's *Deutsche messe*, although the music steadfastly refrains from any hint of nineteenth-century romantic rhetoric.

Wolfgang Fortner was appointed to the faculty of Heidelberg Institute of Church Music in 1931 and participated to great effect in the 1937 Church Music Festival. Joining the Nazi party in 1940, he served in the Wehrmacht, contributed to Hitler Youth songbooks, wrote music for various Nazi celebrations, and published articles condemning Schoenberg's dodecaphonic principles (Kater 1997, 170–171). After the war Fortner became a celebrated composer and teacher in West Germany, eventually becoming professor at

Freiburg Musikhochschule and counting Hans Werner Henze among his long list of celebrated pupils. Fortner's music prior to 1946 reveals an almost generic interest in baroque forms, and it has been argued that his postwar embracing of serial technique was simply a continuation of this predilection. Works include the unaccompanied *Eine deutsche Liedmesse* (1934); a cantata on text by Bertolt Brecht, *An die Nachgeborenen* (1948) for speaker, tenor, mixed chorus, and orchestra; *Gladbacher Te Deum* (1973) for bass-baritone, mixed chorus, orchestra, and tape; and *Petrarca-Sonette* (1979) for mixed chorus.

Distler's case is particularly tragic. In 1933 he and other professors and church leaders signed a declaration calling for Protestant church music to return to the post-reformation ideals exemplified by Bach and Schütz. The idea was to recreate a pure German art free from, in the words of the declaration, "the corrosive forces of liberalism and individualism" and other nineteenth-century romantic musical heresies (Kater 1997, 161). Distler joined the Nazi party about the same time, possibly believing that its platform for social reform and attendant elevation of nationalistic ideals could assist his own church-music agenda. Like David, Pepping, and Fortner, Distler was a major figure at the 1937 Church Music Festival. In 1939 Distler's secular *Mörike-Chorliederbuch* (1938–39) made a great impression at the officially supported Festival of German Choral Music in Graz. During this time Distler occupied good positions, first as cantor and organist at Saint Jacobi, Lübeck, followed by professorships at the Spandau School of Church Music in Berlin and Württemburg Hochschule für Musik in Stuttgart. Two of his pieces were earmarked for use at commemorations of the Munich Beer Hall Putsch and the anniversary of Hitler's assumption of power. In 1942 he was named director of the Berlin State and Cathedral Choir. Over the last years, however, he seems to have become increasingly disillusioned, finally realizing the full implications of Nazi policy and practice. Late in 1942 he killed himself. Still, the evidence refutes any continued claim that Distler's suicide was a result of constant pressure from an increasingly antagonistic government; rather, it appears that he saw the futility of attempting to serve both God and Nazis, and came to terms with his own conscience unequivocally.

As Bartók assimilated folk materials into a distinctive style, so Distler absorbed the music of Bach and Heinrich Schütz. A defining characteristic is that Distler's own objective, neoclassic personality is as recognizable as his models. His music often dispenses with traditional bar lines. Small melodic motives are often fragmented, the smaller portions being repeated to elongate the phrase and create some rhythmic shift. His harmonies are basically triadic, but often rely on open fourths or fifths and occasionally contain added notes. Dissonance results from naturally occurring clashes in the linear counterpoint. He is at his best in smaller, motet-length pieces, such as those that constitute *Geistliche Chormusik*, Opus 12 (1934–36, 1941), of which "Singet dem Herrn ein neues Lied" and "Totentanz" are perhaps best known. Among other works are *Die Weihnachtsgeschichte* (1933), which alternates unaccompanied recitative with choral variations on "Es ist ein' Ros' entsprungen," and *Choral-Passion* (1933), which, like Pepping's Passion setting, follows Schütz's pattern for such works.

While the preceding composers were attempting to balance godly devotion with political pragmatism, Viktor Ullmann (1898–1944), Günter Raphael (1903–1960), Rudolf Wagner-Régeny (1903–1969), Boris Blacher (1903–1975), Zikmund Schul (1916–1944), and others were coming face to face with the cold realities of Nazi racial and artistic policies, and in the process discovering the primacy of artistic creation within the panoply of human endeavor.

Ullmann, a minor Austrian nobleman born and reared in Czechoslovakia, had studied with Schoenberg in Vienna. In September 1942 he was interned in Terezín, the Nazi "paradise ghetto" of Theresienstadt, where he met the Czech choral conductor Raphael Schaechter and others who were organizing concerts there (see chapter 5). Ullmann subsequently maintained a leading role in the development of cultural activities until he was deported and taken to Auschwitz, where he was later murdered. While in Terezín he organized programs of new music, reviewed concerts for the ghetto newspaper, and wrote philosophical articles on the nature of art and its function in times of duress. He declared that in the camp "our efforts in regard to Art were commensurate with our will to live" (Karas 1985, 197). In addition to the opera *Der Kaiser von Atlantis* (1943–44) and numerous songs and chamber works, Ullmann composed several excellent settings of Hebrew and Yiddish folk songs, for treble, men's, and mixed voices, all culled from a copy of the *Makkabi Liederbuch* (Maccabee Songbook, published 1930), which he found in Terezín. Like virtually all music written in the camps, these songs view life's small details through the magnifying lens of more acute, larger issues, among them separation, death, hope, and honor. While they do not quite match the genius of similar pieces by Gideon Klein, their emotional understatement and slightly acerbic harmonies still effectively project an undeniable sense of urgency.

Günter Raphael was a distinguished professor of church music and composition who was highly respected for his grandly conceived *Requiem* (1927–28) for four soloists, mixed chorus, orchestra, and organ. His works were banned, however, after the Nazis gained power, and in 1934 he was forced to resign his positions at the state conservatory and at Church Music Institute in Leipzig. Thereafter, he survived by teaching privately while he continued to compose. He returned to honored academic life in 1949, teaching at conservatories in Duisberg, Mainz, and Cologne. Raphael's early style, of which

Requiem is a prime example, was greatly influenced by Reger. During the war he incorporated neobaroque impulses similar to those espoused by Distler, Pepping, and the other Confessional Church composers. His late compositions test the waters of serial technique, often applying tone rows as ostinatos. Raphael's many choral works include the unaccompanied *Eine deutsche Totenmesse* (1940), written—with no hope of immediate performance—as a lament for his country, *Judica Kantate* (1955) for chorus and orchestra, several other cantatas, and many motets.

Rudolf Wagner-Régeny's direct and conventionally tonal style was officially approved during the early days of Hitler's government, and he, like Orff, accepted an invitation to compose new music for *A Midsummer Night's Dream*. Nevertheless, Wagner-Régeny courted disaster by filling his stage works with unfavorable allusions to the regime and deliberately shifting toward the forbidden style of Kurt Weill. In 1941 a violent demonstration—staged by government functionaries—erupted during one of his operas. Performances of his music ceased, and in 1943 he was conscripted into the army. Surviving the war, Wagner-Régeny, like many others, incorporated aspects of twelve-tone technique into his postwar style. His choral works include the cantatas *Cantica Davidi regis* (1954) for boys' and men's choruses and chamber orchestra, *Genesis* (1955–56) for alto soloist, mixed chorus, and chamber orchestra, and *Schir haschirim* (Song of Songs, 1964) for alto and baritone soloists, female chorus, and chamber orchestra; as well as the "scenic oratorio" *Prometheus* (1957–68) for soloists, chorus, and orchestra.

At the onset of the Nazi regime, Boris Blacher already had a reputation as an innovative composer whose work was informed by the playfulness of Eric Satie, the rhythmic flexibility of Stravinsky, and the expressive qualities of jazz. He was removed from his post at Dresden Conservatory in 1939 because he would not conform his teaching to Nazi policies concerning *Entartete künst*. Thereafter, he supported himself by teaching privately (Gottfried von Einem was an important student at this time). His music was never banned but was in fact occasionally performed, much to the consternation and sadistic delight of official critics who enjoyed beating it with verbal clubs. While his work was condemned, and while he was personally dismissed as a "quarter-Jew," Blacher walked a political tightrope by maintaining risky social and political contacts, and—most dangerous of all—by helping to hide Jews. When he received conscription papers in April 1945, he simply ignored them.

After the war Blacher sought to fuse jazz elements with certain aspects of twelve-tone technique. Following the lead of Frank Martin and others, he usually applied serial procedures either melodically or metrically. This presented a problem for critics who could not visualize the eventual postmodern abandonment of strict serialism in favor of tonally derived alternatives. In 1960 George Perle (1960, 525) attended a New Music festival in Germany, and after attending a performance of Blacher's *Requiem* (1958) for soloists, chorus, and orchestra, commented that the tone row, "almost invariably beginning and ending on D, was reduced to the function of an Alberti bass. . . . If this work is intended as a *reductio ad absurdum* of techniques and values, its bombast and dullness distinguish it most decidedly from earlier examples by French, Russian, and American composers."

Blacher's other important works include the oratorio *Der Grossinquisitor* (1942), *Vier Chöre* (1944) for mixed chorus, and *Die Gesänge des Seeräubers O'Rourke und seiner Geliebten Sally Brown* (1958) for soprano, baritone, female cabaret singer, speaker, speaking chorus, and orchestra. He also participated with Paul Dessau, Karl Hartmann, Hans Werner Henze, and Wagner-Régeny on *Jüdische Chronik* (1961), a work for alto and baritone soloists, two speakers, chorus, and wind orchestra, jointly composed in response to a surge of antisemitic activity in Germany in the late 1950s. Blacher became a very distinguished teacher. Besides Einem, he taught Claude Ballif, Heimo Erbse, Giselher Klebe, Aribert Reimann, and Noam Sheriff.

Zikmund Schul studied with Hindemith in Berlin before moving to Prague in an effort to escape the Nazis. While in Prague he studied with Alois Hába, until the fall of Czechoslovakia in 1939. He was among the first to be incarcerated in Terezín in November 1941. Schul's surviving manuscripts from the ghetto-camp indicate that he began composing almost immediately and continued until 1943, when depression and ill heath brought an end to his creative efforts. He died in Terezín of tuberculosis in 1944.

Schul's music is primarily influenced by Hebrew chant. His surviving choral pieces, the finale from *Cantata Judaica* (1942), a male chorus that may be a fragment of an earlier work, and the three-voice children's (boys') chorus *Ki tavo al-ha'Arez* (When You Go to the Land, 1942), were most likely written for performance after synagogue services in Terezín. Another surviving piece, *Mogen Awaus* (Shield to Our Fathers, 1941) for soprano, baritone, mixed chorus, and organ, was written in Prague and taken to Terezín by the composer.

Herbert Zipper (1905–1997), William Hilsley (b. 1911), and Gottfried von Einem (1918–1996) reached artistic maturity well after the war. That said, they are discussed here because their activities during the Nazi period command admiration and respect.

Herbert Zipper (1905–1997), a member of an affluent Viennese family, was incarcerated in Dachau and Buchenwald, as well as in a Japanese forced-labor camp. Surviving the war, he made significant contributions as conductor of the Manila Symphony Orchestra and as a distinguished music educator in Los Angeles. Though Zipper did not consider himself a composer, in Dachau he organized clandestine concerts, gathering scrap lumber and bribing a guard to obtain wire for makeshift instruments. His *Dachaulied* (1938) for unison men (unaccompanied or with any available instruments) became known throughout the concentration camp system as prisoners were transferred. The martial quality of the music, which was written in the German cabaret style of the thirties, and the text by fellow prisoner Jura Soyfer (translated into English by Herbert Zipper), which was a parody of the Nazis' cynical "Arbeit macht frei" (Work Makes You Free) slogan, testify eloquently to the inmates' predicament:

> Faced with ever threatening rifles
> We exist by night and day.
> Life itself this hell-hole stifles
> Worse than any words can say.
> Days and weeks we leave unnumbered,
> Some forget the count of years,
> And their spirit is encumbered
> With their faces scarred by fears.
>
> But we all learned the motto of Dachau to heed
> And became as hardened as stone.
> Stay humane, Dachau mate,
> Be a man, Dachau mate,
> And work as hard as you can, Dachau mate,
> For work leads to freedom alone.

Shortly before his death Zipper said, in a *Los Angeles Times* interview dated 9 April 1997, "I realized in Dachau that the arts in general have the power to keep you not just alive, but to make your life meaningful even under the most dreadful circumstances." (It is worth noting here that long after the war, while Zipper was still living in Manila, Boris Blacher and Wolfgang Fortner paid him a surprise visit. They had all been friends before the Nazi era, and had remained so in spite of everything [Cummins 1992, 59].)

William Hilsley (originally Hildesheimer) was born in England and lived there until the age of three. After his parents divorced he returned with his mother to her native Germany, and he eventually settled in the Netherlands, teaching music at the International Quaker School in Utrecht. After the Nazi invasion Hilsley was sent to an internment camp for captured noncombatants. Like Zipper, he did not think of himself as a composer, but while imprisoned he wrote and staged several cabaret shows, interesting chamber music, and the thought-provoking male choir *Missa in nativitatis* (1942), composed as a Christmas present for fellow inmates who were Roman Catholic. Internment camps fell under international rules similar to prisoner-of-war camps, so that the Red Cross and other organizations from neutral countries had occasional access to them. Representatives of the Swedish YMCA visited Hilsley's camp

and recorded several performances, including the Mass, which were subsequently broadcast on a Swedish radio program called *From behind Barbed
Wire*. The Mass is an emotional powerhouse of simple expression and pure
tonalities. The diatonic melodic lines are sometimes painfully angular. A Jew,
Hilsley omitted the Credo and kept the other movements extremely compact,
the entire duration being only about nine minutes. The crowning Agnus Dei is
the embodiment of Saint Paul's testimony to the Philippians: "And the peace
of God, which passeth all understanding, shall keep your hearts and minds."
After the war Hilsley returned to the Quaker school, where he was to spend
the rest of his career. While there, he composed other attractive pieces, including *Vervehendes und Bleibendes* (Sounds Fading and Sounds Lingering, 1990)
for mixed choir, and *Seasons* (1992), a cantata dealing with his wartime experiences in broad, rather objective terms.

Gottfried von Einem was a wealthy, young Austrian nobleman whose
political views were shaped by a liberal upbringing, by a visit to England
where he met several refugees from Hitler's Germany, and by Boris Blacher,
with whom he studied from 1941 to 1943. In 1938 both he and his mother,
the Baroness Gerta Louise von Einem, were arrested on suspicion of treason.
Einem lived precariously after being released, cooperating superficially with
the Nazis but continuing to hide Jews and other opponents of the regime even
under frequent Gestapo surveillance. Through his mother's contacts he
secured work as a rehearsal pianist at both the Berlin State Opera and at Bay-
reuth, and managed to have a handful of works performed. After the war he
developed into one of the century's finest opera composers (one opera he
wrote deals with his Gestapo interrogation). He also wrote a few significant
choral works, mostly in large forms, including *Hymnus* (1949) for alto soloist, chorus, and orchestra, *Das Stundenlied* (1958) for chorus and orchestra,
on text by Bertolt Brecht, *Die traumenden Knaben* (1973) for chorus, clarinet,
and bassoon, the cantata *An die Nachgeborenen* (1973–75) for alto and bass
soloists, chorus, and orchestra, and *Missa Claravallensis* (1987–88) for mixed
chorus, winds, and percussion. Among his smaller works, the exquisite partsong cycle *Ünterwegs* (1982–88) is outstanding. Einem's style—always tonal,
and eclectic in the best sense—is influenced by Wagner, Hindemith, Blacher,
and occasionally jazz.

Other German composers active at this time were Franz Schmidt (1874–
1939), whose oratorio on the Apocalypse, *Das Buch mit sieben Siegeln*
(1935–37), is still performed; Werner Egk (1901–1983), who became an official in the Reichs Music Chamber in 1941 (even though he was not a Nazi,
according to the redoubtable Gottfried von Einem), and whose works, including the oratorio *Fürchtlösigkeit und Wohlwollen* (1931, revised 1959) for
tenor, chorus, and orchestra and *Drei Chansons* (1940) for ten-part mixed
chorus, were enthusiastically received by public and government alike; Hein-

rich Spitta (1902–1972), nephew of the great Bach biographer Philipp Spitta, whose *Thanksgiving Cantata* (1935) and other works represented an unfortunate effort to lend spiritual credibility to Hitler youth; Franz Biebl (b. 1906), who created a substantial body of choral music in a gently evocative style, exemplified by the Gregorian-flavored *Ave Maria* for soprano, alto, tenor soloists, and mixed chorus; Helmut Bräutigam (1914–1942), who wrote many fascist-inspired didactic choruses in an attractive popular style before perishing on the Eastern front; and Gottfried Müller (1914–1993), a favorite of Hitler, who composed many political choruses as well as church works.

Austrian and German Composers after World War II

Paul Dessau (1894–1979) and Hanns Eisler (1898–1962) fled the Nazi juggernaut early, working for years in the United States and other countries before returning to East Germany, where they devoted their substantial talents to the service of socialist ideals. Both developed styles freely incorporating twelve-tone technique, and both also established close relationships with Bertolt Brecht, resulting not only in several stage works but also a number of significant choral pieces.

Dessau's style is an intriguing combination of serialism (learned from René Leibowitz in Paris), Jewish folk music, jazz, and in the late works, aleatoric techniques. Profoundly influenced by Brecht, most of Dessau's choral pieces either grapple with injustice, class struggle, and other social issues, or memorialize fallen leftist heroes. While some are only political rhetoric, others reveal a genuinely acute social conscience. His large catalogue contains Jewish works as well as psalm settings. Outstanding examples include *Psalm 15* (1927) and *Psalm 13* (1930–31) for mixed chorus; *Haggada* (1936, revised 1962) for soloists, chorus, children's chorus, and orchestra; *Hawel Hawalim* (1939) for chorus and piano or organ; his first collaboration with Brecht, *Deutsches Miserere* (1944–47) for soloists, chorus, children's chorus, orchestra, organ, and trautonium; *Grabschrift für Gorki* (1947) for unison male voices and winds; *Grabschrift für Rosa Luxemburg* (1948) for chorus and orchestra; *Jüdische Chronik* (1960) for baritone, speaker, chamber chorus, and chamber orchestra, written jointly with Blacher and Henze; *Requiem für Lumumba* (1963) for soprano and baritone soloists, speaker, chorus, and instruments; and others.

Hanns Eisler studied with Schoenberg from 1919 to 1923. Schoenberg promoted his work until 1926, when Eisler joined the German Communist Party and publicly repudiated his teacher's aesthetic because it did not actively seek proletarian victory. During the cold war, Eisler was dismissed in the West as a party hack, but an assessment based on purely musical criteria reveals a refined and unsentimental style devoid of any expressive indulgence.

It is also obvious that Schoenberg's teaching bore fruit, not only in Eisler's tonal application of twelve-tone writing but also in the technical mastery of his materials. In addition to small unaccompanied pieces for every conceivable choral configuration, Eisler wrote several large works, including *Die Mass-nahme* (1930) for tenor, three speakers, male and mixed chorus, and small orchestra, and *Die Mutter* (1931) for chorus and orchestra (later arranged for two pianos), both on texts by Brecht. His largest choral work is the powerful antifascist cantata *Deutsche Sinfonie* for soprano, alto, baritone and bass soloists, two speakers, mixed chorus, and orchestra. Beginning the cantata in 1935, Eisler planned to compose a work primarily utilizing texts by Brecht, to rebuke the Fascist government and to examine horrors already known about Nazi concentration camps. The work was mostly completed by 1937, with an orchestral introduction culled from an earlier piece. Additional instrumental interludes were added in 1939 and 1947, the final form being achieved in 1957 with the incorporation of an additional excerpt from another work. *Deutsche Sinfonie* was finally premiered in 1959. Given its history, the stylistic consistency of this work is remarkable. The music is an objective though sensitive vehicle for the projection of text, accumulating power with each succeeding story of concentration camp life (and death), peasant hardship, and worker disillusionment.

Circumstance spared Günter Bialas (1907–1995) and Bernd Alois Zimmermann (1918–1970) the problem of direct artistic collaboration with the Nazis, but it did not keep them out of the German army.

Bialas occupied a junior music theory position at Breslau University from 1933, apparently under little pressure to produce the kind of propagandistic and didactic pieces his more prominent contemporaries were churning out. He was conscripted in 1941, remaining in military service until war's end, after which he began to devote his energies to composition. His early interests in Hindemith, Stravinsky, and various kinds of folk and popular music were enriched by the undogmatic application of twelve-tone principles and a newly acquired awareness of traditional African techniques (Sadie 1980, 2:671). His nondoctrinaire attitude is a remarkable characteristic. While some works adhere to one compositional principle—for example, the lovely *Eichendorf-Liederbuch* (1965) for mixed chorus and two guitars is primarily twelve-tone—others explore a combination of techniques. His later pieces are often preoccupied with problems of timbre. His choral music includes *Indianische Kantate* (1950) for baritone, mixed chamber chorus, eight instruments, and percussion, *Im Anfang* (1961) for six-part mixed chorus, three-part echo chorus, organ, or orchestra, on texts from Genesis and Martin Buber, *Veni Creator spiritus* (1961) for five-part mixed chorus, *Lobet den Herrn* (1963) for mixed chorus, congregation, and organ, and *Hugenotten-Psalm* (1972) for double mixed chorus.

Bernd Alois Zimmermann was conscripted into the German army at the beginning of the war and served in France where he became acquainted with the music of Stravinsky and Milhaud. After his release from a military hospital in 1942 he resumed his musical studies. Best known for the opera *Die Soldaten*, Zimmermann was a pioneer in the development of collage technique, in which musical and textual materials from varied sources appear together in a single new context. His choral works are few in number but of high quality. The most important is *Requiem für einen jungen Dichter* (1967–69) for speakers, soprano and baritone soloists, three choruses, jazz group, orchestra, organ, and tape. It deals with European history after 1920 by combining Latin liturgical texts with political speeches and other appropriate literary excerpts. Live performers are juxtaposed with recorded excerpts of speeches by Hitler, Stalin, Churchill, Dubček, and Pope John XXIII. Snippets of Beethoven's Ninth, the Beatles' *Hey, Jude,* and other well-known works are heard alongside texts by numerous twentieth-century poets, several of whom committed suicide—as the composer himself would eventually do. Writing in *The New York Times* (18 April 1999) at the time of the American premiere, Johanna Keller rightfully called it "one of the most ambitious and troubling modernist works of the century." Zimmermann's other works include the small *Tantum ergo* (1947) for mixed chorus and the so-called burlesque cantata *Lob der Torheit* (1948) for soloists, chorus, and orchestra, on text by Goethe.

Hans Werner Henze (b. 1926) is perhaps the most important postwar German composer. After serving in the army and being imprisoned in a British prisoner-of-war camp, Henze studied composition with Wolfgang Fortner, who taught him how traditional techniques could be applied to modern compositional problems. The success of Fortner's teaching is apparent in Henze's first choral work, *Fünf Madrigále* (1947) for chamber chorus and eleven instruments. The following year's setting of a large scene from Goethe's *Faust*, *Chor gefangener Trojer* (1948, revised 1964) for chorus and orchestra, bears the obvious imprint of Bergian serialism. Thereafter, Henze developed his own style, freely employing aspects of serial technique within a rhythmic framework guided by Stravinskian principles, and became an extremely well-known composer of opera and symphony.

Henze's best choral works are very impressive, and for different reasons. *The Muses of Sicily* (1966) for chorus, two solo pianos, wind orchestra, and timpani is a most attractive and well-considered work. The composer understood that most schools have choruses, numerous wind players, and competent piano faculty. He further understood that because singers cannot find the right pitch simply by pressing a key, difficulties encountered in performing modern music are more acute for vocalists than for instrumentalists. Therefore he stepped away from the rigors of serial composition and designed a tonal concerto for two pianos accompanied by winds and chorus. The piano writing is virtuosic, the parts for wind and chorus idiomatic and grateful. Rhythms are inviting, harmonies bright and sunny. The brilliant ending is in fact quite reminiscent of the finale of Prokofiev's third piano concerto. Yet the oratorio *Das Floss der "Medusa"* (1968) for soprano and baritone soloists, speaker, boys' chorus, mixed chorus, and orchestra, forces Henze's naturally lyrical dodecaphony into angular and biting shapes of pointed anger. Based on the event depicted in Géricault's famous painting of the same name, the work leaves no doubt as to Henze's position on social justice. In a similar vein, the unaccompanied *Orpheus behind the Wire* (1983), on text by Edward Bond, views the Holocaust (and all potential holocausts) as something more than a Jewish tragedy. The seven brilliantly virtuosic movements of Symphony No. 9 (1995–96) for chorus and orchestra deal with the fate of young German antifascists during the early Nazi years, as described in Anna Seghers's novel *Das Siebte Kreuz*.

Other works include *Moralities* (1967), comprised of three tonally direct "scenic cantatas" designed for school performance, and a reworking of Carissimi's oratorio *Jephte* (1976) for soloists, mixed chorus, four flutes, harp, guitar, mandolin, banjo, and percussion.

Wolfgang Rihm (b. 1952) was catapulted into the attention of choral conductors when he was named one of four composers to write Passion settings for the Stuttgart International Bach Academy's commemoration of the 250th anniversary of Bach's death. The resulting *Deus Passus* (Passion after Saint Luke, 2000) for soloists, chorus, and orchestra received great critical acclaim (see chapter 15). Prior to this, Rihm had composed only two choral works: *Nietzche-fragmente* (1981) for mezzo and baritone soloists, chorus, and flute, and *Dies* (1984) for soloists, chorus, organ, and orchestra. Nicolas Slonimsky (1992, 1514) aptly noted that Rihm's style thrives on "calculated unpredictability; but he does not shrink from producing shockingly euphonious and startlingly pleasurable sounds."

Protestant church music was rejuvenated after the war by Helmut Bornefeld (1906–1990) and Siegfried Reda (1916–1968), who together formed the Heidenheim Arbeitstage für neue Kirchenmusik in 1946. While influenced by the principles of Distler, they also realized the necessity of incorporating modern elements, as exemplified in the music of Bartók, Hindemith, Stravinsky, and others. Bornefeld successfully placed traditional Lutheran melodies within a modern harmonic framework, while Reda applied serial technique to widen the melodic and structural possibilities of liturgical music. Bornefeld's liturgical pieces are published in a series as *Das Chorwerk* (1930–60). Reda composed *Chormusik für das Jahr Kirche* (1947–58); *Die Weihnachtsgeschichte* (Christmas "History," 1949) and *Die Ostergeschichte* (Easter "History," 1950), both for soloists and unaccompanied mixed chorus; and numerous other works, the most important of which are the brilliant motet *Ecce homo aus dem 22. Psalm* (1950), *Te Deum* (1950) for double chorus and brass, and *Requiem* (1963) for soloists, mixed chorus, and orchestra.

A colorful aberration in the development of Protestant music is represented by Heinz Werner Zimmermann (b. 1930), who combined the polyphonic and harmonic ideals of Distler with syncopations and added blues-notes stereotypical of jazz, usually accompanied by percussion and pizzicato bass. Too often this "pluralistic polyphony," to use his term (Stroope 1991, 35), also translated as "polystylistic polyphony" (Sadie 1980, 20:690), only creates an effect of pleasant diversion. Occasionally, however, Zimmermann's music can be overwhelmingly powerful, as in the tremendous unaccompanied motet *Wachet auf!* (1979) for twelve-part mixed chorus, in which the stylistic synthesis, incidentally, leans more toward Distler. Other works include *Psalmkonzert* (1957) for baritone, children's and mixed choruses, brass, vibraphone, and doublebass, *Magnificat* (1970) for chorus, vibraphone, doublebass, and harpsichord, and *Psalm 13* (1973) for chorus, organ, and doublebass.

Other German choral composers include Kurt Hessenberg (1908–1994), Giselher Klebe (b. 1925), Heinrich Poos (b. 1928), Manfred Trojahn (b. 1949), and Ingo Bredenbach (b. 1959).

Hermann Kronsteiner (1914–1994), Josef Friedrich Doppelbauer (1918–1989), Anton Heiller (1923–1979), and others continued the development of Catholic church music in Austria.

Hermann Kronsteiner, continuing the Austro-German *Kapellmeister* tradition, composed many functional church works in a finely crafted but conventionally tonal style. Outstanding examples are *Stille Nacht Messe* (1959) for four-part mixed chorus and organ (with two ad libitum instruments) and *Kleine Stille Nacht Messe* (1976) for three-part treble choir and organ (or three instruments). These two Masses use the famous Christmas carol as a point of departure, with fragments of the tune usually appearing in the accompaniment. Though both works share a common Benedictus, they are otherwise completely different. An interesting structural twist occurs in the more substantial four-part Mass when the contrapuntal ending of Gloria reappears, lavishly elongated, as "Dona nobis pacem." Except for "et incarnatus est," the Credo of the three-part Mass is sung to Gregorian Credo III.

Doppelbauer, a prominent organist and choral conductor, produced a substantial body of choral music of which *Cantate Domino canticum novum* (published 1968) for four-part mixed chorus is typical. In a program note prepared for the Choral Society of Southern California in 1991, Malcolm Cole succinctly described the basic elements of Doppelbauer's style as found in this piece:

This little motet illustrates the role that modal polyphony plays in Doppelbauer's church compositions. . . . Crisp, pointed, syllabic declamation of the word "cantate" provides an ostinato support for melismatic treatment of the same text in the soprano part. The second textual phrase receives its own musical setting, flowing, espressivo, in longer note values, and at a softer dynamic level. A modified return of the opening section, to include more exuberant melismas, a dynamic swell to fortissimo, and a rich five-part final cadence, round out this delightful motet.

Anton Heiller became a well-known Austrian organist after the war and composed a number of works for organ, but his primary compositional interest was sacred choral music. He composed Masses, motets, and other works for both Catholic and Lutheran liturgies, in a modal and often Gregorian-flavored style similar to Hindemith and David. Later works, influenced by Frank Martin, incorporate melodic twelve-tone elements. Representative works are the unaccompanied *Mixolydian Mass* (1944), the little oratorio *Tentatio Jesu* (1952) for soloists, chorus, and two pianos, *Drei kleine geistliche Chöre* (1953) for four-part mixed chorus, *Kleine Messe über Zwölftonmodelle* (1961) for mixed chorus, and *Stabat mater* (1968) for mixed chorus and orchestra. Some of his most delightful pieces are for treble voices, including *Missa in nocte* (1949), with organ; the unaccompanied *Missa super "Erhalt uns Herr"* (1952), *Adventmusik* (1971), with oboe, violin, and organ; and *Passionsmusik* (1973), with organ.

The Austrian partsong tradition was carried forward by Heimo Erbse (b. 1924), Friedrich Cerha (b. 1926), and Heinz Kratochwil (b. 1933). Erbse's *Drei Chöre* (published 1975) for six-part mixed chorus, on texts by Nelly Sachs, is a study in choral textures and frequently biting harmonies, while his *Eine Kleine Heine-Kantate* (published 1979), on text from Heinrich Heine's *Book of Songs*, is more consistently diatonic and Mahlerian in inspiration. Cerha, a serialist primarily noted for his operas and other large concert pieces, successfully incorporated twelve-tone principles in his miniature suite for unaccompanied mixed chorus, *Zehn Rubaijat des Omar Khajjam* (1949/88 [Cerha's indication]). Kratochwil's *Heimliches Vergnugen* (published 1976), on text by Wilhelm Busch, is a complex essay in which the diatonically direct opening language becomes more chromatic and harmonically rich as the piece progresses.

Other interesting Austrian composers include Jenö Takács (b. 1902), Eugene Hartzell (b. 1932), Gerhard Track (b. 1934), Erich Urbanner (b. 1936), and René Staar (b. 1951). The numerous choral works of Takács are influenced by his interest in ethnomusicology and years of teaching in Egypt and the United States. Track also taught for some time in the United States, before resuming his career in Austria as a composer, choral conductor, and director of the Vienna Conservatory. He has composed a substantial body of attractive choral pieces, many designed for the American educational market. Track's clear-cut forms, love of antiphonal effects, and bright, modally flavored harmonies reflect baroque ideals. Yet he stands apart from the more stringent neobaroque style of Distler, Doppelbauer, and others, the generally sumptuous sound of his music being more evocative of the Gabrielis than of Schütz. The motet *Ex Sion species* (From Zion's Beauty, 1980) for double mixed chorus and treble choir is a good example.

Urbanner, an especially talented and creative modernist, excelled in large forms, as exemplified by *Missa Benedicite Gentes* (1958) for four soloists, mixed chorus, and organ, *Lateinisches Requiem* (1982–83) for soprano, alto, tenor, and bass soloists, mixed chorus, and orchestra, and *Three Movements for Cello and Choir* (1995) on texts by Paul Celan.

Hartzell and Staar are representatives of the Viennese serialist tradition, although their choral music is neither similar nor strictly twelve-tone. Hartzell especially has written a number of psalm settings in a highly evocative tonal style, remarkable for the ease with which the mildly chromatic language can be mastered. Perhaps the outstanding example is the lavishly descriptive *Psalm 23* (1983) for unaccompanied mixed chorus, which showcases the composer's ability to text-paint different sentiments of succeeding verses with material built from a single motive. Staar, a violinist in the Vienna Philharmonic and leader of the new music ensemble Wiener Collage, is more adept in instru-

René Staar: portion of *Kyrie I "Durham Cathedral."*

mental idioms. But his three unaccompanied Kyries, each named for a different cathedral, are quite engaging. Designed as a set, *Kyrie I "Durham Cathedral"* (1984) is for six-part male chorus, *Kyrie II "Cathedrale de Lausanne"* (1984) is for six-part women's chorus, and *Kyrie III "Notre Dame de Paris"* (1984–85) is for twelve-part mixed chorus. *Kyrie I "Durham Cathedral"* is typical. A study in major and minor seconds, its angular vocal lines, quickly changing textures, and surprising rhythms conjure up an austere mysticism.

3

FRANCE, SWITZERLAND, AND
THE LOW COUNTRIES

FRANCE

The most prominent French composers at the beginning of the century were Camille Saint-Saëns (1835–1921), Gabriel Fauré (1845–1924), and Vincent d'Indy (1851–1931), composers with nineteenth-century outlooks who, like Max Reger and Sir Edward Elgar, managed to live and compose well into the new century.

After 1900 Saint-Saëns composed no fewer than four Latin motets, a setting of *Psalm 150* for chorus and orchestra (1907), three secular cantatas, the oratorio *The Promised Land* (1913), and numerous other choral works, large and small, including the curious *Hail, California* (1915) for chorus and orchestra. In all likelihood the enduring anonymity of these pieces is a proper assessment of their value; but some, especially the motets and partsongs, are worthy of revival.

Fauré was much less prolific, but the two small church works produced in the twentieth century—*Ave Maria*, Opus 93 (1906) for two voices (or two-part choir) and organ, and *Tantum ergo* (1905) for soprano, tenor, and chorus—are typically exquisite.

In addition to d'Indy's contributions as a teacher, he also contributed several interesting works: *Pentecosten*, Opus 75 (1919), harmonizations of twenty-four Gregorian chants for soloist, unison chorus, and organ; *La vengeance du mari*, Opus 105 (1931) for soloists, chorus, winds, and piano, originally published as Opus 104; and works for different three-part vocal configurations, including *Le bouquet du printemps*, Opus 93 (1928) for female voices, *Les trois fileuses*, Opus 97 (1929) for equal voices, and *Le forgeron*, Opus 104 (1931) for mixed voices and string quartet.

Roger Nichols summed up the importance of Claude Debussy (1862–1918) when he commented, in a fashion as understated as Debussy's music, that "few later composers have been uninfluenced by him" (Sadie 1980, 5:292). Debussy was himself influenced by the French impressionist painters as well as by Balinese gamelan music. There is fascinating promise inherent in the scoring of such pieces as *Petite cantate* (1907) for soloists, chorus, bells, and piano, and *Noël* (1914) for tenor, chorus, bugles, and piano. Unfortunately, like most of Debussy's choral works, these remain unpublished. The few easily available works, however, reveal a complete mastery of the French language with all its subtleties, as well as a predilection toward the chorus— especially female chorus—as another orchestral color. The richly detailed *Trois chansons de Charles d'Orléans* (1898–1908) epitomizes the fluidity of rhythm and texture so typical of French impressionism, while retaining the directness of expression associated with its sixteenth-century models. The transfixed amazement of the female chorus's chanting in the cantata *La damoiselle élue* (1887–88, reorchestrated 1902) only hints at its later importance in *Nocturnes* (1897–99), in which the wordless *sirènes* not only come to hypnotic life but also provide inspiration for later composers, including Gustav Holst, Carl Nielsen, and Ralph Vaughan Williams. *Le martyre de Saint-Sébastien* (1911) was conceived as incidental music for a theatrical extravaganza that included soloists, chorus, orchestra, speakers, mimes, and dancers, and that might have been classified as performance art by the end of the century. It was composed under such severe time constraints that Debussy employed one of his friends to complete the orchestration. Notoriety attached to it immediately when the Archbishop of Paris forbade Catholics from attending the premiere because of, again in Nichols's words, "the glorification of cruelty in D'Annunzio's text and the beautiful legs of Ida Rubinstein, who played the saint." Never successful in the theater, Debussy's music has been occasionally revived as a cantata.

Albert Roussel (1869–1937) was an influential teacher whose importance as a composer did not become internationally recognized until late in his life. Stylistically, his innate lyricism reconciled the impressionism of Debussy with classical French impulses, and to a lesser extent with exotic elements from Southeast Asia and India. These characteristics are easily discernible in his handful of choral pieces: *Evocations*, Opus 15 (1910–12), *Madrigal aux muses*, Opus 25 (1923), *Le bardit des francs* (1926), and the impressive *Psalm 80*, Opus 37 (1928).

The music of Florent Schmitt (1870–1958) was quite popular during Schmitt's lifetime; but it did not survive unscathed by critics' barbs and was infrequently performed by century's end. One critic described Schmitt's works as "overloaded with detail and heavily scored to the point of turgidity. . . . His invention is not particularly memorable, and it may be doubted whether much of his music will be often revived, except by way of curiosity" (Blom 1954,

7:499). Anyone who has experienced the ravishing beauty of *Psalm 47* (1904) for chorus and orchestra, or the textural richness and clarity of the motet *Par le tempête* (1916–17) for double mixed chorus and four soloists, however, will automatically question this view. The same critic (hedging his bets, no doubt) offered an additional comment, which is in fact a better assessment: "The interest of connoisseurs . . . will continue to be justified, not only because Schmitt's music differs from that of other French masters but also because it has many positive qualities to recommend it: vigor, eloquence, passion, understanding of various media and masterly if at times too lavish orchestration, to mention only some of the most immediately striking."

Jean Roger-Ducasse (1873–1954) developed an inviting style that was originally influenced by his teacher, Fauré. In 1901, using his own libretto, he began a new version of the Faust legend, entitled *Au jardín de Marguerite* (1901–05) for soloists, large mixed chorus, and orchestra. At this work's completion Roger-Ducasse's style had moved forward, retaining basic elements of French classicism (structural clarity and emotional reserve) while absorbing the warmth and tonal colorations of Debussy. Like other French composers of the day Roger-Ducasse came under the spell of Spanish music, as demonstrated by *Sarabande* (1910) for offstage chorus (sopranos, altos, tenors) and orchestra. Other choral pieces include the large *Ulysse et les sirènes* (1937) for chorus and orchestra, and several motets.

Maurice Ravel's (1875–1937) *Trois chansons* (1914–15) is sometimes compared to Debussy's *Trois chansons de Charles d'Orléans*, but any similarities in contour and effect are not strong enough to suggest direct inspiration. Rather, the archaic sound of Ravel's set, as well as the date of composition—during World War I, when composers were particularly attentive to the patriotism awakened by antique French forms—suggests that Renaissance chansons were probably Ravel's models. In any case, the originality of the second piece, "Three Lovely Birds from Paradise," is unassailable even in a derivative context. Soprano and tenor soloists present a war-related text, the limpid melody supported by wordless chorus with clear-cut, austere sonorities that bring apprehension, shock, and irreconcilable grief into sharp, though quiet, relief. The occasional reduction of harmony to a single line of counterpoint sung in octaves is excruciatingly beautiful when perfectly performed, and at all other times simply excruciating. Ravel's only other work incorporating chorus is the ballet *Daphnis et Chloé* (1909–1912), in which he followed Debussy's example, utilizing a wordless chorus with spectacular effect.

Edgard Varèse (1885–1965) was a pupil of d'Indy, Roussel, and Charles Marie Widor, though clearly unaffected by them in regard to style, preferring instead to create a new, completely unconventional music that was abrasively dissonant and rhythmically bold, a music that would exert an impact on artists as diverse as Pierre Boulez and Frank Zappa. Even though Varèse was an experienced choral conductor with broad experience—he founded both the Choeur de l'Université Populaire in Paris and the Symphonischer Chor in Berlin (the latter primarily for the performance of Renaissance and early baroque music)—his compositional efforts were predominantly aimed at the expansion of instrumental possibilities, including early experiments with electronic music. Still, Varèse produced three choral works that are powerful expressions of his aesthetic: *Ecuatorial* (1934) for unison male chorus and instruments, *Étude pour Espace* (1937) for chorus, two pianos, and percussion, and *Nocturnal* (1961, completed 1973 by Chou Wen-Chung) for soprano soloist, male chorus, and chamber orchestra.

A different, though equally iconoclastic, music was produced by the poet, painter, essayist, and composer Georges Migot (1891–1976), who pursued a polyphonic course, experimenting with unusual timbres and rhythmically free melodic lines, always couched in a tonally ambiguous diatonic framework. Migot's compositions reflect a deeply spiritual nature. He wrote several works for unaccompanied chorus, such as the *Requiem* (1953), but his most interesting are those that combine various instrumental ensembles with chorus, including *Le sermon sur la montagne* (1936), *La Passion* (1941–42), *L'Annonciation* (1945–46), *La mise au tombeau* (1949), *Psaume 118* (1952) *La Nativité de Notre Seigneur* (1954), *Cantate de la vie meilleure* (1956), *Du ciel et de mer* (1961), *La sulamite* (1969), and *De Christo* (1971–72).

Lili Boulanger (1893–1918)—sister of Nadia, the best-known composition teacher of the twentieth century—wrote numerous excellent choral pieces during her brief life, including psalm settings, works for chorus with piano such as the supple and expressive *Soir sur la plaine* (1913), and several cantatas with orchestra, of which *Du fond de l'abîme* (Psalm 130, 1914–17) and the mildly exotic *Vieille prière bouddhique* (1917) are the most impressive. Reviewing a London performance of *Du fond de l'abîme*, Richard Fairman (*Financial Times*, 23 July 1999) remarked, "It is hard to claim that she had forged a style of her own when there is so little to judge her by, but this lofty and alluring music certainly suggests that she had found time to draw up a book of rules on harmony that had not been plundered by anybody else."

Alexandre Tansman (1897–1986) began composing at the age of eight. During the 1920s his music was championed by Koussevitsky, Stokowski, Toscanini, and other leading conductors, and he toured extensively as a pianist, often performing his own works. He was a great friend and biographer of Stravinsky. He often used folk materials, but his style was not based on them. Rather, they became a prominent element in an arsenal of freely incorporated techniques that included serial procedures, atonality, polytonality, and straightforward conservative tonality. In addition to Tansman's contribution to Nathaniel Shilkret's *Genesis Suite* (see chapter 2), his choral works include

In Memoriam (1943) for chorus and orchestra, the oratorio *Isaïe, le prophète* (1951) for tenor, chorus, and orchestra, *Prologue et cantate* (1956) for women's chorus and orchestra, and *Psaumes* (1961) for tenor, chorus, and orchestra.

Shortly after World War I, a group of six composers (Georges Auric, Louis Durey, Darius Milhaud, Francis Poulenc, and Germaine Tailleferre from France; Arthur Honegger from Switzerland) banded together under the guidance of Eric Satie and Jean Cocteau, whose tract *Le coq et l'arlequin* (1918) seemed to provide the basis for a purely French music, free from foreign (German) influences but open to various societal stimuli, including all kinds of popular music, jazz, and new industrial technologies. During the few years that it hung together as a group, Les Six was also aggressively critical of all established or emerging compositional schools. However, the practical application of Cocteau's philosophy produced compositions that tended to be brief, sardonic, superficial, and eminently forgettable. A more lasting consequence was that the group gained enough notoriety in the press for the individual members to become better known internationally than proponents of similarly anti-German artistic agendas that were springing up in Czechoslovakia (Ervín Schulhoff) and in Germany itself (Kurt Weill), a fact that would only help the great composers Honegger, Milhaud, and Poulenc.

As the group dissolved, beginning in 1921, each composer's personality developed individually, with the three less important members making only limited contributions to the choral repertoire. Georges Auric (1899–1983), still collaborating with Cocteau, concentrated on film scores, ballets, and other theatrical works before turning to music criticism. A representative choral work is the typically urbane setting of fifteenth-century texts for mixed chorus, *Quatre chansons françaises* (1950). Louis Durey (1888–1979) produced *Eloges* (1917–62) for solo voices, chorus, and orchestra, and *Dix choeurs de métiers* (1957) for mixed chorus, two flutes, clarinet, violin, celesta, and piano. Germaine Tailleferre (1892–1983) composed her interesting Concerto for Two Pianos, Chorus, and Orchestra (1934) and *La cantate du Narcisse* (1937) for soloists, female choir, and orchestra.

Darius Milhaud (1892–1974) belonged to a wealthy Jewish family steeped in the culture of Provence. His talent was manifested early, and he received a solid musical training at the Paris Conservatoire, where he studied composition with Widor and Paul Dukas. His lifelong devotion to the songs, dances, and other folk elements of his native region are easily recognized in his work, although polytonality, already present in his earliest major compositions, is invariably regarded as his music's most characteristic feature. From 1916 to 1918, while serving as a secretary at the French embassy in Brazil, Milhaud became familiar with the rhythms and colorations of native Brazilian music.

Two years later, by then an active member of Les Six, he was introduced to American jazz. These influences—in addition to literary and artistic interests cultivated through his friend Paul Claudel and others—produced a richly varied musical style, reflecting the rustic landscape of southern France and the urbane sophistication of Paris, seasoned with exotic American ingredients.

As with all extremely prolific composers, Milhaud's work is of uneven quality. Further, his inspiration diminished somewhat as he aged. Still, there are several outstanding choral pieces that can be considered typical of his best work. Among them are the witty and accessible *Les amours de Ronsard* (1934) for chamber chorus and instruments; the unaccompanied cantatas on texts by Claudel: *Cantique du Rhône* (1936), *Cantate de la paix* (1937), *Les deux cités* (1937), and *Cantate de la guerre* (1940); Symphony No. 3 (*Te Deum*, 1946), written in thanksgiving following World War II; *Service sacré* (1947) for chorus and orchestra, and other smaller pieces for the Jewish liturgy; *Pacem in terris* (1963), a choral symphony on words by Pope John XXIII; the choral comedy *Les momies d'Égypte* (1972); and his last completed work, *Ani maamin* (1972), a cantata written for the 1973 Festival of Israel.

Francis Poulenc (1899–1963) also belonged to a very well-to-do family, and his music reflects the seemingly flippant wit and glib, superficial gloss readily associated with wealth. Much more interesting, however, is the exceptional depth of understanding that exists just below the polished surface. Melody dominates in Poulenc's style, which, though influenced by his study of Bach chorales and early French masters, is mostly the product of a nondoctrinaire attitude (apparently the only common attribute of Les Six) that allowed him to cultivate a deep love of traditional music while appreciating the most advanced composers of the age. He drew on his own inclinations and experiences—the love of comfort, the company of good friends, a vibrant Catholic faith (intensely reawakened by the tragic circumstances of a friend's death in 1935), and the demeaning pressure of existence in occupied France during World War II—to create a large and varied body of choral works, many of which have entered the standard repertoire. All of them display the clear-cut tonalities (with frequent use of diminished seventh chords), unusual cadences, short, clipped phrases, and very angular part-writing—causing chord progressions to glisten in unexpected ways—that are Poulenc's hallmarks.

Most important are Poulenc's sacred works, beginning with *Litanies à la vierge noire* (1936) for treble chorus and organ, in which his ability to place a unique spin on otherwise commonplace material is obvious. This was followed by Mass in G (1937) for unaccompanied mixed chorus; the heartfelt and influential *Quatre motets pour un temps de pénitence* (1938–39); two individual motets written during the war, *Exultate Deo* and *Salve regina* (1941); two works for male voices, *Quatre petites prières de Saint François*

d'Assise (1948) and *Laudes de Saint Antoine de Padoue* (1957–59); the popular *Quatre motets pour le temps de Noël* (1951–52); and the little *Ave verum
corpus* (1952) for treble chorus. His large-scale sacred works with orchestra
consist of *Stabat mater* (1950), a moving work for soprano soloist, chorus,
and orchestra, whose emotional impact is nevertheless muted by the orchestral sheen; *Gloria* (1959), also for soprano, chorus, and orchestra, which
became an extremely popular large work of the century, and which shares
thematic material—as well as a delight in misplaced word accents—with his
earlier Mass; and *Sept répons des ténèbres* (1961), in which Poulenc's profound concentration of thought has been likened to Webern. A good example
of the surprise inherent in Poulenc's music occurs in *Gloria*, in which the
word "miserere" receives sudden and unmistakable commentary through a
fortissimo orchestral chord, simultaneously major and minor.

Francis Poulenc: simultaneous major-minor chord in *Gloria*.

Poulenc's secular works, which exhibit a decided affinity for poetry by
Paul Eluard (1895–1952), include the unaccompanied *Sept chansons* (1936)
and the delightful treble suite *Petite voix* (1936); the infrequently performed
cantata *Sécheresses* (1937) for chorus and orchestra; *Figure humaine* (1943)
for unaccompanied chorus, a difficult and complex essay on the nature of
freedom; the chamber cantata *Un soir de neige* (1944); and the slight and
effervescent *Chansons françaises* (1945–46).

The venerable French tradition of the organist-composer was carried into
the century by Louis Vierne (1870–1937). Best known for his organ works, he
also contributed the impressive *Messe solennelle* (1900) for mixed chorus and
two organs, which was influenced by an earlier, equally effective Mass (1890)

by Charles Marie Widor (1845–1937) for double chorus and two organs. While Vierne's Mass shares with Widor's certain characteristics of French classicism, such as lush late-nineteenth-century harmonies and clearly defined formal structures, it still stands on its own merits, among them handsome proportions, convincing contrapuntal writing, and a refined sense of dynamic balance. It is also more unassuming than Widor's, as there is little division in the straightforward four-part choral writing, and the second organ is used only to reinforce climaxes (a version arranged for one organ was published in the United States by Mark Foster Press in 1979).

The organist-composer tradition was fittingly continued by Maurice Duruflé (1902–1986), Jean Langlais (1907–1991), and Jehan Alain (1911–1940). Their styles are decidedly French, though highly individualistic, Duruflé's being influenced primarily by Gregorian chant and Alain's by older French contemporaries, while Langlais's style is based on rhythmic procedures and added-note harmonies derived from Stravinsky.

Even though Maurice Duruflé was one of history's least prolific composers, two of his three choral works—*Requiem*, Opus 9 (1947) and *Four Motets on Gregorian Themes* (1960)—are among the century's most frequently performed pieces. Indeed, *Requiem* occupies a unique niche in the repertoire, being universally viewed as the twentieth century's counterpart to the Requiem of Gabriel Fauré. Unlike Fauré's, however, Duruflé's Mass for the dead is created from the appropriate Gregorian chants, elaborated in a characteristically clear and uniform style learned from his teacher, Paul Dukas. The popularity of "Ubi caritas" from *Four Motets on Gregorian Themes* is such that many choral conductors remain blissfully unaware that any other settings of that text even exist. This popularity may be justified, too, since Duruflé's succinct setting is a virtually perfect reflection of the text. His third work, *Missa "Cum jubilo"* (1966) for baritone soloist, unison male voices, and orchestra, is equally effective but not as well known as its predecessors.

Jean Langlais composed more extensive chansons and cantatas, and a sizable number of liturgical works. Contrasting examples are the austere *Mass in Ancient Style* (1952) for chorus and organ, and the splashy *Psalm 117* (1976), which is harmonically richer, unleashing root-position triads in frenetic contrary motion to produce unavoidable dissonance, and exploring a mild bitonality, effectively punctuated by trumpets. The final cadence, an E-flat minor–D7 polychord progressing to C major with added sixth, is stereotypically French. Practically conceived and vocally grateful, both works are reinforced throughout by organ doublings.

Jehan Alain composed several Masses, including *Requiem* (1938) and *Missa brevis* (1938), as well as numerous shorter pieces for unaccompanied choir, all reflecting his notion that music is "less charm than mystery" (Sadie 1980, 1:189).

Olivier Messiaen (1908–1991) is an indisputable giant of twentieth-century music. As Debussy embraced orientalism, mostly from Bali, Messiaen also embraced non-European sources to stimulate his imagination: ancient Greek meters, Hindu rhythms (in which he discovered nonretrogradable rhythms), and birdcalls of all kinds and from all places. Additionally, he looked at traditional Western art music in new ways, especially studying the possibilities of rhythmic canons and freely embracing tonality, atonality, modality, and serialism with unique results.

Messiaen's analysis of a piece so apparently simple as the Renaissance chanson *Printemps* by Claude Le Jeune resulted in a work that is among the century's greatest and most complex compositions for chamber chorus, *Cinq rechants* (1948). Written for Marcel Couraud's ensemble, it combines a French text containing many references to Tristan and Isolde with syllables created by Messiaen ("ha yo ka pri ta ma la li la li la li la ssa re no"), as well as rhythmic patterns realized by quickly articulated consonants. Canons and rhythmic canons abound; there are frequent unison passages and passages of great harmonic complexity. The structure of the first movement is typical:

a brief introduction for solo voice
> first refrain:
>> A. two angular, contrasting ideas in unison, repeated
>> B. a very brief rhythmic passage of articulated consonants for men
>> C. a six note passage of rich, vertical harmonies, tutti
>> D. a brief unison passage contrasting with A
> first couplet:
>> a chromatically rich and ornate duet for soprano and contralto: the soprano melody repeats once, with a four note coda, under which the contralto melody repeats four times
> second refrain:
>> as before
> second couplet:
>> soprano and contralto as before, simultaneous with a complex rhythmic pattern of articulated consonants in the tenor, which repeats twice, and new melodic material in the bass, which repeats three times
> third refrain:
>> A. as before, but with a three-voice canon of new material added in the sopranos
>> B. as before
>> C. as before, but with a more dramatic spacing of the final chord
>> D. as before
> coda:
>> same as introduction

Messiaen could also write profoundly simple music, such as the little Communion motet, *O sacrum convivium!* (1937). Constructed homophonically in a basic AAB song form, the supple harmonies present mild challenges that reap great rewards. Obviously conceived as practical church music, it is performable by unaccompanied mixed chorus, mixed chorus with *colla parte* organ, or soprano soloist with organ.

Olivier Messiaen: *O sacrum convivium!*, measures 17–23.

Existing somewhere between the straightforward utterance of *O sacrum convivium!* and the extreme complexities of *Cinq rechants* is the rather large-scale *Trois petites liturgies de la Présence Divine* (1944), which Messiaen (n.d.) referred to as "first and foremost, a tremendous act of faith." Based on sonorities that related in his mind to specific colors, Messiaen mingled them—as if mixing paint—according to various rhythmic procedures developed through his research, and enhanced them with the exotic touch of ondes martenot and pitched percussion. He wrote the scripture-inspired text as he was composing the music, dedicating the first part "to the God who is present within us," the second part "to the God who is present in Himself," and the third part "to the God who is present in all things," adding that "these inexpressible ideas are not expressed but remain of the order of a dazzling display of color." Surely one of his most accessible and popular works, *Trois petites liturgies de la Présence Divine* is now considered basic entry-level Messiaen for the novice listener. Yet its premiere was met by violent and lengthy derision in the press, perhaps because the music's unapologetic sensuousness did not match the critics' religious preconceptions.

Messiaen achieved a new stylistic synthesis in the enormous cantata *La Transfiguration de Notre Seigneur Jésus-Christ* (1969) for ten vocal soloists, a one-hundred-voice chorus, seven instrumental soloists, and large orchestra. Dividing the work into two parts, each containing seven corresponding sections (alternating Gospel texts with commentary and concluding with a chorale), Messiaen abandoned, in André Boucourechliev's words (Sadie 1980, 12:209), "the highly speculative musical ideas he had developed, to return . . . to a greater simplicity of language, with clear structures and even stylistic traits that had been given up in the preceding works. This less hermetic music is enriched with the fruits of long experience; its great clarity and expressive force have reached a large audience." It ends in an enormous blaze of pure E major. Unpublished works by Messiaen include Mass (1933) for eight sopranos and four violins and *Chœurs pour une Jeanne d'Arc* (1941) for unaccompanied double chorus.

Jean Françaix (1912–1997) contributed *Five Chansons* (1932) for children's chorus and orchestra, *Three Epigrammes* (1938) for mixed chorus and string quintet, and *Two Motets* (1946) for unison chorus (or soloist) and organ. His music is generally characterized by grace, wit, and polished charm. However, the oratorio *L'apocalypse selon Saint Jean* (1939) for soloists, mixed chorus, and two orchestras reveals a depth of conception not encountered in his other works. In it the ecstasy of divine revelation is set against agonies of Hell as represented by the unusual second orchestra of saxophones, accordion, mandolin, and guitar.

The works of Maurice Ohana (1914–1992) have been unjustly neglected. Born in Casablanca of Andalusian-Jewish ancestry and Basque upbringing, Ohana settled in Paris after World War II. Never interested in serialism, he found his musical roots in such influences as Greek mythology, Andalusian flamenco, and a multifarious fascination with the rich traditions of Spain, Provence, Greece, Israel, Morocco, Africa, and even Cuba. Among the dozen choral works of note penned by Ohana are *Cantigas* (1953–54) for soprano and mezzo soloists, mixed chorus, winds, piano, and percussion; *Lys de Madrigaux* (1976), a dazzling work for twenty-two-part women's chorus, the text of which is largely made up of various syllabic incantations; *Dies solis* (1982) and *Lux noctis* (1988), both scored for multiple choirs and organ; *Swan Song* (1988) for mixed chorus, the text of which includes Ohana's own epitaph framed around an African American spiritual; and his final work, *Avoaha* (1991), a visceral aural setting for chorus, three percussionists, and two pianos evoking Afro-Cuban religious celebrations.

Other French composers include Charles Koechlin (1867–1950), who contributed several works for female chorus, some with orchestra, as well as *Ten Sacred Choruses in Modal Style* (1935) for mixed chorus, *Quinze motets de style archaïque* (1949) for chorus and woodwind quintet, and numerous other pieces; Jean Cras (1879–1932), a distinguished admiral in the French Navy who somehow found time to compose a variety of choral works both large and small; André Jolivet (1905–1974), whose Mass, oratorio, and several cantatas drew freely from a variety of inspirational sources, including Debussy, Varèse, Bartók, Stravinsky, and Arabic music; René Leibowitz (1913–1972), the first French champion of the Second Viennese School, whose cantatas *The Grip of the Given* (1950) for chorus and six instruments, *The Renegade* (1956) for chorus and eight instruments, and other works display a complete mastery of Schoenbergian serialism; Marcel Landowski (1915–1999), whose works include *Cinq chants d'innocence* (1952) for female choir and *Notes de nuit* (1961) for children's speaking chorus and chamber orchestra; Claude Ballif (b. 1924), a student of Blacher, whose systematization of the predodecaphonic expressionism of Schoenberg is apparent in his choral-orchestral *Requiem* (1953–68), and smaller *Prières* (1971) and *Chapelet* (1971) for mixed chorus; Pierre Boulez (b. 1925), a student of Leibowitz and an extremely influential serialist, who wrote *Séquence* (1952), which he withdrew after performance by Marcel Couraud, and the "work in progress" *e. e. cummings ist der Dichter* (begun 1970) for chamber chorus and twenty-four instruments; and Philippe Leroux (b. 1959), whose workmanlike exploration of avant-garde effects, *Anima Christi* (1985, revised 1990) for mixed chorus or quartet, combines Saint Ignatius Loyola's Latin text with phrases in French, and more awkwardly, English.

SWITZERLAND

Born in Le Havre to Swiss parents, Arthur Honegger (1892–1955) maintained very close associations with Switzerland throughout his life even though he continued to live in France. While his early involvement with Les Six no doubt sharpened his interest in popular idioms and reinforced his natural inclination toward direct, nondoctrinaire forms of communication, it did not diminish his international outlook, and he remained quite open to a variety of foreign influences. His style was aptly described by Aloys Mooser (Stepanek 1988,

13) as "oneness in diversity," a phrase which has also been applied to Charles Ives. Melodically, Honegger's music contains numerous chromatic angularities, the diatonicism and clipped phrasing typical of the French baroque, and the easygoing vigor of French popular song, all in jarringly close proximity. His harmony—sometimes lush, sometimes astringent—is predominately tonal, enriched with added notes, but often reduced to an absolutely basic diatonicism. Favorite cadential formulae resolve on chords with added seconds or sixths.

An outstanding example of Honegger's mature style is the late *Une Cantate de Noël* (1953) for baritone soloist, children's and mixed choruses, and orchestra, in which the compositional details, as well as the originality of concept, are particularly interesting. Initially sketched from 1940 to 1941 as part of a projected oratorio, *Jeu de la Passion*, Honegger later completed the Christmas portion for the twenty-fifth anniversary of Paul Sacher's Bale Chamber Orchestra. Freely combining popular elements with sophisticated harmonic and structural procedures, it begins with a slowly materializing prelude, "De profundis," that culminates in an anguished petition for aid. These cries are interrupted, first by children's choir, then by the baritone soloist, informing the chorus that redemption is near. The central section is a quodlibet on well-known Christmas carols, performed simultaneously in their original languages. The children return with a snippet of Gregorian chant (subtly accenting its common origins with the carol "Es ist ein' Ros' entsprungen"), and the baritone sings a prayerful "Gloria in excelsis" followed by an appropriately joyful choral setting of Psalm 117. The cantata is rounded off by a gradually subsiding orchestral postlude based on the previously heard carols, the last three measures forming a retrograde of the work's opening.

Without the Christmas cantata, Honegger's reputation as a composer of choral music would rest primarily on two large oratorios, *Le roi David* (1921) and *Jeanne d'Arc au bûcher* (1934–35), which were both originally designed to accommodate partial staging. The composition and premiere of *Le roi David* occurred within a very brief span of time. Ernest Ansermet recommended Honegger to the poet René Morax, who was seeking a composer for his drama on King David, scheduled to open Morax's theater in Mezieres, Switzerland, in 1921. Honegger began composing it on 25 February of that year, completing it on 28 April. The first performance took place on 11 June. In 1923 Honegger expanded the original instrumentation of fifteen instruments to full orchestra, and it is in this later version, without staging, that *Le roi David* became most popular. It is designed in three parts of unequal length and independent dramatic unity, presenting (1) the young David and his dealings with the increasingly mad Saul, (2) the coronation of David, and (3) David's reign, including his peccadilloes, mortal sins, family troubles, relationship with God, and finally the coronation of Solomon and David's peaceful death. The action is propelled by a narrator, the chorus and soloists providing commentary and occasional characterizations. The musical interjections, often extremely brief, tend to become more spacious as dramatic conclusions are reached, which not only accentuates the action but also increases the sense of fulfillment at the end of each part. The music is never subtle. Rather, the story's pageantry is presented in bold, obvious strokes of effective and entertaining music-hall color.

Jeanne d'Arc au bûcher was the first collaboration of Honegger and Paul Claudel (1868–1955). Typical of Claudel, the libretto focuses on varied and extreme perceptions—mysticism and reality, faith and cynicism, lyricism and brutality—which Honegger's music matches mood for mood. It contains some novel elements, such as the use of ondes martenot, and a dramatic structure that has Joan of Arc tied to the stake from the beginning, major events in her life being presented as flashbacks commented on by a variety of characters, some singing, some speaking (Joan herself is a spoken role). The chorus plays a dominant part, often interacting directly with the actors. The final scene, in which the choir chants an epitaph while the flames rise up, is unforgettable.

Other choral works include a concert version of the opera *Judith* (1925); the oratorio *Cris du monde* (1930–31); the cantatas *Les mille et une nuits* (1937), *La danse des morts* (1938), and *Hamlet* (1946); and the radio cantatas *Christophe Colomb* (1940), *Les battements du monde* (1944), and *Saint François d'Assise* (1949).

Ernest Bloch (1880–1959) composed only two choral works: *America* (1926), an epic rhapsody for chorus and orchestra, and Sacred Service (*Avodath Hakodesh*, 1930–33) for baritone soloist, chorus, and orchestra. While *America* has fallen into disuse, Sacred Service has become the benchmark by which all other concert settings of Jewish liturgy are measured. Prior to its first performance in San Francisco, Bloch told the audience that the work encompassed the totality of his experience, that he was endeavoring to deliver a message of faith and hope in life, and that, while it was presented from a Jewish perspective, it was written for the entire world. Poignantly modal but with infrequent use of the augmented second typical of Jewish chant, Sacred Service is in turn supplicatory, awestruck, questioning, penitent, and joyful. From the opening moment when the music rises slowly, like incense, into a baritone solo of great expressivity, the listener is hooked. For Jews, this work is a great affirmation of their faith; for others it provides a moving and enlightening introduction to the liturgy. Some of its passages, "Yimloch Adonoy leolom" (The Lord shall reign forevermore) and "Lecho Adonoy hageduloh" (And Thine, Lord, is the greatness) for instance, rank with the most thrilling of the century, while the particularly beautiful "Silent Devotion and Response" leads an independent life, well known in churches and schools as well as synagogues.

Born in Geneva, Frank Martin (1890–1974) was the son of a Calvinist minister whose family had fled from France centuries earlier. Martin began composing at the age of eight and shortly thereafter heard a performance of Bach's *Saint Matthew Passion* that essentially set the direction of his own music. Over the next thirty years he gradually assimilated the styles of Ravel and Debussy, and experimented with folk music and exotic rhythms, gradually refining his own modal language by developing a highly personalized twelve-tone technique supported by harmonies built from perfect triads. As his style developed he composed a number of choral works, including the large *Les dithyrambes* (1918) for soloists, mixed chorus, children's chorus, and orchestra, *Cantate sur la Nativité* (1929), *Musique pour le fêtes du Rhône* (1929) for chorus and band, and *Chansons* (1931) for female chorus with ad libitum cello. Bernhard Billeter provided an engaging analysis of Martin's mature style as it pertains to the secular oratorio on the Tristan legend *Le vin herbé* (1938–41), noting that "in the accompaniment, perfect triads are moved in unusual progressions. Dissonant chords are developed in smooth part-writing, often over a static bass which indicates the momentary tonal centre. As a result of Martin's 'gliding tonality,' a movement rarely ends in its initial key" (Sadie 1980, 11:716). By the end of the century, Martin's best-known work was his Mass for unaccompanied double chorus, which surely has as interesting a history as any work in the repertoire. Written without any external impetus between 1922 and 1926, at the height of the composer's pure modal period, it remained undisturbed in Martin's desk for almost forty years—a matter, he said, between him and God. The Mass was finally performed in 1962, in the Netherlands, and performances have increased ever since as it steadily usurps a place on programs that formerly would have listed the Masses of Vaughan Williams or Poulenc. Why would a Protestant composer such as Martin write such a Mass? As an homage to his beloved Bach, perhaps? Or merely as an exercise? When one hears this piece—spaciously unsentimental, but with a compact structure accentuating at every turn a profound emotional content—it seems that there was surely more to it, for its remarkable serenity and strength exude a sense that real communication is occurring, not only between composer and audience but also between the composer and God. Its ever increasing popularity not only reflects superb craftsmanship but also the artistic and emotional atmosphere of the century's last twenty-five years, when strict serialism and various avant-garde techniques ran dry and many people, including composers, performers, and audiences, were searching for an aesthetic that promised fulfillment rather than empty, unending challenges.

Martin's other works include *Cantate pour le 1er août* (1941) for chorus and organ, written for the 650th anniversary of the Swiss confederation; *In terra pax* (1944), an oratorio commissioned by the Swiss government to celebrate the end of World War II; *Chansons* (1944, 1945) for male voices; *Golgotha* (1945–48), an oratorio that intersperses the Passion narrative with commentary by Saint Augustine of Hippo; *Five Songs of Ariel* (1950), engaging and popular settings of texts from Shakespeare's *The Tempest*; *Psaumes de Genève* (1958) for mixed chorus, boys' chorus, and orchestra; *Ode à la musique* (1961), curiously but effectively scored for baritone soloist, chorus, brass, string bass, and piano; and *Requiem* (1971–72).

Other leading Swiss composers in the first half of the century included Othmar Schoeck (1886–1957) and Willy Burkhard (1900–1955).

Schoeck, a renowned composer of art songs, was also very active as a choral conductor in Zurich. His style is essentially lyrical, an outstanding characteristic being the effortless matching of text to music. Most of his choral pieces are for male voices, but from 1911 to 1917, when he was conducting the Teachers' Chorus, his focus shifted to works for mixed choir. Examples include the interesting *Eichendorff Cantata* (1933) for male chorus, brass, piano, and percussion, and *Dithyrambe* (1911) for double chorus and orchestra.

Willy Burkhard was a composer of considerable spiritual depth and emotional profundity, especially in his choral music. His style is contrapuntal, based on Renaissance and late baroque models, and always relies on modal harmony. His two great works, coming at either end of his creative life, are the oratorio *Das Gesicht Jesajas* (1933–35) and his Mass (1951). Major works in every respect, they are musically convincing and otherwise satisfying essays in large form. The Mass impresses, particularly, in its highly individual approach to the text. Burkhard's other choral pieces, both sacred and secular, represent a comprehensive survey of types and ensembles: cantatas, motets, partsongs, oratorio; unison, treble, and male and mixed voices; organ, orchestra, brass, and percussion. Outstanding examples are *Psalm 93* (1937) for unison chorus and organ, the cantata *Genug ist genug* (1938–39) for chorus, two trumpets, timpani, and strings, *Cantate Domino* (1940) for soprano, chorus, strings, and timpani, *Nine Folk Songs* (1942) for female chorus, the oratorio *Das Jahr* (1942), and *Frühlingsglaube* (1950) for male voices.

Dominique Gesseney-Rappo (b. 1953) stands out among the younger generation of Swiss composers. An experienced music educator and professor in charge of training secondary school music teachers at the Lausanne Music Academy, he has created numerous choral works that reveal an acute sensitivity to the needs of younger adult voices. His compositions are rhythmically vital and tonally accessible, ranging in size from the eighty-minute "choral fresco" *Aujourd'hier Aujoird'hui* (1989) for soloists, chorus, and orchestra to the unaccompanied three-minute motet *Benedic anima mea* (1993). In between are a variety of works, including *Missa brevior* (1994) for chorus and brass, *Le Rondo de Cupidon* (1994) for chorus, baritone soloist, oboe, harp, and cello, *Tibi Gloria Domine* (1998) for chorus and two French horns, and the impressive brief cantata *Dei populus liberatus* (1998), commissioned by the eighteenth Zimriya (World Assembly of Choirs) in Jerusalem in honor of the fiftieth anniversary of Israel.

Other Swiss composers include Hermann Suter (1870–1926), who composed the oratorio *Le laudi di S Francesco d'Assisi* (1923) for soloists, children's and mixed choruses, and orchestra, and other large works; Walther Geiser (1897–1993), whose many partsongs and cantatas were composed in a warm romantic-impressionistic harmonic language flavored by baroque contrapuntal elements; Robert Blum (1900–1994), whose polyphonic and occasionally serial style provided a comfortable framework for numerous psalm settings, cantatas, oratorios, and other sacred pieces, of which *Two Meditations* (1970) for women's choir, woodwind quintet, and organ, is exemplary; Robert Suter (b. 1919), a student of Geiser who composed some Latin motets as well as the interesting *Ballade von des Cortez Leuten* (1960) for speaker, mixed chorus, speaking chorus, and chamber orchestra, on text by Bertolt Brecht; Klaus Huber (b. 1924), whose studies with Blacher and Burkhard influenced both the philosophy and musical technique of his several large choral works, including *Job 14* (1971) for mixed chorus and nine instruments; Rudolf Kelterborn (b. 1931), whose *Kleine Psalmenkantate* (1951) for soprano, chorus, and organ, oratorio *Die Flut* (1963–64) for soloists, speaker, chorus, and orchestra, and unaccompanied *Tres cantiones sacrae* (1967) are representative of an evolving style rooted in baroque procedures but increasingly open to serial and avant-garde techniques; and Heinz Holliger (b. 1939), who contributed the interesting *Scardanelli Zyklus* (Scardanelli Cycle) for mixed chorus, solo flute, and chamber orchestra.

Belgium

The most active choral composer in Belgium at the beginning of the twentieth century was Edgar Tinel (1854–1912). Tinel's work with chant and his resulting opinions on church music influenced the *Motu proprio* of Pope Pius X in 1903, which limited the expressive possibilities available to Catholic composers. Typical of his compositions is *Missa in honorem Beatae Mariae Virginis de Lourdes*, Opus 41 (1905), which combined small doses of nineteenth-century romanticism with Renaissance polyphony. Tinel's *Te Deum* (1905), written for concert performance, abandons this quasi-Renaissance polyphonic style in favor of one more openly romantic and inspired somewhat by Bach. Tinel's musical conservatism was typical of other Belgian composers and conductors. With few exceptions, contemporary music was simply not performed in Belgium until after World War I. Lodewijk de Vocht began giving concerts of new choral music with the Chorale Caecilia in Antwerp in 1921, but for the most part Belgian composers remained under the influence of Wagner and Strauss.

Joseph Jongen (1873–1953) was widely performed during the first half of the century. His attractive style differs from his contemporaries in that it was influenced by Ceasar Franck, Claude Debussy, and other French composers, but lacks a defining personality of its own. His works include Mass (1946) for mixed chorus, several cantatas, and a few motets.

Paul Gilson (1865–1942) wrote cantatas and numerous small pieces but is primarily remembered as the most significant teacher of his generation. Jean Absil (1893–1974), Marcel Poot (1901–1988), and René Bernier (1905–1984) were important students of Gilson. Absil developed a polytonal style noted for its structural clarity and polyphonic richness. Several of his early pieces are grouped in tripartite sets, all bearing the title *Three Choruses*: Opus 6 (1922) for female choir, Opus 14 (1934) for mixed choir, Opus 15 (1934) and Opus 18 (1935) for children's choir and orchestra, and Opus 24 (1936) for female choir. Works for children's choir occupy a dominant position among other numerous cantatas and partsongs. Poot was recognized internationally as leader of Belgium's mainstream neoromantic composers, but he wrote few choral pieces, of which the oratorio *Icare* (1947) and the interesting *Chanson bachique* for speakers and male chorus are examples. Bernier was influenced by late-nineteenth- and early-twentieth-century French masters, as well as by Gilson's teachings. He excelled in choral music, especially unaccompanied works in which his modally colored harmonies and effortless melodic gifts are displayed to good advantage. Among Bernier's best pieces are *Liturgies* (1941–42) and *Incantations* (1954–56) for mixed chorus, as well as the earlier *Sortilèges ingénus* (1939–42) for treble chorus and piano or orchestra.

Flor Peeters (1903–1986) is, at least among church musicians, the most famous Belgian composer of the century. The most salient feature of his style is its abundant optimism. Influenced by Gregorian chant, Belgian folk music, and classical forms, Peeters created music with bright tonalities—enhanced by added notes—that glisten in a fabric that freely alternates rhythmically active counterpoint with more introspective lyrical passages. He wrote many kinds of liturgical music including Masses, Latin motets, and English anthems. Typical are *Jubilee Mass* (1958), the popular *Intrada festiva* (1959) for unison chorus, brass, and organ, and *Jubilate Deo* (1936) for mixed chorus and organ.

Other Belgian composers include Jan Blockx (1851–1912), who contributed two cantatas for children's voices and orchestra, *Gloriae patriae* (1902) and *Feeste in den Lande* (1903), as well as cantatas and shorter unaccompanied works for mixed chorus; Paul Malengreau (1887–1959), who wrote several Masses and motets in addition to the oratorio *The Legend of Saint Augustine* (1934); Staf Nees (1901–1965), an internationally famous carillonneur who composed several oratorios and Masses; Pierre Froidebise (1914–1962), who composed several Latin motets, the cantata *La navigation d'Ulysse* (1943), and other pieces in a style incorporating serialism and, later, aleatoric techniques; Henri Pousseur (b. 1929), who established the first Belgian electronic music studio and produced two very interesting works with chorus: *Invitation a l'utopie* (1970) for speaker, soprano, and mezzo soloists, mixed chorus, piano, and eighteen instruments and *Midi-minuit* (1970) for mixed and children's choruses, jazz group, pop group, folksinger, piano, and orchestra; and Vic Nees (b. 1938), who contributed a *Stabat mater* and *Five Sacred Motets*, both for mixed chorus, as well as other works.

NETHERLANDS

The leaders of Dutch music at the beginning of the century, Bernard Zweers (1854–1924), Alphons Diepenbrock (1862–1921), and Johan Wagenaar (1862–1941), contributed to choral music as teachers, conductors, and composers.

Zweers's greatest contributions were as teacher and choral conductor, but he also composed many small pieces and several cantatas, including *Aan de schoonheid* (To Beauty, 1909) for soloists, chorus, and orchestra, in which a simple melodic style is enriched by thick harmonies. Willem Landré (1874–1948) and Daniel Ruyneman (1886–1963) were important students of Zweers. Landré, unlike most of his Dutch contemporaries, was profoundly influenced by French music. His small catalogue of choral works happens to contain his best piece, the gently elegiac *Requiem in memoriam uxoris* (1931). Ruyneman developed an enormous reputation in the Netherlands for his unquenchable desire to explore new musical territory. Traces of virtually every twentieth-century trend can be found in his works. Typical are his pieces for mixed chorus, *De roep* (1918) and *Sonata* (1931), which handle the voices instrumentally.

By the turn of the century Diepenbrock, the first significant Dutch composer since Sweelinck, had already produced an extremely important work in the Dutch Catholic repertoire, *Missa in die festo* (1891) for chorus and organ, and was at his peak. Influenced by Wagner and later by Debussy, Diepenbrock developed a style that presents an intriguing mixture of Renaissance polyphonic principles and late romantic harmonic considerations. *Carmen saeculare* (1901), on texts by Horace, *Hymnus de Sanctu Spiritu* (1906) for chorus and organ, and *Hymne aan Rembrandt* (1906) for chorus and orchestra are representative of the nine choral works composed in the new century.

Johan Wagenaar (1862–1941) was renowned as music director of Utrecht Cathedral and conductor of the Utrecht and Arnhem Toonkunst choirs. Among his composition students were his son, Bernard Wagenaar (1894–

1971), who would find success on the other side of the Atlantic, and Willem Pijper, who would become the first internationally recognized Dutch composer of the century and an influential teacher in his own right. Johan Wagenaar also composed some interesting pieces, notably *Three Double Canons*, Opus 12 (1902) for female chorus and *Prière au printemps*, Opus 18 (1904) for female chorus and piano.

Hendrik Andriessen (1892–1981) was the most important Catholic composer after Diepenbrock. His genuine gift for expressive melody is balanced by a rather conventional harmonic language supported by clear-cut, though originally conceived, forms. The simple, devotional quality of text setting in *Missa in honorem Ss cordis* (1919) for two-part chorus and organ departed completely from previous Dutch Masses, creating the contemplative style thereafter typical of Andriessen's music. Other Masses include the modal *Missa diatonica* (1935) for six-part mixed chorus and the powerful *Missa Christus Rex* (1938), which encouraged Dutch listeners during the Nazi occupation. In addition to a large quantity of liturgical pieces, Andriessen also composed secular works, of which *Carmen saeculare* (1968) for soloists, chorus, and orchestra, and two unaccompanied works, *Sonnet de Pierre de Ronsard* (1917) and *Omaggio a Marenzio* (1965), are noteworthy.

Willem Pijper (1894–1947) was initially drawn to a mixture of German and French influences before discovering his own unique polytonal and polyrhythmic personality. His style is predominantly contrapuntal, relying on development of a "germ cell" (Pijper's term [Sadie 1980, 14:746]) from which all succeeding material generates. Virtually all of Pijper's choral music is secular. Representative works include *Two Ballades of Paul Fort* (1921) for women's choir and piano, *Heer Halewijn* (1929) for mixed chorus, and *Réveillez-vous, Piccars* (1933) for male chorus and winds.

Jan Mul (1911–1971), Herman Strategier (1912–1988), and Albert de Klerk (1917–1998) studied with Andriessen at the Roman Catholic School of Church Music in Utrecht. Each contributed several Masses and other liturgical pieces. Excellent examples include Klerk's warmly inviting *Missa Mater Sanctae laetitiae* and Mul's little unaccompanied *Pater noster* (published 1980). In a modal style similar to Andriessen's, equally at home in church or concert hall, the quasi-Renaissance language of *Pater noster* projects a vital and contemporary faith. Strategier, who served as conductor of Leiden's Dutch Madrigal Choir, also composed a number of large concert works, among them *Don Ramiro* (1943) for chorus and orchestra, *Rembrandt Cantata* (1956), and *The Shadow out of Time* (1973) for ad libitum chorus, flute, percussion, organ, harp, and tape.

Pupils of Pijper include Guillaume Landré (1905–1968), Henk Badings (1907–1987), and Rudolf Escher (1912–1980).

Landré inherited a gift for elegiac writing from his father, Willem, developing a lyrical style quite different from Pijper's. His large choral-orchestral *Piae memoriae pro patria mortuorum* (1942) is a riveting memorial to those killed in the Nazi invasion. The unusual device of liturgical text eventually supplanted by folk song would be used later in the century by the Swedish composer Nils Lindberg with equally profound effect (see chapter 7).

Henk Badings was born in Java and orphaned at an early age, moving to his parents' native Holland in 1915. After completing a university education in the natural sciences he began composition studies with Pijper. He was not, however, interested in his teacher's concept of "germ cells," preferring instead to explore the possibilities of tonality. To this end Badings devised his own scales and harmonic series, and experimented with quarter tones. His later music also utilized electronic sounds, usually to provide timbres and ranges not otherwise attainable. Widely respected as a composer of orchestral and dramatic music, Badings composed many substantial choral pieces with orchestra. Particularly interesting are *Kantate II* (1937) for soprano, chamber chorus, and chamber orchestra, the oratorio *Apocalypse* (1948) for soloists, chorus, and orchestra, *Psalm 147* (1959) for children's choir, two mixed choirs (chamber and large), and orchestra, *Hymnus ave maris stella* (1965) for female chorus and orchestra, *Kantate VII* (*Ballade van die bloeddorstige Jagter*, 1970) for solo voices, chorus, orchestra, and tape, and *Whitman Cantate* (1973) for narrator, chorus, and wind orchestra. He also produced smaller works, including the well-known *Trois chansons bretonnes* (1946), *Missa brevis* (1946), and *Five Chinese Poems* (1973), all for unaccompanied mixed chorus; *Six Christmas Songs* (1950) and other pieces for female chorus; and many compositions for male chorus, including *Drie Lucebertliederen* (1964), with tape. Like Pijper, Badings also became an influential teacher.

Escher's most important choral pieces were written during the 1950s, including *Le vrai visage de la paix* (1953), *Songs of Love and Eternity* (1955), on texts by Emily Dickinson, and *Ciel, air et vents* (1957), all for unaccompanied chorus. An interest in Debussy and Ravel and an original grasp of polyphonic technique inform these works, as well as the later *Three Poems by W. H. Auden* (1975).

Ton de Leeuw (1926–1996), an important student of Badings, utilized rhythmic and structural concepts he learned in India, as well as Pijper's motivic development ideas. Leeuw's later works are preoccupied with spatial aspects of music. He first attracted attention with the radio oratorio *Job* (1956). Honegger's influence is apparent in the French text, in the use of speakers and singers, and even in the use of electronic sounds with orchestra, although Leeuw's *musique concrete* is quite different from Honegger's ondes martenot. Other impressive pieces are *The Magic of Music* (1958), on text from an Indian music theory book, *Psalm 68* (1966) for chorus and three trombones, and *Cloudy Forms* (1970) for male chorus.

Another important student of Badings, Hans Kox (b. 1930) received his early musical training from his father, an organist and choral conductor. His works prior to 1964 contain an abundance of early-twentieth-century Austrian influences. Thereafter, his interests focus more on controlled improvisation and spatial considerations. Outstanding examples of these later tendencies are *In Those Days* (1969) and *Requiem for Europe* (1971). Written in commemoration of the Battle of Arnhem, *In Those Days* calls for two choruses, three instrumental ensembles, and two conductors, each starting at different times. *Requiem for Europe* requires four choruses, two organs, and orchestra, each placed in separate parts of the room, with some performance aspects left to the conductor's discretion. Other works include the partsong cycle *Chansons cruelles* (1957), on texts by Nicole Louvier, K. Merz, and Rainer Maria Rilke, *De kantate van Sint Juttemis* (1962) for tenor and baritone soloists, male chorus, and piano, and *Litania* (1965) for female chorus and orchestra.

Other important Dutch composers include Ernest Willem Mulder (1898–1959), an important teacher at the Amsterdam Conservatory, who contributed *Requiem* (1932) and *Stabat mater* (1948); Johannes Röntgen (1898–1969), a well-known choral conductor and frequent accompanist to Pablo Casals, who wrote several small choral pieces; Robert Heppener (b. 1925), best known for his exciting and technically innovative cycle on Renaissance carnival poems, *Canti carnascialeschi* (1966) for mixed chorus; and Louis Andriessen (b. 1939), whose choral works became overshadowed by his internationally acclaimed operas.

Important and poignant events in choral music occurred during World War II on the island of Sumatra in the Dutch East Indies (now Indonesia). Although these events were international in character, they are discussed here because the primary chroniclers and many of the participants were Dutch. Dutch, British, and Australian noncombatants who had been captured during the Japanese onslaught were placed in prison camps on Sumatra. Families were torn apart, men separated from women and children. One camp for women and children changed location three times, always moving further into the hinterland. Almost from the beginning of their imprisonment, the inmates of this camp participated in informal singing in the evenings. In early summer of 1942 a British captive named Margaret Dryburgh (1890–1945), who was also a missionary and music teacher, wrote words and music for *The Captive's Hymn*, a short work for unaccompanied four-part women's chorus, which was performed almost immediately. It is a prayer of patience and courage, and its complete lack of bitterness makes the final expression of hope particularly impressive:

Grant that nations under Thee
O'er the world may brothers be,
Cleansed by suffering, know rebirth,
See Thy kingdom come on earth.
(Colijn 1995, 105)

On Christmas of that year the singers performed familiar carols, and later in 1943, under the direction of Dryburgh and fellow British inmate Norah Chambers, a "vocal orchestra" was created that performed folk songs and famous instrumental pieces—"Largo" from Dvořák's *New World Symphony*, Chopin's *Preludes*, Nos. 15 and 20, "Morning" from Grieg's *Peer Gynt Suite*, Bach's "Jesu, Joy of Man's Desiring," and others—all arranged from memory for four-part women's chorus by the remarkable Dryburgh, who unfortunately did not survive the war. Since the war, the accomplishments of this orchestra have been memorialized in print and on television and served as the basis of a major Hollywood film called *Paradise Road*.

✑ 4

BRITISH ISLES

Twentieth-century British choral music is dominated by Ralph Vaughan Williams (1872–1958) and Benjamin Britten (1913–1976), two outstanding figures who not only created a large number of wonderful choral pieces but also profoundly influenced virtually every aspect of British music.

Vaughan Williams composed for every conceivable choral situation, from unison folk song arrangements with piano to very large works for chorus, soloists, and orchestra. His art is a unique distillation of British folk elements, ancient compositional techniques, and twentieth-century sensibilities. Like Janáček and Bartók, whose musical personalities were likewise unlocked by the discovery and absorption of folk materials, Vaughan Williams created a highly individual and original style. However, to critics and intelligentsia who viewed modernity only in terms of expressionistic dissonance and atonal chromaticism, his essential diatonicism and its application often seemed old-fashioned if not downright reactionary. Still, his works remained immensely popular with choruses all over the world, and late in the century, when unabashed tonality once again interested young composers, the innovative and original aspects of his music began to be more fully appreciated.

The essential elements of Vaughan Williams's mature style were already present in his first published anthem, *Psalm 48: O Praise the Lord of Heaven* (1913) for unaccompanied double mixed chorus and semichorus. A study in antiphonal sonorities and textures, the mode alternates between Mixolydian and Aeolian, modulating frequently and occasionally altering notes for harmonic purposes. Following the example of Renaissance motets, the form is created by the psalm's structure, each section having a new point of imitation. Instead of obvious text-painting, the work exudes an abstract delight in the pure sound of words, especially the interplay of sibilants. The opening music and text return at the end, abbreviated but easily recognizable, in keeping with the composer's conviction that statement-departure-return was the basis of all musical form.

An unusual property of Vaughan Williams's art is a consciously applied stylistic pluralism. The composer thought that a technique effective in 1911 or 1934 would still be effective in 1953 if the right opportunity presented itself. Therefore, in some pieces, such as the oratorio *Sancta civitas* (1923–25), a singularity of expression—in this case, harmonies built on fourths—is relentlessly pursued. In others, such as the late Christmas cantata *Hodie* (1953–54), variations in compositional style occur from movement to movement, the composer selecting a musical vocabulary deemed most suitable for a particular text. It is a measure of Vaughan Williams's greatness that this patchwork approach works at all, and that whatever the style, it is always identifiable as his.

In addition to *Sancta civitas*, at least three of Vaughan Williams's large choral-orchestral works—*A Sea Symphony*, *Five Tudor Portraits*, and *Dona nobis pacem*—rank among the best of the century.

A remarkable first essay in symphonic form, *A Sea Symphony* (1905–1910) for soprano and baritone soloists, mixed chorus, and orchestra remains the composer's most popular large work. The influences of Sir Edward Elgar (especially *The Dream of Gerontius*) and French impressionism are easily discernible in the expansive themes, harmonies, and colorful orchestration, but these do not diminish the strength of Vaughan Williams's own emerging personality, which is especially apparent in the wonderfully wrought second movement, "On the Beach at Night Alone," and the cantata-like finale, "A Song for all Seas."

In 1932 Elgar recommended the poetry of John Skelton (1460–1529) to Vaughan Williams. The result was *Five Tudor Portraits* (1936) for contralto and baritone soloists, mixed chorus, and orchestra, a problematic masterpiece requiring a virtuoso chorus and a conductor with an exquisite sense of pacing. It also stands alongside Vaughan Williams's *Magnificat* (1931) as one of the choral repertoire's few pieces containing substantial solo work for contralto. By turns ribald, charming, sarcastic, and tender, *Five Tudor Portraits* brings each of Skelton's characters vividly to life. No other choral work contains so perfect a contrast as that achieved between the movements "Epitaph for John Jayberd of Diss" and "Jane Scroop." Both are Requiems of a sort, one quoting liturgical text, the other the "Dies irae" tune, but they are in no way similar. John Jayberd was so completely rotten that the mere idea of his death sent acquaintances into enthusiastic fits of drunken revelry. Jane Scroop, on the other hand, was a young novice in a convent, devastated when her pet bird was killed by a cat. "Epitaph for John Jayberd" is at least the equal of Orff's famous "In Taberna" (from *Carmina burana*), and in "Jane Scroop" the listener understands that a child's grief, even over a small thing, is still painful indeed.

Vaughan Williams's second great choral work of 1936, *Dona nobis pacem* for soprano and baritone soloists, mixed chorus, and orchestra, is poles apart from its predecessor. Using his early setting (1911) of Walt Whitman's "Dirge for Two Veterans" as a centerpiece, the composer deftly crafted an antiwar statement by combining Latin and biblical texts with poems of Whitman and part of a famous speech by Sir John Bright. It would perhaps have seemed more convincing as a plea for peace had it not so clearly reflected the trendy sentiments of the British intelligentsia. Nevertheless, *Dona nobis pacem* is dazzling in its evocation of war's horrors, noble in its homage to the dead, and uplifting in its affirmation of life.

Five English Folk Songs (1913) and *Three Shakespeare Songs* (1951), both for mixed chorus, are exemplary samples of Vaughan Williams's numerous important unaccompanied works. The culmination of his direct involvement with folk music, *Five English Folk Songs* cannot be considered simply a compilation of arrangements of preexisting tunes. Rather, the songs must be viewed as new works, the old melodies serving as vehicles to excite the composer's imagination. Exceptionally elaborate, the basic nature of each tune remains magically unaffected. The first four songs deal with sailors, either alive or dead, who return to their lovers. The last of these, "The Lover's Ghost," achieves a nobility of utterance seldom encountered. The fifth, "Wassail," has nothing to do textually with the others unless one sees a pun in the title. A Christmas piece, it has independently achieved a universal popularity and provides a satisfying and sprightly ending to the set. *Three Shakespeare Songs* retains the modal influence, love of language, and rich sonorities found earlier in *O Praise the Lord of Heaven*, while masterfully employing additional means of expression the composer had developed over the intervening years. Text-painting here is palpably real and completely effective, employing sophisticated chromatic colorations and exploring the possibilities of the chorus's dark timbres.

The distinguished musicologist Watkins Shaw wrote that Vaughan Williams "composed practically no church music in the narrow sense. There is hardly anything that can be called an anthem" (Blume 1974, 730). When compared to the enormous volume of workmanlike but largely uninspired liturgical pieces produced by lesser composers, Vaughan Williams's output does indeed seem modest. But the situation changes when Vaughan Williams is compared to composers of similar stature. Unlike most major twentieth-century composers, Vaughan Williams in fact wrote a significant number of pieces for the church, and in them his originality is obvious. Particularly noteworthy are his Mass in G Minor (1922), a profound reexamination of Renaissance technique and among the finest Mass settings of the century; the famous anthem *O Clap Your Hands* (1920), which added brass and percussion to the organ accompaniment and introduced pairs of root-position triads moving in contrary motion against each other; *All Hail the Power* (1938), possibly the first example of an English anthem requiring congregational par-

Ralph Vaughan Williams: conclusion of "The Lover's Ghost."

ticipation (Vaughan Williams would revisit this innovation in later anthems); and the lovely little Communion anthem O *Taste and See* (1952), which showcased the composer's love of unusual cadences.

Vaughan Williams also wrote numerous works that do not fit neatly into any standardized choral category. One of his most popular pieces, *Serenade to Music* (1938), commemorated Sir Henry Wood's fiftieth anniversary as a conductor. This setting of text from Shakespeare's *The Merchant of Venice* was originally designed for orchestra and the specific voices of Wood's sixteen favorite soloists. Vaughan Williams later adapted it for chorus and orchestra, and that is how it is most often performed. Likewise, the pastoral episode *The Shepherds of the Delectable Mountains* (1922), though designed for the stage, is sometimes performed as a concert piece for chorus, soloists, and small orchestra, the composer's protestations to the contrary notwithstanding (Michael Kennedy 1980, 158). Another very popular work, *Five Mystical Songs* (1911), is a song-cycle for baritone, orchestra, and optional chorus, on texts by the English mystic and preacher George Herbert (1593–1633). *An Oxford Elegy* (1947–49) for speaker, chorus, and small orchestra is Vaughan Williams's version of the melodrama, with chorus added. The text from "The Scholar Gypsy" and "Thyrsis," by Matthew Arnold, is mostly recited by the speaker, the chorus offering up refrains, interjections, commentary, and an occasional wordless point of color. *Flos campi* (1925), which also utilizes wordless chorus, is a suite for viola, mixed chorus, and small orchestra, based on verses from the Song of Solomon. Here the chorus functions entirely as an additional timbre in the orchestra. The music is highly descriptive, the exotic chromaticism of the viola part and the wordless vocalizations of the chorus combining effectively to evoke the text's implied eroticism. Structurally a set of variations, *Fantasia on the Old 104th Psalm Tune* (1949) is in fact a concerto for piano, chorus, and orchestra. Typical of Vaughan Williams's pragmatic approach to large choral works, the fantasia can be performed by soloist and chorus with (1) full orchestra, (2) strings, brass, and organ, or (3) strings and organ, all contained in the same score. There are three large cadenzas for the piano, and the choral writing is equally brilliant.

Benjamin Britten was profoundly interested in the dramatic and musical possibilities of English texts. These literary and dramatic impulses, combined with a paradoxical inclination toward musical abstraction and a rare ability to paint musical pictures, resulted in some of the most sublime choral music of all time. Even in his earliest compositions Britten exhibited a remarkable understanding of the choral idiom. There is nothing tentative about the unaccompanied *A Hymn to the Virgin* (1930, revised 1934), which solves the problems of macaronic text antiphonally. Likewise, the theme and variations of *A Boy Was Born* (1932–33, revised with organ 1955) reveals an early mastery of large form. In both of these the seeds of Britten's mature lyricism and unique approach to tonality are easily identifiable.

Britten's first two really important choral works, *A Ceremony of Carols* (1942) and *Rejoice in the Lamb* (1943), are somewhat more subtly organized. In *A Ceremony of Carols* the composer accentuates the medieval qualities of the texts by framing the work with a Gregorian chant ("Hodie Christus natus est") and by relying extensively on canonic imitation and pervasive modality. Dramatic pacing is achieved through successively changing textual moods and a carefully constructed tonal plan, hinging on a harp fantasy on the "Hodie" plainchant. In the words of Hans Redlich (1965), *Rejoice in the Lamb* showcases "Britten's amazing ability to find musical equivalents for the most intractable words." Even though the theme—to see God in all things and to rejoice—is easily recognizable, the poem's structure is incoherent, which is not surprising considering that Christopher Smart (1722–1771) wrote it while confined in an asylum. Britten attempts to solve this little problem by isolating coherent thoughts in separate musical sections, superficially unrelated but each utilizing in some way the intervals of major second and perfect fourth, which are prominent in the work's opening chords. He further sustains interest by creating exceptionally vivid musical depictions of two animals, the poet's cat and its mouse nemesis, whose unique worship of God provides a focal point within the poem. While critics have never been convinced of the worthiness of *Rejoice in the Lamb*, it has always been popular with audiences and remains a basic staple in many graduate conducting classes. This piece is also quite important because its distinctive dotted rhythms and partial application of eighteenth-century ritornello form reveal the influence of Purcell for the first time in Britten's music.

Although he turned again and again to religiously inspired texts, Britten composed only a handful of liturgical works for the church, of which his settings of the Latin hymn "Te Deum laudamus" are typical. The only similarities between *Te Deum* in C (1935), which had to wait almost thirty years for its companion *Jubilate Deo* (1961), and *Festival Te Deum* (1944) are a basic ABA form and common requirements for soprano solo. *Festival Te Deum* is more dramatic than its predecessor, and the details of its structure are quite different. Whereas the outer sections of the earlier setting provide a thorough examination of C major triads in various guises, the later work explores the possibilities of pure, chantlike melody and sudden mood changes. It is also Britten's only polyrhythmic composition. While well written and attractive, the comparatively obvious and rather perfunctory nature of the liturgical works belies a certain disinterest on the composer's part. *Missa brevis* in D (1959), however, is an exception. Richly inventive, its harmonic exploration of third relations is illuminating, as is the evolution of its themes, created mostly from plainchant and motives built on fourths, which in the Sanctus are manipulated into a twelve-tone row.

Among the century's greatest masterworks, *War Requiem* (1961) represents the culmination of Britten's style and technique up to that time. By combining the Latin *Missa pro defunctis* with poignant and insightful poems by the World War I poet Wilfred Owen (1893–1918), Britten was following the lead of Arthur Bliss, Vaughan Williams, and Frederick Delius. Beyond that, the concept (in which the Latin text is presented either by soprano soloist, mixed chorus, and large orchestra, or by boys' voices and harmonium, and the English poetry is given to tenor and baritone soloists, with chamber orchestra) is boldly original and quite personal, even though Britten clearly aimed to reach the broadest possible audience. While some of the big effects seem obvious, they are also right for the moment, and the vast problems inherent in the juxtaposition of such different texts simply evaporate in the fluidity of Britten's transitions. The work hinges on an augmented fourth, C and F-sharp, which appears vertically at the outset and at other significant points, resolving into an F major chord at the end of the first movement, "Dies irae," and also at the work's conclusion. This interval also provides an important melodic component, most notably in the first movement's "Te decet hymnus," in which these notes anchor an important melody built from a tone row and its inversion, and in Agnus Dei, the heart of the piece, which is actually permeated by the tritone. Concerning this, Peter Evans (1996, 452) made a keen observation:

> Only the Agnus Dei achieves a final statement of [a tritonal] equipoise in which the strains of the whole movement are balanced out. It is noteworthy that this setting, of the liturgical text and Owen's "At a Calvary near the Ancre" in parallel, demonstrates the closest alliance, of feeling and of musical material, to be found in the work, and in the final tonal resolution a meeting-point is recognized between Owen's salutation of the "greater love" and the liturgy's prayer for "requiem sempiternam": Britten's substitution of the nonliturgical "Dona nobis pacem" in the tenor's cadential phrase underlines this very clearly.

Benjamin Britten: "Te decet hymnus" tune from *War Requiem.*

Britten's *War Requiem* was thoroughly praised in the British press even before it was performed, which prompted Stravinsky to comment that one might as well sit during "God Save the Queen" as criticize it. A typical early review came from Peter Shaffer, who thought it "the most impressive and moving piece of sacred music ever to be composed in this century. . . . It makes criticism impertinent" (Carpenter 1992, 408). But critics, by nature, tend toward impertinence, and before long a backlash occurred. It was noticed that Britten's setting of the Latin texts reminded listeners of Verdi's *Requiem.* Some also thought that the Latin and English portions did not balance. In 1977 the composer Robin Holloway wrote that he became disenchanted by "the public manner" of the work, which seemed to him a betrayal of the private concerns of Britten's greatest music (Cooke 1996). Some felt the sweetness of the ending cheapened the work's message. It was eventually, and perhaps inevitably, claimed that audiences were subconsciously put off by various homo-sexual implications (Michael Kennedy 1986). *War Requiem*, however, has survived the criticism. In Peter Evans's words (1996, 466), "All we know of Britten might have led us to expect . . . one of his most introverted works, val-ued by the connoisseur of his music but estranging in some degree to the less committed listener. In sustaining a manner of address so direct through tran-sitions of mood so problematic, he achieved a feat of a kind that is not paral-leled elsewhere in his work, and which remains undiminished by the critical strictures that have been leveled at the Requiem."

Following *War Requiem*, Britten tended toward greater subtlety of expres-sion, as exemplified in his next choral work, *Cantata Misericordium*, Opus 69 (1963), written for the centenary of the International Red Cross. This com-mission provided Britten with another platform for his inclusionary views, which accented humanism and pacifism instead of dogma. The cantata's sub-ject matter (the parable of the Good Samaritan) and tenor-baritone soloist combination invite comparison with *War Requiem*. However, the cantata's chamber orchestra produces sonorities uniquely its own, and the tonal plan, relying heavily on the third relation between F-sharp major and D major, is quite different from the Requiem. Britten's previous frequent reliance on scales with strong modal implications is replaced by a chromaticism based on scales built of whole steps (implied in the vertical alignment of D major and F-sharp major), alternating half steps and whole steps, and others that take on the rudimentary appearance of tone rows. Purcell is once again recalled through frequent major-minor juxtapositions and ritornelli.

Throughout his career Britten devoted serious attention to music for chil-dren's voices, featuring them effectively in large works such as *Spring Sym-phony* (1949) and *War Requiem*. He also produced impressive pieces for tre-bles alone, beginning with the colorful, mostly unison suite *Friday Afternoons* (1933–35), and including *A Ceremony of Carols* and *Missa brevis* in D. Brit-ten's intent was not to create yet another series of didactic pieces but rather to include young people in the process of music making at the highest artistic lev-els, without compromise, condescension, or the imposition of impossible demands. A striking example is the cantata *Saint Nicolas* (1948), in which his interest extended to adolescent voices. Written for the centenary of Lancing College, the piece was designed specifically for a chorus comprised of boys from three schools and girls from another, a largely amateur string orchestra, percussionists, piano duet, and tenor soloist. Quite beyond the successful inte-gration of material technically appropriate for inexperienced performers with difficult material, requiring professional attention (tenor soloist, piano duet, string section leaders, and principal percussionist), *Saint Nicolas* abounds in other delights as well: the tonal scheme, which progresses steadily from A minor to D major, is enhanced by a characteristic Lydian flavor, while modes transpose and mix with considerable freedom; preexisting tunes (a psalm tone and the hymn tunes "Old Hundredth" and "London New") are effectively used; Purcell's influence is present in ritornelli and certain chromatic colorations.

Other works include *The Company of Heaven* (1937) and *The World of the Spirit* (1938), early cantatas incorporating some spoken text, which were suppressed by Britten and released for publication long after his death; *Ode to Saint Cecilia* (1942), in which the choral writing is instrumentally conceived; *Five Flower Songs* (1950), Britten's homage to the English partsong tradition, in which his descriptive powers are such that the listener can almost smell the blossoms and feel the thorns; *Cantata accademica* (1959), in which serial techniques are prominent; *Sacred and Profane* (1975), a reflective last glance at the British partsong; and the breezy, energetic *Welcome Ode* (1976), Britten's last completed work, which once again confirmed his commitment to music for youth.

BRITISH COMPOSERS BEFORE WORLD WAR II

At the beginning of the century, British choral tastes were essentially dictated by the style of the great Victorian composers Sir Charles Hubert Hastings Parry (1848–1918), Sir Charles Villiers Stanford (1852–1924), and Sir Edward Elgar (1857–1934). Although they continued to compose well into the new century, theirs was a nineteenth-century language, steeped in romantic notions of propriety and beauty. Worthy examples of their late work include Parry's coronation anthem *I Was Glad* (1902), *An Ode to the Nativity* (1912), and *Songs of Farewell* (1916–1918); Stanford's *Three Latin Motets*, Opus 51 (1905) and *Partsongs*, Opus 110, 119, and 127 (1909–1910); and Elgar's *The Music Makers* (1912), *Two Choral Songs*, Opus 71 (1914), *Death on the Hills*, Opus 72 (1914), and *Two Choral Songs*, Opus 73 (1914). Their collective art culminated in 1900 with Elgar's oratorio *The Dream of Gerontius* (1899–1900) for mezzo and tenor soloists, mixed chorus, and orchestra. Based on John Henry Cardinal Newman's lengthy poetic attempt to explain the doctrine of purgatory, *The Dream of Gerontius*, with its free-flowing dramatic dialogue, contrapuntal inventiveness, and exceptional choral outbursts, both angelic and violently devilish, also looks ahead to works by Vaughan Williams, Britten, and others.

Often described as an English impressionist, Frederick Delius (1862–1934) managed to avoid the influence of his Victorian contemporaries altogether. Moving from England in 1884, he became a Florida planter, studying music at leisure before finally settling in Germany, where he became a great friend of Edvard Grieg and took up a formal music education. Delius claimed to have learned little at the Leipzig Conservatory, however, and remained a musical iconoclast. Two of the composers who influenced him most, Edvard Grieg and Percy Grainger, were not among the very great, although he was equally affected by Debussy. His music was virtually unknown in England until 1907, when Sir Thomas Beecham began performing it. The reaction to one of Delius's works was so violent that an audience member actually fired shots at him during a concert. Subsequently, he suffered a lengthy debilitating disease that left him blind and paralyzed years before his death. This colorful history aside, Delius's supporters have always maintained that his was an especially original vision:

> Delius is a solitary figure in music. . . . Much of his music is confessedly pictorial, but it is something much more as well. It is less a painting of nature itself than a study of the influence of nature upon the human soul. Delius views nature, not with that "innocence of eye" which was one of the catchwords of the early impressionistic painters, but in the light of his own temperament, and it is the blending of the psychological with the pictorial element that gives to his music its peculiarly characteristic quality. (Blom 1954)

On the other hand, there are many to whom his music does not speak. The distinguished composer and teacher Ingolf Dahl, while casually talking to students at the University of Southern California (the author among them), simply dismissed Delius's music, likening it to goldfish in pink Jell-O. Still, among his several large choral-orchestral works three can be considered important: *Sea Drift* (1904) for baritone, chorus, and orchestra, *A Mass of Life* (1905), and *A Song of the High Hills* (1911). Delius was among the first composers to embrace the poetry of Walt Whitman, and his quasi-impressionistic settings of these texts, in *Sea Drift*, are quite unlike any others. His treatment of wordless chorus and his often painfully slow harmonic rhythm in *A Song of the High Hills* look forward to the application of similar techniques later in the century. *A Mass of Life*, on texts by Friedrich Nietzsche, is perhaps the earliest twentieth-century musical attempt to wrench the issues of life and death from the hands of the church.

   Gustav Holst (1874–1934) shared an enthusiasm for English folk song with his friend Vaughan Williams, and together they collected many examples; but while Holst's music was influenced by this, other British aspects are more obvious, such as the accentuation of pastoral elements and a reliance on striding basso ostinatos. There are also unusually exotic elements derived from an interest in Eastern religions, which he incorporated, often seamlessly, into a fabric otherwise rooted in the English countryside. Examples of pieces in this vein are *Choral Hymns from the Rig Veda* (first, second, and fourth sets 1908, third set 1910) and *Hymn of Jesus* (1919). The four sets of *Choral Hymns*, each for a different choral-instrumental configuration, are not designed to be performed together. Representative is the third set, for women's chorus and harp. The contrapuntal interplay among the voices and between voices and harp is delightful, the chromatically seasoned harmonies rich and supple. The texts are set sensitively and with considerable imagination, especially in the 7/4 "Hymn to the Waters." It is fortunate that each movement excerpts nicely, for by the last decade of the century many preferred Holst's more exotic style in small doses. As critic Alan Rich pointed out in *L.A. Weekly* (5 August 1993), the four-movement set was "undeniably pretty and three too many." Certainly Holst's best-known large choral work, *Hymn of Jesus* for mixed chorus and orchestra combines the ancient (Gregorian chant), the typically British (basso ostinatos à la Purcell), the exotic (5/4 meter, mild dissonance, and apocryphal text) and the new (speaking chorus). Quite original in conception and realization, its spell nevertheless wore off considerably by the end of the century, perhaps because Holst interrupts the fun to reverently remind us that the mystical Jesus is speaking.

Holst's works of a more conventional English style, however, entertained audiences unconditionally throughout the century. *Christmas Day* (1910), a fantasy on carols for mezzo soloist, chorus, and orchestra, and the little Christmas carol "Lullay, My Liking" (from *Five Partsongs*, 1916) are still frequently performed, their popularity showing no sign of diminishing. Immediately accessible, *Lullay* is a virtually perfect miniature, while the more substantial *Christmas Day* is effortlessly learned when it needs to be, the contrapuntal juxtaposition of "Come Ye Lofty, Come Ye Lowly" and "The First Noël" being especially impressive.

In addition to *Christmas Day*, the numerous pieces that Holst composed for schools contain some of his best. The writing is just challenging enough to instill a sense of accomplishment without discouraging the singers, and the effects invariably work, whether large vertical sonorities or intricate contrapuntal embroidery. Good examples are *Two Psalms* (1912) for mixed chorus, organ, and strings, and *Six Choral Folk Songs* (1916) for mixed chorus. Other pieces worth mentioning are *The Planets* (1914–16), in which the wordless women's chorus lends another color to the orchestral palette, *Nunc dimittis* (1915), which surprises with its loud ending, and the neglected *Choral Symphony* (1923–24), Holst's largest choral work, which deserves an occasional revival.

Another chum of Vaughan Williams, Herbert Howells (1892–1983) differed from him by virtue of a sincere, though perhaps marginal, orthodox Protestant theology, a lack of interest in folk music, and a lesser talent. Even though Howells stated on one occasion that he was not a religious man, he produced a great quantity of liturgical music and preferred religious texts for his large concert works. His several settings of the Anglican canticles are basic repertoire in churches on both sides of the Atlantic.

Of Howells's larger works, *Hymnus Paradisi* (1938) for mixed chorus and orchestra has gained in popularity over the years, especially in the United States where it is highly favored among choral conductors. Written in memory of the composer's son, its rich compilation of texts constitutes a kind of Protestant Requiem. A deep grief, viewed through the eyes of enduring faith and supplanted by sustaining peace, is obvious in every note. Yet each individual page of the score can be mistaken for Vaughan Williams on one of his more impressionistic days. Taken as a whole, *Hymnus Paradisi* is protected from the hard edge of reality—a basic Vaughan Williams ingredient—by a kind of sonic gloss, perhaps indicating that it was composed in a state of lingering shock rather than divine grace. It is revealing therefore to know that Howells supposedly told Vaughan Williams that he composed *Hymnus Paradisi* on his knees, to which Vaughan Williams responded that he composed his Fifth Symphony at the kitchen table.

More original and perhaps even more heartfelt is Howells's *Stabat mater* (1959–1965), begun on the first anniversary of Vaughan Williams's death. The jagged melodies and biting harmony lend the impression that loneliness and desolation have replaced the composer's peace. The shock value of this music, for anyone slightly familiar with Howells's other work, was aptly described by Philip Greenfield (1995), who noted that "before you can say 'Ralph Vaughan Williams,' the strings start to sigh, horns swoop in ominously, and the brasses and chorus enter in a cataclysm of grief that will blast you right out of your chair. From then on, there are solemn dirges [and] interludes of biting anger."

Missa sabrinensis (Mass of the Severn, 1954) is the middle work in Howells's big choral-orchestral triptych, which also includes *Hymnus Paradisi* and *Stabat mater*. It was named for the River Severn, which flows through Howells's native Gloucestershire. The longest of the three works, it seems to be an examination of emotional extremes in an undisciplined structure, and it is seldom performed. If one is in the right mood, though, its impact can be potent.

Howells's most consistently satisfying music can be found in his small pieces, such as the matchless unaccompanied carol *A Spotless Rose* (1919–20), in which the chantlike rhythm and effortlessly soaring cantilena of the baritone solo combine perfectly to express the text, or the freely metered anthem *My Eyes for Beauty Pine* (1925) for mixed chorus and organ, in which the chorus retains an unassuming unison texture until the pivotal moment when God's name is inscribed as Love.

Peter Warlock was the pseudonym of Philip Heseltine (1894–1930), a rather tragic figure in early twentieth-century British music. He wrote many songs and as many as twenty-three choral works during his brief life, but seems to have run completely out of compositional ideas by the time of his mysterious death (it was never decided whether it was accident, suicide, or murder). Among choral musicians, Warlock is well known for his Christmas carols *Balulalow* (1919), *Bethlehem Down* (1927), and others, all imbued with a unique haunting quality. His best secular piece, *The Full Heart* (1916, revised 1921), pays homage to Carlo Gesualdo in its mastery of choral textures and rather difficult chromatic twists and turns.

Other British composers from this period are Ethel Smyth (1858–1944), whose finely crafted partsongs and choral-orchestral works, *A Spring Canticle* (1926) and *The Prison* (1930), never matched the popularity of her operas and impressive, early Mass in D Major (1893); Granville Bantock (1868–1946), whose unaccompanied "choral symphonies," *Atalanta in Calydon* (1911), *Vanity of Vanities* (1913), and *A Pageant of Human Life* (1913), deserve an occasional hearing; Edward Bairstow (1874–1946), whose music for the Anglican Service, especially the delightful Communion anthem *I Sat Down under His Shadow* (published 1925), remains in use; Martin Shaw (1875–1958), whose anthem *With a Voice of Singing* (published 1923) remains standard repertoire in churches worldwide; Havergal Brian (1876–1972), whose gigantic *Gothic Symphony* (1919–27) remains an extremely intriguing work; John Ireland (1879–1962), remembered in the United States for the anthem *No Greater Love* (1912, orchestrated 1924) and highly respected in England for his partsongs and settings of the Anglican Service; George Dyson (1883–1964), whose oratorio *The Canterbury Pilgrims* (1931) for soloists, chorus, and orchestra found a new and enthusiastic audience late in the century; Arthur Bliss (1891–1975), whose cantata *Morning Heroes* (1930) provided a war-memorial prototype for several later composers; and Constant Lambert (1905–1951), whose piano concerto with chorus and orchestra, *The Rio Grande* (1927), is among the earliest successful attempts at symphonic jazz.

British Composers during and after World War II

William Walton (1902–1983) did not compose a lot of choral music—less than two hours' worth if performed end to end—but the quality is such that he is often counted among the twentieth century's great masters of the idiom. His gifts seem particularly miraculous when one considers that he was essentially self-taught. Of the several small choral pieces written when he was very young, only *A Litany* (1917) has remained in the repertoire. This slight, attractive, and unassuming partsong gave scant indication of the masterpiece that would explode from Walton's pen in 1931. In the intervening years his reputation as a composer of instrumental music had been established by his melodrama, *Façade*, and his Viola Concerto, so that audiences at the 1931 Leeds Festival probably expected something dazzling. Given the rather stuffy history of British choral music, however, they surely did not expect anything like *Belshazzar's Feast* (1931) for baritone soloist, mixed chorus, and large orchestra. David Johnson (1963) aptly described the effect: "Closer to choral drama than to either cantata or oratorio, the work proved a gorgeous, barbaric tapestry of sound such as no other British composer had ever conjured from massed choruses and a huge percussion-laden orchestra. . . . *Belshazzar's Feast* is essentially the work of a powerfully original and seminal talent." It was an immediate hit, though its portrayal of wild pagan revelry, divine retribution, and jazzy Israelite rejoicing were too much for the organizers of the Three Choirs Festival in Worcester, who refused to program it the following year, deeming it unsuitable for performance in a cathedral. Still, *Belshazzar's Feast* had—and continues to have—plenty of performances. It remains a perfect introduction to Walton's style: widely varied themes are created from one or two small motives, sophisticated and complex harmonies are built from triads and seventh and ninth chords, the orchestration is brilliant and startling even after repeated hearings, and the vocal writing is expressive and idiomatic.

Walton's succeeding choral works with orchestra do not create the same effect of inevitability and have not captured as large an audience. *In Honour of the City of London* (1937) is an eager but parochial affair, and *Te Deum* (1953) is immediately attractive but harmonically conventional. *Gloria* (1961) is marked by Walton's flashy, sure-handed orchestration, but lacks the driving impulse of *Belshazzar's Feast*. However, Walton's large anthem for mixed chorus and organ (or orchestra), *The Twelve* (1965), is a different matter. W. H. Auden wrote his poetic commentary on Jesus's Apostles expressly for Walton. As in *Belshazzar's Feast*, he relishes the inherent drama, creating bright, sensitive, invigorating music that propels the story forward to a satisfying conclusion. Walton's other choral pieces include three charming and deservedly popular carols, *Make We Joy Now in This Fest* (1931), *What Cheer?* (1961), and *All This Time* (1970); two exquisite unaccompanied part-songs, *Set Me As a Seal upon Thine Heart* (1938) and *Where Does the Uttered Music Go?* (1946); and *Missa brevis* (1966) and *Jubilate* (1972), both for mixed chorus and organ.

Michael Tippett (1905–1998) first broke onto the choral scene with the oratorio *A Child of Our Time* (1939–41) for soloists, mixed chorus, and orchestra. The initial positive reception of the piece was based largely on the clever chorale-like use of African American spirituals and the timeliness of the libretto, based on the assassination of a German diplomat by a young Polish Jew, which resulted in the infamous Krystalnacht of 9 November 1938. *A Child of Our Time* remains interesting for the same reasons, and still has its enthusiastic admirers. But it has not found universal appeal outside Great Britain, an abundance of good press notwithstanding. Nor has Tippett's second large choral work, *The Vision of Saint Augustine* (1963–65), achieved real popularity, even though the British musical establishment considers it a quintessential example of the composer's often-discussed mystical qualities. From 1980 to 1982 Tippett composed an even larger oratorio, *The Mask of Time*, which received numerous performances in England and the United States over the next few years. He also composed a handful of smaller choral pieces, among them *Two Madrigals* (1942), the motet *Plebs angelica* (1943), and the well-known *Magnificat and Nunc dimittis* (1961) for chorus and organ, in which the clean neoclassic lines and knotty harmony so typical of his music are brilliantly displayed.

The choral music of John Tavener (b. 1944) became increasingly well known during the last decade of the century, a situation aided in part by a renewed interest in Eastern Orthodox mysticism, of which his later works are representative, as well as by the advantageous performance of one of his finer small pieces at the close of the 1997 funeral service for Diana, Princess of Wales. Tavener's works divide neatly into two stylistic categories. His early works were influenced by English hymns (which he played weekly as organist in a Presbyterian church), several modern masters (Stravinsky, Messiaen, Cage, Penderecki), and Bach. But after 1977 his works underwent a remarkable transformation, relying heavily on Byzantine drones, Orthodox liturgical chant, and other Eastern influences. The resulting stylistic differences are enormous. For example, *The Whale* (1965–66), his first successful large work, displays the static harmonies, jagged, percussive rhythms, pointillism, ostinatos, angular and disjointed vocal lines, tonal densities, controlled improvisational techniques, and electronically generated sounds then currently in vogue. The biblical story of Jonah becomes a brilliant exercise in dramatic effects, not the least of which is the baritone soloist's shouting into the open piano as if it were the whale's mouth. The chorus is asked to provide all manner of sounds ("clap-hands, neigh, grunt, snort, yawn, make vomiting noises") in addition to singing in more or less traditional ways. On the other hand, Tavener's profoundly mystical *Song for Athene* (1993), built entirely over an F drone in the bass, projects a cleanly defined formal scheme, the emotional and harmonic intensity increasing with each succeeding long-drawn phrase. The tonal language is very conservative, the occasional poignant dissonance occurring more frequently as the piece progresses to its final, inevitable F major resolution.

Introit for March 27, the Feast of Saint John Damascene (1968), which quotes Bach's B Minor Mass, and *Celtic Requiem* (1969), which juxtaposes various children's games with the idea of death, mark the beginning of a transitional period in which Tavener attempted to reconcile his natural inclination toward mysticism with what he regarded as the pervasive humanism of Western art. During this time the struggle to find himself both spiritually and artistically is more evident in his selection of texts than in changes of musical style.

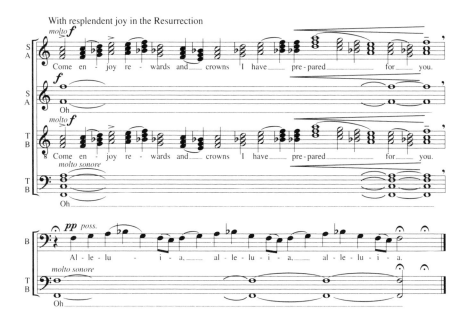

John Tavener: conclusion of *Song for Athene.*

Ma fin est mon commencement (1972), *Responsorium in Memory of Annon Lee Silver* (1972), and the large-scale *Ultimos ritos* (1972), which incorporates two earlier small pieces, *Coplas* (1970) and *Nomine Jesu* (1970), and is entirely based on the B Minor Mass "Cruxifixus," all deal with the Christian idea of dying into life.

By 1977 Tavener had concluded that the artistic heritage defined by the Western church was not adequate for his search. He converted to Eastern Orthodoxy and in the process finally discovered his unique musical personality. Important works written after 1977, in addition to *Song for Athene*, include *Magnificat and Nunc dimittis Collegium Regale* (1986); *The Uncreated Eros* (1988); two small Christmas pieces, *God Is with Us* (1987) and *Today the Virgin* (1989); the large cantata *We Shall See Him As He Is* (1990); *Notre pere* (1996) for children's choirs; *Voices* (1997) for soprano, mixed chorus, Tibetan bowls, and bells; and several more recent works for unaccompanied mixed chorus.

The choral works of Paul McCartney (b. 1942) and Andrew Lloyd Webber (b. 1948) fall into a special category, since neither man is known as a composer of serious concert music.

McCartney's *Liverpool Oratorio* (1991) for soloists, mixed chorus, and orchestra, and his large symphonic poem with chorus, *Standing Stone* (1993–

97), each apparently resulting from an honest and deeply felt creative impulse, must be viewed through a somewhat different critical lens. The timing of their appearance was rather curious. When *Liverpool Oratorio* was written, societal gurus, both secular and religious, had convinced a very large percentage of the public (in the United States at least) that all styles of artistic expression were essentially equal, the only really worthwhile examples being those that reached the largest possible audience with the least amount of fuss. Why then would one of the century's greatest popular songwriters suddenly feel compelled to create works in an idiom supposedly beyond the comprehension of many of his most devoted fans, and apparently foreign to his nature and experience? In the midst of a popular culture, both secular and religious, that aspired mainly to immediate gratification and constant positive reinforcement, why would the same songwriter produce works well over an hour in length and couched in old-fashioned and highfalutin forms that popular culture, both secular and religious, had sought in various ways to discredit? If it was because he realized that there are emotions, ideas, concepts, and spiritual values that simply cannot be adequately articulated, defined, and explored through artistic vehicles designed for easy consumption by the lowest common denominators of society, then *Liverpool Oratorio* and *Standing Stone* deserve to be taken seriously, even though their success as compositions is open to considerable debate. For *Liverpool Oratorio*, a narrative epic, McCartney enlisted the aid of Carl Davis (b. 1936), an expatriate American composer and longtime resident of Liverpool widely respected for his film and television scores. The distinguished British composers Richard Rodney Bennett (b. 1936) and David Matthews (b. 1943) helped shape and score the more aggressively philosophical *Standing Stone*. The music in each tends to be flagrantly rhapsodic if not to say occasionally directionless. Still, both have memorably lovely moments, especially the final, unaccompanied chorale of *Standing Stone*: "High above this overcrowded place a distant blackbird glides through space, and all he does is search for love. Love is the oldest secret of the universe." Creative need and good intentions aside, seventy-one minutes is a long wait for a four-minute partsong.

Because of Lloyd Webber's enormous success in musical theater, his *Requiem* (1984) attracted criticism similar to that which is often attached to Verdi's *Requiem*. Beyond that, however, there is no possible comparison between the two works. Though Lloyd Webber's *Requiem* is stylistically consistent, pleasingly modern, and generally avoids the clichés of musical theater, its inability to sustain emotions without visual stimuli—it has been staged as a ballet by the American Ballet Theatre—is disappointing. Further, its episodic structure lends the impression that the music is searching for a personality. Initially this search is strangely compelling, but just as the listener is convinced of the composer's serious intent, a bizarre and incredibly vulgar "Hosanna" breaks on the scene, followed by a genuinely lovely (and easily excerptable) "Pie Jesu." The exceptional dramatic gesture at the work's end only adds to the confusion.

John Rutter (b. 1945) must also be mentioned because of his impact on choral music in the United States and to a lesser extent in Great Britain. His first widely recognized works, *The Falcon* (1969) for chorus and orchestra and *Gloria* (1974) for mixed chorus, brass, and organ (arranged for orchestra 1988), impressed with warm, generous harmonies and grateful vocal lines. In Rutter's hands, unabashed tonality seemed to produce an honesty and sparkle absent in compositions by other composers attempting to mine the same vein. However, the great promise has remained unfulfilled. With the possible exception of *Requiem* (1985), the most noticeable characteristic of Rutter's later music is an almost casual commercialism—a trait that separates him from most other European composers. He has produced many little pieces with easily singable melodies and idiomatic accompaniments, and reaped the benefits due an astute businessman who correctly identified his market and exploited it fully. While his original music has achieved enormous popularity, his consummate folk song arrangements, superlative editions of Fauré's *Requiem*, and opera choruses by various composers will likely prove a more lasting legacy.

WALES

The Welsh composers Alun Hoddinott (b. 1929) and William Mathias (1934–1992) have produced particularly colorful choral music.

Hoddinott is noted for his sensitive approach to texts, a frequent reliance on ostinato motives, and an uncanny ability to create enormous climaxes. Works include the cantata *Dives and Lazarus* (1965); numerous anthems and motets, of which *Puer natus* (1972) can be considered typical; and *Sinfonia fidei* (Symphony of Faith, 1977), a three-movement setting of medieval Latin texts for soloists, chorus, and orchestra, of which Geraint Lewis (1976, 5) said, "The composer creates an immediate and distinctive sound-world . . . in which the warmly resonant chordal harmony and the high-flying, free-flowing solo lines are underpinned by orchestral pages of glowing Byzantine splendor. Here is Hoddinott at the height of his powers."

Mathias is known for his anthems and other brief sacred pieces, although *This Worlde's Joie* (1974), a four movement choral symphony on the seasons, and the large cantata *Lux aeterna* (1982), a memorial to his mother, also have many admirers. The influences of Hindemith and Stravinsky, as well as a few older English contemporaries, are easily discernible in his works. Two anthems, *Let the People Praise Thee* (1981), written for the wedding of Prince Charles and Lady Diana Spencer, and *Make a Joyful Noise* (1964), are good examples of Mathias's penchant for organizing melodic and harmonic material around a single element. The incessant added-note harmonic structure of the otherwise triadic *Let the People Praise Thee* is created entirely through the use of divided altos singing consistently in parallel seconds; *Make a Joyful Noise* explores the interval of a fourth—vertically and horizontally—against a jazzy, syncopated background.

SCOTLAND

The twentieth century's most important Scottish composers, Iain Hamilton (1922–2000), Thea Musgrave (b. 1928), Kenneth Leighton (1929–1988), and James Macmillan (b. 1959), have written impressive and popular choral works.

Hamilton, perhaps best known as an opera composer, contributed several large-scale pieces, including *Cantata* (1955) for mixed chorus and piano, on text by Robert Burns, and *Epitaph for This World and Time* (1970) for three mixed choruses and three organs. His style, while occasionally revealing the influence of jazz and Caribbean music, was essentially austere and harmonically acerbic.

Several distinct stylistic periods can be discerned in the music of Thea Musgrave. Her early, diatonic language gradually became more chromatic, eventually embracing serialism, and finally evolving into an intensely expressive post-serial style that the composer called "dramatic-abstract." Extremely versatile, Musgrave has produced important operas as well as orchestral and chamber works in addition to impressive compositions for chorus, including *Four Madrigals* (1953), *The Five Ages of Man* (1963), *Memento creatoris* (1967), and the brilliant *Rorate coeli* (1976).

Kenneth Leighton is best known for the finely wrought *A Hymn of the Nativity* (1960), Mass (1964), and other unaccompanied choral pieces. He also composed two very interesting large works: Symphony No. 2 (*Sinfonia mistica*, 1974), which presents an intriguing collection of texts by various British mystics—with an American revivalist text, "Shall We Gather at the River," tacked on for good measure—in a sustained and varied bitonal texture; and the sensuous, sensitive *Columba mea* (1978), a cantata on texts from Song of Solomon, which is otherwise noteworthy because of its inventive, though modest, orchestration and its combination of alto and tenor soloists.

Macmillan composed several Masses incorporating congregational participation, numerous Latin motets, and several cantatas. A most impressive work written at century's end is *Quickening* (1999) for countertenor, two tenors, and baritone soloists, children's and mixed choruses, and orchestra. Commissioned jointly by the BBC and the Philadelphia Orchestra, it sets texts by the British poet Michael Symmons Roberts, as well as the Aramaic Lord's

Prayer, which the composer intended as "an invocation of the future" (Ratcliffe 1999, 42).

IRELAND

Unlike many British composers, the Anglo-Irish E. J. Moeran (1894–1950) wrote only a few pieces for chorus. The unaccompanied *Phyllida and Corydon* (1934) and *Songs of Springtime* (1934), and the larger Nocturne (1934) for baritone, chorus, and orchestra, are warm and convincing examples of a fastidiously crafted style reminiscent of Delius and Vaughan Williams.

Among Irish composers, A. J. Potter (1918–1980) and Gerard Victory (1921–1995) are noteworthy. Potter was a student of Vaughan Williams and served as professor of composition at the Royal Irish Academy of Music. His harmonic conservatism and melodic gifts are well suited, his works containing both romantic sweep and motivic detail. The ability to deliver a considerable emotional impact within the confines of an otherwise conventional style is perhaps the most impressive feature of his music. Among the choral works are an unaccompanied *Missa brevis* (1949); several settings of poems by Hilaire Belloc (1951, 1967); a cantata for male voices, *Saint Patrick's Breastplate* (1966); and *Stabat mater* (1973). Gerard Victory's style ranges from conventionally tonal to serial and other techniques, depending on the nature of the work at hand. Within a particular piece, however, his style is usually quite consistent. His compositions include the important *Kriegslieder* (1966) for tenor, mixed chorus, trumpet, and percussion, and the cantatas he composed on commission: *Hymnus vespertinus* (1965), written for the Heinrich Schütz Festival; *Quartetto* (1966), a "cantata burlesqua" for speaker, soloists, and mixed choir written for the Cork International Choral Festival; and several cantatas for youth written for the BBC.

Among the many others in Great Britain who have contributed to the choral repertoire are Margaret Dryburgh (1890–1945), whose *The Captive's Hymn* (1942) and arrangements of selected instrumental works sustained prisoners in Sumatra during World War II (see chapter 3); Gerald Finzi (1901–1956), whose fascinating anthem *God Is Gone Up* (1945), on text by the colonial American puritan Edward Taylor, ceremonial ode *For Saint Cecilia* (1947), and *Magnificat* (1952) have helped his music to become more recognized; Edmund Rubbra (1901–1986), whose *Missa cantuariensis* (1946) and numerous partsongs and motets display an obvious originality within a very conservative framework; Lennox Berkeley (1903–1989), whose sure-handed melodic and polyphonic technique in the cantata *Domini est terra*, Opus 10 (1937), Mass, Opus 64 (1964), *Magnificat*, Opus 71, and other works, recalls the sacred aesthetic of Poulenc; Alan Rawsthorne (1905–1971), whose large

Carmen vitale (1963) and small *A Rose for Lidice* (1956) are well served by his serially inflected, tonally ambiguous style; Elisabeth Lutyens (1906–1983), whose cantata *Essence of Our Happinesses* (1968), motets, and other works are highly regarded; Dame Elizabeth Maconchy (1907–1994), whose *And Death Shall Have No Dominion* (1969) for choir and brass reveals the influence of Vaughan Williams; George Lloyd (1913–1998), whose unabashed neoromantic style is exemplified in his *A Symphonic Mass* (1992); John Gardner (b. 1917), whose *Herrick Cantata* (1960), Mass in D (1992), and various smaller works reveal an attractive and very eclectic musical personality; David Willcocks (b. 1919), a justly famous choral conductor who contributed numerous arrangements of carols; Michael Hurd (b. 1928), who contributed several cantatas and other works for children; Alexander Goehr (b. 1932), whose *Two Choruses*, Opus 14 (1962) shows the influence of Schoenberg and Messiean; Harrison Birtwistle (b. 1934), whose *Music for Sleep* (1964), dramatic cantata for schools entitled *The Mark of the Goat* (1965–66), and *The Fields of Sorrow* (1971) reveal an uncompromising and inquisitive nature; Peter Maxwell Davies (b. 1934), whose *Veni Sancte Spiritus* (1964), *Ecce manus tradentis* (1965), *Five Carols* (1966), and the more recent oratorio, *Job* (1997), are excellent examples of a style that often combines an aggressively dramatic serialism with parodies of medieval technique and material; Nicholas Maw (b. 1935), who contributed several pieces, including *Hymnus* (1995–56) for mixed chorus and orchestra; Richard Rodney Bennett (b. 1936), whose children's cycles *The Aviary* (1965) and *The Insect World* (1965), large choral-orchestral works *Epithalamion* (1966) and *Spells* (1974–75), and unaccompanied *Four Devotions* (1971) helped establish him as one of the most important composers of his generation; David Matthews (b. 1943), who impressed with the attractive small partsongs for mixed chorus— *Green* (1989), on text by D. H. Lawrence, *Bones* (1992), on text by Miraslav Holub, and *Sky*, on text by Gerard Manley Hopkins, all written as gifts for friends—as well as the large Vespers (1995) for mezzo and tenor soloists, mixed chorus, and orchestra; Michael Finnissy (b. 1946), whose *Seven Sacred Motets* (1991) reflect a consuming interest in Renaissance polyphonic techniques; Giles Swayne (b. 1946), whose impressive catalogue of choral music, some of which is inspired by African influences, includes *The Silent Land* (1998) for forty-part mixed chorus and solo cello; Paul Patterson (b. 1947), an obvious disciple of Penderecki, whose colorful *Kyrie* (1971) and *Mass of the Sea* (1982) contain many bold effects, such as vocal glissandos, handclaps, and slamming piano lids; Oliver Knussen (b. 1952), who contributed *Frammenti da "Chiara"* (1975–86) for two twelve-part women's choruses; Malcolm Singer (b. 1953), whose *Two Psalms* (1995) for mixed chorus and other works are worthy representatives of Britain's vital Jewish community; the King's Singers' Bob Chilcott (b. 1955), who contributed many imaginative works, such as *The Making of the Drum* (1985) for mixed chorus and percussion, as well as idiomatic arrangements of spirituals and folk songs; Roxanna Panufnik (b. 1968), whose *Westminster Mass* (1998) was premiered to great acclaim; and the Grawemeyer Prize–winning wunderkind Thomas Adès (b. 1971), who contributed the troubling cantata *America: A Prophecy* (1999) for mezzo soloist, mixed chorus, and orchestra.

CZECH REPUBLIC, SLOVAKIA, HUNGARY, AND POLAND

Czech Republic

The outstanding Czech composer during the first third of the century was Leoš Janáček (1854–1928). Like Vaughan Williams, Aaron Copland, Zoltán Kodály, and Béla Bartók, Janáček was influenced by folk materials. Yet he went further than any other folk-influenced composer, basing his musical vocabulary entirely on the rhythms of Moravian speech, which he called "speech melodies." In an interview with *Literarni svet* in 1928, he talked about this:

> For me, music as it comes out of the instruments, from the repertoire, whether it is by Beethoven or anyone else, has little truth in it. Perhaps it was like this, strange as it seemed, that whenever someone spoke to me, I may have not grasped the words, but I grasped the rise and fall of the notes! At once I knew what the person was like: I knew how he or she felt, whether he or she was lying, whether he or she was upset. As the person talked to me in a conventional conversation, I knew, I *heard* that, inside himself, the person perhaps wept. Sounds, the intonation of human speech, indeed of every living being, have had for me the deepest truth. And you see—this was my *need in life*. The whole body has to work—it is something different from just working the keys. . . . I have been collecting speech melodies since 1879; I have an enormous collection. You see, these speech melodies are windows into people's souls. (Zemanová 1989, 121–122)

The Augustinian monk, choirmaster, and composer Pavel Křížkovský (1820–1885) also profoundly influenced Janáček. Křížkovský was not only responsible for the young composer's musical training but was also instrumental in the early development of the Czech male chorus tradition that would later benefit from Janáček's genius. During the 1860s Křížkovský ran afoul of the church music reforms instigated by the Cecilian Movement, which advocated a return to Renaissance ideals, and was transferred from Brno to Olomouc. This also had a lasting effect on Janáček.

Janáček's early choral works were mostly small Latin motets and folk song arrangements. These displayed a marked creativity without hinting at the composer's mature style. In *Hospodine!* (1896) his personality began to assert itself, and by the turn of the century, in works such as the cantata *Amarus* (1897, revised 1901–06), *The Lord's Prayer* (1901, revised 1906), *Elegy on the Death of Daughter Olga* (1904), and the Czech *Ave Maria* (*Zdrávas Maria*, 1906), his unique characteristics were present, among them modality, love of ostinato rhythms, and parlando vocal lines (applied according to a technique often referred to as tectonic montage), as well as an uncanny ability to bring dramatic texts to life. He was especially interested in texts concerned with humanity's hopes, fears, and shortcomings. For example, the mood of *The Lord's Prayer*—which is not a devotional work at all, but an accompaniment for tableaux vivants based on paintings by the Polish artist Józef Krzesz-Mêcina (1860–1934)—reflects the angry and acerbic nature of Krzesz-Mêcina's paintings (one, "Give us this day our daily bread," depicts peasants railing at heaven after a storm destroyed their crops).

The choral compositions written at the invitation of Ferdinand Vach, director of the all-male Moravian Teachers Chorus, are among Janáček's most important. These include the masterpieces on texts by Petr Bezruč (1867–1958): *Kantor Halfar* (1906), *Maryčka Magdónova* (1906–07), and *The 70,000* (1909); and the equally effective works for women's voices: *Kašpar Rucky* (1916), *Songs of Hradčany* (1916), and *The Wolf's Track* (1916), which were written when Vach was forced to reorganize his chorus because of a shortage of men during World War I. These pieces deal frankly with various social problems (the persecution of a patriotic schoolmaster, the destruction of a family and death of a girl through forced unemployment and societal neglect, marital infidelity and rakish voyeurism) and clearly demonstrate that Janáček is at his best—perhaps better than anyone else in the century—when setting texts about injustice or sexual indiscretion.

The immediate postwar years saw the completion of the impressive song-cycle *The Diary of One Who Vanished* (1917–1919) for tenor and mezzo soloists, treble chorus, and piano, about a young peasant who leaves his home and family to follow a gypsy girl. The treble chorus sings only briefly, but its role is central to the work, providing one of the greatest dramatic moments in the choral repertoire as it quietly describes the girl lowering her blouse in front of the boy.

Janáček's largest choral work, *Glagolitic Mass* (1926), is among the great masterpieces of the century. The composer had thought about it since 1921 when the Archbishop of Olomouc suggested that he write a large church piece. In August 1926 he finally set to work while on vacation in the Moravian

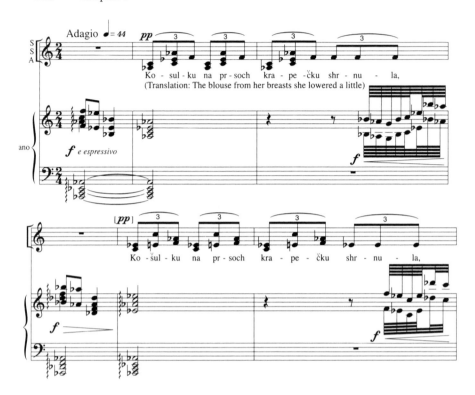

Leoš Janáček: portion of the seduction scene from *The Diary of One Who Vanished*.

spa town of Luhacovice. Incorporating material from an earlier unfinished Mass, he completed it within a month. Rejuvenating an old Czech tradition for festival Masses, *Glagolitic Mass* is framed by orchestral movements, and also contains a fantastic, and justly famous, organ solo movement.

Unconventional in virtually every respect, *Glagolitic Mass* so strikes at the heart of the text's meaning that initial reviewers thought the free-thinking Janáček had converted in his old age. It has been frequently analyzed and discussed, but no one has been better able to explain the roots of its transcendence better than Janáček himself, who wrote about it in *Lidove noviny*, just before the premiere:

> Why did I compose it? It pours, the Luhacovice rain pours down. From the window I look up to the glowering Komon mountain. . . . I sketch nothing more than the quiet motive of a desperate frame of mind to the words "Lord have mercy." Nothing more than the joyous "Glory, Glory!" Nothing more than the heart-rending anguish in the motive "and was crucified also for us, he suffered and was buried!" Nothing

more than the steadfastness of faith and the swearing of allegiance in the motive "I believe!" And all the fervour and excitement of the expressive ending "Amen, Amen!" The holy reverence in the motives "Holy, holy," "Blessed," and "Lamb of God!" Without the gloom of the medieval monastery cells in its motives, without the sound of the usual imitative procedures, without the sound of Bachian fugal tangles, without the sound of Beethovenian pathos, without Haydn's playfulness; against the paper barriers of Witt's reforms [the Caecilian movement]—which have estranged us from Křížkovský. . . . Always the scent of the moist Luhocovice woods—that was the incense. A cathedral grew before me in the colossal expanse of the hills and the vault of the sky, covered in mist into the distance, its little bells were rung by a flock of sheep. I hear in the tenor solo some sort of high priest, in the soprano solo a maiden-angel, in the chorus our people. The candles are high fir trees in the wood, lit up by stars; and in the ritual somewhere out there I see a vision of the princely Saint Wenceslas. And the language is that of the missionaries Cyril and Methodius. And before the evenings of three Luhocovice weeks had flown past, the work was finished. (Wingfield 1992, 118)

After its premiere, the composer had more to say about *Glagolitic Mass*, making the following remarks in *Literarni svet*:

You know what they wrote about me: "the pious old man." I got angry then and said: look here, young man, first of all I am not old, and as for being a believer—well, I am certainly not that, certainly not! Only when I am convinced. It was just that something occurred to me. . . . I wanted to show faith in the certainty of the nation not on a religious basis, but on a moral one; a basis of strength which takes God as its witness. (Zemanová 1989, 122–123)

Other works of Janáček that must be mentioned are the cantatas *Na Soláni Carták* (1911), which describes the seduction of a young school teacher by an innkeeper's daughter, and *The Eternal Gospel* (1914, revised 1924); the fantastic male chorus *The Wandering Madman* (1922); and both versions of the witty and pleasant *Nursery Rhymes*: the first version (1925) for three treble voices, clarinet, and piano; and the expanded second version (1927) for mixed voices, two flutes (one alternating piccolo), two E-flat clarinets, two bassoons (one alternating contrabassoon), ocarina, toy drum, double bass, and piano.

After Janáček, the period between the world wars was dominated by Joseph Bohuslav Foerster (1859–1951), Vitězslav Novák (1870–1949), Josef Suk (1874–1935), and their students. Theirs is an important and worthwhile body of choral music, most notably Foerster's *Mortuis fratribus*, Opus 108 (1918), *Saint Wenceslaus*, Opus 140 (1928), and *May*, Opus 159 (1936); Novák's

The Storm, Opus 42 (1908–1910) and *The Spectre's Bride*, Opus 48 (1912–13); and Suk's *Epilogue* (1920–29, revised 1933). In addition to these large choral-orchestral works, they composed many pieces for mixed and treble choruses, and consciously continued the Czech male chorus tradition. Foerster also made significant contributions to liturgical music and is credited with establishing a new style of choral composition that viewed the chorus as "an ideal medium for the fusion of thought and emotion" (Sadie 1980, 6:684).

Foerster's ideas were expanded by his pupil Emil Burian (1904–1959), who in 1927 organized a performing group that he called a "voice band," in which the chorus recited texts to specified rhythms but indefinite pitch, accompanied by a jazz ensemble and occasionally by whistling. Burian's *Requiem* (1927) is an impressive work in this style.

Vitězslav Novák's most famous students were Ladislav Vycpálek (1882–1969), whose cantatas *Of the Last Things of Man* (1921), *Blessed Is the Man* (1933), and *Czech Requiem* (1940) assured him a successful career; Jaroslav Křička (1887–1969), who excelled in the writing of partsongs and music for children, and whose student Jaromir Weinberger (1896–1967) also contributed to the choral repertoire; and Alois Hába (1893–1973). Hába occupies a unique and important place in Western art music because of his experiments with quarter tones. He did not shrink from using this new system when writing for the chorus. His quarter-tone works for children's chorus, the two sets of *Children's Choruses*, Opus 42 and 43 (1932), effectively demonstrate that music for children need not be patronizing. Also interesting are his later works in the semitone system, examples being the series of male chorus pieces written from 1948 to 1949, some of which became politically obsolete: *Constitution of 9 May*, Opus 64; *Three Male Choruses*, Opus 65; *Meditation*, Opus 66; *Peace*, Opus 67; and the cantata *For Peace*, Opus 68.

Josef Suk's preeminent pupil, for a brief time only, was Bohuslav Martinů (1890–1959), who was extremely well known during the forties and fifties. His mature style is immediately recognizable: Czech folk elements are paired with touches of French color (learned from his other teacher, Albert Roussel), melodic lines in short motives twist and turn around themselves, important chord changes occur on weak beats, tonalities are stretched in distinctive ways, chamber ensembles are created from unorthodox instrumental groupings, and orchestrations usually include piano. Martinů was a tremendously prolific composer, and his output was very uneven. His best compositions, however, several of which are choral, rank among the great.

Extreme examples of Martinů's facile abilities are his last work, *The Prophecy of Isaiah* (1959) for soprano, alto and baritone soloists, male chorus, trumpet, viola, timpani, and piano, and *The Spectre's Bride* (1932) for soprano and baritone soloists, mixed chorus, and orchestra, a previously unknown cantata discovered among his papers in 1990. *The Prophecy of Isaiah* was commissioned by the state of Israel. Because of its highly unusual combinations of voices and instruments, it is compelling at first glance; but it eventually disappoints through lack of musical invention, leaving the impression of an incomplete sketch. On the other hand, the incisive and dramatically charged *The Spectre's Bride*, quickly written as an afterthought for possible inclusion in the ballet *Špalíček*, is a most effective setting of a grotesque folktale—also used by Dvořák and Novák—and is among the composer's most intriguing compositions. Colorfully orchestrated, with highly expressive solos and inventive choral writing, it vividly tells the story of a ghost returning to claim his living bride.

Martinů's best-known choral work is the unusual and moving *Field Mass*, a masterpiece written in 1939 to honor Czech volunteers then fighting in the French army. The librettist Jiří Mucha (b. 1915) combined psalm verses and some liturgical Latin with his own poignant text, which spoke directly to the predicament of those soldiers: Would God recognize them away from their homeland, fighting on foreign soil? The text-derived structure, evocative scoring for baritone soloist, male chorus, and small military band (two piccolos, two clarinets, three trumpets, two trombones, and percussion) augmented by piano and harmonium, fluid vocal lines, and exquisite timing of mood changes (despair, supplication, awe, determination, acceptance) are virtually flawless.

Other important and attractive works by Martinů include *Songs of the Uplands* (1955–59), an imaginatively scored collection of four cantatas on Moravian peasant life: *Opening the Wells* (1955) for speaker, soprano and baritone soloists, treble chorus, two violins, viola, and piano, *The Legend of Smoke from Potato Fires* (1956) for soprano, alto, and baritone soloists, mixed chorus, flute, clarinet, French horn, accordion, and piano, *Dandelion Romance* (1957) for soprano soloist and unaccompanied mixed chorus, and *Mikesh from the Mountains* (1959) for soprano and tenor soloists, mixed chorus, two violins, viola, and piano; *Five Czech Madrigals* (1948) for unaccompanied mixed chorus; the ballet *Špalíček*, which includes chorus and vocal solos; *The Primrose* (1954), five songs for SA soloists or treble chorus, violin, and piano; *The Nativity* (1934) for soprano, alto, baritone, and bass soloists, children's and mixed choruses, and small orchestra, which is one of four one-act operas that make up *The Miracles of Mary* and is often performed unstaged as a cantata; and the unjustly neglected oratorio *The Epic of Gilgamesh* (1955) for soprano, tenor, baritone, and bass soloists, mixed chorus, and orchestra.

After the war, as Martinů and Hába approached the pinnacle of their fame, a new generation of Czech composers burst onto the scene. Many of these composers contributed significantly to the choral repertoire, the most important being Jan Hanuš (b. 1915), Petr Eben (b. 1929), and Karel Husa (b. 1921).

The emotionally charged and highly expressive music of Jan Hanuš is easily recognizable: tonal centers shift frequently and effortlessly, balancing and intermingling traditional Czech elements with the most advanced twentieth-century techniques. Justly famous for symphonies, ballets, and other large instrumental works, Hanuš's innate lyricism also proved ideal for vocal music. Good examples include *Flos florum*, Opus 118 (1992, revised 1999), a set of three Latin motets for unaccompanied mixed chorus that show the composer's contrapuntal skills to good effect; and the oratorio *Ecce homo*, Opus 97 (1977–78), one of the most significant works of the century. The text-derived structures of the first two Opus 118 motets are propelled and unified by small motives associated with specific words. The third is an extensive set of variations on a medieval Slavic hymn. *Ecce homo* brilliantly assimilates traditional material with electronic, aleatoric, serial, sprechstimme, and other avant-garde techniques, creating a dramatically charged and expansive tonal framework of great warmth and substance. In one particularly evocative passage Hanuš enters Mary's mind, and as she watches her son hanging on the cross she also remembers past events. Thus the emotionally wrenching music also hints of angels, far away, singing "Gloria in excelsis." Contemplating *Ecce homo*, one is reminded of an observation attributed to Leonard Bernstein, the idea that "any great work of art is great because it creates a special world of its own. It revives and re-adapts time and space, and the measure of its success is the extent to which it invites you in and lets you breathe its strange, special air."

An active church musician for many years, several of Hanuš's most important choral works are liturgical. His seventh Mass, *Mše Hlaholska*, Opus 106 (Glagolitic Mass, 1986) for bass soloist, mixed chorus, organ, and ad libitum bells, is an impressive setting of the Old Church Slavonic text in modern Czech translation (*Hlaholska* means "Glagolitic"), which accentuates the double meaning of the title through the colorful use of tubular bells (*Hlahol* is Czech for "bells"). Hanuš's concern for the religious and artistic training of children, even during the Communist period, is reflected in *Opus spirituale pro juventute*, Opus 65 (1969–1977), a collection of ten works consisting of motets, a staged Christmas musical, Passions according to Matthew and John, and settings of the Beatitudes, all written for the children's choir at Saint Margaret's Church, Břesnov, Prague. Other important works include *The Earth Is Speaking*, Opus 8 (1940) for soloists, chorus, and orchestra, a cantata honoring Czech students murdered by the Nazis in 1939; *Song of Hope*, Opus 21 (1945–48) for soloists, chorus, and orchestra, a Christmas cantata written in opposition to the big political cantatas that were being promoted by eastern European governments; Symphony No. 7, Opus 116 (*The Keys of the King-*

Manuscript page of Jan Hanuš's *Ecce homo*. Courtesy of Jan Hanuš.

dom, 1989–90), which includes choral settings of the Te Deum and Beatitudes; and *Requiem*, Opus 121 (1991–95) for soloists, chorus, and orchestra, dedicated to friends and colleagues whom the composer referred to as "angels on my way."

The unique combinations of joy, sorrow, compassion, and controlled anger (or righteous indignation, if you will) that distinguish Petr Eben's art result from both his mixed Jewish–Roman Catholic heritage and his experience as a prisoner in the Buchenwald concentration camp, where as a teenager he managed to compose some songs. Routinely hounded by the Czech Communist regime, but allowed essential freedom to compose because of his international reputation, Eben created an impressive body of work recognized for its artistic integrity and emotional expressivity. Medieval influences, which are obvious in a preoccupation with ancient texts, an occasional archaic cadence (such as the under-third), and the frequent use of Gregorian chant inform his works. But Eben, well aware of the Solemnes monks' theories, approached chant in highly individualistic ways, exploring accents peculiar to Czech pronunciation and seeking new rhythmic applications. Freely tonal, his music is often punctuated by biting dissonance and quickly moving vocal lines that seem almost improvised. A good example is *Prague Te Deum* (1989) for mixed chorus and organ (or brass and timpani), composed in thanksgiving for the Velvet Revolution. In 1990 Eben discussed the piece in a personal letter to the author that was later incorporated into the preface of the published score:

> We had—as a nation—not many reasons in the past forty years to sing a Te Deum. What I had written in 1950 was a "Missa Adventus et quadrasisimae" in a strict ascetic style and in D minor, [which] expresses one mood and atmosphere: the fight of our citizens for their faith and freedom, the fight of the church for her existence. But when now suddenly the unexpected change happened, as a real miracle, when we could feel God's leading hand and the prayers of Saint Agnes of Prague, whose sanctification was so connected with the revolution days, I felt that I must write a composition as a thanksgiving, and there was no better text [than] the Te Deum. For a composer the most serious problem in setting this text into music is how to create a contrast, since all the sentences are suggesting a continuous praise in jubilating fortissimo. Thus I used Sanctus, which can be felt in a mysterious way, and all the praying sentences for the piano passages. I used the quotation of the Gregorian chant in the very beginning, bringing the first half sentence with the modern answer in the afterphrase, to show the tradition combined with the present. Almost no words are repeated, but the last sentence, "In Te Domine speravi, non confundar in aeternum," explaining so precisely our longlasting hopes, I composed as a passacaglia, to underline its importance.

After the Soviet invasion of Czechoslovakia in 1968, Eben was asked to write something for a student group that met informally in the evenings. The students did not demand a piece in a particular style but only described their needs and limitations. Without condescension, Eben produced *Trouvere Mass*, a work for unison chorus (congregation) with optional descant, accompanied by keyboard, two recorders, and optional guitar. Popular in tone and immediately accessible, it is profoundly simple.

Liturgical reforms that returned the Ordinary to the realm of congregational participation resulted in Eben's *Missa cum Populo* (1982), in which the congregation, supported by brass instruments, freely interacts with a mixed chorus accompanied by organ, and *Suita liturgica* (1995), which sets propers of important feasts in a chromatic, quasi-chant style for unison chorus and organ. Other important works include *Missa in adventus* (1952) for unison chorus and organ; the cantatas *The Lover's Magic Spell* (1957) for soprano, two alto soloists, and mixed chorus, and *The Bitter Earth* (1959) for baritone soloist, mixed chorus, and organ (or piano); the unaccompanied motet *Ubi caritas et amor* (1964); the oratorios *Apologia Sokrates* (1967) and *Sacred Symbols* (1997); and *Pragensia* (1972), three Renaissance tableaux for chorus and Renaissance instruments.

Karel Husa left Prague in 1946 to study in Paris, eventually settling in the United States in 1954. The recipient of many prestigious awards, including the Pulitzer Prize and the Grawemeyer Award, he is among the most universally celebrated composers of his generation.

Although he became an American citizen, Husa retained an essentially Czech outlook. His first big choral work, *Apotheosis of This Earth* (1970, 1972), was originally written for band alone, then rescored for chorus and orchestra. Written as a warning, it presents a terrifying vision of the future, examining, in Husa's words, "the present desperate stage of mankind and its immense problems with everyday killings, war, hunger, extermination of fauna . . . and critical contamination of the whole environment" (Nott 1990). *An American Te Deum* (1976) for baritone soloist, mixed chorus, and orchestra (or wind ensemble) is another outstanding, and perhaps more accessible, large work. It is as bold and invigorating as *Apotheosis*, but it is also essentially optimistic, combining Latin, Czech, and American texts in a distillation of emigrant experiences. Husa has also written several attractive small pieces, including the unaccompanied partsong *Every Day* (1983) and *Three Moravian Songs* (1980), in which his expressive tonal language is vividly displayed.

Other leading Czech composers include Klement Slavicky (1910–1999), whose works for various choral ensembles are graced by a seemingly spontaneous expressivity; Václav Nelhybel (1919–1996), who wrote the very popular *Estampie natalis* (1976) for double mixed chorus, piccolo, viola, cello, and percussion, and numerous other works for the American educational

Petr Eben: opening of "Offertorium" from *Suita liturgica*.

market; Vladimír Sommer (1921–1997), whose haunting *Vocal Symphony* (1958) for mezzo, mixed chorus, and orchestra is unforgettable; Jiří Ropek (b. 1922), who in spite of frequent persecution by Communist authorities produced functional and warmly personal church works, including several excellent settings of *Pange lingua* (1944, 1956, 1965), the little cantata *Christmas Fantasy* (1979, orchestrated 1983), and *Missa brevis* (1987); Jindřich Feld (b. 1925), whose unaccompanied *Three Inventions* (1966) and *Nonsense Rhymes* (1973) are often performed in western Europe and the United States; Zdeněk Lukáš (b. 1928), whose *Requiem* (1992) and other large unaccompanied works, written in a personal and attractive tonal style, became well known after the Velvet Revolution of 1989; Antonín Tučapsky (b. 1928), whose *The Time of Christemas* (1977) for mixed chorus, two glockenspiels, guitar, and percussion, and unaccompanied choral suites *In honorem vitae* (1977) and *The Year of Grace* (published 1989), are well known on both sides of the Atlantic; Jiří Laburda (b. 1931), whose cantatas *Glagolitica* (1966) and *Metamorphoses* (1968) won important prizes in western Europe; Marek Kopelent (b. 1932), whose *De passione Saint Adalberti Martyris* (1981) integrates rock elements with avant-garde techniques, and whose *Syllabes mouvementées* (1972) for twelve-part mixed chorus was considered by Marcel Couraud to be the best of the avant-garde works premiered by the Soloists of LORT and the Group Vocal du France; Luboš Fišer (1935–1999), whose *Requiem* (1968) and *Sonata for Chorus, Piano, and Orchestra* (1981) were important statements of the Czech avant-garde; Arnošt Parsch (b. 1936), whose works include *Red Sun Rose Once* (1974), an intriguing piece for chorus and jazz band, composed with Miloš Štědroň (b. 1942) on text by Sitting Bull, and *Welcoming the Spring* (1990–93), an impressive cantata for soloists, chorus, and orchestra commemorating the Velvet Revolution of 1989; Ivana Loudová (b. 1941), who impressed early in her career with *Vocal Symphony* (1965) before concentrating her energies on the composition of choral music for children, such as the prize-winning *Little Christmas Cantata* (1976); Peter Graham, pseudonym for Jaroslav Šťastný-Pokorny (b. 1952), whose deeply spiritual works include an impressive *Stabat mater* (1990) and a miniature jewel, *Ave Regina* (1989), both for unaccompanied mixed chorus; and Jiří Gemrot (b. 1957), whose *Psalm 146* (1992) for chorus and orchestra received international attention.

Special consideration must be given to Pavel Haas (1900–1944), Gideon Klein (1919–1945), and others who created moving and extraordinary choral music within the confines of Terezín during World War II. Klein, already a famous pianist in Czechoslovakia before the Nazi invasion, was not known as a composer at the time of his deportation, even though he had been studying with Alois Hába in Prague for some time. Haas, a pupil of Janáček, was well established and respected throughout Czechoslovakia for *Psalm 29* (1931–32) for mixed chorus and chamber orchestra, as well as for other works.

In Terezín, Klein immediately allied with the conductor Raphael Schaechter (1905–1944), who had already begun the process of forming choirs among inmates, and later joined forces with Austrian composer Viktor Ullmann, who was eager to organize concerts, including performances of new music. After some delay Haas joined them. Soon others followed the lead, so that in addition to Schaechter's mixed choir there were several children's choruses, two choirs specializing in Jewish music (one for religious services), at least two that performed folk music, and one that concentrated on oratorio. Henry Oertelt, an oratorio chorister in Terezín, commented on the experience in notes prepared for a special Friday evening service in Minneapolis in 1995:

After the performance of *The Creation*, we started rehearsing for Mendelssohn's *Elijah*. We thought it to be very odd, because all of his works were forbidden to be performed in any German-controlled territory. . . . Also, the contents of the text have passages that are possibly not too comfortable to a Nazi ear. It was time for the performance. The Nazi commander and his SS-uniformed cohorts sat down. The Jewish leaders of the camp, strangely enough, were placed right next to them. . . . We (the choir) took our position, the soloists appeared. The conductor raised his baton. Just try to imagine the anxiety of these performers as . . . the huge choir of inmates cried out in a strong fortissimo: "Help, Lord—Help, Lord! Wilt thou quite destroy us?" We knew it was the most beautiful and most meaningful performance that ever took place anywhere!

Haas completed only one choral work in the ghetto, *Al S'fod* (1942), a setting of a Palestinian Jewish poem, in Hebrew, about the value of work. He was not a religious man and did not read Hebrew. Completely assimilated, he considered himself Czech, and in fact briefly quoted the Hussite "Saint Wenceslas Chorale" in *Al S'fod*. But in an effort to identify with his Jewish heritage, he had someone in Terezín fashion musical notes into Hebrew letters for the title page, which read "Souvenir of the first and last year in the Terezín exile."

While in Terezín, Klein arranged many folk songs for performance by children's choirs, several Russian folk songs for male voices, *Bachuri L'an Tisa* (1942) for treble voices, and three extraordinary original pieces: a pair of SSATB madrigals on texts by François Villon and Friedrich Hölderlin, and the incredible *The First Sin* (1943) for male voices. *Bachuri L'an Tisa* is something of an enigma. The poignant text, "My son, where are you going? My sweetheart, it's all over," does not continue after the first four measures, though the manuscript notation thereafter—sometimes using beams to connect eighths, sometimes using flags—surely indicates that additional text existed. Likewise, the folklike nature of the tune and its setting suggest that this may in fact be a folk song arrangement. Still, the origin of the tune and text is uncertain. The texts of Klein's madrigals are in Czech translation, although it is clear from the manuscript that the Hölderlin setting was composed to the original German, with Czech added later. The text of *The First Sin* is old Moravian folk poetry, retelling the story of Adam, Eve, and the serpent. All three are composed in a highly expressive chromatic language, with subtle rhythmic shifts and masterfully intricate counterpoint. The climax of *The First Sin*, where an A major chord suddenly materializes out of nowhere, like a flash of light, is the work of genius.

Klein was pianist for Schaechter's famous performances of Verdi's *Requiem*, given in Terezín just before they were deported to Auschwitz in 1944,

Manuscript page of Gideon Klein's *Bachuri L'an Tisa*. Courtesy of the Jewish Museum in Prague.

and he may also have collaborated with Schaechter in providing special barracks songs for the children (the nature and function of these little pieces caused the composers to remain anonymous). The songs were never written down, undoubtedly because of their encouraging, anti-Nazi texts, but some lived on in the memories of those who survived. When sung publicly, they were whistled or vocalized on *lai, lai, lai.* Joža Karas (1985, 89–90) quotes the text of one. Another, remembered by Dasha Lewin, is notable for repeated use of the phrase "The truth shall prevail," which, as every Czech child would know, were the last words of Jan Hus (1369–1415) before being burned at the stake as a heretic.

Byt svetem vladla
Even though a power dominates in the world,
Fists raised without rights, in a world of lies,
We will remain loyal and maintain honor
Because truth will prevail.

We are wounded but we will not betray
The faith which remains in our hearts.
A day will come! A day will come!
The truth will prevail!

The world's development continues
In spite of reactionary criticism;
He who lies builds his own destruction,
But we salute the day when the truth will prevail!
The truth will prevail!

Terezín barracks song, "Byt svetem vladla," with translation by Monika Miller and Nick Strimple. Transcription and translation © 1991 by Nick Strimple.

Others who must be mentioned are Ervín Schulhoff (1894–1942), Karel Reiner (1910–1979), and František Domažlicky (1913–1998).

Schulhoff was among the first European composers to experiment with jazz, and he may have been the first to join jazz techniques with Schoenbergian serialism. Primarily a pianist, he contributed a few startling choral works, including the jazz oratorio *HMS Royal Oak* (1930), the large cantata *Communist Manifesto* (1935) for thirteen soloists, double mixed chorus, and wind orchestra, and Symphony No. 6 (1940) for chorus and orchestra, which sets Adalbert von Chamisso's "Ode to Freedom." Schulhoff became a communist during the early thirties, took Soviet citizenship, and moved to Russia in 1939. His political views and Jewish heritage resulted in his arrest by the invading Nazis in 1941, and he died in 1942 in a concentration camp.

Reiner was an important Czech music educator. Prior to his deportation to Terezín in 1943, he composed *The Flowered Horse* (1942), an interesting cycle of children's choruses that was successfully performed in the ghetto. While there, Reiner also provided music as accompaniment to choral readings of Czech literature. Although only *The Flowered Horse* survived Terezín, he composed several choral works after the war, including the cantata *They Were a Thousand Years Old* (1962) and *Peace Madrigal* (1963).

Domažlicky composed *May Song* (1943) for male chorus in Terezín. His best-known choral work is *Czech Songs* (1955) for treble chorus and strings.

Incidentally, Terezín, Dachau, Kreuzberg, and Indonesia were not the only places where choral music was brought forth by the oppression of the Nazis and their allies. The Jewish ghettos of eastern Europe, for example, had a tradition of workers' choruses and singing societies dating from the latter half of the nineteenth century. When these ghettos were sealed off by the Nazis, choral and other musical activities continued wherever possible (sometimes in secret), often including arrangements of new Yiddish songs that spoke directly to the inmates' predicament. In the Sachsenhausen concentration camp, Aleksander Kulisiewicz kept a diary (a facsimile of which is kept at the United States Holocaust Memorial Museum in Washington, D.C.) that documented the efforts of Martin Rosenberg, who secretly formed a chorus that performed newly arranged male-voice versions of German, Polish, Hebrew, and Yiddish folksongs, as well as a few Christmas carols for non-Jewish inmates; it is particularly interesting to note that some of these performances may have included simple choreography. In Buchenwald, secret cabarets, which occasionally included newly arranged choral versions of folk songs, were organized in individual barracks. In 1938 a bizarre example of public singing by the entire camp also took place in Buchenwald, the deputy commandant ordering Hermann Leopoldi, a Viennese cabaret singer, and Fritz Loehner-Beda, one of Franz Lehar's librettists, to compose a camp song on the false pretense that all the other camps had them. Theories as to why this Nazi official actually ordered the song range from simple sadism, since the prisoners were made to stand in the snow while singing, to his need for something that the assembled inmates could sing to drown out the communist prisoners, who had the disconcerting habit of breaking into "The Internationale" during roll call. The resulting *Buchenwald Lied* is similar in sentiment and style to Herbert Zipper's *Dachaulied* (see chapter 2) but does not have its sharp edge. Another, more meaningful occurrence of singing by assembled prisoners took place in Auschwitz in November 1944. In reprisal for an uprising by inmates working in the crematoriums, the Nazis selected some to be gassed as an example. As the prisoners were loaded onto trucks for removal to the gas chamber, they began to sing *Ani Ma-a-nim* and *Tikosenu* (which, in slightly altered form, would eventually become the Israeli national anthem). The other inmates, assembled to witness the executions, spontaneously joined with them in singing.

SLOVAKIA

The most important Slovak composer of the century was Eugen Suchoň (1908–1993), whose contributions to the repertoire include numerous partsongs, folk song arrangements, the masterful cantata *Psalm of the Carpathians*, Opus 12 (1938) for tenor, mixed chorus, and orchestra, and *The Slovak Mass* (1991) for unison chorus. His most representative choral work is the cycle *Of Man* (1962) for unaccompanied mixed chorus, on text by Jan Smrek, in which he successfully explores certain positive aspects of life: optimism, love, and national heritage. Suchoň's little partsong in admiration of the Slovak countryside, *Aka si mi krasna* (How Beautiful You Are), may be the single most beloved choral piece in Slovakia, held in an esteem similar to Randall Thompson's *Alleluia* in the United States, or Lūcija Garūta's "The Lord's Prayer" in Latvia.

Other important Slovak composers include Mikuláš Moyses (1872–1944), whose Masses, folk song arrangements, and other small pieces helped establish Slovak nationalism; his son, Alexander Moyzes (1906–1984), whose impressive early partsongs *Santa Helena* and *Instead of a Wreath* suggested the technical mastery that became apparent in the folk song cycle *Whose Organ Is Playing*, Opus 37 (1947); Ján Cikker (1911–1990), whose best-known choral work is the cantata *Cantus filiorum*, Opus 17; Alfred Zemanovsky (b. 1919), whose numerous compositions for children's, women's, men's, and mixed chorus show a decided predilection for three- and five-voice textures; Jozef Gaher (b. 1934), whose brilliant little cantata, *The Death of Saul* (1967) for chorus and organ, won the 1968 Ernest Bloch Award; and Iris Szeghyová (b. 1956), who has written many successful works for children's chorus.

HUNGARY

When the twentieth century began, Hungarian choristers' ears were full of music by people like Béla Szabados (1867–1936), a famous voice teacher who was also a prolific composer of partsongs. His style, typical of the time, was rooted in nineteenth-century romantic nationalism, which relied heavily on Hungarian popular song for inspiration. Into this environment came Ernst von Dohnányi (1877–1960), Béla Bartók (1881–1945), Zoltán Kodály (1882–1967), László Lajtha (1892–1963), and Lajos Bárdos (1899–1986).

Dohnányi, an important instrumental composer during the century's first half, also maintained a well-deserved reputation as a concert pianist. Practitioner of an old-fashioned nineteenth-century art that eschewed inspiration from popular sources, he was an excellent craftsmen who made small but worthwhile contributions to the choral repertoire. His few works for chorus include the attractive *Missa in Dedicatione Ecclesiae* (1930) for soloists, chorus, and orchestra, and *Stabat mater* for treble chorus and orchestra (1952–53), as well as some smaller pieces that became available only after the collapse of the Eastern Block in 1989.

Béla Bartók was among the greatest composers of the twentieth century. His choral compositions occupy a distinguished, if somewhat peripheral, position in the repertoire. Initially influenced by Richard Strauss and Franz Liszt, he began a systematic study of peasant music in 1905 that resulted in a complete overhaul of his aesthetic principles. From that time forward, his music exhibited a remarkable stylistic consistency. Hungarian peasant rhythms predominate and harmonies are derived from the vertical sonorities inherent in the pentatonic scales of the oldest peasant tunes: two triads, a seventh chord, and chords utilizing seconds and perfect fourths. The use of later heptatonic modal scales expanded the possibilities without changing the basic harmonic foundation. Bartók's interest in Debussy and peasant music other than Magyar—Slovak, Walachian, Turkish, North African, and especially Romanian—further increased his color palette, accounting for his frequent use of chromaticism and augmented fourths. Halsey Stevens (1964, 154) described another interesting characteristic, quite international in nature, which also occurs in music by Randall Thompson, Hugo Distler, and others (including Stevens himself): "In even his earliest choral work, the *Four Old Hungarian Folk Songs* for unaccompanied male chorus (1912), he uses harmonies of somewhat dissonant character; but the individual lines are so logical that it is not difficult to attain the desired sonority. This is the fundamental secret of Bartók's choral writing, as it is of the chorale harmonizations of Bach: the predominance of horizontal motion over vertical harmony." In Bartók's case this "fundamental secret" reflects a total assimilation of peasant music, in which modal melody is propelled by relentless rhythmic considerations, creating harmony as a byproduct (the same phenomenon is also part of other folk traditions, including "claw hammer" banjo playing in the United States).

In addition to several sets of folk song arrangements and the folk-rich *Three Village Scenes* (1926), Bartók's original works consist of *Cantata profana* (1931) for tenor and bass soloists, mixed chorus, and orchestra, a compact and intense essay on freedom couched in the language of a folktale; *From Olden Times* (1935); and *Twenty-seven Choruses* (1935). *Cantata profana* is very difficult and infrequently performed, but it presents a compendium of Bartók's techniques and should be studied closely by every aspiring conductor and composer. Side by side with obvious and elemental materials culled from peasant music are mirror images, intricate fugal writing, and other sophisticated contrapuntal devices used for text-painting and dramatic purposes, as well as a remarkable, outwardly expanding choral chord in seconds, similar to that encountered first in Charles Ives's *Psalm 90* (see chapter 12) and later in Britten's *War Requiem*.

Zoltán Kodály made vast contributions to choral music by collecting and arranging folk songs, developing an educational method for children, composing numerous original works for every conceivable vocal ensemble, and serving as a teacher for several important choral composers. He stands apart from virtually every other major twentieth-century composer in that the majority of his compositions are choral. An eager colleague of Bartók in the collection and codification of peasant music, Kodály never absorbed those materials into the very center of his being as Bartók did (or perhaps in Bartók's case folk music was a key unlocking what was already in his heart), so his music, while strongly colored by peasant rhythms and scales, retains curious stylistic inconsistencies, such as neobaroque passages, frequent use of augmented sixth chords, and modal cadences in otherwise nonmodal tonal environments. These and other anomalies create an interesting pastiche rather than reflecting different aspects of a strong personality as in the stylistic pluralism of Vaughan Williams.

Kodály had little interest in choral music prior to 1923, when he was asked to compose something for the fiftieth anniversary of the unification of Buda and Pest. This invitation acknowledged the composer's full reentry into Hungarian musical life, along with Bartók and Dohnányi, following the overthrow of the short-lived postwar government in which they served. It may have been that during the intervening period of forced inactivity and reflection Kodály had come to new conclusions about choral music. In any case, he surely wanted to give his best for such a prestigious event. The resulting *Psalmus hungaricus*, Opus 13 (1923) for tenor soloist, chorus, and orchestra was an immediate success. The initial Hungarian audience was both comforted and exhilarated by sensations of familiarity in new guise. Kodály's text, a paraphrase of Psalm 55 written during the sixteenth-century Turkish occupation by the poet Mihaly Keczkemeti Veg, accented the Hungarian understanding of persecution and desire for peace. Further, the rhythmic structure of the main theme is identical to that of at least two well-known sixteenth-century Hungarian songs (Stevens 1968, 149–150), and the modal language—without actually quoting tunes—is rooted in Magyar peasant music. The structural balance, harmonic warmth, melodic expressiveness, typically Hungarian rhythmic "snap" (long-short-short-long, the beats falling on the first long and second short note), and eloquently articulated message of *Psalmus hungaricus* helped it to remain popular throughout the century.

The success of this piece vaulted Kodály onto the international scene, but rehearsal problems prior to the premiere may have made an even greater impact on his development, as well as on the development of choral music education. While preparing *Psalmus hungaricus* for performance, the chorus proved so inadequate that Kodály added a boys' choir to double the treble parts. He was so pleased with the sound of the boys that he immediately made two SSAA folk song arrangements for them, *The Straw Guy* and *See the Gypsies*. Thus began an interest that would result in Kodály's choral method and a substantial body of folk song arrangements and partsongs for various vocal configurations and levels of proficiency.

Missa brevis (1942) was originally written as an organ Mass. Kodály recast it for chorus and organ between 1944 and 1945, and orchestrated it some years later. The original subtitle, *in tempore belli*, was omitted from the published score. László Eosze (1962, 161) wrote that this work addressed "the whole tradition of European sacred music, from Gregorian plainsong, through Palestrina and Bach, to the great romantics of the nineteenth century." Less charitably, it can also be viewed as one of the most stylistically inconsistent of Kodály's works. In quick succession he visits the realms of chant, classical oratorio, Handelian oratorio, and nineteenth-century romanticism, the occasional pentatonic scale or other identifiable Hungarian flavoring used only sparingly, like paprika. Of more positive interest is the seemingly haphazard reappearance of themes, quite unlike the connection between Kyrie and "Dona nobis pacem" common to many Mass settings. This intriguing characteristic may result from the origins of *Missa brevis*. As an organ Mass it functioned without the connecting tissue of text, so that themes could appear and reappear with greater freedom. Hence the acute observation of Halsey Stevens (1968, 160):

> Materials from earlier sections are brought back in later stages to provide a feeling of reprise. So the music of "Christe eleison" serves in modified form for the "Hosanna" and for the "Dona nobis pacem"; the last bars of the "Ite missa est" refer to the opening and closing bars of the Credo; the "Deo gratias" is set to the music which served (more polyphonically) for the Sanctus. This transference of musical materials

seems, except for the "Qui tollis" (where the same words recur), to be unrelated to textual demands. It must therefore be considered in reference to *musical* form; if the *Psalmus hungaricus* is designed as a rondo, the *Missa brevis* has, perhaps rather loosely, pretensions to the sonata.

Kodály's last large composition, *Laudes organi* (1965–66), was written for the American Guild of Organists and premiered at their convention in 1966. Since then it has slowly but steadily increased in popularity, mostly because it matches neatly with economic and programming criteria. Here is a moderately large-scale secular concert work by a major composer that requires only chorus and organ. The medieval Latin text, after praising the virtues of the "King of Instruments," includes a few kind words for Guido d'Arezzo (992–1050), whose handsignals for the teaching of solfège were incorporated by Kodály into his own choral method. Structurally, the casual listener may perceive a rondo, but the work is really an elaborate set of variations, one of which returns periodically, like a ritornello. After an organ prelude—which cannot decide between baroque and turn-of-the-century romanticism—the chorus enters, chantlike, and with definite Hungarian touches. However, the piece has already revealed itself to be another stylistic amalgam similar to *Missa brevis*, though lacking the inspiration, and one begins to wonder if this schizophrenic hodgepodge—a little Gregorian, a little baroque, a little romanticism, and a little Magyar—could in fact be Kodály's real style. In any case, *Laudes organi* is a disappointment, in spite of its structural subtlety and effective choral writing.

Like many prolific choral composers, Kodály excelled in small forms. One of his best partsongs is *Jesus and the Traders* (1934), an especially vivid setting of the biblical account of Jesus throwing the moneychangers out of the temple. It begins and ends with a modal progression to D major, serving at first only as a narrative function but finally representing an astonished, approving realization of what Jesus has done. In between, the story rushes ahead at breakneck speed by means of a rustic double fugato (one subject for the whip that Jesus makes, another for the spilling of the changers' coins), colorful text-painting, and bold choral declamations, culminating in Jesus's exasperated cry, "What have ye made it? A den of robbers!" The music gradually calms down, and a variant of the opening material returns to describe both Jesus's consternation and the people's awakened interest in him. Like the similarly unreligious Janáček, Kodály's understanding of moral outrage resulted in wonderfully dramatic musical storytelling.

Other works include the festive, well-balanced, polyphonically masterful, and stylistically consistent *Budavári Te Deum* (1936) for chorus and orchestra, written for the 250th anniversary of the liberation of Buda from the

Turks; the technically skillful, dramatic, and patriotically inflammatory *Hymn of Zrinyi* (1956) for baritone soloist and mixed chorus, which was doomed to oblivion during the Communist regime by the timing of its premiere, just before the unsuccessful anti-Communist revolution in 1956; *Magyar mise* (1966), a simple, vernacular setting of the Mass; and many substantial folk song arrangements and other small pieces for women's and men's ensembles.

László Lajtha was among the more tragic victims of Soviet-style repression. Highly regarded throughout western Europe as a composer and ethnomusicologist, he was, like Liszt before him, elected to membership in the L'Academie Française. The French particularly appreciated his music for its clarity, spontaneity, and dramatic impact, causing the commentator of his French publishers' catalogue (1954) to remark that "Parisians who find him too Hungarian and the latter who find him excessively Parisian forget the essential fact that he is first of all himself." After 1948, however, Lajtha was no longer allowed to go abroad, and lived the rest of his life poverty stricken in Hungary. Devoutly religious, he continued to compose sacred works, of which *Missa in tono phrygio* (*Missa in diebus tribulationis*, 1950) is representative. It was one of the first works recorded in Hungary after the establishment of democracy in 1990. Composing a Mass did not seem paradoxical to the Calvinist Lajtha since he believed that Jesus, as Lord of All, was neither Protestant nor Catholic. Other choral pieces, all of which reflect the composer's interest in folk music (especially that of Transylvania) as well as his command of various twentieth-century techniques, include *Two Choruses on Poems of Charles d'Orléans*, Opus 23 (1936), *Four Madrigals on Poems of Charles d'Orléans*, Opus 29 (1939), *Missa*, Opus 54 (1952) for mixed choir and organ, and *Magnificat*, Opus 60 (1954) for women's choir and organ.

Lajos Bárdos was a choral conductor, musicologist, and composer who, with Kodály, was responsible for the high level of proficiency that characterized Hungarian choirs after World War I. Beginning his teaching and conducting career in 1925, he helped create choirs in villages and rural areas while simultaneously developing some of the country's most prominent choruses, such as the Cecilia Chorus, the Palestrina Chorus, and the Budapest Chorus. His programming was exemplary, incorporating works from the early Renaissance to the most modern, and drawing extensively from the rich heritage of Hungarian folk music. Bárdos's own compositions, based on these same models, are noteworthy for directness of expression and empathetic setting of texts. His works include four volumes of folk song arrangements for mixed chorus (1933), *A nyúl éneke* (Song of the Rabbit, 1946) for double chorus and three timpani, *Twenty Choruses* (1963) for equal voices, four unpublished Masses and other liturgical works, and many small pieces for various vocal configurations.

Prominent composers among Kodály's pupils are Ferenc Szabó (1902–1969), whose *Ave Maria* (1926) for chorus and organ, *Urchin Song* (1929) for children's chorus, and numerous partsongs exhibit a tendency toward well-balanced structures and rather old-fashioned melody; Pál Kadosa (1903–1983), whose style—a mixture of Magyar influences with Hindemithian ideas of objectivity and accessibility—is manifested in several choral works, including the partsongs collected as Opus 24 (1933–36) and the cantata *De amore fatali*, Opus 31 (1940) for soloists, chorus, and orchestra; Ferenc Farkas (1905–2000), whose cantata *Fountain of Saint John* combined Hungarian colors with Italian formal and melodic clarity (learned from his other teacher, Ottorino Respighi); and Sándor Veress (1907–1992), whose cantata *Sancti Augustini psalmus conta partem Donati* (1943–44) and partsongs for all conceivable vocal configurations reflect the Phrygian colorations of Hungarian folk music, as well as the influence of Stravinsky.

Miklós Rózsa (1907–1995) was an established composer of concert works before moving to Hollywood in 1940, thereafter devoting his major efforts to composition for film (sometimes utilizing chorus, as with *Ben-Hur* and *The King of Kings*). Among his concert works are *To Everything There Is a Season* (1946), *The Vanities of Life* (1967), and *Psalm 23* (1972). The composer's designation of these three rather extensive pieces as "motettes" reflects his broad application of Renaissance points of imitation as a basic structural procedure, while at the same time creating unique architectures for each. A fitting description of Rózsa's motets has been succinctly given by Christopher Palmer (1978): "Here, as in all his music, sensuousness is tempered by austerity in a manner peculiar to Rózsa, and the overall impact of the music is positive and life-enhancing." *The Vanities of Life* and *Psalm 23*, both written for Pacific Lutheran University's Choir of the West, are tightly constructed, employing classical ideals of form and balance. *The Vanities of Life* is more actively contrapuntal, and the harmonies more biting; *Psalm 23* is more opulent, and rounded off with an "Alleluia." While sonically rich, *To Everything There Is a Season* is less adventuresome harmonically than the others. Even so, it is perhaps more interesting because its structural sprawl is organized according to cinematic principles: musically independent sections (or scenes), each projecting one thought-picture (a time to live, a time to die, a time to sow), move effortlessly from one to another, gradually accumulating momentum for the final extended climax. Some musical descriptions—war, for instance—are obvious and not particularly original; but like all good film scores, the piece is quite effective.

It should be pointed out here that reliance on musical description in concert works sometimes proves an irresistible temptation to film composers. Louis Gruenberg's (1884–1964) extravagantly descriptive oratorio *A Song of Faith* (1962) comes immediately to mind. Still, other good film composers have managed to write colorful large choral works that avoid the pitfall, among them Erich Wolfgang Korngold's (1897–1957) *Passover Psalm* (1943), Franz Waxman's (1906–1967) *Song of Terezín* (1964–65), Bernard Herrmann's (1911–1975) cantata *Moby Dick* (1940), and Jerry Goldsmith's (b. 1929) *Christus Apollo* (1969), on text by Ray Bradbury.

Important composers of the next generation include András Szöllösy (b. 1921), György Ligeti (b. 1923), Erzsébet Szönyi (b. 1924), and György Kurtág (b. 1926).

András Szöllösy avoided composing choral music of any kind until 1981, when he was asked to write a piece for the Hungarian State Folk Ensemble. The resulting work, *In Phariseos* (1981–82) for mixed chorus and trumpet, pays homage to the spirit of Kodály without reflecting Kodály's sound world in any way. Szöllösy's basic approach is revealed in János Kárpáti's (1989, 11) description of the melodic process. Identifying *In Phariseos* as neo-baroque, Kárpáti also points out that it is different from traditional baroque music, adding, "This skeletal tune reaches extremes of melody at certain points: it repeats a single pitch over heavy rhythm schemes. Occasionally the tune even leaves the realm of pitched musical sounds and is reduced to the rhythmical recitation of plain speech." Rather than relate an event, as does Kodály's *Jesus and the Traders*, Szöllösy's piece is a litany against the various forms of hypocrisy listed in Saint Luke 11:43–52 and 12:1–2. The absence of folk influence is one indication that the composer is attempting, in Kárpáti's words, "to conquer polyphonic vocal music in a framework appropriate to today's language and requirements." Another is the violence of the choral writing, contrasted with the surprising, quiet trumpet entrance that begins the concluding section. It is an altogether convincing first essay in the choral idiom.

In Phariseos was followed quickly by *Planctus Mariae* (1982) for women's chorus, in which Szöllösy made certain assumptions about choral music only to have them shattered in rehearsal. In the composer's words, "I thought I had written something very simple because it was full of second-canons. I thought all there was to do was to learn the melody and then sing it in canon, each part entering a whole tone lower or higher. I learned from Maria Katanics, the choir-mistress, that it was awfully hard to do" (Olsvay 1994a, 18).

Szöllösy's next choral work, *Fabula Phaedri* (1982), was commissioned by the King's Singers. It proved so popular that before long the King's Singers commissioned another work, *Miserere* (1984). Once again, Szöllösy's relative inexperience with ensemble singing caused him to miscalculate the difficulty factor. "The King's Singers said it was one of the most difficult pieces they had ever come across," the composer complained, "although I tried to write easy, singable parts" (Olsvay 1994b, 17). Difficulties aside, *Miserere* has still received numerous performances in continental Europe and Great Britain, suggesting that its message is substantive. A twelve-tone work that at one point introduces the chorale "O Sacred Head Now Wounded" into the serial fabric, *Miserere* effectively conveys deep emotions via intellectual procedures.

György Ligeti is a great composer of the late twentieth century. After years of struggling under the Communists, he fled to the West in 1958. Most people are familiar with his choral music through the slowly evolving sonorities of *Lux aeterna* (1966), made famous by its use in Stanley Kubrick's *2001: A Space Odyssey*; but Ligeti has written other works as well, all displaying the highest levels of artistic integrity and craftsmanship. His largest is *Requiem* (1963–65), an exceptionally thorny affair, requiring sizeable numbers of expert performers. With relentlessly harsh harmonies, sharply angular solo lines (often operating at the extremes of vocal range), thick textures, and nervous canons following so closely on one another as to create swarming masses of sound, it is as if the Jewish Ligeti were reliving existence under Nazis and Communists rather than looking forward to some kind of redemption. The piece ends suddenly with an almost ethereal "Lacrimosa." A startling work, it was aptly described by critic Mark Swed in the *Los Angeles Times* (20 April 1998) as "strange, exciting, compelling, and deeply disturbing music . . . not so much about afterlife as about *life* in the second half of the twentieth century."

Anyone who knows the theatrical *Aventures* (1962) and *Nuovelles Aventures* (1962–65) realizes that Ligeti can also be accessible and witty. These aspects are found in his choral music, too, most obviously in the early unaccompanied choruses *Night* and *Morning* (1955) and several folk song arrangements and other small pieces, which are indebted in some ways to folk sources. The unaccompanied *Three Fantasies after Friedrich Hölderlin* (1982) finds common ground between the more radical tonal language of the 1960s and the folk-derived works. Here the exploration of new diatonic and chromatic harmonic combinations creates the overall effect of very dense diatonicism with rich, edgy sonorities and the kind of agitated, close counterpoint typical of Ligeti.

Erzsébet Szönyi studied in Paris with Boulanger and Messiaen, and returned to Budapest, where she became head of teacher training and choral conducting at the Academy of Music. Her works in large forms, including the children's oratorio *The Shivering King* (1959) and the youth oratorio *Tinodi's Song about Eger* (1963), have been especially successful.

György Kurtág disavowed most of his music written prior to 1959. Of the early works remaining in his catalogue, three are choral: *Beads* (1949) for mixed chorus, *Dance Song* (1952) for children's chorus and piano, and *Korean Cantata* (1952–53) for bass soloist, mixed chorus, and orchestra. Following the Hungarian uprising of 1956, Kurtág studied in Paris with Milhaud and Messiaen, gradually progressing from a rigidly dissonant style to one incorporating melodies more improvisational in nature, Hungarian folk instruments (notably the cimbalom), and extreme concentration of form. According to Kurtág, his goal was "to strip away all that is unimportant, or, in other words, to express the most with the fewest notes" (Halász 1996). A master of vocal composition, he nevertheless completed only three choral works after 1959, all typical of his mature style: *Omaggio a Luigi Nono*, Opus 16 (1979) for mixed chorus, *Songs of Despair and Sorrow*, Opus 18 (1980–1995) for mixed chorus and chamber ensemble, and *Eight Choruses to Poems by Dezso Tandori*, Opus 23 (1981–84) for mixed chorus.

Two notable younger composers are Ivan Eröd (b. 1936) and György Orbán (b. 1947). Since immigrating to Austria, Eröd has produced numerous choral pieces in a mildly chromatic and harmonically satisfying style, of which the unaccompanied cycle *Drei Gedichte aus Goethes "West-Oestlicher Divan"* (published 1990) is an outstanding example. Orbán, a professor of composition at the Lizst Academy in Budapest, was born in Romanian Transylvania and immigrated to his ethnic homeland in 1979. His Masses and motets became popular in the West, especially the United States, after the European political events of 1989–90. His music, which has been described as "neo-romantic or neo-something," relies on an eclectic combination of musical styles, including classical impulses, waltzes, and other types of dance, as well as the musical theater of Leonard Bernstein and Andrew Lloyd Webber, resulting in works that are "somewhat controversial" but "nevertheless extremely powerful" (Boronkay 1992, 12). A particularly fine example is the motet *Daemon irrepit callidus* (published 1997), which convincingly portrays Satan's attempts to make worldly pleasures more important than the heart of Jesus. Hyperintense motor rhythms, sparse harmonies, and sharp, pointed exclamations create the effect of an hysterical preacher shouting hellfire and damnation. The anonymous medieval text, incidentally, coins some Latin words of its own. For example, *impinguo* is not a Latin verb; in "Inescatur impinguatur dilatatur" (It is enticed, is made fat, is made dull), "impinguatur" has been created out of the adjective *pinguis*, which means "fat."

Other Hungarian choral composers include Mátyás Seiber (1905–1960), who settled in England in 1935, becoming a respected teacher and choral conductor as well as a composer known for his many folk song arrangements and cantatas on texts by James Joyce; József Karai (b. 1927), whose very large catalogue of choral works includes folk song arrangements as well as extended works utilizing avant-garde procedures; Kamilló Lendvay (b. 1928), who wrote two oratorios, *Orogenesis* (1969–70) and *Pro libertate* (1975), as well as numerous smaller pieces, of which *Winter Morning* (1966) for mixed chorus and *Three Male Choruses* (1959) may be considered representative; József Soproni (b. 1930), whose Symphony No. 3 (*Sinfonia da Requiem*, 1983) for chorus and orchestra received extended commentary in the Hungarian press; and Zoltán Jeney (b. 1943), who wrote the emotionally involving and interesting *Absolve Domine* (1990) for sixteen-part mixed chorus, which he has unfortunately described with the intellectual detachment of an auto mechanic explaining how a transmission works: "The first four parts are the original melody and its mirror-, crab-, and mirror-crab inversions; the other parts are subtly accelerating canons of these four, on different tones. The whole piece does not contain a single tone alien to the original, while the sound is of extreme rhythmic diversity and contains the complete twelve-tone scale" (Olsvay 1993, 17).

POLAND

Two giants of the age, Witold Lutoslawski (1913–1997) and Krzysztof Penderecki (b. 1933), dominated Polish music in the twentieth century.

Lutoslawski, who exerted tremendous influence on a generation of younger composers throughout the world, briefly described his own development (Tom Carlson 1970): "I consider myself a follower of the Debussy-Bartók tradition. I don't follow the second Viennese school. While I do use the twelve-tone technique, I don't use it in the serial way. The basic element in my technique is not the row, but the chord containing the twelve notes." Lutoslawski first encountered the music and philosophies of John Cage in 1961, a powerful experience that led him to incorporate Cage's principles into his own style. *Trè poèmes d'Henri Michaux* (1963) for twenty-part chorus (one singer to a part, or multiples thereof) and orchestra of winds and percussion is an early example of this. Exceptionally complex, requiring two conductors, its individual components are so well conceived that coordination of the two performing groups—instruments and singers—is not particularly difficult. This is not to say that *Trè poèmes* is a walk in the park for performers, but rather that Lutoslawski had them in mind when he made sure numerous technical challenges would not be insurmountable. For example, much of the choral writing consists of rhythmically free ostinato-like passages of indeterminate pitch, or of one or two simple intervals (usually a second or third) and pitch cells of four to seven notes, freely repeated.

Lutoslawski's only other choral work is *Twenty Polish Christmas Carols* (1946), originally composed for treble chorus or solo voice and piano. Seventeen songs were orchestrated in 1985, the remainder in 1989, for performance by soprano soloist, chamber chorus, and orchestra. An English translation by Charles Bodman Rae was published in 1990. Couched in sophisticated harmonies that anticipate Lutoslawski's later procedures, the carol melodies are retained in their original form.

Penderecki may be the most acclaimed composer of the century's second half. Choral conductors in the early sixties knew him for two works: *Psalmy Dawida* (1958), with its aggressive, jazzy rhythms, fascinating instrumental

* Immediately upon the conductor's signal Soprano I begins to sing alone. The entries of the other sopranos are indicated by cues given in the parts. The whole section should be spoken rather than sung, though keeping in the pitches indicated. This applies both to short as well as longer notes. Particular care should be taken to execute the latter with the minimum of force and without vibrato.

Witold Lutoslawski: portion of *Trè poèmes d'Henri Michaux*.

ensemble of percussion, pianos, and pizzicato string basses, and surprisingly easy-to-sing chord clusters; and *Stabat mater* (1963) for three unaccompanied mixed choruses, its bold array of avant-garde techniques ending in a dazzling D major chord. In 1966, however, Penderecki arrived full force on the scene with a commission honoring the 700th anniversary of the Münster Cathedral. For this event Penderecki created *Passio et mors Domini Nostri Jesu Christi secundum Lucam* (1963–66), better known ever since simply as the *Saint Luke Passion*. Considering the large scale of its vision, combined with the virtually complete realization of its artistic goals (including compositional craft, depth of feeling, and expressiveness), only two or three other twentieth-century choral works can possibly bear comparison with it: Britten's *War Requiem*, perhaps Mahler's Eighth Symphony, and possibly Hanuš's *Ecce homo*. The authenticity of its musical language, the grasp of technique, the exquisite sense of drama, the panoply of emotions, the well-considered homage to Bach in the work's structure, and use of the B-A-C-H motive claim it as a masterpiece among masterpieces. No one before had thought to follow simultaneously the logical consequences of Charles Ives, the impressionists, the serialists, Alois Hába, John Cage, Emil Burian, and other vocal experimenters, thereby liberating the chorus to all manner of expression. Before the premiere, Penderecki told the press, "I am a Roman Catholic. In my opinion, however, one does not have to belong to a church to compose religious music. The only condition is that one is willing to confess one's religious convictions. Therefore, you can without any objection consider my music as 'avowal' music: in that respect I am a Romanticist" (Hogarth n.d.).

Succeeding choral-orchestral works, such as the Auschwitz oratorio *Dies irae* (1966–67), *Kosmogonia* (1970), and *Utrenja* (1970), a gigantic contemplation on the death of Christ, represent a continuation of the same aesthetic, although some change of direction is obvious in *Magnificat* (1973–74), where there is less emphasis on avant-garde effects, rhythms are more clearly defined, and traditional forms such as fugue and passacaglia are present. Later pieces, the large *Polish Requiem* (1980–84) and the unaccompanied *Agnus Dei* (1981) for instance, further reveal a shift toward more direct expression, culminating in *Seven Gates of Jerusalem* (1996). Here certain elements from Penderecki's earlier works, such as thematic metamorphoses from small, seminal motives and a major-minor triad with raised fourth in the bass (first used in *Magnificat*), are included in an all-embracing neoromantic harmonic style with clearly defined tonal centers and prescribed rhythms. Another nod to Bach is present in the composer's use of numerology. As Ray Robinson (1998a) has pointed out, "The unison theme that commences the work contains five notes in its first part and seven in the answer. . . . The number seven in the work's title, its seven movements, and the passacaglia theme in movements two and four [derived from seven notes] . . . indicate that the number seven has a special importance."

Other works include *Canticum canticorum Salomonis* (1970–73); *Ecloga VIII* (1972), written for the King's Singers; *Te Deum* (1979–80); *Lacrymosa* (1980); the unabashedly tonal *Izhe zeruvimy* (Song of Cherubim, 1987) for unaccompanied mixed chorus; and the large *Credo* (1996–98) for five soloists, boys' and mixed choruses, and orchestra, which further develops the stylistic accessibility found in *Seven Gates of Jerusalem*.

Karol Szymanowski (1882–1937) was the most important Polish composer in the first half of the century. His style is a distillation of nineteenth-century romanticism and elements culled from Middle Eastern cultures, although he never quotes oriental materials directly. His love of female voices, both as soloists and in chorus, is reflected in his choral works. His best-known piece outside of Poland, *Stabat mater* (1925–26) for soprano, mixed chorus, and orchestra, enjoyed a renewed popularity during the 1990s, when enterprising young conductors began performing it with Janáček's *Glagolitic Mass*. The two make an interesting pairing because, while contemporaneous, they are not alike: *Stabat mater* is more compact, much more lyrical, and does not emanate from any sense of Polish ethnicity. The orchestration is polished, and the chromatic quasi-modal harmonies lend an impressionistic sheen.

Krzysztof Penderecki and Helmuth Rilling at the Oregon Bach Festival for the world premiere of Penderecki's *Credo*, 1998. Photo by Juretta Nidever. Courtesy of the Oregon Bach Festival.

Other choral works, all with orchestra, include Symphony No. 3 (*The Song of the Night*, 1914–16); *Demeter* (1917), *Agave* (1917), and *Litany to the Virgin Mary* (1930–33), all three for female chorus; and *Veni Creator* (1930).

Jan Adam Maklakiewicz (1899–1954) was a prominent choral conductor whose compositions were much admired by Szymanowski. A good example of Maklakiewicz's dissonant early style is the large Symphony No. 2 (*O Holy Lord*, 1928) for baritone, chorus, and orchestra. After World War II, he composed a quantity of church music in a more conventional style.

Artur Malawski (1904–1957) was initially influenced by Debussy and other late-nineteenth-century composers, though his style developed along rather individual lines, aware of trends but following none slavishly. His music displays a gift for lyrical melody, a fondness for ostinatos, and a predilection toward motivic development. Examples of his choral writing are the cantata *Gorgon's Island* (1939) for soprano and baritone soloists, chorus, and orchestra, and the four-movement *Little Choral Suite* (1952), on texts by Polish poets.

Grażyna Bacewicz (1909–1969) was considered by Witold Lutoslawski to be "one of the foremost women composers of all time" (Rosen 1984, 13). In an interview in 1960, answering a question about Schoenbergian serialism and other new musical directions, Bacewicz briefly discussed the impetus for her searching, dramatically vital style:

> I am very interested [in these developments], because in music like everything else, something new must come along from time to time. The [twelve-tone] technique itself is very important to me because it provides the necessary rigor and formal technique for the composer. Without this base, improvisation could not be created. As a drawback, I find that often the works that have been written all sound alike. In [my compositions] I want to maintain certain sections in the serial technique, but by the same token I want to give them a different character. I am not interested in pointillism because I believe the road to be too narrow, but I feel directed by the coloring of sounds and the new rhythms of electronic music. (Rosen 1984)

Bacewicz's choral works consist of the very early *Fugue for Double Chorus* (1928) and the cantatas *De profundis* (1932) for soloists, mixed chorus, and orchestra, *Olympic Cantata* (1948) for mixed chorus and orchestra, and *Acropolis* (1964) for mixed chorus and orchestra.

The choral music of Andrzej Koszewski (b. 1922) ranges from rather simple folk song settings to works of substantial complexity incorporating various avant-garde techniques. Representative of the latter style are *Muzyka fa-re-mi-do-si* (1960), in which the musical material is derived from letters in Chopin's name, and the double chorus *La espero* (1963), an intriguing bitonal exploration of a pentatonic scale.

Tadeusz Baird (b. 1928) developed a lyrical style based on romantic models, into which a variety of modern techniques were assimilated. Particularly interesting are *Egzorta* (1956), a cantata on old Hebrew texts; and *Etiuda* (1961) for "vocal orchestra," percussion, and piano.

Edward Bury (b. 1919) and Jozef Swider (b. 1930) specialized in choral composition. Bury concentrated on functional liturgical music, also contributing the large oratorio *Saint Francis of Assisi* (1975). His music, full of Gregorian implications, tends to the conventionally diatonic, although his notational system lends a more avant-garde look to the page. A good example of Swider's work is *Cantate Domino* (1989), in which aleatoric technique further enlivens a vigorous diatonic language enriched by added-note chords. In a preface to the published American edition (1989), Polish critic Ryszard Gabrys aptly described the effect of such music on listeners and performers:

"When I hear or watch performances of Swider's choir music—sung by professionals, amateurs, students, or children—I always see a great joy of singing, a joy of creating living music, a pleasure of singing that is deeply founded so that it emerges from the musical score as if also a part of human nature."

The New Grove Dictionary of Music and Musicians (Sadie 1980) declared the music of Henryk Górecki (b. 1933) to be "among the most original to have emerged in the third quarter of the twentieth century." Still, he remained essentially unknown in the West until 1992, when recordings of his Third Symphony (1976) catapulted him to international fame. His style was influenced more by inwardly troubling nonmusical occurrences, such as World War II, persecution by the Communist government, and ill health, than by any teacher or other composer. This style—modal, with sustained textures, thick counterpoint, and generally slow tempos—is easy to describe but difficult to define. The musical and psychological complexities are immediately sensed and somewhat unsettling, though the sounds, even in the midst of great chord clusters, are traditional and unthreatening. Often, an immense sadness is almost palpable. A strong vocal quality permeates the music, so the choral works especially are idiomatic. Górecki's writing for unaccompanied choir is particularly adept. Of his choral compositions, the best-known are Symphony No. 2 (*Copernicus*, 1972); the motets *Amen* (1975), *Euntes ibant et flebant* (1977), and *Totus tuus* (1987); the folk song suite *Broad Waters* (1979); and the large *Miserere* (1980).

Other Polish choral composers include the famous choirmaster Stanislaw Kazuro (1881–1961), who contributed many partsongs for mixed and children's choruses, several choral suites, and three large oratorios; and Ryszard Kwiatkowski (b. 1931), who impressed with *Prayer of a Blind Somnambulist* (1969) for twenty-part male chorus.

ᗡ 6

RUSSIA AND OTHER FORMER
SOVIET REPUBLICS

Sergey I. Taneyev (1856–1915) was the most prominent Russian choral composer at the turn of the century. From 1903 until his death he composed thirty-two unaccompanied pieces as well as the large cantata *At the Reading of a Psalm* (1915) for chorus and orchestra, his last composition. Unlike that of many of his contemporaries, the bulk of Taneyev's work is secular and informed by an abiding interest in the music of Bach and the great masters of Renaissance polyphony. A student and lifelong friend of Tchaikovsky, Taneyev was a fastidious technician who conceived each composition from the outside in, so that the overall concept and structure were complete in his mind before he began and the details were gradually added as he composed. This approach naturally lends itself to abstract, contrapuntal ideas. An outstanding example is *Hori* (Choruses, 1909), a cycle of twelve partsongs for unaccompanied mixed chorus on texts by Jakov Polansky. Extremely difficult, each partsong is a real tour de force of the a cappella art, with thick, sonorous choral writing alternating with extremely complex counterpoint. Such is the case with "Prometheus," a highly dramatic work in which Taneyev writes a double fugue for five voices with two themes and two counterthemes simultaneously.

Of the several composers responsible for the international popularity of late-nineteenth-century Russian music, only Mily Alexeyevich Balakirev (1837–1910), Nicolai Rimsky-Korsakov (1844–1908), and Alexsander Glazunov (1865–1936) lived into the new century.

Balakirev seemed disinterested in choral music, although he was an ardent nationalist and had done some work with folk songs. In addition to a few early choral pieces, he composed, after his retirement, *Cantata for the Unveiling of the Glinka Memorial in Saint Petersburg* (1904), followed by a choral arrangement of a Chopin mazurka. At his death Balakirev was essentially a forgotten figure in Russian music.

Glazunov composed mostly abstract instrumental music, although he did compose a handful of choral pieces as well, most of them in the twentieth century. Like his other works, they are conceived according to German classical concepts of form and proportion, always highly polished and attractive, and infrequently substantive. After the 1917 Revolution, Glazunov helped reorganize the Leningrad Conservatory, leaving Russia in 1928 and eventually settling in Paris. His interest in an old-fashioned western European aesthetic placed him outside the mainstream of Russian musical thought (both official and otherwise), and his example was not emulated by younger Russian composers.

Rimsky-Korsakov composed numerous choral pieces, including two after 1900, but none are considered among his best works. However, the heritage embodied in his style was carried forward, quite literally, by his younger contemporaries Alexander Gretchaninoff and Sergei Rachmaninoff, and in a more cosmopolitan way by his student, Igor Stravinsky.

Alexander Gretchaninoff (1864–1956) steadfastly retained the musical language and sensibilities of the nineteenth century, except for some influence of impressionism that can be found in works composed following the First World War. After his first large sacred works—in particular Liturgy No. 2 (1902), which marked a significant evolution in musical styles, a link between the sacred works of Tchaikovsky and those of Rachmaninoff—he stands somewhat outside the Russian church music tradition in that his use of chant is sporadic, and his occasional inclusion of instrumental accompaniment prohibits those works from liturgical use. *Strastnaya sedmitsa* (Passion Week, 1911) is unusual in reflecting not a single service but a collection of thirteen pieces selected from a number of different offices of Holy Week, from matins of Great and Holy Monday through the vesperal liturgy of Great and Holy Saturday. Written for a choir of up to twelve parts, with numerous written low B-flats and even a written low A for bassi profundi, it reflects the type of "choral orchestration" prevalent in the a cappella writing of the late Moscow School composers.

In addition to many small sacred and secular works in Russian, Latin, and German, Gretchaninoff composed an All-Night Vigil (1912); *Liturgia domestica* (1917), originally for solo voice alone but reworked by the composer for tenor and bass soloists, chorus, strings, harp, and organ; and *Missa oecumenica* (1944) for soloists, chorus, and orchestra, a Latin Mass with some Russian elements, first performed in Boston. Gretchaninoff himself described his Liturgy No. 4 (1943), a simple setting for four voices, as "easy to perform . . . even [for ensembles] consisting of amateurs who are inexperienced in reading music" (Skans 1995). In a 1945 letter to Charles C. Hirt (1946), he expressed the hope that it would rid Russian Orthodox Church music of German and Italian influences.

Like Gretchaninoff, Sergei Rachmaninoff (1873–1944) emigrated from Russia during the October 1917 Revolution. Although he too retained a nineteenth-century musical vocabulary, he somehow managed to inject it with a new vitality and, despite the old-fashioned rhetoric, became a great composer of the century. It took many years, however, for the popularity of Rachmaninoff's choral works to catch up with his piano concertos and symphonies, even though *The Bells* (1913) for soprano, tenor, and bass soloists, mixed chorus, and orchestra was his personal favorite. The composer's opinion notwithstanding, *The Bells* (based on the poem by Edgar Allan Poe), for all its flashy orchestration and obvious craft, is too relentlessly gloomy and noisy to be thought of as more than an acquired taste. On the contrary, his undisputed masterpiece, *All-Night Vigil* ("Vespers," 1915), is, in Alexander Ruggieri's words, "arguably the epitome of sacred Russian choral art" (personal letter, 1998). A setting of the ordinary portions of the Orthodox evening service celebrated on Saturday nights and eves of feasts, consisting of vespers, matins, and prime, *All-Night Vigil* effortlessly conveys a profound message to a very broad audience. The first performances by the Moscow Synodal Choir were in concert form, and the lack of litanies and other short responses seems to indicate that Rachmaninoff intended the work for the concert hall rather than for use in church services. The piece is almost entirely based on chants. Ten movements are based on actual ancient chants, such as Kievan and Znamenny, and three are based on counterfeits of the composer's own creation that are so true in style and ethos as to be almost indistinguishable from the authentic chants. Only two movements are through-composed. One movement that might serve as an example is the Introductory Psalm of the vespers, "Blagoslovi, dushe moya, Gospoda" (Bless the Lord, O My Soul). Rachmaninoff employs the commonly used, so-called Greek chant. The ancient melody moves back and forth between psalm verses stated by the alto soloist and refrains sung first by the first tenors and later by the first sopranos. The men of the choir support the soloist with rich harmonies and imitative lines, while the refrains are relegated to higher voices (women and tenors) in more active counterpoint. The result is moving and mystical in its seamless and quiet motion.

One of two movements of *All-Night Vigil* to eschew the use of chant, "Virgin Mary, Rejoice" has become quite popular as an independent piece. From the first notes one is drawn into a deep contemplation of the mystery of the annunciation. Here, Rachmaninoff impresses with a simple ABA form. The opening section is appropriately contemplative, and the middle is quietly startling, with its alto melody in parallel thirds framed—quite literally—by a unison countermelody in soprano and tenor. The sudden climax, accentuated by the basses' fortissimo entrance, is well timed, and the leisurely denouement quite satisfying.

Rachmaninoff's first mature effort at a large work for mixed chorus was

Divine Liturgy of Saint John Chrysostom (1913). Unlike *All-Night Vigil, Divine Liturgy of Saint John Chrysostom* is freely through-composed. It includes the elements (litanies, responses, and so forth) necessary for liturgical use, although the musical writing is quite sophisticated and demanding, amplifying the structural and expressive dimensions beyond liturgical norms. His other choral works consist of the student composition *Concerto for Chorus* (1893), the early *Six Songs for Children's Voices* (published 1896) for treble chorus and piano, and the cantata *Spring* (1902) for baritone soloist, chorus, and orchestra.

Igor Stravinsky

Igor Stravinsky (1882–1971) ranks with Schoenberg as one of the most important composers of the century. His compositions and other writings had enormous influence on composers as diverse as Luciano Berio, Benjamin Britten, Alfredo Casella, George Dreyfus, Jean Langlais, Carl Orff, and Einojuhani Rautavaara. After Schoenberg's death, Stravinsky fell under the spell of Schoenbergian dodecaphony, as filtered through Webern. He also proved a convenient whipping boy for Soviet critics who considered him "an important and near-comprehensive artistic ideologue of the imperialist bourgeoisie" (Lang 1963, 80). Stravinsky was the first non-French composer since the baroque to seriously regard the chorus in terms of dance. His choral music is free of the jazz elements that colored much of his music during the thirties and forties, with the exception of the use of flügelhorn in *Threni: id est Lamentationes Jeremiae prophetae*. Of particular interest are his views that music is unable to express anything and that sacred music should be completely free of subjective influence.

Stravinsky's earliest choral work, *Cantata* (1904) for mixed chorus and piano, was written for the sixtieth birthday of Rimsky-Korsakov. Unfortunately, after a private performance in Rimsky-Korsakov's home, the score was lost. The next choral piece, the cantata *Zvezdoliki* (Starface, 1911–12) for male chorus and orchestra, waited until 1939 for performance and then failed to win an audience. Initially its neglect was blamed on intonation problems inherent in the choral writing—almost always homophonic triads with an added note, often resulting in the simultaneous sounding of a major-minor triad. The continued obscurity of *Zvezdoliki* may also rest in the uneconomical distribution of forces—the large orchestra never plays tutti—and the otherwise uninteresting layout, which some have called sluggish. The piece does feature some interesting excursions into bitonality, the final chord being a composite of C7 and G major 7, but its lack of rhythmic vitality is surprising, especially considering that it was composed at the same time as *Le sacre du printemps* (Rite of Spring, 1911–13).

Over the next several years Stravinsky produced three works seminal to the development of choral music later in the century: the dance cantata *Les noces* (The Wedding, 1914–1923) for SATB soloists and chorus, four pianos, and a host of percussion, the opera-oratorio *Oedipus Rex* (1926–27, revised 1948) for speaker, soloists, male chorus, and orchestra, and *Symphony of Psalms* (1930, revised 1948) for mixed chorus and orchestra without violins or violas.

The short score of *Les noces* was completed in 1917, but it took considerable time for Stravinsky to finalize the instrumentation. The full score was eventually finished in April 1923. Undoubtedly his most "Russian" choral work, *Les noces* is based on Russian folk poems, some of which may have been written by Aleksandr Pushkin, retains the modalities of Russian folk music, and follows the natural, often irregular poetic rhythmic patterns of the texts. Stravinsky described it as "a suite of typical wedding episodes told through typical talk . . . in which the reader seems to be overhearing scraps of conversation" (White 1979). The work was initially celebrated by early Soviet critics, who praised the composer's return to Russian folk materials, but this view was short lived. By the early 1930s Stravinsky's increasing cosmopolitanism had become anathema to the Soviets, who then considered even his earlier Russian works to be "mockery and distortion of Russian historical reality" (Lang 1963, 82). The rhythmic vitality and orchestration of *Les noces* had a profound impact on Carl Orff, paving the way for *Carmina burana*, *Catulli carmina*, and the development of primitivism.

Stravinsky's *Oedipus Rex* also influenced Orff, and to a somewhat lesser degree Goffredo Petrassi (especially *Psalm IX*), as well as others; but for many, this great evocation of Greek ritual drama remained enigmatic. The text is a Latin translation of Jean Cocteau's French adaptation (made to order for the composer) of Sophocles's tragedy. Superficially a pastiche of many styles, *Oedipus Rex* came as something of a shock: except for a total reliance on music to propel the otherwise static action, its regular rhythms and clear-cut, relatively simple harmonies were not exactly what was expected from Stravinsky. Schoenberg and Roger Sessions both commented on the piece (Harbison 1989, 4), Schoenberg more critically: "I do not know what I am supposed to like in *Oedipus*. At least, it is all negative: unusual theatre, unusual setting, unusual resolution of the action, unusual vocal writing, unusual acting, unusual melody, unusual harmony, unusual counterpoint, unusual instrumentation—all this 'un' without *being* anything in particular." A more positive reaction was voiced by Sessions, who noted that "the power of *Oedipus* never depends on effects of association. In each case the analogy holds good only up to a certain point, beyond which we find ourselves in the presence of a style whose individuality is so pervasive and compelling as to thoroughly escape analysis."

In contrast, Stravinsky's *Symphony of Psalms* has been almost universally appreciated. The struggle toward the G major conclusion of the first movement, the masterful double fugue of the second, and the sublime catharsis of the finale are frequently cited as marks of genius. This is not to say, however, that the piece is without detractors. Wallace Brockway and Herbert Weinstock (1958, 604–605), who thought it to be in "bad taste," reflect in their criticism the inability of many average concertgoers to comprehend Stravinsky's increasingly objective aesthetic:

Stravinsky, with a complete lack of humor, had put on the title page "composed for the glory of God and dedicated to the Boston Symphony on the occasion of the fiftieth anniversary of its existence." As Stravinsky is an intensely religious man, it seemed reasonable to suppose that he would have written deeply felt religious music, which—despite his many pronouncements against emotional content in music—might move the listener as well as the composing artist. Actually, except in those portions when his sheer musical talent momentarily released him from the grip of his own aesthetic, the *Symphonie de psaumes* must be chalked up as just another experiment. For two movements, the good things are spaced closely enough to make it impressive, and occasionally moving, as nothing of Stravinsky's had been since *Les noces*. The third movement has been dismissed by some critics as sentimental trifling: this would in itself be egregious in a setting of the fortieth Psalm. But the sad truth is that even the sentimentality is not genuine. It rings about as true as the halo Del Sarto put about the head of his peasant mistress when he was manufacturing a religious picture.

On the other hand, Wilfred Mellers (Lang 1963, 45) pointedly synthesized the prevailing favorable view:

In [*Symphony of Psalms*] he again starts from the baroque conventions of toccata and fugue. The similarity to baroque techniques is, however, no more than superficial: for the work shows little evidence of the baroque sense of harmonic momentum. Indeed, in so far as the themes tend to oscillate around a nodal point and the structures to be organized by linear and rhythmic pattern rather than by harmonic and tonal architecture, the Symphony is strictly comparable with some aspects of medieval technique; and the seemingly preordained or "doctrinal" system of key-relationships is also in principle, if not in practice, appropriate to an age of faith. And here, in the marvelous lyrical expansion of the last movement, the faith is fulfilled, the music being at once an evocation of "the chime and symphony of Nature" and an act of worship. . . . One may question, too, whether Stravinsky's music has ever again achieved the lyrical fulfillment it reaches in *Symphony of Psalms*. That work, which is certainly among the two or three supreme masterpieces of the twentieth century, is a revelation of God's love because the creator attains, in the last movement, to the love of God. In comparison, Stravinsky's later works seem to be in love with the idea of God, rather than with God Himself.

In 1933 Ida Rubinstein approached Stravinsky with the idea of setting André Gide's melodrama, *Persephone* (1933–34, revised 1949), as a vehicle for her dance company. Stravinsky liked the idea and initially got along quite well with the poet. This changed, however, when Gide realized too late that Stravinsky's syllabic treatment of text was antithetical to his views of natural speech rhythm, which, according to Eric Walter White (1979), Stravinsky characterized as "loose and formless prosodies." The music, for tenor soloist, speaker, mixed chorus, children's chorus, and orchestra, is full of rhythmic interest and bright major keys. White described

> the occasional use of an aerated style of writing, in which notes and phrases are separated and punctuated by rests and pauses that introduce silence as a musical element. Stravinsky had already experimented with this style in the duet between the shepherd and the messenger in *Oedipus Rex*; but now he made more extended use of it, particularly in some of the choruses. . . . In the chorus, "Ivresse matinale," the rests sometimes cut through the words and give the effect of consummate lightness and transparency. Elsewhere, the musical pauses coincide with the natural pauses of the words and phrases and help the meaning.

Maurice Perrin's recollection of Stravinsky's reaction to rehearsals at the Ecole Normale de Musique may serve as a general guide to the performance of Stravinsky's music: "He told us that at the first rehearsal of *Persephone* the chorus sang 'Reste avec nous' sentimentally. When he asked why, they said that 'the music seems particularly expressive.' His response was: 'Then why do you want to *make* what already *is*?'" (Kenyon 1982). This comment suggests that Stravinsky was already formulating the famous "Excelsior manifesto" in which he defended his approach to setting Gide's text (and in fact all texts) with the comment, "One does not criticise anyone that is functioning. A nose is not manufactured—a nose just *is*. Thus, too, my art" (White 1979).

The brief cantata "Babel" (1944) for narrator, male chorus, and orchestra was Stravinsky's contribution to Nathaniel Shilkret's *Genesis Suite* and his first attempt to set English words. He resisted Shilkret's desire for descriptive, representational music on aesthetic as well as religious grounds, believing that no attempt should be made to dramatically portray the voice of God. Instead, he typically relied on abstract musical form to objectively present the text. Robert Craft described "Babel" as "a passacaglia in which a fugue serves as one of the variations" (White 1979).

Stravinsky's Mass (1944, 1948) for mixed chorus, two oboes, English horn, two bassoons, two trumpets, and three trombones is surely his most frequently performed choral work after *Symphony of Psalms*. He composed the work specifically for liturgical use and specified children's voices for the treble parts. Most performances, therefore, fall well outside the composer's intentions, since they usually occur with women's and men's voices in concert situations (the premiere, in fact, was given in Milan's Teatro alla Scala). The work's genesis is rather interesting. According to Eric Walter White (1979), around 1943 Stravinsky became acquainted with some of Mozart's Masses, which he referred to as "rococo-operatic sweets-of-sin." Opposed to "the Platonic tradition, which has been the Church's tradition through Plotinus and Erigena, of music as anti-moral," and seeing Mozart as exemplary of the causes for the Church's view, he determined to write a Mass of his own that would correct the sentimental excesses of Mozart and virtually every other composer; it would be, in his own words, "very cold music, absolutely cold, that will appeal directly to the spirit." Since the Orthodox Church, to which Stravinsky belonged, forbade the use of instruments, he wrote for the Roman rite instead. His comment in this regard, that he could "endure unaccompanied singing in only the most harmonically primitive music," may, like Schoenberg's similar remark concerning *Friede auf Erden*, reveal a negative attitude toward the state of choral singing at the time. But since the instruments in Stravinsky's Mass almost never double the vocal lines, there may have been other reasons for his dissatisfaction with unaccompanied choral sound. In any event, somewhat extended a cappella singing does occur in the Agnus Dei, where the tripartite text is presented by chorus alone, separated by instrumental ritornelli. In terms of allocation of performing forces, Stravinsky's Mass forms an arch similar to that found in Dvořák's *Stabat mater*: the Gloria and Sanctus movements, showcasing soloists, surround the central Credo, and the opening Kyrie and concluding Agnus Dei are purely choral. The structural and melodic variety of the outer movements is accentuated by the melodic stasis in Credo, in which the lengthy text is quietly chanted against very slow-moving harmonies. Though well known, Mass, like the composer's other choral works excepting *Symphony of Psalms*, has never achieved real popularity. Humphrey Burton's (1994, 439–440) comment about a 1977 performance is telling: "For the English Bach Festival in London [Leonard Bernstein] conducted Bach's *Magnificat* and two works by Stravinsky, *Les noces* and Mass, a program of such austerity that even with Bernstein's advocacy it failed to sell out the Royal Festival Hall."

Stravinsky's Mass was followed by the secular opera *The Rake's Progress*, which was followed in turn by *Cantata* (1951–52) for soprano and tenor soloists, female chorus, two flutes, two oboes (one doubling English horn), and cello. The combination of secular and semireligious texts as well as the unique performing ensemble in *Cantata* can be viewed superficially as a synthesis of the impulses that drove the two works preceding it. A more profound glance backward, toward Bach, is revealed in Stravinsky's use of old contrapuntal forms, while the antique qualities of the fifteenth- and sixteenth-century English texts are further accentuated by a rather severe modality. Still, the most interesting aspects of *Cantata* are hints of the future: a new reliance on canons that utilize retrograde and inverted motion clearly demonstrates Stravinsky's awakening interest in serial procedures.

Canticum sacrum ad honorem Sancti Marci nominis (1955) for tenor and baritone soloists, mixed chorus, organ, and orchestra (without percussion, clarinets, French horns, or violins) was written for Saint Mark's Cathedral in Stravinsky's beloved Venice. Many aspects of this cantata, including its choice of biblical texts, orchestration, various antiphonal effects, and well-timed acoustic pauses, show the composer's knowledge of, and respect for, Venetian musical tradition. Structurally, *Canticum sacrum* is cyclical, the last movement being a retrograde of the opening, and like *Cantata* it contains an abundance of canonic writing. Beyond this, it is Stravinsky's first choral work to seriously delve into serial procedures, utilizing several rows of varying lengths, all with very strong tonal implications. Now highly regarded, the premiere met with critical disaster. American and western European reviews tended toward the same hysterical tone as a somewhat later Soviet appraisal (Lang 1963, 85), which called *Canticum sacrum* "the graveyard of decomposed musical composition."

For the premiere of *Canticum sacrum* Stravinsky provided a marvelous companion piece, *Chorale Variations on "Vom Himmel hoch" by J. S. Bach* (1956) for mixed chorus and orchestra. The orchestra is virtually the same as *Canticum sacrum*; otherwise, the pieces are quite different. For some time Stravinsky had been clearly indebted to Bach in contrapuntal matters. Now he paid unveiled homage to his master with a full-fledged cantata based on Bach's organ variations. The chorus sings the chorale tune in unison while the variations swirl around it. Stravinsky enriched Bach's harmonic structure by varying the keys of each variation, and enriched the texture by adding new contrapuntal lines at will, with stunning results.

The next two choral works are also companions, although they do not form an uninterrupted line of succession, being separated chronologically by *Movements* (1958–59) for piano and orchestra, and a couple of small instrumental pieces. *Threni: id est Lamentationes Jeremiae prophetae* (1957–58) for soprano, alto, two tenor, baritone, and bass soloists, mixed chorus, and large orchestra (including sarrusophone and flügelhorn) shares some structural similarities with *Canticum sacrum* but is otherwise serially conceived throughout. At about thirty-five minutes, it is also the longest of his serial compositions. Based on a row sung at the beginning by the soprano soloist, inversions, retrogrades, permutations, and canons abound. In a more effective application of a technique first encountered in *Zvezdoliki*, the orchestra is never used tutti but rather becomes an ever changing chamber ensemble, thereby placing emphasis on the vocal elements. In addition to the normally encountered give-and-take between soloists and chorus, the chorus sings the Hebrew letters designating the verses of text and is asked to chant on single pitches that are sometimes prescribed and sometimes indeterminate. *A Sermon, a Narrative, and a Prayer* (1960–61) for alto and tenor soloists, speaker, mixed chorus, and orchestra provides a New Testament balance to Jeremiah's lamentations. The text, which was chosen from the authorized version of the Book of Acts, the Pauline Epistles, and an early-seventeenth-century prayer by Thomas Dekker, presents the story of Saint Stephen, the first Christian martyr, who was able to pray for his killers even as they stoned him. While not as elaborate overall as *Threni*, the technique of pitched and unpitched chanting is much more highly developed, with the soloists and chorus moving freely from unpitched declamation to singing.

Stravinsky's *Anthem* ("The dove descending breaks the air," 1962) for unaccompanied mixed chorus is among the century's more fascinating four-minute pieces. Interest is held not only because of the composer's technical mastery of serial composition but also because of his steadfast refusal to explore any of the expressive or coloristic opportunities provided by T. S. Eliot's poem. Unlike Krenek's *O Holy Ghost*, which treats John Donne's similar text with an emotional wash of sonic color, Stravinsky maintains complete objectivity.

Requiem Canticles (1965–66) for alto and bass soloists, mixed chorus, and orchestra was Stravinsky's last major composition. It is a work with strong merits that has been unjustly neglected. Like *Symphony of Psalms* it was choreographed with great effect by George Ballanchine, and later by Jerome Robbins. The texts are brief extracts from the Roman Catholic liturgy. The structure is symmetrical, three instrumental movements framing and centering six vocal movements. The most unusual feature is the presence of two separate tone rows. The varied choral writing contains massive vertical sonorities, echo effects, the murmuring of text with indeterminate rhythm, and highly chromatic, angular vocal lines reminiscent of the chromatically awkward tenor lines occasionally found in choruses by Bach.

Other choral works by Stravinsky include *Four Russian Peasant Songs* (1917, 1954), the first version for unaccompanied female voices and the newer version for four equal voices and four horns; the little motets originally written for the Orthodox liturgy, *Pater noster* (1926 Slavonic, 1949 Latin), *Credo* (1932 Slavonic, 1949 Latin, 1964 Slavonic), and *Ave Maria* (1934 Slavonic, 1949 Latin), all for unaccompanied mixed chorus; an arrangement for orchestra and ad libitum chorus of the *Star-Spangled Banner* (1941), which offended Boston's sense of civic propriety enough for city officials to ban further performances there; *Tres sacrae cantiones* (1957) for mixed chorus, a reconstruction of three motets by Carlo Gesualdo; and the brooding *Introitus* (1965) for male chorus, harp, piano, timpani, two tam-tams, solo viola, and doublebass, written in memory of T. S. Eliot.

THE TRANSITIONAL PERIOD

Many composers wrote music for the Russian Orthodox Church in the period preceding the Russian Revolution of 1917. Although their style typically continued from the musical language prevalent in the late nineteenth century, some showed remarkable creativity. Examples include Nikolai Kompanelsky (1848–1910), perhaps the most original, who fused the ethos of folk song with that of sacred music, and who wrote *Divine Liturgy* as well as fifty-eight smaller works; Semyon Panchenko (1867–1937), who composed *Liturgy* (1902) and *Vigil* (1908) as well as *Panikhida* (Funeral Service, 1908) and *Wedding Service* (1913); Alexander Nikolsky (1874–1943), who contributed *Vigil* (1909), Liturgy No. 1 (1909), *Wedding Service* (1913), and *Liturgy of Pre-Sanctified Gifts* (1906–08); Nikolai Golovanov (1891–1935), later a director of the Bolshoi Opera, who wrote a set of twenty-three sacred works —full of color and originality—that were published on the eve of the revolution, in 1917; and Georgy Izvekov (d. 1930), who published thirty-one anthems.

In order to avoid censure or imprisonment, several important composers active at the time of the revolution changed their emphasis from sacred music to folk song arrangements and the setting of patriotic texts. The most significant of these composers were Alexandr Kastal'sky (1856–1926) and Pavel Chesnokov (1877–1944). Their task was somewhat simplified by three influential conductors who formed ensembles specializing in folk songs and patriotic pieces: Mitrofan Pyatnitsky (1864–1927), whose Pyatnitsky Folk Ensemble was the prototype for similar ensembles throughout eastern Europe, including the famed Bulgarian Women's Chorus; Aleksandr V. Aleksandrov (1883–1946), founder of the Red Army Chorus and composer of the Soviet Union's National Anthem; and Alexander Sveshnikov (1890–1980), founder of the State Chorus of Russian Folk Song, later renamed the Academic Chorus of the Soviet Union. These conductors were quite important arrangers of choral music as well (both folk and patriotic), and their influence on choral music in Russia and the perception of it outside of Russia was enormous throughout the century. The straightforward and often sentimental folk song arrangements of Sveshnikov in particular became part of every Soviet choir's repertoire.

Alexandr Kastal'sky conducted extensive and influential studies of old Orthodox chants and the compositions based on them, developing a distinctive Russian style based on modal harmonies, pedal points, and doublings at the octave and fifth (with resultant overtones). He composed over a hundred hymns for the church, several interesting secular works including *Glory!* (1902) and *Songs to the Motherland* (1904), *Liturgy of Saint John Chrysostom* (1905) for treble chorus, and the large *Requiem to the Fallen Heroes* (1916) for chorus and orchestra, written in memory of Russian soldiers killed in World War I. Kastal'sky was among the first composers to fall in with the Soviet regime. His numerous later patriotic works include *To Lenin: At His Graveside* (1924), *The Year 1905* (1925), and numerous folk song settings accompanied by peasant instruments. Also of interest is *The Railway Train* (1924) for chorus, piano, trumpet, and percussion.

Pavel Chesnokov was a most prolific Russian composer, producing about four hundred sacred and one hundred secular choral works, including two Divine Liturgies, two All-Night Vigils, two Orthodox Memorial Services, *Prayers in Time of War* (1913–15), and numerous folk song settings. His style varied from a stark use of unisons, octaves, and open fifths to chromatic harmonies involving ninth and eleventh chords. After the Russian Revolution he also composed patriotic pieces and in 1940 published a book, *The Choir and How to Direct It*, which he considered his greatest contribution to the choral art. The book was the first major attempt to synthesize and describe the art of choral music and choral conducting in Russia, and gives a great deal of information on the performance practice of the period.

Other important composers of the transitional period include Mikhail Ippolitov-Ivanov (1859–1935), who contributed a Liturgy (1903), an All-Night Vigil (1907), of which "Bless the Lord, O My Soul" is standard repertoire in churches of all denominations outside Russia, and *Hymn of the Pythagoreans to the Rising Sun* (1904), which is accompanied by a fantastic ensemble of ten flutes, tuba, two harps, and ad libitum organ; Vladimir Rebikov (1866–1920), sometimes referred to as the father of Russian modernism (his style is best described as musical primitivism), who composed a Divine Liturgy (1910–11) and a Vigil (1911); Yuri Sergeyevich Sakhnovsky (1866–1930), who abandoned the modal implications of chant in favor of a more lush harmonic style; Viktor Kalinnikov (1870–1927), whose *Cherubic Hymn* (1904) and *Hymn to the Mother of God* (1904) are typical of his style, which stresses sonority and harmony, and whose *Beatitudes* shows a use of imitation and counterpoint rarely found in Russian sacred music of the late nineteenth and twentieth centuries; Nikolai Tcherepnin (1873–1945), who wrote two Divine Liturgies and an All-Night Vigil, as well as the oratorio *La descente de la Sainte Vierge à l'enfer*; the very important teacher and composer Nikolay Myaskovsky (1881–1950), whose several cantatas and smaller pieces reflect his own observation (Sadie 1980, 13:4) that "the tireless quest for the 'final word' in technique and invention did not constitute an end in itself for me"; and Konstantin Shvedov (1886–1954), who composed a Divine Liturgy

(1913) for mixed chorus that reflected his opinion that folk music and occasional oriental effects had a rightful place in church music, and a Divine Liturgy (1935) for male chorus.

Russian Composers during the Soviet Era

The works of Sergei Prokofiev (1891–1953), while spanning the transitional and formative years of the Soviet period, are at the same time removed from those events. His music, which Rita McAllister (Sadie 1980, 15:292) described as a "mixture of sophisticated elements with a sort of home-grown innocence, of steely dissonance with almost tender lyricism," is the product of an exceptionally original mind. He drew no inspiration from church music or the great Russian romanticists, his early music already projecting the brash individualism that would characterize his mature works.

Immediately after the revolution Prokofiev moved to the United States, where he lived until moving to Paris in 1922. In 1933 he began sporadic visits to the Soviet Union, finally moving his family and resuming permanent residence there in 1936, exactly when Stalin's government was solidifying its hold on the arts. Prokofiev immediately attempted to adjust to socialist realism by composing the enormous *Cantata for the Twentieth Anniversary of the October Revolution* (1937), but ran afoul of the censors anyway. The cantata, scored for two choirs (one amateur, one professional), military band, accordions, and percussion, never reached the concert stage due to questions about the composer's motives and the supposed vulgarity of the music. When it was finally performed in 1966, the cantata proved to be vintage Prokofiev.

Prokofiev was most comfortable in the realm of opera, ballet, and large, abstract instrumental forms, so his choral music does not occupy the front ranks of his catalogue. However, *Alexander Nevsky* (1939), a cantata reworked from his score for the Sergei Eisenstein film, is a major contribution to twentieth-century repertoire. In it can be heard several important elements of the composer's style, including his sense of drama, rhythmic drive, the ability to project irony, and an unconventional use of tonality—as well as the seeds of inspiration for several younger film composers. The juxtaposition of Latin chant with Russian patriotic themes is brilliant, as is the chilling battle scene on a frozen lake.

Prokofiev's other choral music includes the early *Two Poems* (1909–10) for women's chorus and orchestra; a setting of an incantation from a Sumerian ritual, *They Are Seven* (1917–18); *Ballad of an Unknown Boy* (1938); *Flourish, Powerful Land* (1947), all for soloists, mixed chorus, and orchestra; *On Guard for Peace* (1950) for mezzo soprano, narrators, mixed and boys' choruses, and orchestra; *Winter Bonfire* (1950) for narrators, boys' chorus, and orchestra; and another film score utilizing chorus and orchestra, *Ivan the*

Terrible (1942–45). The later, overtly political pieces share a lack of inspiration common to most politically motivated works.

Nikolai Tcherepnin's son, Alexander Tcherepnin (1899–1977), also went abroad, studying and settling in Paris. Influenced by his father and Prokofiev, he created compositions that contain some French and oriental elements as well (perhaps the result of his marriage to a Chinese musician) and reveal him to be an early experimenter with tone rows and new scales. Typical works include *Le jeu de la Nativité* (1945), *Pan kéou* (1945), on text by Hsieh Yu, Mass (1966) for women's voices, and *Baptism Cantata* (1972).

Others close in age to Prokofiev and Tcherepnin weathered the revolution and stayed at home to become leading Soviet composers as the transitional figures died out, including Yuri Shaporin (1889–1966), whose important cantata *On the Field of Kolikovo* (1941) and oratorio *The Story of the Fight for Russian Earth* (1944) reveal a sturdy and distinct talent capable of flourishing within a system that frowned on innovation; Boris Liatoshenski (1895–1968), who as a professor at Moscow Conservatory trained many younger Soviet composers and whose works did not escape the influence of impressionism and expressionism; Dimitri Kabelevsky (1904–1987), whose naturally conservative musical personality was well suited to the demands of socialist realism, as shown through his several cantatas and symphonies with chorus, all on patriotic or political texts; Gavriil Popov (1904–1972), whose *Heroic Intermezzo* (1944) is representative of wartime patriotic works; and Alexey Kozlovsky (1905–1977), whose *Two Suites* (1934) for chorus predates his attempts to synthesize Azbek folk traditions with European art music.

The most formidable work produced by these composers is surely Dmitri Kabalevsky's *Requiem* (1961–63) for soloists, chorus, and orchestra. Kabalevsky conceived the project as a memorial to those who died in Russia during World War II. He pondered it for many years before asking the poet Robert Rozhdestvensky to provide a text, and then spent over two years composing it. Artists and audiences are only too familiar with the beloved, long-considered, and painfully created work, which somehow meets neither dreams nor expectations. Indeed, failures and near misses in this regard are common, especially among artists not usually counted in the first rank. Kabelevsky's *Requiem* comes therefore as something of a surprise. It cannot be considered a towering masterpiece of the century because, among other reasons, it takes no risks: it is obviously designed for immediate appreciation by the broadest possible audience. But it is a masterpiece nonetheless. Its traditional harmonic language and sure-handed orchestration are perfectly suited to the realization of the composer's intentions. Kabelevsky's melodic and dramatic inspiration virtually never fails, there are plenty of engrossing surprises, and the emotional tension—tightly controlled in spite of numerous large climaxes—is maintained until the final catharsis. Even though the technical means employed are primarily of the nineteenth century, *Requiem* still impresses, like the best works of Rachmaninoff, as a heartfelt twentieth-century utterance.

The most gifted composer of this generation was Dmitri Shostakovich (1906–1975), who had the biggest international reputation of any Soviet composer and who has come to be regarded, after Stravinsky, as the most important Russian composer of the twentieth century. His originality and artistic integrity are unassailable, even though he was constantly hounded during his life by communists because of his "formalism" and occasional "bourgeois" experimentation, and by Western critics for his conservatism and seemingly transparent attempts to satisfy Soviet authorities.

Symphony No. 13 (*Babiy Yar*, 1962) and the stunning *The Execution of Stepan Razin* (1964), both on texts by Yevgeny Yevteshenko, may be considered representative of Shostakovich's work. *Babiy Yar* is big, somber, and very Russian—impressions magnified by the bass soloist and chorus of basses accompanied by a very large orchestra. The texts, dealing with World War II genocide, offended Soviet authorities. Performances scheduled after the premiere were cancelled until Yevteshenko made changes in the poetry. Shostakovich set Yevteshenko's words sensitively, and the balance between lyrical episodes and dramatic outbursts is admirable. Still, even though the symphony is quite moving and generally interesting, it is also exhausting, perhaps because the music takes itself so very seriously. *The Execution of Stepan Razin*, however, about an eighteenth-century Russian libertarian anti-Czarist hero, is exciting and invigorating. The narration of the bass soloist and the commentary of the mixed choir combine with the colorful orchestration to create handsome storytelling. It is well balanced, the climaxes are satisfying, and the musical picturization of the grotesquely surprising ending is very effective. Critics have complained that it does not represent the composer at his most original, but everything in the piece dazzles.

Shostakovich's other choral works include Symphony No. 2 (*To October*, 1927) and Symphony No. 3 (*The First of May*, 1929), which the composer considered to be youthful experiments; the lovely, though often pedestrian, oratorio *The Song of the Forests* (1949); *Ten Poems* (1951) for unaccompanied mixed chorus, on nineteenth- and early-twentieth-century revolutionary verse; the children's cantata *The Sun Shines on Our Motherland* (1952); and eight ballads for male chorus, entitled *Faithfulness* (1970).

Georgy Sviridov (1915–1998) was the only important composer of this generation to live beyond the Soviet era. His early works are full of melodic and harmonic elements derived from folk music. In 1964 the focus of this interest narrowed. According to Peter Jermihov (1993), Sviridov adopted a "native musical vocabulary almost exclusively [to] reveal strong ties to medieval Russia, the Moscow Synodal School [of Kastal'sky], and Stravinsky's 'Russian period' compositions. Sviridov consciously [shifted] his compositional style from a musical system in which peasant elements are merely present to one in which peasant roots dominate." Representative works include *Land of the Fathers* (1950), *My Father the Peasant* (1957), *Oratorio pathétique* (1959), the large cantata *Kursk Songs* (1964), *Small Triptych* (1966), *Spring Cantata* (1974) for chorus, oboe, and percussion, and the important *Poema pamyati Sergeya Yesenina* (1981).

RUSSIAN COMPOSERS AFTER THE SOVIET ERA

After the collapse of the Soviet Union, the music of Sofia Gubaidulina (b. 1931) was performed with increasing frequency in Europe and America. Her unique and almost naïve use of widely varied musical elements such as pure triads, dissonant harmonies and tone clusters, Webernesque string effects, sprechstimme, improvisation, and various avant-garde techniques including new kinds of vocal sounds and imprecise methods of notation, have caused her to be identified as a "polystylist." In any event, Gubaidulina's music has the ability to speak directly on simultaneous layers. Good examples are *Allelujah* (1990) for boys' and mixed choruses, organ, and orchestra; the German-language concerto *Aus dem Stundenbuch* (1991) for cello with speaker, male chorus, and orchestra; *Jetzt immer Schnee* (1993) for mixed choir and chamber ensemble, also in German; and *Johannes Passion* (2000) for soloists, mixed chorus, and orchestra (see chapter 15).

Rodion Shchedrin (b. 1932) never joined the Communist Party and had to endure the prohibition of many of his works within the Soviet Union. Nevertheless, his international prestige and personal acumen allowed him to survive within the Soviet system. While Shchedrin favors the poetry of Aleksandr Pushkin for partsongs and larger unaccompanied choral pieces, his works for chorus and orchestra range from the politically placating oratorio *Lenin Lives in the People's Heart* (1969) to the politically acute *Prayer* (1991), on text by Yehudi Menuhin. A particularly important work is *The Sealed Angel* (1988), the composer's first published sacred work, which operates on several levels at once (religious, emotional, sociological) to accurately reflect the people's state of mind throughout the Eastern Block just prior to the collapse of Communism. Shchedrin's aesthetic, held in common with many end-of-the-century composers, was shared in a 1992 interview with John Stuhr-Rommereim (11): "I am not a conservative, but I think atonality and excessive experimentation was an illness that we had. It was a disease that one must get as a child in order to become immune. . . . It's very good that we 'had it,' but it was unnatural."

Alfred Schnittke (d. 1998) preferred working in large forms. His choral works, all written rather late in his career, include *Requiem* (1975) for alto, tenor, and three sopranos, chorus, and instrumental ensemble, Symphony

No. 2 (*Saint Florian*, 1979) for chamber chorus and orchestra, the Faust cantata *Seid nüchtern und wachet . . .* (1983) for soloists, chorus, and orchestra, and Symphony No. 4 (1984) for chorus and large orchestra (or SATB soloists and chamber orchestra).

COMPOSERS FROM OTHER SOVIET REPUBLICS

Komitas (1869–1935), also known as Komitas Gevork'ian, was among the first Armenians to study in the West. He was active as a composer, folk song collector, and choral conductor, and his contribution to Armenian music was extensive. His compositions are based on folk models but contain highly original aspects, including his great achievement of effectively adapting Western polyphonic technique to enhance the unique characteristics of Armenian monody. In addition to partsongs reflecting virtually every aspect of Armenian life, Komitas's sacred works, *Chants of the Sacred Liturgy* (1933) for male voices and *Tagher and Alleluias* (published 1946) for mixed chorus, are very important.

One of the most famous composers during the Soviet period was Aram Khachaturian (1903–1978), whose choral works such as the symphonic poem *Song of Stalin* (1937) never matched the international success of his piano concerto or ballets. His nephew Karen Khachaturian (b. 1920) was somewhat more interested in choral music, producing two successful cantatas and the oratorio *A Moment in History* (1971).

Edgar Sergeyi Hovhanesyan (b. 1930) combined ethnic Armenian elements with western European neoclassicism in the cantatas *Erku ap'* (1951) and *Erebuni* (1968). His *Antuni* (1969), a ballet with chorus composed for the centinary of Komitas's birth, sets a portion of the Armenian liturgy as a memorial to the victims of the 1915 genocide.

Another Armenian active in the composition of choral music was Alexander Arutyunian (b. 1920), whose style, based on folk music and the improvisations of wandering Armenian folk minstrels, found useful application in several patriotic-political cantatas, among them *Cantata on the Homeland* (1948), *The Tale of the Armenian People* (1960), *Ode to Lenin* (1967), and *Hymn to the Brotherhood* (1970).

An important work by the Georgian composer Giya Kancheli (b. 1935) is the cantata *Light Sorrow* (1984), which contrasts lyrically tender sections with violent orchestral eruptions in a musical fabric dominated by Georgian folk song and religious influences. In this regard, Kancheli's music follows the lead of Zakhary Paliashvili (1871–1933), whose incorporation of folk elements into his own music—such as *Festival Cantata* (1927) and many small choral pieces, including arrangements of the Georgian liturgy—caused him to be regarded as the father of Georgian nationalism in music.

Other Georgian composers include Alexei Machavariani (b. 1913), whose oratorio *The Day of My Motherland* (1954) explored new applications of distinctly Georgian folk intonations; and Sulkhan F. Tsintsadze (b. 1925), whose oratorio *Immortality* (1970) and cantata *The Great Way* (1975), both for soprano, mixed chorus, and orchestra, combined Georgian folk materials with more advanced developmental ideas derived from Shostakovich and Prokofiev in a style of great popular appeal.

Important Ukrainian composers include David Nowakowsky (1848–1921), Alyexandr Krein (1883–1951), Levko Revutsky (1889–1977), German Zhukovsky (1913–1976), and Leonid Grabovsky (b. 1935).

Nowakowsky, an ethnic Russian, composed many outstanding choral works for Jewish worship during his fifty years as cantor and choirmaster at Brody Synagogue in Odessa. He became famous in Jewish communities around the world because of his unique ability to combine traditional cantorial melodies with modern harmonies and formal structures in such a way that the original character of the tunes was preserved. He did not shrink from increasing the number of choral parts from the standard four to as many as eight if the situation called for it, and like Sigmund Schlessinger in the United States (see chapter 12), he experimented with liturgical music patterned on secular and non-Jewish models. Two collections of Nowakowsky's music were published during his life: *Closing Service for Yom Kippur* ("Ne'ilah," 1895) and *Preliminary Service and Evening Prayer for Sabbath Eve* (1901), both for cantor, mixed chorus, and organ. Among his best works are the famous *Adonai Z'charanu* for cantor, mixed chorus, and organ, and the cantata-length *Psalm 115* for soprano, mixed chorus, and organ. Nowakowsky stopped composing around 1917.

Alyexandr Krein was described by Leonid Sabaneyeff (1927, 181) as "one of the most gifted composers of contemporary Russia. His vitality and actuality are based on his live contact with folk elements. It is an old truth that art always gains vitality from contact with the earth of folk music. The element fructifying the art of Alyexandr Krein, giving it life, freshness, and 'full-bloodedness,' is the element of the Jewish folk melody." Krein was eventually prohibited by the Soviets from writing music derived from his Jewish roots and survived by writing propaganda pieces like *The Soviet Shock Brigade* (1932) for chorus and orchestra, on texts by Marx, Lenin, and Stalin, and by studying the ethnic music of central Asia, Volga-Ural, and other Soviet regions. Surely his most interesting work is the symphonic cantata *Kaddish* (1922) for tenor, mixed chorus, and orchestra, which was apparently successfully performed in the Ukraine shortly after its composition. Sabaneyeff (1927, 183) provided a succinct commentary, calling *Kaddish* "a kind of grand symphonic cantata in which the solo tenor personifies the struggling and protesting 'earthly personality,' while the chorus symbolizes the religious and pas-

Choir of the Brody Synagogue, Odessa, Ukraine, c. 1902. Courtesy of the David Nowakowsky Foundation.

sionless law. But if Krein's melodies are drawn from synagogue melodies and their ornamentation, his harmony is of mixed origin. Herein are influences of Skryabin, Ravel, and even of the Russian composers of the National School, chiefly Rimsky-Korsakov." *Kaddish* disappeared sometime after 1927, only to be discovered late in the century in the cellar of Universal Edition in Vienna. It was performed in 1993 at the Second International Festival of Jewish Music in Odessa.

Levko Revutsky wrote many partsongs, as well as a couple of cantatas for soloists, chorus, and piano, in a warmly approachable style influenced by impressionism. German Zhukovsky composed several cantatas in a style that conformed well to the imperatives of socialist realism, among them *Hail, My Fatherland* (1949), *Prayer of World Youth* (1951), and *The Knieper Ripples* (1957). Leonid Grabovsky was among the first Soviet composers to experiment with serialism, graphic notation, and other advanced Western techniques during the 1960s, thereby challenging the stylistic hegemony of socialist realism. Among his choral works are the more conventional *Four Ukrainian Songs* (1959) for chorus and orchestra.

Kara Karayev (1918–1982) was the leading composer in Azerbaijan. His awareness of Prokofiev, Schoenberg, and neoclassicism, as well as the folk music of his own republic, resulted in a unique style that was nationalistic but with longing glances beyond the border. The unaccompanied *Osen* (Autumn, 1947) can be considered typical.

❧ 7

SCANDINAVIA AND THE BALTICS

DENMARK

Carl Nielsen (1865–1931) influenced virtually all Danish music in the twentieth century. Two hallmarks of his mature style, the juxtaposition of unrelated keys and a highly personalized approach to contrapuntal technique, were already evident in the early *Hymnus amoris*, Opus 12 (1896). After 1900 Nielsen wrote ten cantatas and several other works for chorus and orchestra. Of these, *Springtime in Funen*, Opus 42 (1921) for soloists, chorus, and orchestra, and *Sleep*, Opus 18 (1904) for chorus and orchestra are internationally known. Most of the others were designed for very specific occasions and have not remained in the repertoire (who now, for instance, would be seriously interested in hearing *Cantata for the Fiftieth Anniversary of the Danish Cremation Union?*).

Nielsen's only unaccompanied choral work, the masterful *Three Motets*, Opus 55 (1929), supports Knud Jeppesen's view that the "novelty in his music consisted . . . in a new, spontaneous way of applying tried procedures, a way that made old devices appear surprising mainly because the context was unexpected" (Blom 1954, 6:86). Like Mozart, Beethoven, Grieg, and others, Nielsen composed incidental music for a number of plays, which effectively utilized the chorus. The best-known of these is *Aladdin* (1918). Nielsen's approach to opera also created unique opportunities for choral writing, as shown in *Saul and David* (1900–02), which has proven quite effective in concert version.

Opportunities for Danish choral performance were dominated by churches and large choral societies during the first two decades of the century. This began to change when conductor Mogens Wöldike (1897–1988) formed the Palestrina Choir in 1922 and the Copenhagen Boys' Choir in 1924. The 1932 establishment of the Danish National Radio Choir was followed by the creation of several other ensembles, among them the famous Danish Radio Chamber Choir. The existence of these fine choruses, coinciding with the Danish folk song movement of the thirties, not only provided composers with numerous new outlets for their works but also allowed a shift in emphasis toward partsongs, folk song arrangements, and secular works accompanied by small combinations of instruments. Outstanding ensembles continued to be formed throughout the century, among them the internationally acclaimed Vox Danica and Gaia.

The first generation to benefit from this situation included Knud Jeppesen (1892–1974), Vagn Holmboe (1909–1996), and Svend S. Schultz (1913–1998). Jeppesen's cantatas, many partsongs, motets, and English-language *Four Shakespeare Songs* reflect his extensive knowledge of Palestrina. Holmboe impressed early in his career with two works for boys' voices: *Requiem* (1931) for chamber orchestra, on text by Friedrich Hebbel, and *Psalm 62* (1937). His Latin motets *Expectavimus pacem* (1951–52) for six-part mixed choir, *Benedic Domino* (1952), *Dedique cor meum* (1953) for bass soloist and chorus, *Hominis dies* (1984), and *Laudate Dominum* (1984)—all from a large collection called *Liber canticorum* begun in 1951—are internationally known. Schultz, the longtime director of the Danish Radio Choir, composed many fine partsongs in Danish as well as the impressive *Quattuor fragmenta ex Ovidii "Ars amandi"* (1972) for mixed choir and optional flute, the lovely *Four Latin Madrigals* (1974), and the large *Three Pastorales* for solo voices, choir, and orchestra, on text by John Milton.

Others include Finn Høffding (1899–1997), whose partsongs and *Das Eisenbahngleichnis* (1934) for mixed choir, double bass, and percussion were influenced by the Danish folk music revival; and Otto Mortensen (1907–1986), whose accessible style helped ensure the popularity of his partsongs (in both Danish and English) and folk song arrangements, the best-known of which are *Seven Choir Songs* and *Det var en lordag uften*, a favorite at international choral festivals.

Outstanding among the succeeding generation are the Catholic composers Leif Kayser (b. 1919) and Bernhard Lewkowitch (b. 1927) as well as the primary pupils of Vagn Holmboe: Ib Nørholm (b. 1931) and Per Nørgård (b. 1932).

Leif Kayser studied music in Copenhagen and Stockholm before entering seminary in Rome. He returned to Copenhagen in 1949 as a priest attached to Saint Ansgar's Cathedral, at the same time resuming his composition. His numerous unaccompanied motets, in addition to a Christmas oratorio, Te Deum, and several Masses, are written in a conservative style influenced by Gregorian chant.

In his capacities as organist at Saint Ansgar's and founding conductor of the Copenhagen Schola Cantorum and Schola Gregoriana, Bernhard Lewkowitch worked closely with Leif Kayser. While his contributions to the secular repertoire are impressive, he is considered the most important Danish composer of sacred music since the eighteenth century. His style relies to some extent on classical instrumental forms, occasionally incorporating serial and other advanced techniques, which are, however, always subservient to an essentially traditional harmonic language. Representative works include *Five Danish Madrigals*, Opus 12 (1952); *Three Psalms*, Opus 9 (1952); the Masses, Opus 10 and Opus 15 (1952, 1954); *Improperia* (1963); *Three Songs for Male Chorus* (1965); *Stabat mater* (1970); four English madrigals collectively entitled *Apollo's Art* (1993); *De Lamentatione Jeremiae Prophetae* (1994); and *Three Motets*, Opus 11.

Ib Nørholm approached radical twentieth-century techniques with a certain reservation until about 1960, when he turned first to serialism and then to collage technique before freely incorporating everything in a style often referred to as "pluralism." Representative works include *Kenotafium*, Opus 23 (1961) for chorus and orchestra, *Light and Praise*, Opus 55 (1971) for soloists, chorus, and orchestra, and *Songs*, Opus 59 (1971) for equal voices.

Per Nørgård is arguably the greatest Danish composer since Nielsen. Through his compositions, writings, and teachings he has exerted substantial influence on Danish musical life. Perceptible in his complex style are the rhythmic and harmonic application of infinity concepts (a process by which a short motive and its inversion can be repeated indefinitely by beginning the process anew on each succeeding pitch) as well as ideas of contrast and conflict derived from the work of Swiss painter Adolf Wolffli (1864–1930). A particularly interesting and accessible piece is *Three Motets* (1982), written on the Agnus Dei text: single syllables of text inspire occasional flights of fantasy while the diatonic theme is expanded and then contracted by half steps and subjected to various contrapuntal devices such as canon in elongation. Other works by Nørgård include the children's Christmas oratorio *It Happened in Those Days* (1960), with narrators, chorus, and instruments; the oratorios *Dommen* ("The Judgement," 1962) and *Babel* (1964) for soloists, chorus, and orchestra; *Wie ein Kind* (1980), regarded by many in Denmark as the greatest unaccompanied choral work of the century; and *Og der skal ikke mere gives tid* (And Time Shall Be No More, 1993), written for the Europa Cantat on a macaronic text (Danish, Swedish, German, and Turkish).

Other composers include Finn Viderø (1906–1987), Bent Lorentzen (b. 1935), and Karl Aage Rasmussen (b. 1947). Viderø was the most acclaimed Danish organist of his generation, an important scholar of Gregorian chant and early music performance practice, and an accomplished composer. His works include two cantatas (1937, 1938) and numerous smaller works, including *Three Choral Songs* (1954). Bent Lorentzen became well known outside Denmark, especially in the United States, for *New Choral Dramatics* (Dimensions in choral speech and movement, 1971). His works also include more traditionally conceived pieces, such as the German-language *Two*

Per Nørgård: thematic manipulation in *Three Motets* (theme variants 1–3).

Choral Songs to Ensensberger (1988–89) for unaccompanied mixed chorus. Karl Aage Rasmussen has written several choral pieces with interesting instrumental combinations, including Mass (1966) for mixed chorus, horn, and bell chimes, and *Parade* for male voices and Renaissance instruments (1968).

ICELAND

Because of the country's isolation, choral music in Iceland developed late. After the publication of Iceland's first hymnal in 1861, an emerging interest in partsinging resulted in the formation of choirs. For these new ensembles, the first Icelandic composer, Sveinbjörn Sveinbjörnsson (1847–1927), wrote thirty choral pieces, mostly partsongs, several of which are in English. Among his works, *Royal Cantata* (1907) for chorus and piano marks the first successful attempt by an Icelandic composer to write in large forms.

Following Sveinbjörnsson's lead, most of the country's handful of composers developed styles that relied heavily on nationalistic elements, while simultaneously demonstrating a facile awareness of serial, electronic, and other advanced techniques. Prominent composers include Páll Ísólfsson (1895–1974), whose *Althing Festival Cantata* (1930) for chorus and orchestra celebrated the 1000th anniversary of Iceland's parliament; Skúli Halldórsson (b. 1914), whose *Pourquoi pas?* (1960) for soprano and tenor soloists, male chorus, and orchestra reflects nationalistic and romantic impulses; and Thorkell Sigurbjörnsson (b. 1938), whose attractive eclecticism is exhibited in *Missa miniscule* (1971) for female chorus, *Ode* (1975) for male chorus, and other works.

NORWAY

During the first two-thirds of the twentieth century, progressive international trends gradually replaced Grieg and folk sources as primary influences on Norwegian composers. Arne Eggen (1881–1955), Klaus Egge (1906–1979), Knut Nystedt (b. 1915), and Øistein Sommerfeldt (1919–1994) are representative.

Arne Eggen was an organist and composer whose style was greatly influenced by Grieg. He composed an oratorio, *King Olav* (1930), as well as a number of church pieces, including the lovely *Ave maris stella* (1927) for soprano, chorus, and organ.

Klaus Egge, a voice teacher and choirmaster in Oslo, became an internationally recognized composer of instrumental music. His style progressed from one based on folk materials to a rather pure twelve-tone technique. Egge produced some interesting choral music early in his career, including *Lyric Suite*, Opus 8 (1938) for male voices and *Noreg-songer*, Opus 16 (1941) for chorus and orchestra.

Knut Nystedt studied composition with Aaron Copland after he completed conservatory training in Norway. A highly competent choral conductor, he created recordings with the Norwegian Soloist Choir that contributed to the international popularization of twentieth-century Scandinavian choral music. His own music is eclectic, ranging from functional pieces in a conventional style for church and school (many composed for the North American market), to more challenging concert pieces incorporating traditional, avant-garde, and serial techniques in colorful combinations. This eclecticism, unlike the stylistic inconsistencies of Kodály, has much in common with the varied impulses encountered in the work of Ernst Krenek: individual pieces, each written in a particular style, coexist within a larger catalogue of great stylistic variety. Important works include *The Burnt Sacrifice*, Opus 36 (1954) for narrator, chorus, and orchestra, *De profundis*, Opus 54 (1964) for mixed chorus, *Lucis creator optime*, Opus 58 (1968) for soloists, chorus, and orchestra, and *Suoni*, Opus 62 (1970) for women's chorus, flute, and marimba. Nystedt's best-known piece, perhaps, is *The Path of the Just* (1968). For many choirs in the United States during the 1970s, its tightly controlled motivic canons, whole-tone chords, and satisfying A major ending created a necessary and grateful bridge into more adventurous musical realms.

Øistein Sommerfeldt was greatly influenced by his teacher, Nadia Boulanger, developing a diatonic style that, while reminiscent of folk music, was uniquely personal (much like that of Aaron Copland, another Boulanger pupil). Sommerfeldt excelled in smaller forms such as *Three Blake Songs*, Opus 13 (1967) for mixed choir.

Antonio Bibalo (b. 1922) emigrated from his native Trieste in 1957. In the words of John Yoell (1974, 54), "Diverse currents flow into Bibalo's work: his Italian-Slavic heritage, Japanese poetry, the prose of Henry Miller, a whiff of impressionism, the precise logic of Elizabeth Lutyens (perhaps his most influential teacher), and the crisp bite of northern air." Representative choral works include *Elegia per un'era spaziale* (1963) for soprano and baritone soloists, mixed chorus, and instruments, and *Serenata* for baritone soloist and male chorus.

Egil Hovland (b. 1927), who numbered Copland and Luigi Dallapiccola among his teachers, became very well known in the United States during the 1970s for his extraordinary church music, including the remarkably visual *Missa vigilate*, Opus 59 (1967) for soloists, mixed chorus, organ, tape, and two female dancers, and the powerful and stimulating *Saul* (1972) for narrator, mixed chorus, and organ, a stunning depiction of Saint Paul's experience on the road to Damascus that brilliantly combines traditional elements with avant-garde techniques in a manner unthreatening to amateur performers.

Arne Nordheim (b. 1931) was mostly interested in instrumental music, including the use of electronic tape, but he also composed a few significant choral works that display the workings of a technically adept and visionary imagination. Good examples include the Nordic Prize–winning *Éco* (1967) for soprano, children's and mixed choruses, and orchestra, and the cantata *Wirkliches Wald* (1983), in which the separate and conflicting texts of the soprano soloist and chorus are contrasted with the cello soloist and orchestra.

Alfred Janson (b. 1937) is best known for the textless *Tema* (1966), a gripping homage to those who survived Nazi concentration camps. Quite apart from its lingering emotional impact, *Tema* provided both functional experience in basic entry-level avant-garde technique and introduction to the Holocaust for a generation of American collegiate singers. Janson's *Nocturne* (1967) was commissioned for the fiftieth anniversary of the Norwegian Composers Association and was enthusiastically received throughout Europe. A setting of excerpts from Friedrich Nietzsche's *Also sprach Zarathustra*, its double chorus, two cellos, two percussion groups, and harp must be placed symmetrically on the stage. Other works include *Voices in a Human Landscape* (1969) for chorus, ten instruments, and three actors.

An accomplished choral composer, Trond Kverno (b. 1945) studied organ at the Oslo Conservatory of Music. His works such as the unaccompanied *Corpus Christi Carol* reflect the influence of medieval forms.

SWEDEN

The best-known Swedish composer during the first decades of the century was Hugo Alfvén (1872–1960), whose stature in Sweden was similar to Nielsen's in Denmark. From 1900 until his death, he composed ten cantatas for soloists, chorus, and orchestra; two cantatas for male chorus and orchestra; the popular patriotic piece *Sveriges flagga* (1916); several male-voice quartets; and several smaller works, including the international favorite *Aftonen* (1942).

Wilhelm Stenhammer (1871–1927), a contemporary of Alfvén, is best remembered for *Three Choral Ballads* (1890) and the cantata *The Song* (1920–21), his last major work, which was written for the 150th anniversary of the Royal Academy of Music on text by the influential composer Ture Rangström (1884–1947). Infrequently performed, owing perhaps to the substantial performing forces required, complexity of the score, and what Bo Wallner (1982) described as "a general Swedish indifference to nationalistic poetry," *The Song* is nevertheless among the best Swedish choral works composed during the first half of the century. While its harmonic conservatism lends an old-fashioned flavor, the overall aspects of its style reveal a closer kinship to the aesthetics of Sibelius and Mahler than to other nineteenth-century composers—Amy Beach, Max Reger, Camille Saint-Saëns, and Sir Charles Villiers Stanford, for instance—who also wrote well into the new century.

Otto Olsson (1879–1964) was an important church musician and great organist of the century. His affinity for French organ music is apparent in his own compositions, which, in addition to their otherwise contrapuntal characteristics and inclination toward classical forms, are infused with touches of French harmonic color. *Six Latin Hymns*, Opus 40 (1919) for mixed chorus is particularly interesting because it contains perhaps the earliest example of Swedish bitonal choral writing: "Song of Simeon" is sung by a baritone soloist on Gregorian psalm tone III (for Introits), the reciting tone being C, and the chorus repeats each phrase with newly composed music based on the psalm tone in E major. Other works include the large *Te Deum*, Opus 26 (1906) for chorus, strings, harp, and organ, considered a masterpiece in Sweden, and many folk song arrangements and original pieces for male voices.

Oskar Lindberg (1887–1955), editor of the Church of Sweden Hymnbook (1939), made major contributions to choral music as a composer. A primary figure in the romantic-nationalist school of Swedish music, Lindberg produced works characterized by irrepressible lyricism. His *Requiem* (1912) provided the standard to which subsequent large Swedish liturgical works have been held. Of his many cantatas and partsongs for all vocal configurations, *Skansenkantat* (1918) for mixed chorus and instruments, *Sommar jag in med blicken fast* (1926) for female chorus and instruments, and the unaccompanied *Stjärntandning* (1926) for mixed chorus are exemplary.

Hilding Rosenberg (1892–1985) was influenced by Stenhammer on the one hand and Schoenberg on the other, developing a style with clearly defined rhythms and long melodic lines. He approached twelve-tone technique in his own way, stating, "It is the melodic and polyphonic in this technique that has inspired me, not so much the sonorous aspect" (Percy 1967, 77). In addition to motets for mixed choir (1949) and the Christmas oratorio *Den Heliga natten* (1936), Rosenberg also included chorus in two of his symphonies, Symphony No. 4 (*The Revelation of Saint John*, 1940) and Symphony No. 5 (*The Keeper of the Garden*, 1944) for alto soloist, chorus, and orchestra.

Moses Pergament (1893–1977) was a master of Jewish liturgical music. He composed many pieces still in use, including his important Holocaust-related choral symphony, *Den judiska sången* (The Jewish Song, 1944) for soprano and tenor soloists, mixed chorus, and orchestra, which effectively contrasts Nazi brutality with the Jewish people's hope for the future.

Sven-Erik Bäck (1919–1994) was among the greatest Swedish composers of the century, active in virtually all genres. A student of Rosenberg, he was profoundly influenced by the idea that music is a spiritual force. His exceptionally expressive style draws freely from elements as diverse as Gregorian chant, Renaissance and baroque polyphony, and Webernian serialism. A lengthy series of unaccompanied motets for mixed chorus constitutes a highpoint in twentieth-century choral composition and can be considered an extension of the motets composed by Josquin Des Prez, Palestrina, and Tomás Luis de Victoria, though Bäck's works are far removed from the quasi-Renaissance modality cultivated by several other twentieth-century composers. Rather, Bäck aims for direct and poignant reflection of each text's meaning. His natural lyricism and sense of dramatic clarity make the motets highly accessible for listeners, even though the harmonic language is often severe. Traditionally conceived, there is no use of avant-garde vocal techniques. Good examples include *Ego sum panis vitae* (1959), the more intricate, English-language *Behold I Am Making All Things New* (1969), and the relatively simple *Utrannsaka mig* (Search Me, 1970), a setting of verses from Psalm 139, unusually lovely with its forthright harmonic scheme, elastic vocal lines, and brief, cleverly hidden quote from Bach's "Bist du bei mir."

After World War II, Ingvar Lidholm (b. 1921) became prominent enough as a Swedish composer to have his views included with Ligeti and Lutoslawski in Ligeti's *Three Aspects of New Music* (1968). A student of Hilding Rosenberg and Mátyás Seiber, Lidholm's works were critical to the growth of Swe-

Sven-Erik Bäck: opening measures of *Utrannsaka mig.*

dish choral music during the second half of the century, and his own compositional development can be easily observed in them, from the Stravinskian *Laudi* (1947) through the more homophonic though quite difficult . . . *a riveder le stelle* (1973), a setting from Dante's *Divine Comedy* in which narrative alternates with textless passages describing the mood of the poem.

Lars Edlund (b. 1922) achieved prominence for his expertise in early music and ear training as well as for his compositions. As a member of Eric Ericson's Chamber Choir in the late forties, he became interested in newly emerging choral techniques. Still, much of his work remained in a more traditional idiom, as with the motet *Mea culpa* (1955) and the large devotional cantata *Maria* (1955) for mixed choir, tenor, and baritone soloists, which derives from the style and structure of Schütz's Passions. The international success of Edlund's ear training books, *Modus novus* (1963) and *Modus vetus* (1966), naturally encouraged his interest in combining ear training exercises with compositions utilizing the most advanced techniques. The result was *Choir Studies I–III* (1972–73), which resembles Bartók's *Mikrokosmos*. Since the late sixties Edlund's compositions have tended to look forward, not only in terms of sonic design but also in structure and ensemble configuration. Outstanding examples include *Gloria* (1969) for unaccompanied mixed choir, notable for clusters built in quarter tones; *The Beatitudes* (1971) for children's and mixed choruses, flute, guitar, double bass, and organ; *Elegy* (1971, revised 1972), which requires the choir to act; and *Triad* (1973) for mixed chorus and stage band.

The avant-garde choral work of Jan Bark (b. 1934) and Folke Rabe (b. 1935) is entwined with the Culture Quartet, a trombone ensemble which they cofounded and which became famous for "integrated" concerts with Karl-Eric Andersson's Bel Canto Choir of Stockholm. For these concerts Bark and Rabe jointly created several large works, including *Air-Power Supply for Voices and Trombones* (1969) and *Disturbances in the Atmosphere* (1971). Individually, each composer produced choral pieces that achieved international popularity during the last third of the century, particularly Bark's choreographic *Nota* (1964) and *Light Music* (1968), both for mixed chorus, and Rabe's *Piece* (1961) for speech choir, *Rondes* (1964) for male or mixed choir, and *Joe's Harp* (1970), in which the singers are required to produce overtones.

Though Bo Nilsson (b. 1937) was essentially self-taught as a composer, he was possessed of an immense talent and his avant-garde compositions began receiving international acclaim when he was still a teenager. An outstanding example is *Nazm* (1973) for reciter, soloists, chorus, orchestra, and jazz ensemble (all amplified), in which a Turkish *magam* forms the basis of lengthy variations, alternating improvisation with prescribed events. Other works include the little partsong *Ayiasma* (1967) for mixed chorus and flute, and the somewhat larger *Vi Kommer att Traffas i Morgan* for soprano, mixed chorus, and triangles.

Eskil Hemberg (b. 1934) devoted himself almost totally to vocal music. His work as director of choirs for the Swedish Broadcasting Corporation, and later as conductor of the Stockholm University Chorus, provided valuable insight into new compositional possibilities. Hemberg's works combine clusters, glissandos, sprechstimme, spatial realignment of singers, and so on, with traditional polyphonic techniques, producing always colorful and occasionally startling effects. A fine example is *Messa d'oggi* (1968–70) for five soloists and unaccompanied mixed chorus, which combines portions of the Latin Mass with texts by Quasimodo and Dag Hammarskjöld. The Gloria is particularly interesting, the purposely antique diatonic counterpoint of the soloists engaging in dialogue with the choir's recurring textually aleatoric clusters. The final resolution of these disparate elements is achieved through slow glissandos into a C major chord. Other works include the choreographic choral suite *Eighteen Movements* (1968), the popular *Signposts* (1968), *Love* (1969–70) for three soloists and unaccompanied mixed chorus, based on poems by

Robert Graves and described by the composer as an "opera in four acts," and numerous other small pieces.

In addition to several partsongs, Nils Lindberg (b. 1933) produced one of the most interesting compositions of the 1990s. *Requiem* (1993) for soloists, chorus, and jazz band, augmented with French horns, flutes, and extra percussion, remains a startling work both in its overall effect and the details of its composition. Influenced by his Uncle Oskar's Requiem and remembering that jazz has always been used as funeral music in New Orleans, Lindberg managed to avoid both the stylistic self-consciousness that hampers the choral works of Brubeck, Ellington, and Zimmermann, and the overt commercialism that stains most other sacred works written in jazz or popular style. By combining jazz with Swedish folk song, a primitive form of peasant communication called *kulning* (in effect, high-pitched screams), and a parochial form of Gregorian chant unique to his native province of Dalecarlia, Lindberg created a fascinating and stunningly beautiful cultural synthesis.

Important younger composers include Anders Hillborg (b. 1954) and Peter Bengtson (b. 1961), whose *Songs to Lilith* has received international attention. Hillborg's *mua:aa:yiy::oum* (1983–86) was precisely described by the Eric Ericson Chamber Choir's anonymous program annotator in 1997:

> Is there anybody who has not been fascinated, at some time or other, by the myriad of small particles in the air, visible only in very bright sunlight? Or who has not heard tales of experiences of sound and light in connection with transcending the boundaries of consciousness? Hillborg's composition for unaccompanied sixteen-part mixed choir . . . invokes associations with microscopic movements, intense light, and both natural and supernatural experiences. The piece has no words and is to be sung entirely without vibrato. A phonetic formula, a kind of mantra, allows the sound to expand and contract, imparting life to long, sustained phrases surrounded by rapidly pulsating voices. In the ostensibly uneventful but at the same time mystically eventful, time appears to stand still.

Other worthy Swedish composers include Ture Rangström (1884–1947), whose lyric gifts and genius for setting the Swedish language, so obvious in his many songs, are also prominently displayed in his little choral pieces; Gunnar de Frumerie (1908–1987), whose settings of the *Lord's Prayer* and *Psalm 23*, both for mixed chorus, are good examples of a melodic style enhanced by French colorations; Lars-Eric Larsson (1908–1986), whose *Missa brevis* (1954) for SAB chorus, oratorio *The Disguised God* (1940), and various delightful partsongs on diverse texts (Blake, Horace, Nietzsche, and others) assured him an international following; Lars Johan Werle (b. 1926), whose *Canzone 126 di Francesco Petrarca* (1966) for unaccompanied mixed chorus and other works explore avant-garde techniques within a rather traditional tonal framework; Arne Mellnäs (b. 1933), whose *Aglepta* (1969) for children's chorus, a clever setting of an old Swedish incantation to frustrate one's enemies, became an immediate hit in London, Moscow, and other places; and Sven-David Sandström (b. 1942), who impressed with numerous varied choral works.

FINLAND

Like their neighbors in the Baltics, Finns have always been particularly fond of the choral song, an interest that continued, along with the composition of numerous significant large works, throughout the twentieth century. In the first decades composers naturally wrote in the language of a previous generation, with strong nationalistic features. Later, composers fell under the spell of Stravinsky, Hindemith, and to a somewhat lesser extent Schoenberg; several younger composers studied in the United States, often with Aaron Copland or Vincent Persichetti; and all were nurtured by the immense example of Jean Sibelius (1865–1957).

Sibelius was, without doubt, the most important Finnish composer of the twentieth century. Best known for his symphonies and other orchestral works, he also produced a sizeable quantity of choral music: some forty-eight works, of which about half were considered important enough to include Opus numbers. His first, the early five-movement symphony, *Kullervo* (1892) for soprano, baritone, male chorus, and orchestra, not only established his credentials as a great symphonist but also clearly revealed his undying nationalism and love of Finnish folk legends. Though the premiere in April 1892 was a great success, Sibelius forbade further performances of *Kullervo* during his lifetime, so its real impact on Finnish music did not occur until its rediscovery after 1957. Throughout the 1890s Sibelius dutifully composed cantatas, including two for ceremonies at Helsinki University (1894, 1897) and one for the coronation of Czar Nicholas II (1896), as well as numerous small choral pieces; but it was clear by 1900 that his heart belonged to symphonic music. Still, he continued to do his part to feed the Finnish hunger for partsongs (in the usual vocal configurations) and even contributed to the budding educational market in the United States with the English-language *Three Songs for American Schools* (1913). Sibelius's late works include three cantatas for mixed chorus and orchestra: *Our Native Land* (1918), *Song of the Earth* (1919), and *Hymn of the Earth* (1920). His last compositions are partsongs: *Karelia's Fate* (1930) and *The Bridge Guard* (1938), both for male voices, and *Two Italian Songs* for mixed voices. After *Kullervo*, Sibelius's most important choral work may be *The Origin of Fire* (1902, revised 1910), a cantata for baritone, male voices, and orchestra, which possesses a rich and vital expressiveness similar to the roughly contemporaneous Symphony No. 2.

Others from Sibelius's generation who made significant contributions to the choral repertoire include the musicologist and choral conductor Ilmari Krohn (1867–1960), who wrote a number of oratorios and several small sacred pieces; Selim Palmgren (1878–1951), who composed approximately one hundred partsongs and other works for mixed chorus; and Leevi Madetoja (1887–1947), whose numerous choral-orchestral cantatas, church pieces, and partsongs are influenced jointly by French music and the folk songs of his native region.

Of the several composers active during the century's latter half, Erik Bergman (1911–1996), Bengt Johansson (1914–1989), Einar Englund (1916–1999), Joonas Kokkonen (1921–1996), and Einojuhani Rautavaara (b. 1928) are particularly impressive.

Erik Bergman's early experience as a choral conductor resulted in numerous idiomatic choral pieces. The influences in his work, beyond his exploration of twelve-tone technique, were widely varied and obvious, from the Egyptology of *Aton* (1959) for baritone, speaker, chorus, and orchestra, to *The Birds* (1962) for male chorus and percussion, which is obviously indebted to Messiaen. While capable of being quite humorous, as in *Vier Galgenlieder* (1960) for three reciters and speaking chorus, and appropriately pious, as in his Mass (1971) for chorus and organ, Bergman also did not shrink from making musical comments on pressing issues. For example, the cantata *Noah* (1976) for baritone, chorus, and orchestra, considered one of Finland's most significant works, has also been viewed as a warning against nuclear holocaust. In one continuous movement it sets only a few Hebrew words dealing with the threat of deluge and, ultimately, rescue. The piece ends with a lovely song of praise.

Bengt Johansson devoted most of his energies to choral composition. Much of his work is designed for amateur singers, although the tonal language, usually built on fourths and fifths and often employing simultaneous major-minor chords, is challenging. His compositions for more advanced ensembles extend the harmonic palette and apply a variety of new techniques. An outstanding example is *The Tomb at Akr Çaar* (1964), an exceptional setting of Ezra Pound's poem for mixed chorus and bass soloist. It is built from a four-note row of adjacent half steps, which are constantly realigned, expanded, and verticalized in ways that achieve a glistening harmonic language of substantial variety and power, enhanced by various nonpitched vocal effects. It is altogether stunning, arguably the best Scandinavian choral work of the century's third quarter. Other pieces include *Stabat mater* (1953) for unaccompanied mixed chorus, *Missa sacra* (1960) for tenor, mixed chorus, and orchestra, *Requiem* (1967) for baritone, double mixed chorus, and three instrumental groups, and *Cantata humana* (1969) for baritone, chorus, piano, orchestra, and four prerecorded speakers, on text by Dag Hammarskjöld.

Einar Englund developed a polished, texturally transparent, and melodically expansive style, quite unselfconscious in its use of jazz rhythms and influenced in subtle ways by Stravinsky, Bartók, and Shostokovich. Noteworthy examples of Englund's choral music include *Chaconne* (1969) for mixed chorus, trombone, and doublebass, and Symphony No. 6 (*Aphorisms*, 1984) for mixed chorus and orchestra.

Largely self-taught as a composer, Joonas Kokkonen retained a stylistic dichotomy between his serially influenced, mostly atonal instrumental music and the tonal, quasi-Renaissance style of his choral works, of which *Missa a cappella* (1963) and *Laudatio Domini* (1966) are typical. A stylistic synthesis was achieved in *Requiem* (1981) for soloists, chorus, and orchestra, widely praised for its logic and structural clarity as well as for its transcendental qualities.

It has been said that Einojuhani Rautavaara is stylistically a wandering eclectic, drawing inspiration from Hindemith and Stravinsky, Debussy and Mussorgsky, and Berg and Bruckner without assimilating them into an individually identifiable style. Still, at century's end critics began to view Rautavaara as a distinctive voice, perhaps because his choral music was finding larger audiences internationally, impressing concert goers and professional musicians alike with its vitality and well-crafted approachability. The cantata *The True and False Unicorn* (1971) for mixed chorus, orchestra, and tape, and his most popular work, *Suite de Lorca* (1973) for unaccompanied mixed chorus, are among his very best pieces. Other works include *Missa Duodecanonica* (1963), *Two Preludes* (1967), on text by T. S. Eliot, and *Canticum Mariae Virginis* (1978), all for unaccompanied mixed chorus.

Younger Finnish composers include Kari Rydman (b. 1936), whose unaccompanied sacred choruses *Sancta Maria ora pro nobis* (1957) and *Dona nobis pacem* (1963) barely hint at his otherwise active interest in pop styles and collage technique; Paavo Heininen (b. 1938), who contributed the unaccompanied *The Autumns* (1970); Henrik Otto Donner (b. 1939), who impressed with his cantata *XC* for soprano, mixed chorus, and orchestra; Pehr Henrik Nordgren (b. 1944), whose early oratorio inspired by environmental issues, *Agnus Dei* (1970) for soprano, baritone, mixed chorus, and orchestra, showed immense promise; Kaija Saariaho (b. 1952), Finland's foremost female composer; Olli Kortekangas (b. 1955); and Jaakko Mäntyjärvi (b. 1963).

ESTONIA

It is difficult to overestimate the importance of choral singing in Estonia. Every town has a choir, and the choir is usually excellent. Children are encouraged to sing, and composers—who are often also choral conductors—

eagerly provide new works for the repertoire. The popularity of the national song festival, which began in 1869 with 845 singers and increased in size to 28,000 singers by 1990, testifies to the vital role played by choral music in Estonian life.

Rudolf Tobias (1873–1918) was a significant figure early in the century. After study in Saint Petersburg with Rimsky-Korsakov, he composed the first Estonian cantata, *Johannes Damascenus* (1897) for soloists, mixed chorus, organ, and orchestra; the first Estonian oratorio, *Des Jona Sendung* (1909) for soloists, mixed chorus, and orchestra; and *Twelve German Motets* for unaccompanied mixed chorus.

Other Estonian choral composers include Miina Harma (1864–1941), Mart Saar (1882–1963), Cyrillus Kreek (1889–1962), Gustav Ernesaks (1908–1993), Ester Mägi (b. 1922), Velio Tormis (b. 1930), Jaan Rääts (b. 1932), and Arvo Pärt (b. 1935).

Miina Harma studied organ, choral conducting, and composition at Saint Petersburg Conservatory before returning to Estonia, where she founded an important touring choir. She composed many partsongs in a quasi-romantic style similar to those found in other countries in which budding artistic nationalism was only then beginning to emerge.

Mart Saar and Cyrillus Kreek also studied at Saint Petersburg Conservatory. Together they are credited with establishing a distinctive Estonian choral style, based on the somewhat irregular rhythms of Estonian folk song and freely incorporating the rich vertical sonorities and chromatic flavoring often employed by their Russian teachers. Saar wrote several cantatas and hundreds of small choral pieces, the most important of which were collected into *Children's Choruses* (two volumes, 1921), *Mixed Choruses* (five volumes, 1933–35), and *Men's Choruses* (three volumes, 1935). Kreek was not quite as prolific but still produced a significant number of sacred and secular partsongs, of which the lovely *Blessed Are They* (1923) is internationally known. Of particular importance is Kreek's *Estonian Requiem* (1927) for tenor soloist, mixed chorus, and orchestra, in Estonian with the original Latin added later. Based largely on themes derived from Estonian folk song, Kreek's work is the earliest example of a Requiem Mass by an Estonian.

Gustav Ernesaks's style was more immediately accessible than that of Saar or Kreek, relying almost exclusively on very simple rhythms and harmonies. In addition to the Estonian national anthem, Ernesaks composed over two hundred partsongs and several cantatas.

Ester Mägi is perhaps best known for her cantata *Kalevipoeg's Journey into Finland* (1954) for chorus and orchestra. She also composed partsongs.

Velio Tormis developed a dissonant and rhythmically vigorous style based largely on Estonian folk music. His earliest important work, *Meestelaulud* (Men's Songs, 1965) for unaccompanied male voices, includes whistling and footstomping among the colorful devices employed to establish a rustic and humorous mood. *Eesti kalendrilaulud* (Estonian Calendar Songs, 1967) for mixed chorus is a cycle based on ancient runic folk song forms, from which "Saint John's Day Song" is particularly impressive. In addition to other part-song cycles, Tormis composed over twenty cantatas, including *Kalevipoeg* (1955) and *Sun, Sea, Earth* (1970). His work with Estonian folk music has been compared to Béla Bartók's work in Hungary, and he is held in very high esteem by the Estonian public.

Jaan Rääts is somewhat unusual in that he did not contribute significantly to the partsong repertoire. However, he did produce the intriguingly innovative cantata *Karl Marx* (1962–64) for speaker, chorus, and orchestra, which combines elements of jazz, Estonian folk music, and western European neoclassicism, as well as *School Cantata* (1968).

The music of Arvo Pärt (b. 1935) exerted an international influence in realms quite removed from the Estonian partsong. The first Estonian composer to grapple with dodecaphony, Pärt's serialism gradually evolved into minimalism. He is often considered a great mystic of the twentieth century, though his music is quite distinguishable from that of others with similar inclinations: Jani Christou's metaphysical explorations seem more emotional than spiritual; neoclassic principles are always implied in Morten Lauridsen's compositions; Georges Migot's incessantly diatonic atonality can sound, to the uninitiated, suspiciously like cats on piano keys; Giacinto Scelsi's work abounds in eclectic mannerisms; and John Tavener's early works are fixated on Bach, while his later works all contain some easily identifiable element of Eastern Orthodox chant. But Pärt's mysticism generates, like life itself, from small, profoundly complex structures presented in deceptively simple guise.

Pärt's compositional procedures are similar, in fact, to Stravinsky's, but the aesthetics and results are polls apart. Stravinsky conceived of God as objective thought, while Pärt seeks a sensory communion. In Stravinsky's music the process is everything, but Pärt delights in the effect created by the process. Hence, while serial structures in Stravinsky's later sacred works issue a challenge to the listener, serial structures in Pärt's works offer an invitation to lose oneself in the music. Pärt achieves these results by working mostly with familiar sounds. This does not make him a better composer than Stravinsky; the ultimate primacy of effect over process (or perhaps *through* process) is simply a defining element of his art.

A frequently performed piece is the small, superficially unassuming *Magnificat* (1989) for soprano soloist and mixed chorus, which includes deceptively few technical demands other than a requisite ability to sing long, sustained phrases with good intonation. Melodic, harmonic, and formal structures are delineated by the composer's use of double bars: four units with four sequential repeats, each compressed, expanded, or otherwise varied. Beyond

Arvo Pärt: the five manifestations of the second thematic unit in *Magnificat*.

this are unusually rich analytic possibilities: serialist roots are revealed at every turn, and the extensive exploration of sonorities built from the components of an F minor triad brings to mind the remarkable variety of uses of a single chord in Palestrina's *Pope Marcellus Mass*. Among Pärt's other numerous works are *Solfeggio* (1964), an exhaustive exploration of a G major scale; the unaccompanied *De profundis* (1980); *Saint John Passion* (1982) for chorus, six vocal soloists, and five instruments; the well-known *Te Deum* (1984–86) for mixed chorus and chamber orchestra; the English-language *And One of the Pharisees* (1990); *Berliner Messe* (1990–92) for chorus and chamber orchestra; *I Am the True Vine* (1996) for unaccompanied chorus; *Tribute to Caesar* (1997) for unaccompanied chorus; and *The Woman with the Alabaster Box* (1997) for unaccompanied chorus.

Younger Estonian composers include René Eespere (b. 1953), Erkkisven Tuur (b. 1959), and Urmas Sisask (b. 1960). Like his colleague Arvo Pärt, Eespere is noted for the spiritual dimensions of his music. Unlike Pärt, however, he frequently incorporates elements borrowed from pop styles. Highly regarded works include *Glorificatio* (1995) and *Two Jubilations* (1995), both for mixed chorus. Erkkisven Tuur has combined a variety of late-twentieth-century techniques, such as minimalism and aleatorism, with brilliant effect. Like his teacher Rääts, Tuur is primarily interested in larger forms, as exemplified by *Oratorio ante finem saeculi* (1985), Symphony No. 2 (1987), *Missa lumen et cantus* (1989), and other works for chorus and orchestra. Urmas Sisask developed an aesthetic based on a highly imaginative interest in astronomy and cosmology, which is vividly evoked in his numerous unaccompanied sacred pieces, including the *Estonian Mass* (1994), and other Masses and motets.

Latvia

The leading Latvian composer at the beginning of the century was Andrejs Jurjāns (1856–1922), an avid and systematic collector of folk materials whose numerous partsongs accentuated the naturalistic and folkloristic aspects of Latvian culture. At the same time, Emīls Dārziņš (1875–1910), Jānis Zālītis (1884–1943), and others dedicated to setting texts by Latvian poets produced many fine partsongs of a uniformly high quality.

As World War I embroiled them, about a quarter of the Latvian population fled to Russia, virtually destroying cultural life in their own country. During the war, however, choirs were formed in Latvian churches in Russia and among Latvian regiments serving in the Russian army. Teodors Reiters (1884–1956), who as a student conducted a Latvian choir in Saint Petersburg, Teodors Kalniņš (1890–1962), who participated in a Russian army chorus, and others returning to Riga following the war reorganized Latvian choral life. The Latvian National Opera Chorus was formed, university and other amateur choruses began flourishing, and by 1926 the tradition of the Latvian National Song Festival, which had begun in 1873, was reinstituted. In this atmosphere composers began once again to produce choral works. The leaders of the resurgence were Emīlis Melngailis (1874–1954) and Jāzeps Vītols (1863–1948).

A gifted composer, Melngailis was also the foremost Latvian ethnomusicologist of the age. He produced many choral arrangements of folk songs and in 1920 formed a choir that traveled throughout the country giving concerts, accompanying his lectures, and generally enlisting enormous and eager audiences for choral singing based on folk music. Melngailis used his considerable influence to lobby for the idea that Latvian folk music not only could but should be the foundation of newly written pieces, offering his own works as examples. Fortunately, he was no charlatan. An obvious master of the little partsong (always built on clear-cut Latvian folk forms), Melngailis created a new Latvian choral repertoire that spoke to the broadest possible audience without alienating professional musicians or intellectuals. Representative works include *Nature and the Soul* (1921), on text by the great Latvian poet Jānis Rainis (1865–1929); *Midsummer Eve* (1928), an elaborate setting that represents the pinnacle of Latvian folk song arrangements; and *Skylark's Wedding* (1934), which exemplifies the composer's later interest in equally balanced six-part textures (soprano-mezzo-alto and tenor-baritone-bass). Also important are four earlier partsongs, *Move Gently and Quietly* (1906), *Doomsday* (1911), *Gently, Slowly* (1912), and *The Sun Is Setting* (1921), which Melngailis referred to as parts of his "Latvian Requiem." It is not known, however, if the composer actually planned for these pieces to constitute all or part of a larger work, and they are usually performed separately.

Most Latvian composers who reached maturity in the decades between the world wars were students of Jāzeps Vītols. Their considerable success in establishing a new classically based repertoire, which balanced and complimented the folk-derived style of Melngailis, is largely a result of the demanding standards Vītols placed on them. As a composer himself, Vītols was particularly adept at writing narrative ballads for unaccompanied chorus. The most popular of these works, *The Castle of Light* (1899), has been widely used as an allegorical symbol of the Latvian people. Among the best choral ballads is *David before Saul* (1928), which relates the biblical account of the shepherd David barely escaping with his life after playing the harp for a sleepless King Saul. Vividly descriptive and emotionally involving, the music brings a jealous Saul to fire-breathing life. The vocal and dramatic techniques are reminiscent of Janáček's *Kantor Halfar* or *Maryčka Magdónova*—portions of the score even look like something Janáček could have written—and the terrifying climax is well timed and effectively understated. Janáček, though, would probably not have rounded off the story (or the musical form) as neatly as does Vītols, repeating the opening description of Saul's fitful slumber.

Outstanding—and contrasting—students of Vītols include Jānis Kalniņš (1904–2000) and Pēteris Barisons (1904–1947), both of whom excelled in partsongs. Kalniņš strove for a conscious objectivity in his work, which naturally led him to descriptive texts, good examples being *The Story of Pikamice*

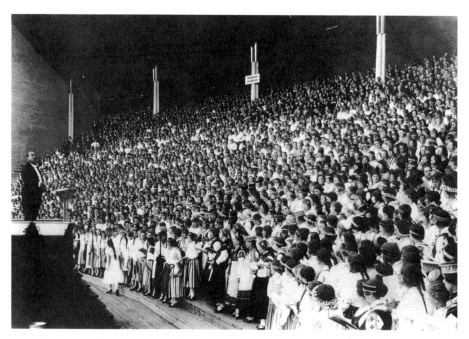

Emīlis Melngailis conducting the Latvian National Song Festival, 1926. Courtesy of the Rainis Museum of Literature and Art History, Riga, Latvia.

(1932) and *The Shiny Sea* (1939). Barisons was more interested in controlled emotional impact and variegated moods; hence his predilection for setting impressionistic texts such as *Harbinger of Spring* (1937) and *Blue Dream-Hill* (1939). Both composer's styles are essentially diatonic, but Kalniņš's occasional chromatic effects are used for dramatic emphasis, while Barisons's occur as points of color.

The most important Latvian work written during World War II is *God, Your Earth Is Burning* (1943) by Lūcija Garūta (1902–1977). Even though the tape of the 1944 premiere also records the sounds of battle outside Riga's Dom, twenty-first-century listeners can only guess at the impact this work had for those who were there. Survivors of the Leningrad siege who remember wartime broadcasts of Shostokovich's Seventh Symphony, and perhaps British listeners who either attended the premiere of Vaughan Williams's Fifth Symphony or heard it broadcast during German air raids, have some frame of reference for the emotional glue that attaches this cantata to the hearts of Latvians. The text, subtitled "Latvian Prayer," was written by Andrejs Eglītis in 1943 and set to music almost immediately by Garūta. She kept the musical forces modest—tenor and baritone soloists, chorus, and organ—and the musical language direct. The most overpowering section is the unaccompanied and otherwise understated Lord's Prayer, which comes toward the end, glistening like a jewel amid the corrosive and decaying influences of evil, unspeakable violence and creating a bridge into the cantata's hopeful conclusion.

Lūcija Garūta: opening of the Lord's Prayer from *God, Your Earth Is Burning.*

Other composers active during the first half of the century include Alfreds Kalniņš (1879–1951), who, in addition to founding the national opera, teaching at the Latvian Conservatory, and conducting, found time to compose over a hundred choral pieces; Jēkabs Graubiņš (1886–1961), who wrote some 150 partsongs and folk song arrangements for schoolchildren; and Jānis Mediņš (1890–1966), whose late motet *To Our Lady of Aglona* (1960) is particularly lovely.

In addition to continuing the Latvian partsong tradition, the younger generation of composers also turned to liturgical texts and large forms. Perhaps the most important of these composers is Maija Einfelde (b. 1939), winner of the 1997 Barlow International Competition, whose treble choruses *Ave Maria* with organ and *Peo persona* with piccolo reveal somewhat different aspects of her confident technique and fertile imagination. Others include Romualds Jermaks (b. 1931), whose *Missa solemnis* in honor of Pope John Paul II, written in a slick popular style, immediately reached a large and appreciative audience; Pēteris Plakidis (b. 1947), whose impressive, unaccompanied choral symphony, *Destiny* (1985), explores varied rhythmic textures and delights in syllabic interplay; and Rihards Dubra (b. 1964), whose collection of ten motets, *Ave Maria* (1989–94), uses a diatonic style similar to Garūta's as a fixed point from which all manner of avant-garde techniques emanate.

Lithuania

As in Latvia, the prevailing Lithuanian interest in choral music can be traced to its folk music. Particularly conducive to the development of choral singing were two polyphonic folk song genres: an interestingly dissonant contrapuntal type in which the individual lines together form a chain of unresolved seconds (*sutartine*), and a homophonic type in which harmonies are created from the first, fourth, and fifth notes of the scale. Another factor in the development of choral music was the rise of nationalism during the second half of the nineteenth century. Lithuania had been ruled by Russia since 1795. In 1864 the establishment of more severe constrictions on Lithuanian culture naturally resulted in the development of a national school of composition and the creation of many amateur choral societies, which thrived by the time Lithuania achieved independence in 1919. The Lithuanian Song Festival, modeled after those of Latvia and Estonia, was established in 1924.

The most important composers early in the century were Juozas Naujalis (1869–1934), Mikolajus Čiurlionis (1875–1911), and Stasys Šimkus (1887–1943). Naujalis made many important contributions as a choral conductor, teacher, and publisher. In addition to numerous folk song arrangements and partsongs he is remembered for his attractive Mass in C Minor for chorus and orchestra. Mikolajus Čiurlionis, perhaps the greatest Lithuanian composer, was also an accomplished painter. His natural romanticism was enhanced by musical effects rooted in the disciplines of visual art and enlarged by his own interest in folk music, chromaticism, and new modes. In addition to a significant body of folk song arrangements and partsongs, Čiurlionis composed a large *De profundis* (1899–1900) for chorus and orchestra, and *Kyrie, Gloria, and Sanctus* (1902) for mixed chorus, which uses liturgical texts as vehicles to develop musical form. Stasys Šimkus was an avid collector of folk songs and an important music educator who also composed several large choral works including *Farewell to Motherland* and other cantatas.

During World War II choral activities were curtailed. But immediately after, two important composers, Balis Dvarionas (1904–1972) and Antanas Račiūnas (1905–1984), fell in line with Soviet wishes to produce overtly communistic pieces. Dvarionas, whose brother was a well-known choral director, composed the cantata *Salute to Moscow* (1953) for chorus and orchestra, and several melodiously unthreatening partsongs, of which the atmospheric *Raigardo Saltinelis* for mixed chorus is exemplary. Račiūnas, who studied in Paris with Boulanger, Stravinsky, and Koechlin, became one of Lithuania's most honored teachers and composers, his highly refined technique and naturally conservative inclinations combining to form a near-perfect musical conduit for socialist realism. Besides an oratorio, *Tarybu Lietuva* (1948), and a couple of cantatas, Račiūnas wrote many partsongs, some of which utilize the dissonant elements of the old *sutartines*.

A student of Račiūnas, Eduardas Balsys (1919–1984) was among the first composers to openly disregard Soviet artistic policy, although he himself was a rather high-ranking member of the Lithuanian Communist Party. Balsys's rebellion mostly took the form of mild experimentation with various new Western musical techniques. Among his numerous large choral works is the touching oratorio *Don't Touch the Blue Globe* (1969) for mezzo and baritone

Mikolajus Čiurlionis: opening of the double fugue from *Kyrie, Gloria, and Sanctus.*

soloists, children's chorus, two pianos, doublebass, and percussion, which deals with the Nazi murder of children at camp on the first day of World War II.

Vytautas Barkauskas (b. 1931) is the most outstanding Lithuanian composer to be completely trained under the Soviet system. Though apparently devoted to the audience-pleasing tenets of socialist realism, his works are occasionally tempered by the use of serialism and aleatoric techniques. Representative compositions include *Pathetic Thoughts* (1962) and *Prelude and Fugue* (1974), both for unaccompanied mixed chorus.

Among younger composers, Vytautas Miskinis (b. 1954) and Vaclovas Augustinas (b. 1959) are especially noteworthy.

Vytautas Miskinis composed ten Masses, many motets, and partsongs, several of which are in the repertoire of choruses throughout Europe. His music communicates easily by means of a direct diatonic style that freely incorporates avant-garde techniques. A good example is *Pater noster* (1994), which begins in E Dorian, creating a succession of quickly moving canons from small motives. At length, Miskinis aligns the mode vertically into large clusters and modulates quickly, via canonic imitation, into a six-voice chordal section in a hybrid Mixolydian and Ionian mode on E-flat, before returning effortlessly to the opening material in E Dorian.

Primarily a choral composer, Vaclovas Augustinas won important competitions in Lithuania, Russia, and France. Typical works, such as the cantata-like *Gloria* (1990, revised 1996) for soprano soloist, mixed chorus, and organ, and the double-choir motet *Hymn to Saint Martin* (1996), reveal a predilection for classical forms and dimensions, clean and sometimes angular melodies, lilting rhythms, and strong tonal impulses.

Others include Jonas Tamulionis (b. 1949), whose works for women's chorus are particularly adept; Vidmantas Bartulis (b. 1954), whose *Missa brevis* uses only the first lines of each text; Kristina Vasiliauskaite (b. 1956), who impressed with her *Missa brevis* and other works for children's chorus; and Giedrius Svilainis (b. 1972), whose motet *O quam tristis* (1994) for mixed chorus, timpani, and bongos demonstrates a sure grasp of late-twentieth-century procedures within the context of chromatically expanded modality.

➳ 8

GREECE AND THE BALKANS

GREECE

With one staggering exception, the composition of choral music in Greece during the twentieth century was dominated by attempts to come to terms with the specter of Greek folk music, either by integrating it into the perceived mainstream of European art music or by celebrating it on its own terms.

The exception was Iannis Xenakis (1922–2001), among the century's most original composers, who, according to Maurice Fleuret (1972, 20), "invents absolutely, like Adam in the Garden." Xenakis based his art on mathematical theories. His music is generally thought of as inordinately complicated, a view encouraged by a famous 1964 incident in which Leonard Bernstein supposedly held a Xenakis score open for the audience to see and announced, "Today, the New York Philharmonic is on the honor system!" Even so, Xenakis has also composed important works for children's choir and orchestra, such as *Polla ta dhina* (Hymn to Man, 1961). His best-known unaccompanied choral piece, *Nuits* (1967), was composed for Marcel Couraud and the Soloists of LORT. A blistering indictment of political injustice, it became immediately known all over the world despite vocal and musical demands that obviously require a virtuoso ensemble. Xenakis's *Medea* (incidental music, 1967) is full of colorful effects and engaging dancelike passages. Here the composer attempts to replicate the imagined sounds of ancient Greek performers while indulging in some literal tone-painting by banging stones together to describe the protected entrance of the Euxine Sea. *Serment* (1981) for unaccompanied mixed chorus is Xenakis's most accessible work. Written for the International Society of Cardiovascular Surgeons, its choral wails, moans, and barking may not seem intended, at first, to promote confidence in the medical profession, but repeated hearings reveal many inventive and entertaining ideas. Bright, sunny, and relatively brief, its boundless enthusiasm creates the illusion of a great, primitive tribal ceremony. A more recent work,

174

Knephas (1990) for unaccompanied mixed chorus is also noteworthy because of its sustained, dense, crystalline, and incredibly beautiful sonorities.

At the other end of the spectrum is Yannis Markopoulos (b. 1939), who founded the "Return to the Roots" movement in 1980 for the purpose of creating a new music based almost entirely on ethnic elements. A typical work, permeated with the scales and rhythms of Greek folk music, is *The Liturgy of Orpheus* (1993) for mixed chorus and ensemble of strings, winds, and percussion, including several traditional Greek instruments: pipe, zournas (a kind of clarinet), shephard's pipes, tamboura, psalterion, lyre, and rattles.

Other leading composers occupy a very broad middle ground between Xenakis and Markopoulos. Of the older generation, the most important are Manolis Kalomiris (1883–1962), whose Symphony No. 1 (*Of Manliness,* 1920) for chorus and orchestra successfully integrates traditional dance rhythms into a large symphonic work based on western European models; and Petros Petridis (1892–1977), whose mastery of counterpoint, incisive rhythmic sense, and warm, pointed harmonic language inform the oratorio *Saint Paul* (1950), *Requiem for the Last Emperor of Byzantium* (1952–64), and the cantata *La belle dame sans merci* (1965). In 1916 Petridis noted the importance of teaching harmony, but added that Greeks were "being taught harmony in a way incompatible to the Greek music color and ideas" (Fidetzis 1995). He sought to establish a new national style that was based on Greek scales but that included tonal elements held in common with western European music, pointing out that "once this system is formed, then we can quite safely say that we have overcome the danger of our music being 'absorbed' by foreign kinds of music."

One composer who followed this path was Mikis Theodorakis (b. 1925), who composed a handful of unaccompanied liturgical pieces for the Greek Orthodox Church as well as several oratorios and symphonies with chorus. More important perhaps is his *Requiem* (1984–85), which sets the traditional sixth-century text of John of Damascus in a nonliturgical way, requiring soprano, alto, tenor, and bass soloists, as well as children's chorus, mixed chorus, and orchestra. However, instead of seeking the common ties that Petridis envisioned, many composers of Theodorakis's generation sought to create an East–West synthesis through dodecaphonic and other serial means. In this atmosphere a number of worthwhile pieces appeared by composers such as Yannis Papaioannou (1910–1989), Yorgos Sicilianos (b. 1922), and Jani Christou (1926–1970).

Papaioannou, a leader in the movement to explore new Western techniques within a specifically Greek context, successively applied principles of Hindemith, Schoenberg, and Penderecki, while occasionally also employing Byzantine modes. His choral works include the large *Daphnis and Chloe* (1934) for chorus and orchestra, *Songs of the Night* (1954) for female chorus, the cantata *The Funeral of Sarpedon* (1965) for mezzo soloist, narrator, mixed chorus, and chamber orchestra, and *Trihelikton* (1976) for mixed chorus.

Sicilianos studied with Boris Blacher, Darius Milhaud, Vincent Persichetti, Walter Piston, and Ildebrando Pizzetti, developing a nationalistic style freely incorporating serialism. Among his choral works are *Epitaphion: in memoriam Nikos Marangopoulos* (1971) for mixed chorus, children's chorus, narrator, and orchestra, and two textless pieces: *Episodia II* (1971) for double chorus, piano, doublebass, percussion, and tape, and *Parable* (1973) for chorus, flute, tuba, percussion, and tape.

Christou's metaphysical music evolved from Bergian serialism into a kind of irrational performance art requiring a completely new notational system, best exemplified by the oratorio *Mysterion* (1965–66).

Theodore Antoniou (b. 1935) is outstanding among the next generation of composers. A student of Papaioannou and Günter Bialas, Antoniou also absorbed folk influences and utilized more advanced techniques derived from Christou and Penderecki. A prolific composer, Antoniou's numerous choral works include the German-language *Greichische Volkslieder* (1961) for unaccompanied mixed chorus, *Kontakion* (1965) for SATB soloists, mixed chorus, and strings, *Three Choruses* (1971–72), and the cantata *Die weisse Rose* (1974–75) for baritone soloist, three narrators, mixed chorus, children's chorus, and orchestra.

BULGARIA

As in Lithuania, choral music in Bulgaria was influenced by the polyphonic nature of its folk songs, which, like the Lithuanian *sutartine*, often delight in the sound of parallel seconds. The distinctiveness of Bulgarian folk music is further enhanced by frequent reliance on asymmetrical meters (an important influence on Béla Bartók, Leonard Bernstein, and other composers). Organized choral singing developed rapidly after Bulgaria's liberation from the Turks in 1878, the first music school opened in 1904, and professionally trained composers began to have impact after World War I and the September 1923 uprising. Although more composers were formally trained, their prevailing styles still clung to the traditions of Bulgarian folk music. Younger composers influenced by the socialist revolution of 1944 retained folk impulses but strove, in the manner of socialist realism, for even more direct and accessible expression.

Important choral composers at the beginning of the century included Angel Bukureshtliev (1870–1951), a pianist and choral conductor who wrote choruses based on Bulgarian folk music; Panayot Pipkov (1871–1942), an important choral director and teacher who composed, in addition to many other partsongs for mixed and children's choirs, the very popular *Go, Enlightened People*, which is sung throughout Bulgaria each year on Slavonic Literature Day, May 24; and Dobri Christov (1875–1941), who composed fifty choral works, mostly sacred.

Petko Staynov (1896–1977), blind from the age of five, composed a large number of partsongs and larger unaccompanied choral works in addition to many orchestral pieces, all in a rich harmonic language with clear-cut formal schemes. In style and technique he is closely associated with the older Dobri Christov.

Pancho Vladigerov (1899–1978) was an important teacher who wrote many small partsongs. His style was initially based on western European thought, but later works explore more fully the peculiar features of Bulgarian peasant music.

Georgi Dimitrov (1904–1979) studied in Poland and became a well-known choral conductor there before returning to Bulgaria in 1939. He composed over five hundred choral pieces, many for children's chorus. His humorous works are particularly effective, some of which were compiled in 1968 in a volume called *Selected Choral Songs*. The same year, Dimitrov published an important book, *Conversations on the Question of the Choral Art*.

Lyubomir Pipkov (1904–1974), son and student of Panayot Pipkov, was interested equally in folk music and social themes. His music is therefore permeated by the rhythms, harmonies, and melodic contours of Bulgarian peasant music and dominated by themes of patriotism and justice. In addition to many partsongs for mixed chorus, Pipkov's catalogue contains numerous unison choruses and other pieces for use in schools. Representative large compositions include *Wedding* (1934), *Soldier's Cantata* (1958), and *Oratorio for Our Time* (1959), all for chorus and orchestra.

Marin Goleminov (1908–2000) combined the various elements of Bulgarian folk song with certain French influences learned during his study in Paris with Vincent d'Indy. In addition to unaccompanied partsongs, an oratorio, and some cantatas, he composed *Five Christmas Songs* (1938) for mezzo, women's chorus, and chamber orchestra.

Todor Popov (b. 1921) composed hundreds of partsongs for various vocal configurations, including many for children's voices. Melody is the most important aspect of his easily accessible style, which also contains elements derived from folk music. Typical of Popov's larger works are the cantatas *Bright Festival* (1959) for soloists, mixed chorus, and orchestra, and *Song for the Great Day* (1968) for baritone, children's, and mixed choruses, and orchestra.

The music of Konstantin Iliev (1924–1988) effectively combined serial and aleatoric techniques with folk elements. His choral works include *Chudnoto choro* (The Miraculous Dance, 1956) for children's chorus, wind quintet, and piano, the cantata *Septemvri 1923* (1963) for soprano and bass soloists, mixed chorus, and orchestra, and several pieces for unaccompanied chorus.

Especially noteworthy for his frequent use of humor, Alexander Tanev (1928–1996) composed more than two hundred choral works in a style that leans heavily on folk music for inspiration. Representative works include *Old Bulgarian Dances* (1974) for male chorus and the oratorio *Chronicle of Freedom* (1975) for baritone, speaker, mixed chorus, and orchestra.

Perhaps the most internationally known Bulgarian composer is Henri Lazarof (b. 1932), who immigrated first to Israel and then to the United States, settling in Los Angeles. His music, written in an individualistic atonal style free of folk influences, includes three choral works: *Cantata* (1958) for speaker, mixed chorus, and instruments, *The First Day* (1959) for unaccompanied mixed choir, and *Canti* (1971), which requires an unaccompanied mixed chorus to make unusual sounds and stomp their feet.

Another composer to provide an international dimension to Bulgarian music was the jazz pianist Milcho Leviev (b. 1937), who immigrated to Los Angeles in 1971. His jazz cantata *The Green House* (1991) for mixed chorus (twelve singers or more), trap drums, string bass, and piano combines Bulgarian, Latin, and English texts. The libretto by Scott Guy sets the opportunities and responsibilities of freedom against the human tendency to seek affluence at the expense of the underprivileged. The music calls for jazz soloists from within the choir (one from each voice part), freely combines speech chorus with traditional singing, and explores a sometimes overlooked harmonic capability of jazz by mixing Dorian and Phrygian modes.

Other composers include Boyan Georgiev Ikonomov (1900–1973), whose choral works include two oratorios; Lazar Pironkov (b. 1927) and Krasimir Kyurkchiiski (b. 1936), who each wrote several partsongs; and Tsvetan Tsvetanov (b. 1931), who contributed *Stalbata* (Ladder, 1966) for alto soloist, male chorus, and orchestra, a cantata in peasant style.

CROATIA

Jakov Gotovac (1895–1982) was a leading conductor of opera and choral music from the beginning of his career in 1922. Very active in the promotion of Croatian musical nationalism, Gotovac's first great work was the folk oratorio *Koleda* (1925). Other choral works, all on Croatian folk texts, include *Two Songs of Laughter and Wonder* (1924), *Three Choruses for Young Men* (1932), *Songs of Eternal Sorrow* (1939), and *Songs of Inspiration* (1955).

Other important composers include Boris Papandopulo (1906–1991), Branimir Sakač (1918–1979), Ivo Malec (b. 1925), and Petar Bergamo (b. 1930).

Boris Papandopulo's significantly large output of cantatas and other choral pieces makes him somewhat unique among Croatian composers. Particularly noteworthy is *The Passion of Our Lord Jesus Christ* (1935) for male chorus and soloists, which uses metrically free elements of Dalmatian peasant music with profound effect.

Branimir Sakač was influenced by expressionism, *musique concrete*, Lutoslawski, and Penderecki. He produced a number of choral works that reveal a forceful and dramatic musical personality, including *Seven Movements* (1963) for mixed chorus, *Omaggio—canto della commedia* (1969) for chorus, violin, and percussion, and *Umbrana* (1971) for twelve voices.

Ivo Malec was primarily interested in electronic and other avant-garde applications separate from choral music, though he did write one important work for Marcel Couraud: *Dodecameron* (1970) for twelve mixed voices, which treats the rather controlled aleatoric procedures of Witold Lutoslawski's *Trè poèmes d'Henri Michaux* as a point of departure in order to create a more improvisational and virtuosic structure.

Petar Bergamo's strong dramatic sense is revealed in the two-movement *Farewell and Sailors of Podgora* (1955) and *The Nameless* (1955), a suite for unaccompanied mixed chorus.

ROMANIA

George Enescu (1881–1955) dominated Romanian music during the first half of the century, thanks mainly to the international popularity of his Romanian Rhapsodies and other orchestral works. His choral music includes the symphonic poem *Vox maris* (1929–51) for soprano and tenor soloists, mixed chorus, and orchestra, and a few smaller pieces, such as *Silence* (1946) for three equal voices.

Gheorghe Cucu (1882–1932), Dimitrie Cuclin (1885–1978), and Marţian Negrea (1893–1973) also composed choral music during the early decades of the century.

Cucu was a church musician and choral conductor who effectively assimilated a classical contrapuntal technique into a largely folk-derived style. Of his numerous works, the large *I Cannot Understand, Curata* (1920) for baritone soloist and mixed chorus is particularly important because it created a stylistic synthesis that would be fully explored by Paul Constantinescu and others.

Cuclin remained somewhat outside the Romanian mainstream as a composer for reasons similar to those that led to the alienation of Havergal Brian from the British establishment: his works tended to be enormous and philosophically ponderous. They include several cantatas, two partsong collections, the oratorio *David and Goliath* (1928), and three symphonies with chorus: No. 5 (1947), No. 10 (1949), and No. 12 (1951).

Negrea evoked the landscapes of his native Transylvania by using folk materials combined variously with late-nineteenth-century tonal harmonies and twelve-tone serialism. Examples of his work include the partsong collections *Album for Mixed Choir*, Opus 10 and *Album for Children's Choir*, Opus 11, as well as the larger *Requiem*, Opus 25 (1957) for soloists, chorus, and orchestra.

Production of choral music was especially important for the next generation of composers because of an increased demand from numerous flourishing Romanian choral societies, which had sprung into being during the late nineteenth century, and a newly enflamed nationalism. Paul Constantinescu (1909–1963) expanded on the previous achievements of Gheorghe Cucu through his large sacred works, including *Liturghia în stil psaltic* (1935) and the oratorios *The Passion and Resurrection of Our Lord* (1946, revised 1948) and *The Birth of Our Lord* (1947), in addition to his choral cycles *Four Madrigals* (1954) and *Seven Songs from Our Street* (1959).

Many Romanian composers cultivated a highly specialized form of patriotic oratorio. The leading practitioners of this form were Alfred Mendelsohn (1910–1966), whose *1907* honored the rural Romanian uprising; Gheorghe Dumitrescu (b. 1914), whose *Tudor Vladimirescu* (1952), about the hero of the Romanian struggle for independence from the Ottoman Empire, is the best-known of his several works in this form; and Ovidiu Varga (b. 1913), who was particularly adept at choral composition, and whose oratorios courted popularity by blatantly tugging the nationalistic heartstrings of his listeners. Among others who popularized the genre are Anatol Vieru (1926–1998) and Tiberiu Olah (b. 1928). Vieru, the most important composer of his generation, created the legendary oratorio *Miorița* (1957) on folk texts dealing with lost sheep, as well as *Cantata anilor lumină* (Cantata of the Luminous Years, 1960) for chorus and orchestra, and pieces for unaccompanied chorus. In a brief analysis of *Miorița*, Nicolas Slonimsky noted that

> the entire score is based on two six-note tropes, mutually exclusive and aggregating to a twelve-tone series: 1) C, D, F sharp, G, B, and C sharp and 2) E flat, E, F, A flat, A, and B flat. Both tropes are mirror formations, the first being symmetrically built around the central interval of a semitone, and the second around the central interval of a minor third. The interplay of these two tropes creates a fruitful engagement of melodic elements, with ingenious allusions to authentic Rumanian [sic] modes that contain intervals involved in the series. (Lang and Broder 1965, 242)

A representative example of Olah's work is *The Galaxy of Man* (1960), which uses Balkanized scales and asymmetrical meters.

Laurențiu Profeta (b. 1925) realized that his melodious style was well suited to children's voices. Among his large catalogue are several cantatas, the oratorio *Adventures in the Garden* (1958) for baritone soloist, narrator, children's chorus, and orchestra, and *Six Pieces* (1966) for solo voices, children's chorus, and tape.

Myriam Marbé (b. 1931) contributed several impressive works, including *Ritual for the Thirst of the Land* for soloists, mixed chorus, and percussion, a ceremonial reenactment of the ancient Romanian custom of praying for rain during drought and expressing frenzied joy when rain comes. The piece calls for performers to be spaced in the hall so that the audience can be involved in the ceremonial process.

Among younger composers, Adrian Pop (b. 1951), son of the highly regarded choral conductor Dorin Pop, is perhaps representative. An experienced composer of orchestral and chamber music, an artist adept in modern techniques including electronic media, and winner of several international prizes, Pop's numerous choral pieces are nevertheless remarkably conservative (American publishers would refer to them as "functional"). He has concentrated on small pieces, often grouped into cycles on texts by a single poet: Quasimodo, Christian Morgenstern, Rainer Maria Rilke. His partsong, *Song of Peace* (1981) for unaccompanied mixed chorus, gained international popularity following the European transformation of 1989. Written in what Pop's publisher called a "naiv-romantic [sic] style," it is somewhat reminiscent of the American gospel song "All to Jesus I Surrender."

SLOVENIA

Throughout the century, Slovenian composers embraced virtually every modern compositional trend, even as they concentrated on instrumental and stage music. Slavko Osterc (1895–1941) is typical. After study in Prague he developed a wide-ranging style: free atonality, serialism, and quarter-tone constructions gradually supplanting the quasi-romanticism of his early works. Although Osterc's instrumental music is considered his primary achievement, he did not completely neglect the choral idiom, producing some cantatas and partsongs. This trend continued as only two composers of the next generation, Milan Stibilj (b. 1929) and Alojz Srebotnjak (b. 1931), produced significant choral works. Stibilj impressed with his Slovene Requiem, *Apokatastasis* (1967) for tenor, mixed chorus, and orchestra. Srebotnjak contributed a handful of rather important cantatas, of which *The Mother* (1955) for chorus and orchestra became internationally known.

YUGOSLAVIA (SERBIA AND MONTENEGRO)

The most recognizable name in Serbian choral music is Stevan Mokranjac (1856–1914), who conducted the Serbian Choral Society from 1887 until his death. Under his leadership this choir became famous throughout central

Europe and Russia for its high performance standards and repertoire, which contained many Serbian folk songs collected by Mokranjac as well as his original compositions, mostly based on folk elements. While his best-known works date from the late nineteenth century, Mokranjac continued to compose well into the new century. Among his works are *Divine Liturgy of Saint John Crysostom* (published 1901, English version published 1909); *Ivkova slava* (1901), eight dramatic scenes for soloist, chorus, and orchestra; a mixed chorus version (1906) of *The Glorification of Saint Sava* (1893) for male chorus; the last piece of his famous *Rukoveti* (Folk Melodies), entitled "Zimski dani" (Winter Days, 1913); and numerous songs for children's chorus.

Stanislav Binički (1872–1942) was also a famous conductor. He became the first director of the National Theater, and, with the choir of Stankovic Music School, he gave the first Serbian performances of Haydn's *Creation* and Beethoven's Ninth. Binički's music for instruments and stage freely mixes Serbian, Middle Eastern, and European (mostly Italian) elements, but his choral works confine themselves to the style of Serbian folk music. In addition to many partsongs, he composed a Memorial Service (1912) and settings of the Serbian Orthodox Liturgy (1923). His ode *Marš na Drinu* (March on the Drina, 1914), which celebrates a World War I victory by the Serbs, is particularly well known.

Binički's successor at the National Theater was Stevan Hristić (1885–1958), who studied the Russian church style briefly with Alexandr Kastal'sky in Moscow. Later works show the influence of impressionism. His unusually fine melodic gifts are displayed in the oratorio *Resurrection* (1912), his important setting of *Opello* (Orthodox Memorial Service: E minor n.d., B-flat minor 1918), *Dubrovaki Rekvijem* for mixed chorus and soprano soloist, and *Jesen* (Autumn), his most popular choral work.

Petar Konjović (1883–1970) studied in Prague before returning to Serbia to become a music teacher and choral conductor. His Czech experience encouraged his natural inclination toward folk sources, and he began developing melodies, like Janáček, out of the inflections of speech. Konjović's mature style strives for direct communication with a broad audience while incorporating a sophisticated harmonic vocabulary. His works include over one hundred folk song arrangements and twenty original choral pieces.

Miloje Milojević (1884–1946) wrote many partsongs for various vocal configurations, those for children's choir being particularly popular. He was a knowledgeable choral conductor and critic, and his style progressed through several stages, corresponding with the major compositional developments occurring in Europe during the first third of the twentieth century. His best-known work for mixed chorus is the cycle *Pir iluzije* (The Feast of Illusion).

Marko Tajčević (1900–1984), also a leading choral conductor, synthesized Western polyphonic technique with Eastern Orthodox ethos and musical language. Like Janáček, Tajčević created melodies greatly influenced by the natural rhythms of the spoken Serbo-Croat language. Tajčević composed numerous choral songs for children's choir and was particularly appreciated for his secular partsongs, of which *Dvadeset srpskih narodnih pesama* (Twenty Serbian Folk Songs), *Pesme od kola* for male chorus, and *Three Madrigals* may be considered typical. He also composed several psalm settings and *Liturgija* (Liturgy of Saint John Chrysostom), as well as *Cetiri duhovna stiha* (Four Spiritual Verses, 1927), from which the highly popular motet "Vospoite jemu" emanates.

Ljubica Marić (b. 1909), the leading female composer of her generation in the former Yugoslavia, studied in Prague with Josef Suk and was influenced by Alois Hába. Her music is freely tonal, often incorporating elements as disparate as serial technique and Orthodox Church modes. Everett Helm found her cantata *Pesme prostora* (Songs of Space, 1956) for chorus and orchestra to be "a thoroughly impressive work of large dimensions" (Lang and Broder 1965) and provided a succinct description:

> This cantata is imbued with the spirit of Serbian folk music, although no direct quotations occur; Marić has here approached that ideal synthesis of folk spirit and personal expression that marks the compositions of Bartók. The cantata's seven sections are settings of simple and naïvely touching inscriptions from tombstones of the thirteenth century. The texts are treated at times polyphonically, at times homophonically but always with appropriate sobriety. The expert choral writing is kept relatively simple, while the orchestra part is often very complex. Marić displays great sensitivity in the orchestral and harmonic coloring.

Other interesting Serbian composers include Aleksandar Obradović (b. 1927), Dušan Radíc (b. 1929), and Aleksandar Vujic (b. 1945). Obradović's choral music, beginning with *Little Choral Suite* (1948) for unaccompanied mixed chorus, display an active interest in expanding tonalities and motivic development. Later works also utilize serial and electronic techniques. Radíc's large *Symphonic Picture No. 2* (1964), a moody and rhythmically invigorating polytonal affair for violin, women's chorus, and orchestra, received positive attention from critics after its premiere. Vujic, the winner of several international prizes and commissions for choral composition, commands a starkly beautiful diatonic style occasionally flavored by Balkan scales supported by open sonorities and surprising, though fleeting, dissonance. His effortless contrapuntal writing, as exemplified in the exquisite little *Ave Maria* (published 1997) for unaccompanied mixed chorus, is particularly impressive.

∽ 9

ITALY AND THE IBERIAN PENINSULA

ITALY

Italian composers have always been interested in vocal music. However, this interest has usually been aimed at opera and other solo vehicles. In the early twentieth century most opera composers, following the nineteenth-century examples of Bellini, Donizetti, Rossini, and Verdi, dutifully turned out a few large, quasi-liturgical or patriotic choral works inspired by the vocal imperatives of stage music. Representative examples include the oratorios *Inno alla Croce rossa* (1901) by Ruggero Leoncavallo (1857–1919) and *Golgotha* (1909) by Franco Leoni (1864–1949). Giacomo Puccini (1858–1924) also belongs in this group, although his few choral works, all written toward the end of the nineteenth century, tend to be quite understated.

Vito Carnevali (b. 1888) is typical of composers who devoted their efforts to the Roman Catholic Church. He was organist for many years at Saint Anne's Parish Church in Vatican City, and his numerous motets and Masses, often based on Gregorian chant, are perfect examples of functional music written within the confines of the aesthetic principles laid down by Pope Pius X in his famous Bull *Motu proprio*. *Missa "Rosa Mystica"* may be considered representative. Written in versions for three-part male, three-part treble, or four-part mixed chorus and organ, it eschews every operatic tendency: the vocal lines are clean and simple, the text is clearly presented even in contrapuntal passages, the organ supports the voices and occasionally provides simple melodic embroidery, and the harmonic language is absolutely traditional.

Functioning between the polarities of opera and church were Ferruccio Busoni (1866–1924), Ottorino Respighi (1879–1936), Ildebrando Pizzetti (1880–1968), Gian Francesco Malipiero (1882–1973), and Alfredo Casella (1883–1947).

A somewhat isolated figure in Italian music, Ferruccio Busoni lived most of his professional career in Berlin, concentrating on composition for the piano. As a teacher and thinker he was quite influential, his ideas being often presented as tonal alternatives to Schoenberg's methods. His one great choral work was his Piano Concerto (1903–04), which includes male chorus in the finale. When Busoni composed the piece, the presence of chorus in a solo concerto was not entirely new (obvious examples including Beethoven's Choral Fantasy and Bach's Cantata 147, in which the opening Sinfonia is an organ concerto movement). However, the structural conception of Busoni's concerto was without precedent, as was the function of the chorus therein, which, in the composer's words (Dent 1981), "does not break away from the previous mood to an opposite extreme of feeling, as it does in the Ninth Symphony; it resembles rather some original inborn quality of a person which in the course of years comes out again in him purified and matured as he reaches the last phase of his transformations."

Ottorino Respighi found inspiration in a conscious application of archaic principles within a colorful, totally conservative harmonic palette. Best known for his orchestral pieces, he composed very little choral music; but his charming cantata, *Laud to the Nativity* (1928–30) for soprano, mezzo, and tenor soloists, mixed chorus, and instrumental ensemble of piccolo, flute, oboe, English horn, two bassoons, and piano four-hands, remains an international favorite.

Because of their love for the chorus, Ildebrando Pizzetti and Gian Francesco Malipiero, like Busoni, stood somewhat outside the Italian mainstream. Even Pizzetti's operas, for which he is best known, are driven by forceful choral writing. A prominent critic and teacher, Pizzetti's style remained quite conservative. His numerous attractive works for soloists, chorus, and orchestra, including *Epithalamium* (1939), the intriguing *Attollite portas* (1948) for three choruses, twenty-two winds, two pianos, and percussion, *Vanitas vanitatum* (1958) for male chorus, and *Filiae Jerusalem, adjuro vos* (1966) for female chorus, do not overshadow his unaccompanied pieces, especially the fine *Messa di requiem* (1922) for mixed chorus. Malipiero, in addition to his editions of works by Monteverdi and Vivaldi, contributed no fewer than eleven large works for chorus and orchestra, mostly on secular texts but including *Missa pro mortuis* (1938). His style, which has been called "an act of rebellion against nineteenth-century music" (Blom 1954, 5:534), is derived from Gregorian and Renaissance melodic impulses. Counterpoint is simply not an issue in Malipiero's music, which may explain his disinterest in serial procedures.

Alfredo Casella passed through several abrupt stylistic changes, the first revealing the influence of Mahler, the second turning toward expressionism, and the third settling into a more Italianate diatonicism somewhat influenced by Stravinsky and culminating in Casella's one important choral work, the *Missa solemnis* (1944) for soprano and bass soloists, mixed chorus, and orchestra, which hints at a budding, though unrealized, interest in serial technique.

Mario Castelnuovo-Tedesco (1895–1968) studied with Pizzetti and was greatly encouraged by Casella. In 1939 he fled to the United States, eventually settling in Beverly Hills, California. His prolific and uneven output contains many choral works, including a Sacred Service (1943, expanded 1950) for baritone, mixed chorus, and organ, and several other Jewish liturgical works; Kol nidre (1944) for cantor, mixed chorus, organ, and cello; the cantatas Naomi and Ruth (1947) and The Queen of Sheba (1953), both for female chorus and piano; the biblical oratorios Ruth (1949), Jonah (1951), and Esther (1962); the small cantata The Fiery Furnace (1958) for baritone solo-ist, children's chorus, organ, and percussion; and numerous unaccompanied pieces. Castelnuovo-Tedesco's cycle of three poems by Federico García Lorca, Romancero gitano (1951) for mixed chorus and guitar, is outstanding. In it he makes very good use of the guitar's natural sonorities, producing challenging, invigorating, structurally taut, and vocally idiomatic music, which should be considered among the best of the century's several Lorca settings.

As a choral composer, Goffredo Petrassi (b. 1904) was perhaps best known for his setting of five limericks by Edward Lear, Nonsense (1952) for unac-companied mixed chorus. Effectively witty, it proved a perfect choice for con-ductors who wanted to lighten the content of a concert's second half without sacrificing musical substance in favor of the flagrant gimmicks of novelty pieces. It still occupies a secure place in the international repertoire; but, except for the challenging and grateful choral writing, it is not typical of Petrassi's work, which tends toward large pieces on sacred or otherwise seri-ous texts. Stylistically, his music was always evolving. Elements derived from Stravinsky, Orff, the early Italian baroque, Gregorian chant, and Renaissance polyphony gradually replaced the earlier influences of jazz and Hindemith. The one constant was a juxtaposition of diatonic modal choral writing with an instrumental chromaticism that Petrassi described as "centrifugal" (Sadie 1980, 14:583). Among his works are some of the more significant Italian choral compositions of the century, including Psalm IX (1934–36) for mixed chorus, brass, percussion, two pianos, and strings; Magnificat (1939–40) for soprano soloist, mixed chorus, and orchestra; Coro di morti (1940–41) for male chorus, brass, three pianos, percussion, and doublebasses; his master-piece, the cantata Noche oscura (1950–51) for mixed chorus and orchestra; and Orationes Christi (1974–75) for chorus, brass, violas, and celli.

Luigi Dallapiccola (1904–1975) was the first master of serialism in Italy. Although he studied with several Italian teachers, his early influences were Wagner and Debussy, followed by Busoni, and ultimately Berg. Dallapic-cola's preserialist period culminated with Sei cori di Michelangelo Buonarroti (1933–36). Though apparently intended to be performed as a set, the choruses that make up this piece fall easily into three pairs that can be performed alone, the first and last demonstrating definitive steps in the composer's development. The first pair (1933), for unaccompanied mixed chorus, remains Dal-lapiccola's most frequently performed choral work. Its essentially diatonic language and various coloristic devices borrowed from early Italian madrigals clearly reveal the composer's interest in old music. The second pair (1934–35) explores sonorities produced by treble chorus (boys' or female) and an ensem-ble of seventeen instruments. The last pair (1935–36), for mixed chorus and orchestra, introduces serial technique although it is still mixed with a more diatonic style. The serialism exhibited in *Canti di prigionia* (1938–41) for mixed chorus, two harps, two pianos, and percussion extends beyond melody, harmony, and rhythm to include structure as well, a large portion of the third movement being an exact mirror of itself. The "Dies irae" chant is also effec-tively worked into the fabric, and the sonorities of chorus, percussion, harps, and pianos leave a lasting and poignant impression.

Other serialists include Giacinto Scelsi (1905–1988), Riccardo Malipiero (b. 1914), Bruno Maderna (1920–1973), and Luigi Nono (1924–1990).

Giacinto Scelsi has been called "a composer who defines enigma" (*Los Angeles Times*, 14 June 1999). For him, serialism was one of several tech-niques used in attempts to commune with the transcendental. These efforts translated mostly into an eclectic mannerist style with pretensions to meta-physical depth. Typical works include the cantata *La naissance du Verbe* (1948) for chorus and orchestra, *Tre canti sacri* (1958) for unaccompanied mixed chorus, *Yliam* (1964) for unaccompanied women's chorus, *Tkrdg* (1968) for six-part male chorus, amplified guitar, and percussion, and *Litanie* (1975) for unaccompanied women's chorus.

Riccardo Malipiero, nephew of Gian Francesco Malipiero, contributed a twelve-tone *Cantata sacra* (1947) for soloists, chorus, and orchestra on words by Saint Catherine of Siena.

Composer and conductor Bruno Maderna was quite interested in assimi-lating new techniques, from strict serialism to the inclusion of folk elements, combined with aleatoric methods and electronic media. The stated purpose of his music was "to entertain and to interest" (Sadie 1980, 11:454). After a very early unpublished Requiem he composed only two significant choral works: *Three Greek Lyrics* (1948) for soprano, mixed chorus, and instru-ments, and *All the World's a Stage* (1972) for mixed chorus.

Luigi Nono, who not only married Schoenberg's daughter Nuria but also took a very public stand against the aesthetics of John Cage, was both a com-mitted serialist and a committed communist seeking to use his art as a vehicle for social commentary. His most successful work in this area is *Il canto sos-peso* (1955–56) for soprano, mezzo, and tenor soloists, mixed chorus, and orchestra. Setting letters from condemned antifascist resistance fighters, it strikes a beautifully delicate balance between political and emotional sensi-bilities. *Prometeo, tragedia dell'ascolto* (1984, revised 1985) for vocal and instrumental soloists, two speakers, chorus, four orchestral groups, and live electronics is considered a masterwork of Nono's last years. Originally conceiving the piece as an opera, he eventually scrapped the idea of conventional staging in favor of a visually static work for widely separated performing groups, which he called a "Tragedy of Listening." Based on the myth of Prometheus, *Prometeo, tragedia dell'ascolto* utilizes ancient and modern texts (by Aeschylus, Friedrich Hölderlin, and others), in combination with electronic effects created by the experimental studio Sudwestfunks Freiburg, to create a haunting exploration of spatial acoustics. Other important works include the three-part *Epitaffio per Federico Lorca* (1951–53): part 1 for soprano and baritone soloists, chamber chorus, and instruments, part 2 for flute and chamber orchestra, and part 3 for speaker, speaking chorus, mixed chorus, and orchestra; *La terra e la compagna* (1957–58) for soprano and tenor soloists, chorus, and instruments; *Cori di Didone* (1958) for chorus and percussion; and *Y entonces comprendió* (1969–70) for six female soloists, mixed chorus, and tape.

Luciano Berio (b. 1925) was the most influential Italian composer and teacher during the last third of the century. His eclectic style, indebted to models as diverse as Mahler and Stravinsky, gradually became rooted in electronic and aleatoric principles. His music always seems to be exploring new possibilities. *Questo vuol dire che* (1969) for soloists, chamber chorus, instruments, and tape consists of an open-fifth drone and simultaneous electronic collage, over which various styles of folk music performance and other live materials are superimposed. Folk materials are also the focus of *Coro* (1975–76, revised 1977) for mixed chorus and orchestra. The text combines lines by Pablo Neruda with American Indian, Italian, Persian, Hebrew, Polynesian, Croatian, and African folk song texts. According to Berio (1980), "it is not only a question of a *chorus* of voice and instruments but also a *chorus* of different techniques extending from song to *lied*, from African heterophony (as analyzed by Simha Arom) to polyphony. In the rather wide range of techniques adopted in *Coro*, the folk element is certainly not the only one."

Berio's most popular choral work is *Magnificat* (1949) for two soprano soloists, mixed chorus, eight winds, two pianos, two doublebasses, and percussion. Student origins are obvious in its pronounced eclecticism: the piano writing is occasionally like Dallapiccola's in *Canti di prigionia*; otherwise, everything is very reminiscent of preserial Stravinsky, especially the sixth section, which even looks on the page like *Symphony of Psalms*. But unlike Copland's very early *Four Motets*, which bears no trace of that composer's mature genius, the stamp of Berio's formidable personality can be traced in this attractive and energetic music as it proceeds from a long held, lightly embellished unison C to a rich harmonic fabric built from juxtaposed F major and A major triads.

Luciano Berio: orchestral segment from the sixth section of *Magnificat*.

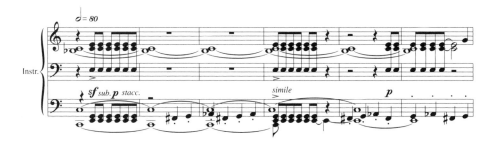

Igor Stravinsky: orchestral segment from the last movement of *Symphony of Psalms*.

Berio's influential *Sinfonia* (1968) for large orchestra and eight singers must also be mentioned because the singers are used as an eight-part ensemble rather than as eight soloists. Written with the jazz-oriented Swingle Singers in mind, the work draws inspiration from wildly different sources including jazz, Bach, Samuel Beckett, Beethoven, Debussy, Martin Luther King, Jr., the French anthropologist Claude Lévi-Strauss, Mahler (lengthy sections of Mahler's Second Symphony are quoted note-for note), Stockhausen, and Stravinsky. John Rockwell (1983, 78–79) observed that

> composers are now incorporating elements of popular music with a newly organic felicity. "Serious" composers have made use of popular music for a long time; some of the great medieval and Renaissance Masses are based on popular songs of the day. But this new kind of usage is different—a giddy potpourri of disparate elements. Ives is the real progenitor here. Berio, while he taught at the Juilliard School, became especially interested in the idea, and in his *Sinfonia* of 1968 he worked it out with a typically European precision—pleasing, but very different from the rougher exuberance of an Ives or a Cage.

Spain

Manuel de Falla (1876–1946) wrote two choral works: *Atlántida* (1925–46) for chorus and orchestra, which was left unfinished; and the unpublished *Balada de Mallorca* (1933), a choral transcription of Chopin's F major Ballade. After his death, Falla's family invited Ernesto Halffter (1905–1989) to complete *Atlántida*. Halffter's later large choral pieces, most notably *Canticum in memoriam P. P. Johannem XXIII* (1964) for soprano and baritone soloists, chorus, and orchestra, and *Gozos de Nuestra Señora* (1970) for chorus and orchestra, reflect a profound influence of Falla, as well as an abiding interest in Renaissance polyphony.

The blind Valencian Joaquín Rodrigo (1901–1999) was best known for *Concierto de Aranjuez* (1939) and other works for guitar but also made important contributions to the choral repertoire. His largest piece is a setting of Miguel de Unamuno's "Ode to Salamanca," *Musica para un Codice Salmantino sobre letra de Miguel de Unamuno* (1953) for bass soloist, four-part mixed chorus, and eleven instruments (two violins, viola, cello, contrabass, piccolo, flute, English horn, trumpet, French horn, harp), written to commemorate the 700th anniversary of the University of Salamanca. The formal structure is similar to a motet with, in the composer's words, an occasional "involuntary lyrical escapade" (Chase 1959, 313). Beginning with an eight-part canon at octave, its melodies are derived from Gregorian chant and Castillian folk song. Rodrigo's comments provide further insight into his harmonic vocabulary: "The generative harmonic factor is the perfect chord [major triad] which stretches itself lazily up to the major seventh that punctuates the Sapphic cadence of Unamuno's verse. This whole harmonic atmosphere is maintained in the same 'climate' to the end, extended over the bimodalism of an ambiguous tonality" (Chase 1959, 313–314). Another important work is *Triste estaba el Rey David* (1950) for mixed chorus.

The Spanish Civil War (1936–1939) caused a number of important composers to leave the country. Known as "the dispersed generation," this group included Rodolfo Halffter (1900–1987), who became a Mexican citizen, and Julián Bautista (1901–1961), who moved to Buenas Aires. Halffter's style was largely derived from Falla, with the addition of asymmetrical rhythms and occasional polytonality. He became the first composer in Mexico to explore twelve-tone technique. Choral works include *La nuez* (1944) for children's chorus, *Three Epitaphs* (1958) for mixed chorus, on texts by Cervantes, and *Pregón para una Pascua pobre* (1968) for mixed chorus, brass, and percussion. Bautista's cantata *Cantar del Mío Cid* (1947) for soloists, chorus, and orchestra and *Romance del Rey Rodrigo* (1955–56) for unaccompanied chorus are good examples of his dissonant, polyrhythmic style, rooted in the traditions of Spanish polyphony.

Cristóbal Halffter (b. 1930) and Juan Alfonso García (b. 1937) are representative of a transitional group of composers that emerged after the Civil War. Halffter, nephew of Rodolfo and Ernesto, developed a tonal style, freely incorporating modality and serial techniques. Important works include *Antifona pascual a la virgen "Regina coeli"* (1952) for four solo voices, mixed chorus, and orchestra, *Two Motets* (1954) for unaccompanied mixed choir, *Misa ducal* (1956) for chorus and organ (or small orchestra of woodwinds and low strings), *Gaudium et spes* (1972) for thirty-two voice chorus and tape, and *Oración a Platero* (1975) for speaker, children's chorus, mixed chorus, and percussion. Juan Alfonso García served as organist at the cathedral in Granada and contributed many small choral pieces of a practical nature. Also highly respected as a composer outside the church, he produced the impressive cantata *Campanos para Federico* (1971) and the "symphonic cantata" *Paraíso cerrado* (1982) for soloists, chorus, and orchestra, possibly his greatest work. García's style was briefly described by Tomás Marco (1993) as "abstract but retaining ties to Andalusian music."

Luis de Pablo (b. 1930), a master of the avant-garde, wrote the brilliant *Yo lo vi* (1970) for Marcel Couraud's unaccompanied Group Vocal du France. The shock value of this piece is not in the plethoric avant-garde twists but rather in the frequently recurring A-flat major triads, which not only establish some feeling of tonality but also enhance the structural unity.

Among younger composers, Javier Busto (b. 1949) and José Ramon Encinar (b. 1954) command attention. Busto, a physician and choral conductor, scored an international hit with the unassuming added-note tonalities of *Ave Maria* (1980). His other small pieces display an eclectic compositional style, often incorporting the more common avant-garde techniques. Encinar composed several significant choral pieces, including the lovely *Por gracia y galania* (1975) for mixed choir and *Canción* (1980) for women's chorus and instrumental ensemble, which is noteworthy for its "rare beauty and enormous delicacy within a complex construction" (Marco 1993).

The best-known composers from Catalonia are Pablo Casals (1876–1973) and Carlos Surinach (1915–1997). A member of the dispersed generation, Casals was forced by General Franco to leave Spain in 1936, living at first in a Catalan village on the French side of the border and finally settling in Puerto Rico in 1956. In addition to being among the century's greatest cellists, he composed a large quantity of choral music, much of it designed for use at the Montserrat monastery. Casals's style is traditional in the extreme, making "no concession to twentieth-century developments" (Sadie 1980, 3:847). Characteristic works include *Eucaristica* (1934) for three-part treble or mixed chorus and organ, *Nigra sum* (1942) for six-part chorus (treble or male) and organ, *Tota pulchra es* (1942) for mixed chorus, the Christmas oratorio *El pessebre* (1943–60) for mixed chorus and orchestra, and *Hymn to the United*

Nations (1971) for mixed chorus (SSTB) and orchestra, on text by W. H. Auden. Carlos Surinach—Spanish, although born in Barcelona—immigrated to the United States in 1951, becoming a United States citizen in 1959. As Gilbert Chase (1959, 323–324) has pointed out, Surinach "achieves an effect of novelty by exploring all the familiar clichés of the 'Spanish idiom' with new technical resources and with a completely nonimpressionistic sensibility. Sharply etched lines, dissonant clashes, emphasis on the sheer primitive power of rhythm, and strong reliance on percussion, give his music a mid-twentieth-century accent that contrasts with the post-impressionistic language prevalent in most contemporary Spanish composition." Among Surinach's works are *Cantata de San Juan* (1963) for mixed chorus and percussion, *Songs of the Soul* (1964) for unaccompanied mixed chorus, *Missions of San Antonio* (1969) for male chorus and orchestra, and the very effective *Via crucis* (1972) for mixed chorus and guitar.

Other Catalan composers include Xavier Montsalvatge Bassols (b. 1912), who wrote the symphonic poem *Egloga del Tajo* (Eclogue of the River Tagus) for chorus, soloists, and orchestra, and many attractive smaller works such as *Tres canciones negras* (1946) for soprano, mixed chorus, and piano; and Narciso Bonet (b. 1933), who composed choral arrangements of many Catalonian folk songs, as well as the cantata *Canco de bressol de la Verge* (1951) for chorus and orchestra, and the large *Missa in Epiphanie Domini* (1956–57) for chorus, soloists, and orchestra.

PORTUGAL

Although choirs have functioned in the cathedral churches of Portugal for centuries, secular choral singing was a new development in the twentieth century. The country's oldest secular choir, Orfeão do Porto, was not organized in the city of Porto (or Oporto) until 1910, an event which coincided with the establishment of the Portuguese Federation. Lisbon did not have a major chorus until Ivo Cruz (1901–1985) established the Sociedade Coral Duarte Lobo in 1931. Cruz followed this by founding the Lisbon Philharmonic Orchestra in 1937, thereby providing stable ensembles for the regular performance of major choral or orchestral works.

José Vianna da Motta (1868–1948) was among the better-known European pianists of his generation. He was the first Portuguese composer to utilize folk materials in his music. His only important choral work is the cantata *Lusiads* for chorus and orchestra.

Ruy Coelho (1892–1986) studied with Bruch and Schoenberg in Berlin and with Paul Vidal in Paris. An ardent nationalist, Coelho's stated purpose was "to make known to the world the Portuguese spirit" (Sadie 1980, 4:517). His choral works include the oratorios *Fátima* (1931) and *Oratória da paz*

(1967) for chorus and orchestra; and *Missa a Santa Terezinha* (1934) for unaccompanied mixed chorus.

Claudio Carneyro (1895–1963), a native of Porto, studied there with Lucien Lambert (1858–1945) before moving to Paris, where he studied with Charles Marie Widor and later with Paul Dukas. Carneyro succeeded Lambert at the Oporto Conservatory, becoming director in 1955. Best known for his chamber music, he nevertheless contributed numerous small pieces for mixed chorus and female chorus. His style is noted for its expressive delicacy and an emphasis on popular Portuguese themes. Representative works include *Ave Maria* (1935), *Musa popular* (1939), *Oracoes populares* (1940–51), and *Quatro romances populares* (1942), all for female chorus; and *Três poemas de Fernando Pessoa* (1948–51) for mixed chorus.

Frederico de Freitas Branco (1902–1980) exerted a broad influence on Portuguese musical life through his activities as composer, teacher, and conductor. As a composer his eclecticism ranged from polytonality to a more traditional nationalistic style. A certain affinity for choral composition, especially for women's voices, was provided by his experience as a choral conductor (he founded the Lisbon Choral Society in 1940). Works include *Missa solene* (1940) for soloists, mixed chorus, and orchestra, *Missa "Regina mundi"* (1954) for female chorus, the "lyric scene" *Don João e as sombras* (1960) for soloists, female chorus, and orchestra, and *Stabat mater* (1971) for female chorus and organ.

Fernando Lopes-Graça (1906–1994) studied in Lisbon with Freitas Branco and in Paris with Charles Koechlin before developing, after the example of Bartók, a style based entirely on Portuguese literature and folk music. His many choral pieces include cantatas, partsongs, and folk song arrangements.

Jorgé Croner de Vasconcellos (1910–1974) studied in Paris with Dukas and Boulanger. Works include *Vilancico para a festa de Santa Cecilia* (1967) for chorus and orchestra, *Erros meus* (1972) for chorus and organ, and several four- and five-part madrigals on texts by Luíz Vaz de Camões.

Emanuel Nunes (b. 1941) also studied in Paris, becoming a champion of the avant-garde and creating works such as *Voyage du corps* (1973–74) for mixed chorus and tape, and *Minnesang* (1975) for twelve-part mixed chorus.

Following Nunes, younger Portuguese composers showed particular interest in electroacoustic applications, as exemplified by Miguel Azguime's (b. 1960) *Yuan Zhi Yuan* (1998) for soprano, mixed chamber chorus, six traditional Chinese instruments, and live electronics on a Taoist Chinese text.

ᗧ 10

AFRICA AND THE MIDDLE EAST

European musical influences, including choral singing, were not widely accepted in twentieth-century Africa or the Middle East, excepting South Africa, Israel, and to a much lesser degree Turkey. However, the tribal group-singing prevalent in many parts of Africa, as well as African polyrhythms, fascinated numerous non-African composers who created works based on these styles. The best-known of these is David Fanshawe's (b. 1942) *African Sanctus* (1973) for soprano, mixed chorus, percussion, piano, and tape (or optional instruments such as guitars, African percussion, electronic organ). But works such as this are African only in the sense that various works with "español" in the title, by Ravel, Rimsky-Korsakov, and others, are Spanish. More authentic perhaps is the "Mass in Congolese style," *Missa luba* (published 1964), compiled and arranged by the Belgian missionary priest Guido Haazen. Haazen worked with native singers to record their celebration of Mass, stating in the score's preface that "the music of the *Missa luba* is mainly the product of a collective improvisation. What is recorded [and published] is simply and solely a reproduction of the concrete improvisation that took place during the recording."

In several countries, black churches of all denominations formed choirs that, in addition to learning non-African music, created vibrant choral arrangements of folk songs. Still, at century's end, new works by African composers were relatively rare. Examples include the several works of Fela Sowande (1905–1987), which combine Nigerian folk materials with Western structures; Ugandan composer Anthony Okelo's contrasting Masses: the Latin *Missa Mayot* (1978) for mixed chorus and congregation, which combines Gregorian chant with new material, and the Acholi *Missa Maleng* (1976) for mixed chorus and traditional percussion instruments; and the Eurocentric English-language cantata *Samuel* (1944) for soloists, mixed chorus, and organ by T. K. E. Phillips, from Nigeria.

Middle Eastern cultures showed little interest in Western art music, whose reliance on polyphony and vertical harmonies is diametrically opposed to their traditionally linear and predominately monodic music. Further, fundamentalist Muslim clerics often condemned the seductive and decadent qualities assumed to inhabit Western music. The work of Abu-Bakr Khaïrat (1910–1963) therefore comes as something of a surprise. Although he was thoroughly aware of traditional Egyptian music from birth, he also showed an early interest in Western music, studying violin and piano and composing pieces based on European models. He eventually enriched his otherwise romantic musical vocabulary with Egyptian elements, which are especially prominent in his choral works. Typical is his cantata *Lamma bada* for chorus and orchestra, which develops a monodic Egyptian strophic song form according to European polyphonic principles.

Western music was officially introduced into Turkey in 1828, when Giuseppe Donizetti, brother of the famous opera composer, became director of Turkish court music. Leading composers of Western-style art music included Lemi Ath (1869–1945), Tanburi Cemil Bey (1871–1916), Ulvi Cemel Erkin (1906–1973), and Adnan Saygun (1907–1991). Saygun's oratorio, *Yunus Emre* (1946) for chorus and orchestra, sets selections of text by the thirteenth-century Turkish poet Yunus Emre in a style combining romantic and impressionistic elements.

The outstanding South African composer of the century was John Joubert (b. 1927), who was catapulted to fame when his anthem *O Lorde, the Maker of Al Thing* (1952) for mixed chorus and organ, on text by Henry VIII, won the Novello Anthem Competition in 1952. Self-assured craftsmanship and bold invention set this work apart from many other twentieth-century anthems: a unison melody, stark and expressively angular, evolves into a canon at the fifth over gradually enriched harmonies, and the dramatic climax dissolves quickly in an evocative denouement. Among Joubert's numerous choral works are the choral symphony *The Choir Invisible* (1968) for baritone, mixed chorus, and orchestra, the cantata *The Martyrdom of Saint Alban* (1969) for tenor and baritone soloists, speaker, mixed chorus, and chamber orchestra, the oratorio *The Raising of Lazarus* (1971) for mezzo and tenor soloists, mixed chorus, and orchestra, *Four Stations on the Road to Freedom* (1972) for eight-part mixed chorus, and many other anthems and canticles for the Anglican Service.

ISRAEL

Twentieth-century choral music in Israel represented the successful creation of a body of work based on elements that were accepted as traditional, but that in reality were newly derived from a variety of sources. This "invented tradition" (Hirshberg 1995) was largely the result of pioneering efforts by Abraham Zevi Idelsohn (1882–1938), Menashe Rabinowitz, and David Schorr.

Born in Latvia, Abraham Zevi Idelsohn immigrated to Jerusalem in 1906 and almost immediately began to research the music of native Sephardic Jewish communities. David Schorr emigrated from Russia and obtained work teaching at Miriam Levit's music school in Jerusalem. His journeys through the countryside, where living conditions were still quite primitive and where there was no organized music, convinced him that music instruction had to be developed for all of Jewish Palestine. In 1927 he began adult courses at the school and founded the Institute for the Promotion of Music among the People. Working with Schorr, Menashe Rabinowitz organized local choruses for the institute along the lines of European models. By 1930 there were twenty active choruses in Jewish Palestine, all in need of repertoire; and by century's end virtually every city, town, or kibbutz could boast at least one organized choir, included among them the famous Rinat Choir, founded by the redoubtable maestro Gary Bertini, the Tel Aviv Chamber Choir, and the extraordinary Efroni Children's Choir.

It was easy to recognize that repertoire for the emerging choruses had not only to fulfill musical needs but would also be invaluable in helping to establish a national identity. The entire community of early composers came from eastern and central Europe and were mostly trained in Germany and France. Encouraged by Schorr, Rabinowitz, and others, they cooperated in consciously developing a new folk style—which became known as Eastern Mediterranean—based partly on European Ashkenazi and Yiddish songs, and partly on elements of liturgical chant and Sephardic song as revealed through Idelsohn's studies. Some easily identifiable elements include the interchangeable use of eastern European and Middle Eastern modes; varied rhythms based on Hebrew word accents (even in instrumental music), the irregular meter of Hebrew chant and Sephardic song, and the regular rhythm of the hora dance (imported from Romania); omission or lowering of the leading tone; harmonies based only on notes found in the melodic mode of a given piece; preference for parallel motion in part-writing, with only limited use of Western polyphony; and the use of melodic motives taken directly from Hebrew chant and Sephardic song.

This first generation of composers included Idelsohn himself, who contributed the musical drama *Jephtah* (1908–12) for six soloists, mixed chorus, and piano; Erich Walter Sternberg (1891–1974), still remembered for *Praise Ye* (1929, revised 1961) for baritone soloist, unaccompanied six-part mixed chorus, and speaker; and Karel Salomon (1897–1974), who wrote several cantatas as well as two volumes of folk songs for voice and piano.

A large number of new folk songs were written on kibbutzim by pioneer emigrants who were not trained musicians. During the early 1930s large numbers of these songs were published on postcards by the Zionist organization Keren Kayemeth and distributed to Jewish organizations around the world.

Late in the decade, Hans Nathan (1910–1989) enlisted the aid of several composers outside of Palestine to provide piano accompaniments for about thirty of these songs, thereby creating arrangements for solo voice or unison chorus. Aaron Copland, Paul Dessau, Arthur Honegger, Darius Milhaud, Ernst Toch, Kurt Weill, and Stefan Wolpe were among those who contributed to the resulting *Folk Songs of the New Palestine* (1938). Seventeen songs were republished in 1994 by A-R Editions in Madison, Wisconsin, as the fourth volume of *Recent Researches in the Oral Traditions of Music*: "Israeli Folk Music: Songs of the Early Pioneers."

By 1949 a total of 4073 collected and newly devised folk songs appeared in compilations, copies of which were sold commercially. The songs were also taught in public schools and further disseminated through recordings, radio broadcasts, sessions of coached communal singing organized by Schorr's institute, and public performances of choral arrangements. A wonderful example is Moshe Wilenski's (1910–1997) *Uri Tsiyon* (1959) for unaccompanied mixed chorus. After a brilliant introduction, its rousing, hora-inspired tune is presented alone, followed by various canonic imitations and a quiet midsection. It ends with the tune in bold relief over an irregularly syncopated accompaniment in the lower voices.

Moshe Wilenski: *Uri Tsiyon*, measures 73–80.

The outstanding exponent of Eastern Mediterranean style was Paul Ben-Haim (1897–1984), who became Israel's preeminent composer, well known abroad and adored at home. Born in Munich as Paul Frankenburger, he enjoyed the early stages of a promising career in Germany and was highly respected as the choral director of the Augsburg Opera; but with the advent of Nazi power he moved to Palestine and changed his name to Ben-Haim. By this time his music already revealed an interest in modality, antique cadences on open fifths, and melodies with descending augmented seconds, components that would be important in the new style. Examples include *Drei motteten* (1928) for unaccompanied mixed chorus on German-language texts from the Old Testament, *Zwei Lieder* (1931) for male chorus, on texts from *Des Knaben Wunderhorn*, and the oratorio *Joram* (1933) for soprano, tenor, and baritone soloists, mixed chorus, and orchestra, which was first performed in 1979.

Joram is particularly interesting. An early work of the philosopher and poet Rudolf Borchardt (1877–1945), it attempted to synthesize the Jewish concept of righteous suffering (Job) with the Christian concept of redemption (Jesus). Joram is a good man who endures a series of unhappy events. He is sold into slavery, murders a handmaiden in a fit of rage, and his wife becomes a prostitute. When finally freed he complains to God and reconciles with his wife, who bears him a son. Joram and his wife are then consumed by fire sent from heaven, leaving the boy alone to supposedly grow into the Messiah. In adapting the book into an oratorio libretto Ben-Haim omitted the murder, prostitution, and heavenly fire and inserted a poem by Borchardt about the universal suffering of Jesus. This poem is set as a large chorale, which, according to Jehoash Hirshberg (1990), "marks the turning point. Until this moment Joram has been sinking deeper. From here onward he begins to struggle, remonstrating with God to His face, regaining his beloved and purified wife, and finally attaining the realization of his soul's desire—the birth of a son." In addition to the modality, open fifths, and descending augmented seconds, *Joram* demonstrates a paneclectic synthesis similar to that encountered later in Judith Lang Zaimont's Sacred Service (see chapter 12): homage is paid to Bach, Brahms, Debussy, Strauss, and Stravinsky, choir melodies are derived from Gregorian psalm tones, and there are numerous instances of baroque text-painting.

Ben-Haim's first large choral work composed after his emigration was commissioned by the new Israel Radio. For this he patched together two pieces previously composed for Sabbath services and added three new ones. The resulting *Liturgical Cantata* (1948) for baritone, mixed chorus, and orchestra (or organ) was apparently inspired by Mordecai Seter's *Sabbath Cantata* (1940) and by Ernest Bloch's Sacred Service, for which Ben-Haim had written program notes. But there are substantial differences in these works. While Seter's cantata relies on Sephardic melodies for inspiration,

Liturgical Cantata is rooted in the more diatonic modes of the European Ashkenaz; and unlike Bloch's service, which is intended for Sabbath morning, Ben-Haim's cantata mixes texts from evening and morning services and is therefore not suited, as a whole, for liturgical use. It is, however, an effective concert piece, the hora rhythms and fugue of the Hallelujah movement being especially memorable.

Other excellent works in Ben-Haim's significantly large catalogue include *A Book of Verses: Three Choral Studies from the Rubayiat of Omar Khayyam* (1953) for unaccompanied mixed chorus, the cantata *The Vision of a Prophet* (1959) for soloists, mixed chorus, male speaking choir, three trumpets, and orchestra, *Three Psalms* (1962) for baritone, mixed chorus, and orchestra (or organ), *Hymn from the Desert* (1963) for soprano, baritone, mixed chorus, and orchestra, on text from Dead Sea Scrolls, *Six Sephardic Folk Songs* (1969) for unaccompanied mixed chorus, and many smaller pieces.

Oedoen Partos (1907–1977), Menahem Avidom (1908–1995), and Josef Tal (b. 1910) were important younger contemporaries of Ben-Haim.

Partos grew up in Hungary, where he was greatly influenced by Bartók and Kodály, so that when he immigrated to Palestine in 1938 he was well equipped to assimilate Jewish folk materials into his own musical language. In 1960 he embraced twelve-tone technique, eventually also including many other Eastern and avant-garde elements, such as microtones, into his compositional vocabulary. Even so, Partos never abandoned his interest in Israeli folk music, which remained an important characteristic of his style. Choral works include *Six Songs* (1941) for unaccompanied mixed chorus, based on Sephardic melodies; *Cantata* (1960) for soprano, mixed chorus, and orchestra, on text by Hayyim Nahman Bialik; and *Rabat tsraruni* (Many Times They Have Afflicted Me, 1965) for unaccompanied mixed chorus, arranged in 1966 for chorus and chamber orchestra.

Menahem Avidom came to Palestine from Poland in 1925. The French influence of his early works quickly gave way to the new Eastern Mediterranean aesthetic, into which he eventually incorporated a free melodic application of twelve-tone technique. Among his choral works are *Psalm Cantata* (1955) and *Jerusalem Songs* (1987) for three-part children's chorus.

Josef Tal wrote numerous small choral works; the symphonic cantata *A Mother Rejoices* (1948–49) for soloists, mixed chorus, piano soloist, and orchestra, about a woman who takes her own life when her sons are killed for refusing to convert to Christianity; and the large oratorio *The Death of Moses* (1967) for soloists, mixed chorus, orchestra, and tape.

In addition to his *Sabbath Cantata* (1940), Mordecai Seter (1916–1994), composed *Mo'adim* (1946), *Motets* (1951), *Dithyramb* (1965), and *Jerusalem* (1966), all for unaccompanied mixed chorus and all in a style that combines Sephardic melodic materials with Western polyphonic techniques.

Tzvi Avni (b. 1927) was born in Saarbrücken, Germany, and moved to Israel in 1933. A student of Paul Ben-Heim, Aaron Copland, Lukas Foss, and Vladimir Ussachevsky, Avni's style progressed from one obviously indebted to Eastern Mediterranean style to one influenced by electronic sounds, Japanese music, and the late-twentieth-century Polish avant-garde. In a 1968 interview (Gradenwitz 1996, 402–403) the composer attempted to describe his own musical style: "I don't consider myself to be an avant-gardist. What is most pronounced in my attitude toward music today as compared with the period eight years ago is that I have thrown off the bonds of definitions as regards form, orchestration, and the whole general conception. I live in a freer world." He also commented on two large works for mixed chorus and orchestra that he had completed in 1968, describing *The Destruction of the Temple in Jerusalem* as "a narrative piece with dramatic outbursts, moments of crisis, and a lamentation to end," and *The Heavenly Jerusalem*, its three parts sung in Aramaic, as

> a description of the generation of the wilderness who need to cleanse themselves from original sin by grave-digging by day, their self-interment by night, and their resurrection in new bodies every morning; the description of a hidden spring which has its source in the Garden of Eden and then flows to the Temple, on the floor of which it leaves traces of mysterious drawings from the hand of God; a description of 350 columns in the Temple, decorated with all types of brilliant gems . . . between the columns are 2100 lamps and in each of these 2100 candles shine by day and are extinguished by night for the sorrows of Israel.

The orchestra dominates *The Destruction of the Temple in Jerusalem*, while the chorus dominates *The Heavenly Jerusalem*. Both utilize a very free serial technique. Other works by Avni include *On Mercy* (1973), *Three Madrigals* (1978), and *Song of Degrees* (1987), all for unaccompanied mixed chorus; *The City Plays Hide and Seek* (1986) for three-part treble chorus; and the cantata *Deep Calleth unto Deep* (1989) for soprano, mixed chorus, and organ.

Gil Aldema (b. 1928) made many choral settings of existing songs, in addition to composing original works. An outstanding personality in the later development of Israeli choral music, Aldema's imaginative arrangements, like those of Bartók, Percy Grainger, John Rutter, Schoenberg, Velio Tormis, and Vaughan Williams, are infused with qualities of craftsmanship and originality that lift them quite above the norm. Examples include the traditional Chassidic song *Ai, di, di, di, dai* for mixed chorus, and *Jerusalem of Gold* (1967) for mixed chorus on a song by Naomi Shemer, which in popularity almost constitutes a second national anthem.

Aharon Harlap (b. 1941) was born and trained in Canada, immigrating to Israel in 1961. His music combines attractive lyricism with profound dramatic gesture. Like Janáček, he has a particular gift for establishing the emotional foundation of his musical rhetoric in only a few notes. For instance, the melodic tritones that permeate the brief motet *Shiru Ladonai* (O Sing unto the Lord, 1979) for unaccompanied mixed chorus project a determination to praise God even under constant threat of war and terrorism, rather than a bizarre juxtaposition of incompatibilities. The brilliant *Cain and Abel* (1989) for soprano and tenor soloists, mixed chorus, and piano or orchestra (original version for SSSAAATBB soloists and piano) progresses effortlessly from sacrifice, to jealous rage, to vividly portrayed murder, to righteous judgment, culminating in the anguished terror of a guilt-ridden and exiled Cain. The oratorio *The Fire and the Mountains* (1980) for mezzo and baritone soloists, two children soloists (boy and girl), narrator, children's and mixed choruses, and large orchestra deals with the subject of holocaust and rebirth. Other works include *Three Songs* (1978) for unaccompanied mixed chorus, *Still Remembering Names* (1987) for three-part treble choir, *My Friend Tintan* (1990) for two-part children's chorus, and *For Dust You Are, and to Dust You Shall Return* (1991) for soprano, alto, baritone, narrator, mixed chorus, and piano, written as a companion to *Cain and Abel*.

Many younger Israeli composers, following the example of Partos and Tal,

Aharon Harlap: opening of *Shiru Ladonai*.

sought to enhance the Eastern Mediterranean style by adapting serial or avant-garde elements to fit their needs. Two works exemplify the resulting high level of achievement: Meir Mindel's (b. 1946) *A Maya Prophecy* (1985) for unaccompanied mixed chorus and Michael Meltzer's (b. 1956) *Porke Yorash* (Why Do You Weep, Girl?) for soprano soloist, treble chorus, and drum. *A Maya Prophecy* sets a bone-chilling Mayan text (which at the very end of the century would also capture the attention of young British composer Thomas Adès) that predicts the annihilation of that civilization—a message well understood by post-Holocaust Jews. Melodies are built from whole-tone scales; sustained, empty octaves grow into vertical sonorities built from sevenths and tritones, which move slowly in parallel motion; unpitched rhythmic canons and graphically notated wailing are employed. The visual effect of the opening measures is most striking: the text, mimed in rhythm, gradually materializes as whispered sibilants are added, followed by complete words. The tonal foundation on D is well defined. Extremes of range are avoided. The part-writing is so logical that the piece's various difficulties are relatively easy to rehearse and master. The effect in performance is absolutely stunning. *Porke Yorash* is a remarkable setting of a traditional Sephardic song about the meeting of a wandering knight and a weeping girl. The tune is first given over a sound-collage of whispering and humming, then in canons so close together that a shimmering effect of tone clusters is produced, growing from and returning to a unison. As the girl realizes the knight is her long-absent husband, the song transforms into a dance, and the piece ends with highly stylized humming that sounds more like bowed strings than voices, evaporating in spirals of ascending glissandos, lighter than air.

Throughout the twentieth century certain talented composers dedicated their energies almost exclusively to music for amateur performers in kibbutzim. Outstanding among them were Dov Carmel (b. 1933), who composed many small choral works for various ensemble configurations as well as *Festival Cantata* for soloists, mixed chorus, and orchestra, and Yehuda Sharett, whose numerous choruses include the famous *Kumu to'ei midbar* (Rise Ye, Who Err in the Desert).

Other significant Israeli composers include Shula Doniach (b. 1905), whose two volumes of *Rhymes from Carmel* (1947) for two- or three-part treble chorus and piano became standard repertoire; Leon Schidlowsky (b. 1931), who contributed *Three Pieces* (1966) for unaccompanied mixed chorus, on Hebrew and Spanish texts from Psalms and Moses Maimonides, as well as two Latin Masses, *Missa in nomine Bach* (1984) for mixed choir, flute, oboe, clarinet, bass clarinet, violin, viola, cello, and percussion, and *Missa dona nobis pacem* (1987) for unaccompanied mixed chorus; Tsippi Fleischer (b. 1946), who impressed with *A Girl Dreamed* (1977, revised 1984) for unaccompanied unison chorus on Arab texts, and *Lamentations* (1985) for soprano, female chorus, two harps, and percussion; Max Stern (b. 1947), who wrote many works for various choral configurations; and Moshe Rasiuk (b. 1954), whose works include *Five Children's Songs* (1978), *The Market Street* (1981), and *In Gratitude* (1994), all for unaccompanied mixed chorus, *Sodom Square* (1987) for mixed chorus and percussion, and several works for children's chorus.

MEXICO, THE CARIBBEAN, CENTRAL AMERICA, AND SOUTH AMERICA

MEXICO

Although he was a successful composer and organist at Aguas Calientes Cathedral for many years, Manuel Ponce (1882–1928), considered to be the father of Mexican nationalist music, showed no interest in the choral medium. His only extant choral piece, *Six Motets* for chorus and organ, remains in manuscript.

However, Ponce's student Carlos Chávez (1899–1978), who would become the most famous of all Mexican composers, was quite interested in choral music even though he became much better known for his symphonies and ballets. The duel characteristics of nationalism and romanticism are present throughout Chávez's music, though seldom simultaneously. The more popular, nationalistic style is aptly represented by the "proletarian symphony" *Llamadas* (1934) and the "Mexican ballad" *El sol* (1934), both for chorus and orchestra, as well as by the folklike *La paloma azul* (1940) for chorus and chamber orchestra or piano. Among his other works are four interesting pieces on English texts: *Ah, Freedom!* (1942) and *A Woman Is a Worthy Thing* (1942), both for mixed chorus, *Three Nocturnes* (1942) for mixed chorus, on texts by British romantic poets, and the cantata *Prometheus Bound* (1956).

Ramón Noble (1925–1998) was an important choral conductor and organizer of choral activities in Mexico. Founder of the National Institute of Fine Arts Choir and cofounder (with Amelia Hernandez) of the Ballet Folklorico Choir, he also coordinated the visits of hundreds of foreign choirs. The Spanish-language *La Misa en México* for unaccompanied mixed chorus is representative of Noble's numerous choral compositions.

Other Mexican composers include Rafel J. Tello (1872–1946), Julián Carrillo (1875–1965), and Miguel Bernal Jiménez (1910–1956), who each wrote many pieces of functional church music; Arnulfo Miramontes (1882–1960), who studied with Nadia Boulanger and wrote many sacred works; Julián Zuniga (b. 1893), choirmaster at Mexico City's Basilica of Guadalupe for many years, whose several Masses and many motets reinforced his reputation as the "best twentieth-century composer of sacred music in Mexico" (Tiemstra 1992, 166); Luis Sandi Meneses (b. 1905), who directed the madrigal choir at Mexico City Conservatory and wrote numerous pieces; and Blas Galindo Dimas (1910–1993), who studied with Aaron Copland and impressed with the little *Dos corazones* for mixed chorus.

THE CARIBBEAN

In twentieth-century Cuba, composers generally sought to balance the varied elements of Cuban folk music with European techniques and other Latin American and African influences. Unlike China and the Soviet block, Cuba did not force its composers into the artistic mold of socialist realism after the Communist revolution, and artists continued to combine serial and avant-garde ideas with nationalistic elements.

An important composer early in the century was Guillermo Tomás (1868–1933), who also achieved fame as an important conductor and promoter of new music. Influenced by German operatic tendencies (primarily Wagner and Strauss) as well as by the French neoclassicism of d'Indy, Tomás created music that contains virtually no nationalistic elements, as with the cantata *La oración del creyente* (1896) for tenor, mixed chorus, and winds, and *Canto de guerra* (1896) for mixed chorus.

The most important nationalistic composers were Almadeo Roldán (1900–1939), who wrote Stravinsky-flavored music in Afro-Cuban style, and Alejandro García Caturla (1906–1940), whose incessant Afro-Cuban rhythms propel a wildly dissonant, rough-hewn style. Roldán's best-known choral work is *Curujey* (1931) for mixed chorus, two pianos, and percussion. A representative work of Caturla's is the black liturgy, *Yamba-ó* (1931) for chorus and orchestra.

Serafín Pro (1906–1978) was a very active conductor of municipal and collegiate choruses. Although a member of the avant-garde Grupo de Renovación Musical, he showed little interest in the academic notions of his colleagues. Rather, Pro's music, including the excellent Lorca setting *Las siete doncellas* (1940) for mixed chorus, is more concerned with the expressive and practical.

Cuba's leading avant-garde composer and organizer of Grupo de Renovación Musical, Spanish-born José Ardévol (1911–1981) was also a leader in the Cuban Revolution. His choral works were composed toward the end of his career and with notable exceptions, such as the Lorca cantata *Burla de Don Pedro a Caballo* for mixed chorus and orchestra, *Forma-Ballet* for four six-part choruses and orchestra, and *Tres romances antiguos* for mixed chorus, are political in nature.

Argeliers León (1918–1988) combined Afro-Cuban rhythms with twelve-tone techniques in over twenty choral works, including the cantata *Creador del hombre nuevo* for solo voices, chorus, narrator, woodwinds, and percussion.

Julián Orbón (1925–1991), like his teacher Ardévol, was born in Spain. In 1964 he settled in New York. Perhaps the most internationally known of Cuban composers, Orbón received substantial commissions from the Fromm and Kousevitsky Foundations. His music, occasionally incorporating "white" Cuban folk elements, is marked by an awareness of international trends. Choral works include *Crucifixus* (1953) for unaccompanied mixed chorus and *Liturgia de tres días* (1975) for chorus and orchestra.

Tania León (b. 1943), who also moved to New York, is perhaps the most outstanding younger Cuban composer. Of mixed French, Spanish, African, Chinese, and Cuban descent, León creates music that reflects a very broad multicultural perspective, utilizing a wide variety of ethnic, popular, and jazz elements. Works include *De-Orishas* for six-part mixed chorus and *Heart of Ours—A Piece* for male chorus, flute, two piccolos, and four trumpets.

Choral music in the Dominican Republic was vigorously promoted early in the century by José Arredondo (1840–1924), chapelmaster at Santo Domingo, who wrote 135 Masses, 58 litanies, and many other works for the church. The most important mid-century composer was the prominent choral conductor Luis Emilio Mena (1895–1964), who composed several fine works for church and school. Margarita Luna (b. 1921) trained at the Juilliard School, returning in 1977 to a position at the National Conservatory, where she became known as the Nadia Boulanger of the Dominican Republic. Luna's works include *Alleluya* and *Amor secreta*, both for unaccompanied mixed chorus; *Misa quisqueyana* for mixed chorus and organ; the large oratorio *Vigilia eterna* for three soloists, mixed and male chorus, narrator, and orchestra; and two cantatas.

Important Puerto Rican composers include Héctor Campos-Parsi (b. 1922) and Raymond Torres-Santos (b. 1958). Campos-Parsi studied with Copland, Messiaen, and Boulanger, and his style combines neoclassic tendencies with nationalistic, electronic, and avant-garde elements. He has received several international prizes. Of his numerous choral works, *Ave Maria* for unaccompanied mixed chorus can be considered representative. Torres-Santos served as chancellor of the Puerto Rico Conservatory of Music and had a significant impact on music education there during the last years of the twentieth century. Among his choral works is the impressive *Requiem* (1994) for soloists, mixed chorus, and orchestra.

CENTRAL AMERICA AND VENEZUELA

Leading composers of choral music in Costa Rica included José Ignacio Quintón (1881–1925), whose works, including *Luzid fragrante Rosa* for mixed chorus and *Misa de requiem* for mixed chorus and orchestra, were written in an eclectic style influenced by Beethoven, Debussy, and Hindemith; the Italian-trained Julio Fonseca (1895–1950); Julio Mata Oreamuno (b. 1899); Alcides Prado (b. 1900), who composed *Missa de requiem* for three-part chorus, organ, and orchestra; the outstanding music educator Bernal Flores (b. 1937), who developed an atonal style after study at Eastman; and Roberto Siera (b. 1953), whose *Idilio* (1990) for chorus and orchestra effectively recreates the atmosphere of the jungle.

In El Salvador, Domingo Santos (b. 1892) wrote six Requiems for mixed chorus. The Guatemalan Raul Paniagua (b. 1898) lived in New York, taught in Panama, and composed choral music such as *Misa* for soloists, mixed chorus, and orchestra in a nationalistic-impressionistic style. In Honduras, Rafael Coello Ramos (1877–1967) established choir schools and composed many choral works for church and educational use. Italian-trained Nicaraguan conductor Luis Abraham Delgadillo (1887–1962) composed five Masses for mixed chorus. A Panamanian of Afro-American descent, Roque Cordero (b. 1917) composed several choral works, including the dramatic *Cantata para la paz* (Cantata for Peace) for mixed chorus, on texts by Mahatma Gandhi, John F. Kennedy, Martin Luther King, Jr., and Abraham Lincoln. Another composer from Panama, Carlos Efraín Arias Quintero (b. 1903), contributed many pieces for church.

Early in the century the production of church music was of primary importance to Venezuelan composers such as Vidal Calderon (1877–1936) and Juan Vicente Lecuna (1899–1954). Other composers wrote numerous secular choral works in addition to their contributions to church music. Among them are the folklorist Juan Bautista Plaza (1898–1965), who composed the small *Nocturno* and *Soneto*, both for mixed chorus, and the cantata *Campanas de Pascua* for mixed chorus and orchestra; Evencio Castellanos (1915–1984), who composed madrigals and two Masses for unaccompanied mixed chorus, as well as *El tirano Aguirre* (1984) for soloists, mixed chorus, and orchestra; and Antonio Estévez (b. 1917), who composed several madrigals and the large, significant cantata *Florentino, el que cantó con el diablo* (1954) for tenor and bass soloists, mixed choir, and orchestra.

Younger Venezuelan composers proved quite receptive to musical innovations and responded to the popularity of Venezuela's annual choral festivals by writing numerous choral pieces. José Luis Muñoz (b. 1928) and Alfredo del Monaco (b. 1938) incorporated electronic and aleatoric elements into their compositions. Girolamo Arrigo (b. 1930), besides making many choral arrangements of folk songs, composed several highly original works, most favoring a five-voice (SSATB) texture, including *Tre madrigali* (1973) for five voices and *Due epigrami* (1974), both unaccompanied, and the large *La cantata Hurbinek* (1972) for four clarinets, four trombones, four doublebasses, and harmonicas played by the singers.

Alberto Grau (b. 1937) became quite popular at the end of the century. Among his growing catalogue of choral compositions is *Stabat mater* (1997) for unaccompanied eight-part mixed chorus.

ANDEAN COUNTRIES

The most important musical personality in Chile during the first two-thirds of the century was Domingo Santa Cruz Wilson (1899–1987), who formed the Bach Society in 1917. Until its dissolution in 1932, this choir took a leading role in Chilean musical life and introduced audiences to Renaissance polyphony and major works by Bach and other European composers. It also presented pieces by Chileans, including Santa Cruz Wilson's own works, the first being *Te Deum*, Opus 4 (1919). Influenced by Hindemith, Hispanic elements, and the Renaissance and baroque works in the repertory of the Bach Society, Santa Cruz Wilson created music that is highly chromatic and densely contrapuntal. Other choral works include *Cantata de los rios de Chile*, Opus 19 (1941) for chorus and orchestra; *Alabanzas de adviento*, Opus 30 (1950) for children's chorus and organ; and several sets of partsongs, some on his own texts.

Other Chilean composers include the choral conductor Alfonso Letelier-Llona (1912–1994), who wrote *Vitrales de la anunciación* for SSA and four instruments, on text by Paul Claudel, as well as other fine pieces for choir and instruments; Leni Alexander (b. 1924), whose cantata *From Death to Morning* (1958) for baritone, female chorus, and chamber orchestra "handles a difficult medium with finesse and sensibility" (Perle 1960, 517); Gustavo Becerra Schmidt (b. 1925), who wrote the oratorio *La araucana* (1965) for chorus and orchestra on an epic poem about the Aruacanan Indians; and Juan Allende-Blin (b. 1928), who created his own instruments for the multimedia *Open Air and Water Music* for chorus and "organ."

Three important Chilean composers immigrated to the United States: Juan Orrego-Salas (b. 1919), who taught at Indiana University, where he established the Latin American Music Center, Claudio Spies (b. 1925), who taught at Princeton University, and Joaquín Nin-Culmell (b. 1908), who taught at the University of California, Berkeley.

Orrego-Salas studied with Domingo Santa Cruz Wilson, Randall Thompson, and Aaron Copland. As might be expected from a student of Copland, Orrego-Salas's music freely mingles nationalistic and strictly modal elements with serial techniques, all tempered by an innate neoclassicism. The selection of texts in his works is delightfully eclectic, including words by Emily Dickinson and Saint John of the Cross to Pablo Nerudo and Lope de Vega. His ability to successfully combine such poetry with liturgical or biblical texts is obvious in two large works, *Missa in tempore discordiae* (1969) and the oratorio *The Days of God* (1976).

The music of Spies, who studied with Boulanger and Walter Piston, lacks nationalistic tendencies and is much more influenced by progressive trends. His choral works include the unaccompanied mixed choir motet, *In paradisum* (1950); *Verses from the Book of Ruth* (1959) for women's voices and piano; and *Proverbs on Wisdom* (1964) for male voices.

Nin-Culmell's choral music includes *Three Traditional Cuban Songs* (1952) for mixed chorus and *Dedication Mass* (1970) for mixed chorus and organ, composed for the dedication of Saint Mary's Cathedral in San Francisco.

Production of church music was also very important for composers in Colombia. Jesús Bermúdez Silva (1884–1969) wrote several large-scale Masses in a full-blown romantic style. Antonio María Valencia (1902–1952) composed *Requiem* (1943) for mixed chorus and orchestra, among other works. Roberto Pineda-Duque (1910–1977) wrote the important dodecaphonic oratorios *Cristo en el seno de Abraham* and *Piecitos*. There was also a lively interest in classically framed compositions on secular or quasi-sacred texts. Carlos Posada-Amador (b. 1908) composed *Cantata al miedo* (1981) and other such works in a nationalistic-impressionistic style. Blas Emilio Atehortúa (b. 1933) contributed *Cántico delle creature* for double chorus, bass soloist, percussion, tape, and contrabass.

Perhaps the most vital center of choral music in the country was the Universidad de los Andes, Bogota. During the 1970s the founding choral director, Amalia Samper, developed a thriving program with the aid of her teacher, the American conductor Alfred Greenfield. Numerous outstanding folk song arrangements were made for Samper's choir, which effectively showcased various indigenous elements of Colombian music. As an outgrowth of this, composers created original pieces based entirely on the choral style prevalent in the folk song arrangements. An outstanding example is the textless *Toccata* for unaccompanied mixed chorus by Jesús Pinzón.

In Ecuador, nationalistic music was encouraged early in the century by the influential head of the National Conservatory, Domenico Brescia. Following suit, Segundo Moreno (1881–1972) developed a style based on popular and folk elements, exemplified by *Ave Maria* for mixed chorus and strings; *Stabat mater* for mixed chorus and organ; the cantata *La emancipación* (1920) for soprano, tenor, and bass soloists, mixed chorus, and orchestra; and the patriotic *Cuatro marchas triunfales* for mixed chorus and orchestra, including "A Bolivar," "García el grande," "A Maldenado," and "Imbabura." Brescia's

Jesús Pinzón: opening of *Toccata.*

successor at the conservatory, Pedro Traversari (1874–1956), continued this trend with *Himno pentatónico de la raza indígena de la América* (Pentatonic Hymn of the Indian Race) for mixed chorus. Mesías Maiguashca (b. 1938) was outstanding among younger composers acutely aware of international developments. His *A Mouth-Piece* for amplified mixed chorus remains an especially impressive Latin American avant-garde work.

The Bolivian composer Téofilo Vargas (b. 1868) created numerous sacred works while choirmaster at Cochabamba Cathedral, including the Mass *Niño Dios* for choir and orchestra. In Peru, Pablo Chávez Aguilar (1898–1950) was also celebrated for his large church works.

THE RIO PLATE REGION

Constanino Gaito (1878–1945) was an important influence on Argentine music. After study in Italy he became a prominent teacher at the Buenas Aires

Conservatory. Primarily a theatrical composer, he produced only a few choral works, including a large oratorio. But his views on artistic nationalism had a very positive impact on later Argentine composers.

Gaito's student Hector Iglesias Villoud (b. 1913) began studying the indigenous music of northern Argentina and neighboring countries in 1943. As a result he developed an almost purely nationalistic compositional style full of the rhythms and harmonies of his native region. His choral works include *Concierto universitario* (1952) for soprano and baritone soloists, double mixed chorus, clarinet, harp, two guitars, two pianos, and string quartet, and the unaccompanied *Estampas corales* (1956).

The most important Argentine composer of the century was Alberto Ginastera (1916–1983), whose international reputation as a primary representative of Latin American music was eclipsed perhaps only by Heitor Villa-Lobos and Carlos Chávez. His early neoclassic music, of which the popular *Lamentations of Jeremiah* (1946) for unaccompanied chorus and *Psalm 150* (1938) for chorus and orchestra are exemplary, was noted for its lean muscular lines, effortless melding of European and Argentine forms, and vibrant use of native rhythms. With the appearance of his operas *Don Rodrigo* (1964) and *Bomarzo* (1967) his style took a turn toward the avant-garde, incorporating serial and other advanced techniques, with a corresponding enrichment of his harmonic palette. The Passion oratorio, *Turbae ad passionem gregorianam* (1970–74), was a product of the same new creative impulse. Following its premiere by the Philadelphia Orchestra, James Felton of the *Philadelphia Evening Bulletin* commented that "there are moments so intense and virile as to cause a kind of white blindness in the hearer."

Mauricio Kagel (b. 1931) lived and worked in Buenos Aires until 1957, when he moved to Cologne, Germany. Essentially self-taught as a composer, he was influenced by virtually every modernist impulse of the century, from Schoenberg and Cage to the visual and literary directives of surrealism and dadaism. Kagel also made contributions as a filmmaker, often in combination with his work as a composer. As Josef Hausler pointed out (Sadie 1980, 9:766–769), Kagel's earliest works were permeated with experiments, from *Palimsestos* (1950), which plays with "elements of word dissociation and . . . the interplay of different speech patterns," to *Anagrama* (1955–58), in which "the sound of words [is] more important than their sense. The resulting vocal treatment ranges from whispering to shouting by way of a considerable number of abnormal means of utterance." The composer's interest in the dramatic and visual is obvious in the unfinished *Die Frauen* (1962–64), in which female performers are specified for all parts: soloists, chorus, two actors, dancer, and instrumentalists; and the vocally innovative *Hallelujah* (1967–68), later translated into a film of the same name (1969). Hence, the immediate accessibility and old-fashioned feel of *Sankt-Bach-Passion* (1981–85) for soloists, mixed chorus, and orchestra is a surprise. The original text—in which Bach is himself the focal point, being eventually crucified by the obstructions and indifference of his employers—is pure Kagel. Likewise, Kagel uses the numerology of Bach's name to serialize the work's musical elements. Even so, the work is primarily colored by traditional aspects, including a strong sense of tonality.

Lalo Schifrin (b. 1932) studied with Juan Carlos Paz and Olivier Messiaen before moving to the United States in 1958. Internationally acclaimed as a jazz musician and film composer, he also composed several large choral works, including one of the earliest jazz Masses, *Jazz Suite on Mass Texts* (1965); an oratorio, *The Rise and Fall of the Third Reich* (1967); *Rock Requiem* (1969); *Madrigals for the Space Age* (1976); *Cantos Aztecas* (1989) for soloists, chorus, and orchestra; and *Cantionas Argentinas* (1992) for chorus and orchestra.

Other composers include Alberto Williams (1862–1952), considered the father of Argentine musical nationalism, whose works, like those of many other South American composers, freely mix impressionism with native elements; Gilardo Gilardi (1889–1963) and Carlos Guastavino (1914–2000), who wrote many small pieces for unaccompanied chorus; Ariel Ramirez (b. 1921), whose polyrhythmic *Misa criolla* (1964), in which each movement is based on a different Indian folk dance, and Christmas cantata *Navidad nuestra* (1964) are perhaps the best-known pieces of twentieth-century Latin American choral music; the internationally esteemed avant-gardist Mario Davidovsky (b. 1934), whose *Synchronisms No. 4* (1967) for chorus and tape is an important work; and Osvaldo Golijov (b. 1960), who moved to the United States before contributing the riveting *La pasión según San Marco* (2000) for soloists, folk groups, mixed chorus, and orchestra (see chapter 15).

Eduardo Fabini (1882–1950), perhaps the best Uruguayan composer, is remembered for his ballet with chorus and narrator, *Patria vieja*. Alfonso Broqua (1876–1946), a contemporary of Fabini's, helped further the careers of other Latin American composers while living in France. Broqua's best-known works are *Tabaré* (1910) for chorus and orchestra, an early example of the use of Uruguayan folk materials in art music, and *Tres cantos Uruguayos*. Vicente Ascone (1897–1979) also made contributions to the choral repertoire.

Other Uruguayan composers include Guido Santórsola (1904–1994), whose *Concerto for Chorus without Words* for chorus and viola d'amore is an important avant-garde work; Hector A. Tosar Errecart (b. 1923), who produced the impressive *Te Deum* (1960) and other works after studying with Copland, Honegger, and Milhaud; and the important conductor José Serebrier (b. 1938), whose impressive choral compositions include *Vocalise* for wordless chorus and *Partita* for chorus and orchestra.

After studying in Germany, Italy, and France, Alberto Nepomuceno (1886–1920) returned to Brazil opposed to European domination in the arts and determined to promote native Brazilian modes of expression (Tiemstra 1992, 113). He was the first composer to introduce Afro-Brazilian elements into orchestral music, and in addition to several Masses produced *As Uyaras* for soprano, chorus, and orchestra, on text by Mello Morais Filho; *Nonetto* for chorus and orchestra, and other works, many of which had a profound impact on the young Heitor Villa-Lobos (1881–1959), who would become one of the most acclaimed Latin American composers in history.

Villa-Lobos developed a vital, colorful style influenced by his study of Indian music in eastern Brazil, by the Brazilian popular music he learned as an itinerant danceband musician, and by his love of Bach. Bach was, in Villa-Lobos's words, "a universal folkloric source, rich and profound, with all popular sound materials from all countries, intermediary between all peoples. The music of Bach comes from the astral infinite to infiltrate itself in the earth as folk music" (Wright 1996, 6). He lived in Paris from 1923 to 1930, before

Eleazar de Carvalho conducting the New York Philharmonic with the Schola Cantorum at the United Nations General Assembly, 1959. The program included Heitor Villa-Lobos's Suite No. 4 (*Descobrimento do Brasil*) and the finale of Beethoven's Ninth. Courtesy of the New York Philharmonic Archives.

becoming Brazil's director of public music education. Although Villa-Lobos's works often use European formal structures, nationalistic elements always dominate the musical thought. He was a prolific composer, creating more than 150 choral works, almost a third of them sacred. Deservedly famous are *Chôro No. 10* (1925) for chorus and orchestra, in which Brazil's urban and rural characteristics are successfully mingled, the lovely *Mass of Saint Sebastion* (1937) for three- or six-part chorus, Suite No. 4 (*Descobrimento do Brasil*, 1937) for orchestra and chorus, and the cantata *Forest of the Amazon* (1958) for soprano soloist, chorus, and orchestra.

Other choral composers of Villa-Lobos's generation include Francisco Mignone (1897–1980), whose *Cantiga de ninar* (1925) for treble choir, *Cataretê* (1930), several Masses (1962–1968, one each year), and other small pieces present a mixture of impressionism, Italian verismo, and native Brazilian elements; and Camargo Guarnieri (1907–1993), whose sacred works—the little *Ave Maria* and *Misa diligite* (1972)—are overshadowed by numerous attractive secular pieces such as the cantatas *Cantata trágica* (1932) and *Sêca* (1958), both with chamber orchestra, Sinfonia No. 5 (1977) for chorus and orchestra, and his partsongs on pop texts (all used in the film *Rebelião em Vila Rica*): *Perpetua* (1958), *Roda Morena* (1958), *Tim-Tim* (1958), and *Voce diz que vai embora* (1958).

After the death of Villa-Lobos, an important development in the composition of choral music occurred with the formation of the Bahia Group in 1966. Members included Ernst Widmer (b. 1927) and his student Lindembergue Cardoso (1939–1989), both gifted and prolific composers of choral music in a cosmopolitan style incorporating serial and various avant-garde techniques. Cardoso's best-known work is a cantata about grieving women entitled *Procissão das carpideiras* (1969). Additional works include the colorful *Caleidoscopio* (1975), *Chromaphonetikos* (1978), *Minimalisticamixolidicosaxvox* (1988), and numerous sacred works. Widmer produced the unaccompanied *Ceremony after a Fire Raid* (1962), and *Rumo Sol-Espirial* (Direction to the Sun Spiral) for choir, orchestra, prerecorded tape, audience participation, and special instruments developed by his Bahia Group colleague Walter Smetak (1913–1984), in addition to various other secular pieces and many sacred works in Portuguese, English, and Latin.

Other important composers include Gilberto Mendes (b. 1922), who became famous for his avant-garde *Beba Coca-Cola* (1967) for mixed chorus, and other pieces; German-born Bruno Kiefer (b. 1923), whose sympathetic choral settings of Brazilian texts are outstanding; the prolific José Penalva (b. 1924), who wrote several madrigals and various liturgical works in a dramatic nationalistic style; Copland's student Osvaldo Lacerda (b. 1927), the first Brazilian to win a Guggenheim grant, whose numerous choral works include four Masses for various vocal configurations and organ; Ernest Mahle

(b. 1929), also born in Germany, who contributed a large number of liturgical works; Sergio Vasconcellos Correa (b. 1934), who developed music education courses for television and composed many choral works in a popular style; Aylton Escobar (b. 1943), whose numerous works include the internationally popular *Alle Psallite cum luya* for mixed chorus and *Missa Breve on Brazilian Folk Rhythms* for mixed chorus and chamber orchestra; and Ernani Aguiar (b. 1950), whose harmonically direct and rhythmically vital *Salmo 150* (1993) for unaccompanied mixed chorus (also arranged for women's chorus) became an international favorite.

∽ 12

UNITED STATES

At the beginning of the century American choral music was dominated by a few composers in the Second New England School whose music was designed for large metropolitan churches, amateur choral societies, and to a lesser extent collegiate glee clubs. At the end of his career, Edward MacDowell (1860–1908) added six songs collectively entitled *College Songs for Male Voices* (1901), *Summer Wind* (1902) for female chorus, and *Two College Songs* (1902) for female chorus to his lengthy list of partsongs. The prolific Horatio Parker (1863–1919), whose choral masterpiece *Hora novissima* was written in 1893, continued to compose oratorios, cantatas, and partsongs of all kinds, including *Hymnos Andron* (1901), whose rhythms and formal structures derive from Greek poetry; the cantatas *King Gorm the Grim* (1908) and *The Dream of Mary* (1918); *School Songs* (1911–1919); *Seven Greek Pastoral Scenes* (1912) for female choir with two soloists, oboe, harp, and strings; and the oratorio *Morven and the Grail* (1915). While Parker wrote many of his early works for the church, almost all the music he wrote in the new century is secular, more purely diatonic and less adventuresome in nature. Writing in a similar style but showing more interest in uniquely American rhythms, syncopation, and scales, George Whitefield Chadwick (1854–1931) composed the Christmas oratorio *Noël* (1909), among other large works, numerous partsongs (especially for treble chorus), and anthems. Amy Beach (1867–1944), whose first choral work was the impressive Mass in E-flat (1890), produced thereafter a steady stream of beautiful music, including the very attractive Service in A, Opus 63 (1905–06), *The Chambered Nautilus*, Opus 66 (1907), *The Canticle of the Sun*, Opus 123 (1928), and many partsongs, anthems, and other service music. Beach's essentially diatonic style— with heavy doses of augmented sixth chords—remained remarkably consistent throughout her career.

Charles Martin Loeffler (1861–1935) was of German ancestry and trained in Germany, but he came to the United States in 1881 and it was there that he enjoyed a lengthy career as violinist and composer. Although records indicate that Berlin was his birthplace, Loeffler claimed to have been born in Alsace, and his predilection for all things French placed him somewhat outside the Second New England School mainstream. Primarily an instrumental composer, he was also famous for his art songs, many of which were set to French texts. He composed several choral works, some accompanied by rather unusual instrumental ensembles, among them *Psalm 137* (1901) for female chorus, two flutes, violin, harp, and organ (a version with piano accompaniment was published in 1906), and *Poème mystique* (1907) for boys' chorus, mixed chorus, four horns, two oboes, harp, and organ.

The slightly younger Arthur Farwell (1872–1952) and Charles Wakefield Cadman (1881–1946) were both very active in the study of American Indian music. Although their arrangements of American Indian songs were idealized in a European manner, they still proved valuable in bringing the tunes before a wide audience. Both also composed cantatas, anthems, and other choral music. Farwell is particularly important because he was the first American composer in the twentieth century to take an active interest in community music, composing many partsongs, folk song arrangements, and pageants for amateur production. Further, his experiments with polytonality and interest in visual arts anticipated John Cage.

The composers of the Second New England School, as well as Loeffler, Farwell, and Cadman, were either trained in Germany or by teachers with German outlooks, and their music obviously reflects late-nineteenth-century European influences (Beach especially is indebted to Brahms). Yet there is a peculiar attitude in their music, a desire to appear proper and learned, that seems more Victorian than Continental. MacDowell died without knowing of the musical revolution that occurred early in the twentieth century, but Parker, Chadwick, and Beach were quite aware of it, and their reaction was to remain conservative to the end.

Charles Ives (1874–1954), however, also born and bred into the traditions of the Second New England School, did not react to the revolution at all—he created it. In 1945, when most Americans had yet to hear of Ives, Arnold Schoenberg wrote, "There is a great man living in this country—a composer. He has solved the problem of how to preserve one's self and to learn. He responds to negligence by contempt. He is not forced to accept praise or blame. His name is Ives" (Johnson n.d.). Virtually every major composer in the world who reached artistic maturity after World War II was indebted in some way to Ives. Among the most original composers in history, he created unique and easily identifiable music that cannot be stylistically pigeonholed and that remains quintessentially American even while standing somewhat outside the mainstream of American musical thought. He freely appropriated whatever musical elements seemed necessary for his vision at the moment—popular songs, impressionistic chords, hymn tunes, traditional counterpoint, the simultaneous sounds of competing bands in a parade, previously inconceivable rhythmic constructs—and combined them in ingenious ways. Robert Sabin (Jacobs 1963, 371) attempted to describe the inherent power of Ives's music in comments about the important *Three Harvest Home Chorales* (1898–1912) for mixed chorus, brass, and organ: "These three relatively short pieces with their strange vocal lines combining semitones and leaps of a seventh, their free rhythms, their fantastic dissonances and harmonic combinations, are like all of Ives's music—so powerfully expressive that one forgets the idiosyncrasies. There is something almost pagan and pantheistic about them, and one senses the splendor and profusion of nature in these hymns of thankfulness." Robert Shaw (Mussulman 1996, 77) also provided apt commentary in a letter to the Collegiate Chorale just after their first rehearsal of *Three Harvest Home Chorales* in January 1948:

> Well—The Ives *Chorales* are at least *different.* . . . I'm still plenty perplexed by this set of Ives's pieces. . . . It isn't smug music, and no smug choir is ever going to perform it, and no smug audience is ever going to like it.
>
> Actually, the sounds are very exciting. Most of you are so immersed in the struggle for your own lines that you don't get to hear the overall avalanche. And while I can't yet figure the pieces mentally, the sum total is very exciting emotionally. . . . This music is a little like a forest fire, and you have to be willing to go up in smoke to be a part of it.

Ives's outstanding and influential *Psalm 90* (1894–1924) for mixed chorus, organ, and chimes boldly ushered in several concepts—chords built from seconds, serialized rhythm, mirror images—that would eventually become standard twentieth-century vocabulary. The music gradually unfolds over an incessantly repeating C octave in the pedal (a representation of God's ever present unchangeableness), mood, technique, and musical elements changing verse by verse. According to Ives's wife, *Psalm 90* was the only composition with which he was really pleased.

Ives was an exemplary song composer, and some of his best choral pieces are songs designed either for solo voice or unison chorus with piano. Two outstanding examples are *Serenity* (1919) and the brilliantly descriptive *General William Booth Enters into Heaven* (1914). In *Serenity* two verses of John Greenleaf Whittier's text are presented as if in a trance. An undiluted impressionism permeates the piece, its calm incantation-like melody seeming to float over an unhurried ostinato of two repeated whole-tone-flavored chords. Subtle variety is achieved by a single application of hemiola in the accompaniment's otherwise hypnotic rhythm. *General William Booth Enters into Heaven* is completely different. A setting of Vachel Lindsay's famous poem about the founder of the Salvation Army, the choral version retains the bari-

Charles Ives: serialized tone cluster in *Psalm 90*.

tone solo voice to project the narrative while the chorus interjects "Hallelujah, Lord!" and snippets of the gospel song "Are You Washed in the Blood?" as if they were excited congregants at a revival meeting. Rhythms and harmonies are complicated; hymn quotes abound. Ives, obviously acquainted with the highly emotional style of itinerant evangelists, brings everything to a fever pitch before Booth and his ragtag army of converts quietly disappear beyond the clouds. The vocal solo is difficult and the piano writing virtuosic. The work is also very effective in its string orchestra version.

Other significant works include the bitonal *Psalm 67* (1894) for unaccompanied mixed chorus; the cantata *The Celestial Country* (1898–99) for soloists, mixed chorus, string quartet, trumpet, euphonium, timpani, and organ, written in a style indebted to the Second New England School; the exuberant *The Circus Band* (1904) for mixed chorus and orchestra (or piano four-hands); and *Holidays Symphony* (1904–13) and Symphony No. 4 (1910–1916), both of which incorporate very simple choral writing into a remarkably complex orchestral fabric.

THE CONCERT MARKET

American composers in the generation after Ives had the unique good fortune to reach artistic maturity just as two of the century's greatest choral conductors emerged on the scene. Roger Wagner (1914–1992) and Robert Shaw (1916–1999) dominated American choral music from the late forties until their deaths. Neither man was a composer, but each was responsible for the composition or premieres of many new works. Through extensive editions of older music and arrangements of folk songs and spirituals, made either by them or by their colleagues Robert Hunter, Alice Parker, and Salli Terri, Wagner and Shaw made high-quality repertoire easily available to high schools and colleges throughout the country. Further, the Roger Wagner Chorale and the Robert Shaw Chorale provided the inspiration for Gregg Smith, Dale Warland, and others to form similar professional or semiprofessional ensembles, thereby greatly increasing the performance opportunities available to serious American composers.

Several Americans born around the turn of the century started a trend by studying in Paris with the young Nadia Boulanger. Her first students, Walter Piston (1894–1976), Virgil Thomson (1896–1989), Roy Harris (1898–1979), and Aaron Copland (1900–1990), are among the most important American composers of the century. Boulanger's unique gift was to develop in each student a strong individual musical personality with an awareness of nationalistic elements and a solid, though nondoctrinaire (i.e. non-German), approach to form and technique. Possessed of unique ability, energy, and vision, she continued teaching until her death in 1979. Her students comprise a veritable *Who's Who* of American music, including among others Ross Lee Finney, Donald Grantham, Daniel Pinkham, and Robert Xavier Rodríguez.

Walter Piston, in his professorship at Harvard, also influenced numerous important composers, such as Leonard Bernstein and Elliott Carter. The most neoclassic of all American composers, Piston, like his contemporaries, was primarily interested in symphonic and other instrumental forms. His contribution to the choral repertoire is confined to two works: *Carnival Song* (1938) for male chorus and brass, and *A Psalm and Prayer of David* (1958) for mixed chorus, flute, clarinet, bassoon, violin, viola, cello, and doublebass. Both are difficult to perform but powerful in effect. Audience appreciation of *Carnival Song* is immediate since the rhetoric is direct and rousing. *A Psalm and Prayer of David* is less accessible, being hampered somewhat by its fast-slow structure, though thoughtful listeners will find many delights within the intricate contrapuntal fabric.

The basic ingredients of Virgil Thomson's choral music were described by the anonymous author of the centennial catalogue published by the Virgil Thomson Foundation in 1996:

> For a composer who claimed he had no metaphysical beliefs, and was only a "nominal Christian," Thomson wrote a considerable quantity of sacred music from his Harvard days to the neglected *Missa pro defunctis* (1960). This Requiem Mass is defrocked church music, part secular, part sacred, connoting an attitude toward the church devoid of piety and unctuousness. It is apparent also that this music, which runs the gamut from simple arrangements of hymns . . . to choral works like *The Nativity As Sung by the Shepherds* (1967), is conceived as pure theater. The ritual of the liturgy fascinated him, he says, not the theological, philosophical, or mystical ecstasies. This music, like everything else he wrote, is an admixture of all the ingredients of his secular style (it even includes an occasional touch of jazz in the Mass), yet in spite of its diversity it conveys a warm, reverent attitude toward humanity. Thomson may not have been a reverend, but his church music is never irreverent.

His best-known choral work is *Four Southern Folk Hymns* (1937, 1949) for unaccompanied mixed chorus. The oldest of this set, "My Shepherd Will Supply My Need," is standard repertoire in schools and churches throughout the country. Its uncluttered straightforwardness is very attractive, though it seems rather earthbound when compared to the pure, ecstatic rapture of "How Tedious and Tasteless the Hours" and the virtually flawless sense of awe and mystery achieved in "The Morning Star."

Roy Harris was immensely important during the first two-thirds of the century. *Symphony for Voices* (1935) for unaccompanied mixed chorus, *A Whitman Triptych* (1939) for unaccompanied female chorus, Symphony No. 4 (*Folk Song Symphony*, 1940) for chorus and orchestra, and a few other works were considered significant additions to the repertoire when they were written. They evoked national pride through the use of folk music and poetry by Walt Whitman; they were innovative, with occasionally daring harmonies and passages for speech chorus or wordless ostinatos. But these pieces, on the whole, did not wear well. Harris's essential harmonic language, while not functional in the strict tonal sense, was based on pure triads, often coming to repose on second inversion chords. This was altogether anathema to serialists and often disconcerting to more conservative listeners who longed for music whose harmonic secrets could be revealed through traditional bass line analysis. Furthermore, the choral works, as a rule, consisted primarily of homophonic declamation of text and clever contrapuntal twists rather than the long, spun-out melodies found in Harris's symphonies. During the nineties, after decades of relative neglect, recordings of several of his major choral works brought with them the potential of new life in the concert hall. In some cases this possibility was most welcome. Works such as *Freedom's Land* (1941), on text by Archibald MacLeish, and *Three Songs of Democracy* (1941) for soprano and mixed chorus, on texts by Walt Whitman, deserve frequent performance. Others, such as Symphony No. 4 (*Folk Song Symphony*) and various other folk song arrangements for mixed chorus, may have run their course. Still others have a curiously unfinished quality, victims of the composer's willingness to allow first performances in versions that did not represent his final thoughts. This is especially true of Harris's Mass (1948) for male chorus and organ, and of Symphony No. 10 (*Abraham Lincoln Symphony*, 1965) for mixed chorus, brass, percussion, and two pianos. The Mass has a brilliantly realized Sanctus–Benedictus, but the Credo, inadequately notated for expression and dynamics, wanders aimlessly. In Harris's score even the first chord has been tied over from something—but from what? Symphony No. 10, conceived as a kind of concerto for two pianos with chorus and brass accompaniment, effectively borrows material from *Freedom's Land*. In revising it, however, Harris cannibalized the performing materials and did not make a definitive new score, so that any subsequent performance has been problematic at best.

Harris clearly understood the cultural importance of choral music. Circa 1960 he delivered the following remarks at University of California, Los Angeles:

A very large American audience is interested in choruses of all kinds. I have been told that America has more than thirty thousand choruses. I know that choral music keeps many American publishers in business. The choral audience is divided into two divergent publics: ecclesiastical and secular.

The church audience was almost 100 per cent reactionary until quite recently. . . . This is an important audience. There is here, I believe, a large potential for those composers who are not ashamed or afraid to try to capture the larger emotions of mankind in tonal beauty. Certainly the church was a willing and resourceful mother to music for more centuries than not. It has only been since the social-industrial revolution that the church has faltered.

The thousands of choruses sponsored and trained for education are one of the most important resources for the development of a native music. In fact, nature has fashioned the voice as an instrument of man's most undiluted, most honest emotions . . . an instrument far beyond the cunning of man to create. These multitudes of voices are one of our nation's most precious legacies. We could work miracles with them. This audience is the most personally interested audience in America . . . because it is comprised of the parents, relatives, and friends of American youth.

But let me again emphasize that the vast choral audience of America has not yet been developed, either in perspective, quality, or magnitude; it is a potential beyond our wildest dreams. (Strimple 1982, 17)

Harris took his own advice only in a limited way. Besides the Mass there are three pieces of functional sacred music: *Alleluia* (1943), an Easter motet for mixed chorus, brass (or strings), and organ; *Mi Chomocho* (1946) for tenor, mixed chorus, and organ, in Hebrew; and *Psalm 150* (1957) for unaccompanied mixed chorus. He showed a more substantial interest in educational music, composing a number of patriotic choruses and folk song arrangements, all within reach of high school performers, and several versions of *Freedom's Land* (for unaccompanied mixed chorus; female or male voices with optional piano; baritone soloist, mixed chorus, and orchestra; and male chorus and band).

Aaron Copland wrote relatively little choral music, and the quality is uneven. The very early *Four Motets* (1921) for unaccompanied mixed chorus is a student work that, in spite of its workmanlike craftsmanship, provides absolutely no clues to the composer's budding genius or unique mature personality. *An Immorality* (1925) for soprano soloist, treble chorus, and piano is an impressive early effort marked by the invigorating rhythms and edgy diatonic harmonies that would become typical of Copland's style. In the same vein, the Spanish folk song arrangement *Las agachadas* (1942) for mixed chorus deserves more frequent performances. Copland's two choruses on texts by Ira Gershwin—*Song of the Guerrillas* for baritone soloist, male chorus, and piano, and *The Younger Generation* for mixed chorus and piano, both written in 1943 for the film *The North Star*—are virtually unknown. The popular choral arrangements of his *Old American Songs* (1950, 1952) for chorus and orchestra (or piano), including the famous "Ching-a-Ring Chaw," "Zion's Walls," "The Little Horses," and "At the River," are not his, but are rather the work of Irving Fine and Glenn Koponen, who labored with Copland's approval. *Canticle of Freedom* (1955) for chorus and orchestra is not one of his happiest creations. The clever and rousing choral excerpts from the opera *The Tender Land* (1954), "Stomp Your Foot" and "The Promise of Living," while often performed, are also not indicative of his best work.

In contrast, Copland's *Lark* (1938) for unaccompanied mixed chorus and baritone soloist, on a brilliant text by Genevieve Taggard, and the cantata *In the Beginning* (1947) for mixed chorus with alto soloist, on text from Genesis chapters 1 and 2, are exceptional compositions. As Beethoven's *Choral Fantasy* anticipates his Ninth Symphony, so *Lark* anticipates *In the Beginning*; only in this case the earlier piece may be the stronger. *Lark* presents a bright vision of America's future by combining typically open sonorities, the swaggering confidence of bright, parallel triads, and jazzy rhythms, which at one point become so exuberantly complicated that the piece threatens to explode. *In the Beginning* is much more extended. Better known than *Lark*, it uses many of the same devices, reining in the rhythmic complexities somewhat and adding the dimension of massed vertical sonorities. It also utilizes a brief connecting ritornello, slightly varied with each appearance, to count off the succeeding days of creation, sometimes with purposefully misplaced word accents. Like *Lark*, *In the Beginning* is a showcase vehicle for the soloist. Structurally, however, it presents the conductor with severe problems in pacing. The structural and emotional culmination occurs, properly, at the creation of man in God's image, at which point the music builds to an exciting and satisfying conclusion. But Copland pulls everything back, starts afresh with the parallel creation narrative of man being formed from dust (Genesis chapter 2), and proceeds, rather leisurely, to a massive ending.

Howard Hanson (1896–1981) differed from most of his contemporaries in that he was an avowed romantic, which colored not only his harmonic language but also his approach to form. As the first president of Eastman School of Music, he influenced several generations of composers. His music is notable for expressive breadth and harmonic richness, touched with occasional impressionistic colorings. A great American symphonist, Hanson also composed choral works that were very popular through the second third of the century, especially *The Lament for Beowulf* (1925) for chorus and orchestra, *The Cherubic Hymn* (1950) for chorus and orchestra, and the Whitman cantatas: *Drum Taps* (1935) for baritone, chorus, and orchestra, and *Song of Democracy* (1957) for soloists, chorus, and orchestra. These pieces later declined in prestige, only to be rediscovered during the nineties by a young and eager audience. Other substantial works include the exquisite anthem *How Excellent Thy Name* (1952) for female or mixed chorus and organ, and *The Mystic Trumpeter* (1970) for speaker, chorus, and orchestra. Less successful is the late *A Sea Symphony* (1977) for chorus and orchestra.

During his tenure at Princeton, Roger Sessions (1896–1985) deliberately developed a reputation as the most difficult American composer of his generation. His writings, especially *The Musical Experience of Composer, Performer, Listener* (1950, revised 1962), provide valuable insight into the need for loyalty to one's aesthetic convictions, but occasionally confuse difficulty

Aaron Copland: from *Lark*.

with profundity. His compositions, however, contain many authentic high points well worth the immense effort required to master them. Sessions's most accessible choral work, *Turn, O Libertad* (1944) for mixed chorus and piano four-hands, is a wonderful setting of Walt Whitman's text. The kinetic energy of the instrumental writing is balanced by a more controlled but gradually released excitement in the chorus. The D major ending is simultaneously inevitable and surprising. Sessions's cantata, *When Lilacs Last in the Dooryard Bloom'd* (1964–70) for soprano, alto, and bass soloists, mixed chorus, and orchestra, written in his most lavish, expressionistic twelve-tone style, is considered by some commentators to be a pinnacle of American composition. Andrew Porter (1981) even called it "a piece many would put into Columbia's hand if she could hold but a single score representing this country's highest musical achievement." Other works include Sessions's Mass (1955) for unison chorus and organ, and *Three Choruses on Biblical Texts* (1971–72) for mixed chorus and orchestra.

Henry Cowell (1897–1965) stands with Ives and John Cage as one of America's greatest musical innovators. He was the first composer to systematize the use of chord clusters and other modern techniques such as free dissonant counterpoint, polychords, and counter rhythms. During the thirties, however, he became interested in composing music that could be used for teaching purposes and easily performed by amateurs, so much of his choral music was composed in a direct, rather conservative style, not particularly indicative of the innovations on which his reputation rests. Sometimes, though, Cowell's innovations occurred so naturally within the musical context that no one noticed (or at least no one was shocked). In reviewing his cantata . . . *if He please* (1955) for mixed chorus and orchestra, which is rife with chord clusters, *The New York Times* noted that it "starts with a Handelian flourish and follows with harmonies with an archaic flavor (though a flavor definitely dictated by contemporary taste buds)" (Dox 1989, 5–6). Other representative works include *The Morning Cometh* (1937) for unaccompanied mixed chorus, *Fire and Ice* (1943) for male chorus and band, *Do, Do, Do, Is C, C, C* (1948) for children's chorus and piano, *To a White Birch* (1950) for mixed chorus, *With Choirs Divine* (1952) for treble chorus and optional piano, *Lines from the Dead Sea Scrolls* (1956) for male chorus and orchestra, the oratorio *The Creator* (1963) for soprano, alto, tenor, and bass soloists, mixed chorus, and orchestra, and *Zapados sonidos* (1964) for eight-part mixed chorus and tap dancer.

Until the 1990s the choral music of Randall Thompson (1899–1984) was probably performed more frequently than any other American composer. Virtually everyone who sang in a high school or college choir in the United States after 1936 performed some portion of Thompson's work. The elements of his diatonic style are well known: expressively supple melodies, idiomatic vocal writing, occasional fleeting dissonance resulting from natural clashes in the linear counterpoint, pronounced sensitivity to words, frequent modal harmonies, well-timed climaxes.

Two of Thompson's most famous compositions, *Alleluia* (1940) for unaccompanied mixed chorus and *The Last Words of David* (1949) for mixed chorus and orchestra (or piano), were commissioned by Serge Koussivitsky to begin Tanglewood Music Festival concerts. *Alleluia* begins with a harmonic sequence so typically American—close position second inversion tonic chords, alternating with first inversion supertonic sevenths—that one commentator dubbed it the "Paumanok pattern" after a 1938 Whitman setting by Normand Lockwood (Norton 1991, 55–56). Thereafter, the piece is Thompson's own: an exercise in pure musical form, cascading melismas and striding bass octaves building to an inexorable climax and denouement. *The Last Words of David*, obviously the work of the same composer, is completely different in form and substance but similar in effect. The dramatic opening, quite unlike the previous piece, dissolves into marvelous modal modulations and almost whispered, chantlike "Alleluias."

Thompson's best-known large works are *The Peaceable Kingdom* (1936), a cantata for unaccompanied mixed chorus on text from Isaiah, whose individual movements are often employed separately in concerts and worship; *The Testament of Freedom* (1943) for male chorus and orchestra or piano, on text by Thomas Jefferson, which was arranged for band in 1960 and for mixed chorus in 1976; and *Frostiana* (1959), a cycle of seven partsongs (five for mixed chorus, one for male chorus, one for female chorus) with piano or orchestra on texts by Robert Frost. Other important works from his large catalogue include the startlingly descriptive *Tarantella* (1937) for male chorus and piano, on text by Hilaire Belloc, *The Best of Rooms* (1963) for unaccompanied mixed chorus, on text by Robert Herrick, and *The Passion According to Saint Luke* (1964–65) for soloists, mixed chorus, and orchestra.

Ross Lee Finney (1906–1998) was among the country's most influential composer-teachers. He studied with Boulanger, Berg, and Sessions, and counted among his own students several Pulitzer Prize winners, including George Crumb, Roger Reynolds, and Leslie Bassett. Finney's early pieces reflect an interest in colonial American hymnody; after 1950 his music became purely dodecaphonic, some later works also incorporating electronic tape. His twelve-tone vocabulary is tonally conceived but not at all like the melodic tone-row techniques of Martin or Blacher. Rather, Finney's music is designed, like Berg's, so that tonal elements inherent in the rows are revealed through common Schoenbergian manipulations. For example, the middle section of the little cantata *Edge of Shadow* (1959) for mixed chorus and percussion, on text by Archibald MacLeish, uses the original form of the row, vertically two pitches at a time, starting on D in the tenor and bass voices, and on A in the soprano and alto. The resulting tonal implications are obvious. Among his other choral works are the early *Pilgrim Psalms* (1945) for mixed chorus and orchestra (or organ); the masterful and deservedly popular *Spherical Madrigals* (1947) for unaccompanied mixed chorus, in which the cover art—a canon notated in a circle—can be sung as the first madrigal; and a collection of three large cantatas, collectively titled *Earthrise: A Trilogy Concerned with the Human Dilemma: Still Are New Worlds* (1962) for baritone, mixed chorus, orchestra, and tape, *The Martyr's Elegy* (1967) for soprano, mixed cho-

Ross Lee Finney: twelve-tone construction in "Love Song" from *Edge of Shadow*.

rus, and orchestra, and *Earthrise* (1978) for solo voices, mixed chorus, and orchestra.

Normand Lockwood (b. 1906), another student of Boulanger, composed in an accessible tonal style partially characterized by the frequent use of preexisting tunes. While he set liturgical texts and texts by W. H. Auden, John Donne, and Dylan Thomas, Lockwood had a real affinity for American poetry. He realized the need to create music that could be performed by amateurs of all ages. The most significant of his approximately eighty choral works are *Out of the Cradle Endlessly Rocking* (1938) for unaccompanied mixed chorus; *The Birth of Moses* (1947) for treble chorus, flute, and piano; *The Closing Doxology* (1952) for mixed chorus and band; *Prairie* (1952) for mixed chorus and orchestra; *Choreographic Cantata* (1968) for mixed chorus and organ; *Mass for Children and Orchestra* (1976); *Donne's Last Sermon* (1978) for mixed chorus and organ; *A Child's Christmas in Wales* (1982) for children's chorus and piano; *Thought of Him I Love* (1982) for children's chorus and orchestra; and several oratorios.

Louise Talma (1906–1996), yet another student of Boulanger, eventually incorporated twelve-tone techniques into her otherwise neoclassic style. Her best-known choral work is the charming cycle *Let's Touch the Sky* (1952) for mixed chorus, flute, oboe, and clarinet. Other worthwhile pieces include *In principio erat verbum* (1939) for mixed chorus and organ, *A Time to Remember* (1966–67) for mixed chorus and orchestra, and *Celebration* (1976–77) for female chorus and chamber orchestra.

Halsey Stevens (1908–1989) was, like Roger Sessions and George Antheil, a student of Ernest Bloch. He spent virtually all of his professional career at the University of Southern California. A distinguished composer of instrumental music and biographer of Bartók, Stevens also understood the choral idiom as few other American composers have, an understanding he was only to happy to share with his students Donald Grantham, Morten Lauridsen, Robert Xavier Rodríguez, Williametta Spencer, and others. His numerous small works for unaccompanied mixed chorus, including *Go, Lovely Rose* (1942), *Like As the Culver* (1954), *Lady As Thy Fair Swan* (1966), and *An Epitaph for Sara and Roland Cotton* (1972), established Stevens as a great master of the partsong. His church music, though less well known, is equally effective, especially the extraordinary anthems for mixed chorus and organ: *The Way of Jehovah* (1963), in which a constant eighth-note pulse fluctuates irregularly between 3/4 and 6/8, and *In te, Domine, speravi* (1964), whose elastic rhythms and changing meters make it a favorite examination piece among conducting professors.

A convinced neoclassicist, Stevens moved easily from homophonic declamation of text, as in *Go, Lovely Rose*, to rather strict contrapuntal writing, as in the double canons found in *Campion Suite* (1967) for unaccompanied mixed chorus and *An Epitaph for Sara and Roland Cotton*. At times both techniques appear simultaneously, as in *Lady As Thy Fair Swan*, which is a mirror canon built from root-position triads moving in contrary motion. In addition to *Campion Suite*, the most successful of his larger works include *The Ballad of William Sycamore* (1955) for mixed chorus and orchestra, the popular *Magnificat* (1962) for soprano, trumpet, mixed chorus, and strings (or organ), and *Songs from the Paiute* (1976) for tenor, mixed chorus, four flutes, and timpani.

By century's end Elliott Carter (b. 1908), also a Boulanger pupil, had become one of the most respected, even revered, composers in American history. Festivals of his music were held in the United States and abroad, and he basked in the well-deserved adulation. Early in his career, after returning from Paris where he conducted a madrigal group, Carter produced some of the best choral music of the United States. The two Emily Dickinson madrigals,

Heart Not So Heavy As Mine (1938) and *Musicians Wrestle Everywhere* (1945), both for mixed chorus, became well known among better American choirs. The return of opening material, wistfully separated by the poem's closing lines in *Heart Not So Heavy As Mine*, and the few measures of rapid, closely followed canons, which vividly describe the cloud of celestial musicians in *Musicians Wrestle Everywhere*, are enough to demonstrate Carter's genius. The witty *The Defense of Corinth* (1941) for male chorus and piano four-hands, and the sparkling, effervescent *The Harmony of Morning* (1944) for female chorus and chamber orchestra, were widely studied if not widely performed. His last choral work, *Emblems* for male chorus and piano, was written in 1947. Thereafter, as his aesthetic moved away from neoclassicism, Carter abandoned all vocal writing, finding it inadequate for his expressive needs, and eventually returned to composition for solo voice and instruments in 1975. Interviewed by the *Los Angeles Times* (15 November 1998), he was asked what it meant to be a twentieth-century composer. In his honest and articulate response, Carter said that, for him, it had to do with reflecting current life. He recalled the unhurried and uncluttered days of his childhood in New York City, and the societal and technological havoc caused by two world wars: "By the time of the Second World War neoclassicism didn't express to me the tension and worry and stress of the time; I wanted to write something more adult and significant." These comments perhaps reveal more about lingering, almost subliminal, feelings of cultural inadequacy among America's artistic and intellectual elite than they do about Carter's music. It is quite normal for a composer's style to develop—even change radically—over the course of his or her life. But it is inconceivable that a composer from any other country would refer to this maturation as "more adult and significant." Maturity is a naturally occurring process. Being "more adult" is something adolescents aspire to. From the earliest Colonial period, American intellectuals have aspired to cultural equality with their European forebears, disdaining most things homegrown or imported from non-European sources. At the end of the twentieth century many American music schools still promoted Eurocentric art in an environment where students were encouraged to seek egocentric "significance" rather than to be of service to one's society and its culture (see Nettl 1995). This may explain why many serious American composers have had neither the time nor the inclination to compose music for children or other amateur ensembles.

Elie Siegmeister (1909–1991) represented a considerably different point of view from Carter. Founder of the vocal ensemble American Ballad Singers, which promoted the performance of American folk music during World War II, Siegmeister developed an often dissonant style, influenced by jazz and highly evocative of American folk and popular music. His many folk song arrangements, partsongs, and cantatas, including *In Our Time* (1965) for chorus and orchestra, *I Have a Dream* (1967) for baritone, narrator, chorus, and orchestra, and *Cantata for FDR* (1981) for baritone, chorus, and wind ensemble, reflect his belief that "Art with a capital A is a menace: music must relate to life, not be imposed on it" (Hitchcock and Sadie 1986, 4:224).

Samuel Barber (1910–1981), though not prolific, was among the most frequently performed American composers of the century, and one of only a handful—including Bernstein, Copland, and Gershwin—well known to foreign audiences. His music, which retains a late-nineteenth-century harmonic foundation, is known for lyricism and dramatic sweep. Like Copland's, Barber's choral works are of uneven quality. The three movements of *Reincarnations* (1937–40) for unaccompanied mixed chorus are wonderfully wrought studies of the Irish character. The difficult and complex *Prayers of Kierkegaard* (1954) for soprano, mixed chorus, and orchestra (later arranged for organ) combines the best of Barber's lyrical and dramatic qualities to good effect. *Agnus Dei* (1967), his curious adaptation for mixed chorus of the famous *Adagio for Strings*, is not well suited to voices but is frequently performed anyway. The two unaccompanied choruses of Opus 42 (1968), *Twelfth Night* and *To Be Sung on the Water*, are brilliantly contrasted as a set but are almost never performed together. *Twelfth Night*, in fact, is so brooding as to make it almost inappropriate for the Christmas season. Barber's last choral work was the unfortunate cantata *The Lovers* (1971) for baritone soloist, mixed chorus, and orchestra, on texts by Pablo Neruda. The composer badly miscalculated the capacity of audiences to respond positively to overtly erotic poetry, and his muse, then very much in decline, could not compensate for it.

William Schuman (1910–1992), a student of Roy Harris, taught at Sarah Lawrence College and Juilliard before becoming the first president of Lincoln Center. Among the most honored American composers, Schuman, like many of his contemporaries, was an accomplished symphonist. Yet he made numerous and lasting contributions to the choral repertoire. He received the first Pulitzer Prize in music for *A Free Song* (Secular Cantata No. 2, 1943) for mixed chorus and orchestra (or two pianos), on text by Walt Whitman. In two masterful movements the composer paints, in bold colors, the tragic face of war's destruction and the exuberant optimism of freedom.

In 1958 Schuman's continued affinity for Walt Whitman resulted in *Carols of Death* for unaccompanied mixed chorus, a great masterpiece of American choral music. The three movements ("The Last Invocation," "The Unknown Region," "To All, To Each") are often performed separately as partsongs, though the effect of the set as a whole is extremely powerful. The harsh harmonies of the declaimed text in the opening chorus serve as prelude to the others. The second movement's harmonically static rhythmic canons—an undiluted musical force—drive relentlessly into the release and resignation of the last movement's serene parallel sixths.

Among Schuman's other works are *Prologue* (1939) for chorus and orchestra and *This Is Our Time* (Secular Cantata No. 1, 1940) for chorus and orchestra, both on texts by Genevieve Taggard; the witty *Five Rounds on Famous Words* (Nos. 1–4, 1956; No. 5, 1969) and *Mail Order Madrigals* (1971), both for unaccompanied mixed chorus; *Concerto on Old English Rounds* (1974) for solo viola, female chorus, and orchestra; *Casey at the Bat* (1976) for soprano, baritone, mixed chorus, and orchestra, a cantata culled from his opera, *The Mighty Casey*; another Whitman cycle, *Perceptions* (1982) for unaccompanied mixed chorus; and the cantata *On Freedom's Ground* (1985) for baritone, mixed chorus, and orchestra, on text by Richard Wilbur. A practical result of Schuman's affiliation with Sarah Lawrence College was the composition of pieces that can be performed either by female or mixed chorus, among them *Prelude* (1939), with soprano solo; *Holiday Song* (1942), with piano; *Requiescat* (1942), with piano; and *The Lord Has a Child* (1956), with piano. He also composed several other choral works for various ensemble configurations.

Cecil Effinger (1911–1990) invented and patented the music typewriter, but he was also known as a skillful composer, at home in church and school as well as the concert hall. His compact, easily recognizable tonal constructions, frequently utilizing parallel thirds, never sound sparse. In addition to anthems and partsongs he composed several large works, such as the oratorio *The Christmas Story According to Saint Luke* (1953) for soloists, mixed chorus, and organ (or organ and chamber orchestra), and *Paul of Tarsus: Three Episodes in the Life of Paul the Apostle* (1968) for baritone, mixed chorus, strings, and organ. Effinger's most famous work is *Four Pastorales* (1962) for mixed chorus and oboe, which is among the century's more satisfying small choral suites.

Alan Hovhaness (1911–2000) was exceptionally prolific. His style varies considerably, from the neo-Renaissance of his early *Missa brevis* (1935) for mixed chorus, organ, and strings, to the more boldly experimental *Magnificat* (1958) for soloists, mixed chorus, and orchestra (among the first works to utilize choral aleatoric passages), to the intriguing cantata *And God Created Great Whales* (1970) for mixed chorus and orchestra, which includes taped recordings of whale vocalizations. Many other works, such as the rather lengthy *Wind Drum* (1962) for unison chorus and chamber orchestra, are noteworthy for their basis in Armenian chant and other Middle Eastern modes. Most of Hovhaness's music is on sacred texts, and he composed many anthems and other functional works for the church, including the folk Mass *The Way of Jesus* (1974) for mixed chorus, congregation (or unison chorus), three guitars, and orchestra, and *A Simple Mass* (1975) for soloists, mixed chorus, and organ. A remark made by Hovhaness in which he explained his artistic creed was reprinted for his obituary in the *Los Angeles Times*, 23 June

2000: "My purpose is to create music, not for snobs but for all people—music which is beautiful and healing, to attempt what old Chinese painters called spirit resonance in melody and sound."

Though Gian Carlo Menotti (b. 1911) was born in Italy, his mother brought him to the United States in 1928 so that he could attend the new Curtis Institute of Music in Philadelphia. There he established what was to become a deep, lifelong friendship with Samuel Barber and served notice that he was an opera composer-librettist to be reckoned with. Although influenced by earlier radicals—Debussy, Mussorgsky, Stravinsky—Menotti created music that is stylistically very conservative. His first substantial choral piece was the popular quasi-dramatic fable for mixed chorus and instruments, *The Unicorn, the Gorgon, and the Manticore* (1956). Comprised of twelve madrigals and a march, interspersed with instrumental interludes, it established his credentials as a choral composer of finesse and charm. Next came the dramatic cantata *The Death of the Bishop of Brindisi* (1963) for mezzo and bass soloists, children's and mixed choruses, and orchestra, which effectively brought together the finest aspects of Menotti's lyrical and dramatic gifts. These were followed by several rather large-scale works, including the cantatas *Landscapes and Remembrances* (1976) for four soloists, mixed chorus, and orchestra, *A Song of Hope* (1980) for baritone, mixed chorus, and orchestra, *Muero porque no muero* (1982) for soprano, chorus, and orchestra, on text by Saint Teresa of Avila, *For the Death of Orpheus* (1990) for tenor, mixed chorus, and orchestra, *Llama de amor viva* (1991) for baritone, chorus, and orchestra, on text by Saint John of the Cross, and *Jacob's Prayer* (1997) for mixed chorus and orchestra; two works for boys' chorus, *The Trial of the Gypsy* (1978), with piano, and *Miracles* (1979), with orchestra; two Masses, *Missa O Pulchritudo in honorem Sacratissimi Cordis Jesus* (1979) for four soloists, mixed chorus, and orchestra, and *Mass for the Contemporary English Liturgy* (1985) for congregation, optional mixed chorus, and organ; the six-part unaccompanied motet *Moans, Groans, Cries and Sighs* (1981), written for the King's Singers; and the male chorus *My Christmas* (1987), with flute, oboe, clarinet, horn, harp, and doublebass.

Norman Dello Joio (b. 1913) created an easily identifiable style by fusing romantic melodies with tonal, though often dissonant, harmonies and energetic, extroverted rhythms. A prolific composer of choral music, he created works further characterized by a natural expressivity, equally at home with humor or pathos, and a sensitivity to text. He had an affinity for American poets. His most important and enduring works are large settings of poems by Walt Whitman, including *The Mystic Trumpeter* (1943) for mixed chorus and horn, *A Jubilant Song* (1945) for mixed chorus (or female chorus) and piano, *Song of the Open Road* (1952) for mixed chorus, trumpet, and piano, *Four Songs of Walt Whitman* (1966) for baritone, mixed chorus, and orchestra, *Proud Music of the Storm* (1967) for mixed chorus, organ, and brass, *Years of the Modern* (1968) for mixed chorus, brass, and organ (or piano), and the "modern masque" *As of a Dream* (1978) for soloists, narrator, mixed chorus, dancers, and orchestra. Dello Joio also composed several sacred works, among them *A Psalm of David* (1950) for mixed chorus, strings, brass, and percussion, *Prayers of Cardinal Newman* (1960) for mixed chorus and organ, Mass (1969) for mixed chorus, brass, and organ, *Psalm of Peace* (1972) for mixed chorus, trumpet, horn, and organ, *Mass in Honor of the Eucharist* (1975) for cantor, congregation, mixed chorus, brass, and organ, and *Mass in Honor of the Blessed Virgin Mary* (1984) for cantor, congregation, mixed chorus, organ, and optional brass.

The premature death of Irving Fine (1914–1962) was an unfortunate loss to American music. His choral works, often witty and always refined and elegant, are usually organized into suites. These include two suites from *Alice in Wonderland*, the first (1942) for mixed chorus and piano (including one movement each for men's and women's voices, orchestrated 1949) and the second (1953) for treble chorus and piano; *The Choral New Yorker* (1944) for soprano, alto, and baritone soloists, mixed chorus (including one movement each for men's and women's voices), and piano; and *The Hour Glass Suite* (1949) for unaccompanied mixed chorus.

Gail Kubik (1914–1984) composed several partsongs and effective folk song arrangements in addition to the cantatas *In Praise of Johnny Appleseed* (1938) for bass soloist, mixed chorus, and orchestra, on text by Vachel Lindsay, *Litany and Prayer* (1943–45) for male chorus, brass, and percussion, *A Christmas Set* (1968) for mixed chorus and chamber orchestra, *A Record of Our Time* (1970) for narrator, chorus, and orchestra, and *Magic, Magic, Magic!* (1976) for mixed chorus and chamber orchestra—all in a jazzy, often witty, neoclassic style.

Vincent Persichetti (1915–1987) composed many works for different ensemble configurations. Exceptionally facile, he composed in a variety of styles that he loosely categorized as either "graceful" or "gritty" (Rubin 1980, 12). Generally, his choral works combine diatonic melodies with pandiatonic or polytonal harmonies. Persichetti's particular affinity for the poetry of e. e. cummings asserted itself in *Two Cummings Choruses* (1948) for two-part chorus and piano, *Two Cummings Choruses* (1950) for four-part treble chorus, *Spring Cantata* (1963) for four-part treble chorus and piano, *Four Cummings Choruses* (1964) for two-part chorus and piano, and *Glad and Very* (1974) for two-part chorus. The two-part configuration, which can be performed by any combination of voices, is as close as Persichetti came to writing for children. One of his best-known pieces is his Mass (1960) for unaccompanied mixed chorus, which contains a wonderfully poignant and often performed Agnus Dei. Among his other works are *Hymns and Responses for the Church Year*

(1950) for mixed chorus, *Te Deum* (1963) for mixed chorus and orchestra, *Winter Cantata* (1964) for four-part treble chorus, flute, and marimba, *Celebrations* (1966) for mixed chorus and band, *The Creation* (1969) for soprano, alto, tenor, and baritone soloists, mixed chorus, and orchestra, and *Flower Songs* (Cantata No. 6, 1983) for mixed chorus and strings.

David Diamond (b. 1915) contributed several secular pieces to the choral repertoire as well as significant works for Jewish worship. In addition to part-songs and other small works his catalogue includes *A Song for Shabuoth* (1935) for children's chorus and piano; the sacred service *Mizmor L'David* (1951) for tenor, mixed chorus, and organ; *Two Anthems* (1955) and *Prayer for Peace* (1960), both for unaccompanied mixed chorus; *This Sacred Ground* (1962) for baritone, children's chorus, mixed chorus, and orchestra, on text by Abraham Lincoln; the choral symphony *To Music* (1967) for tenor and bass soloists, mixed chorus, and orchestra; and *A Secular Cantata* (1976) for tenor, baritone, mixed chorus, and chamber orchestra, on text by James Agee.

Lou Harrison (b. 1917) established himself as a multicultural icon long before the term *multicultural* was in vogue. Possessed of an unquenchable musical curiosity, Harrison created his own instruments, explored the sonic worlds of widely divergent cultures, upheld the idea of just intonation, and joyfully composed music that utilized whatever resources happened to strike his fancy. His almost childlike delight in creating sounds is exemplified in a performance instruction for *A Joyous Procession and a Solemn Procession* (1962) for chorus ("high and low voices"), two trombones, and percussion. In this piece a gong is to be hung with Chinese wind chimes and other small bells so that, in the composer's words, "the whole affair jangles happily with every step" (Brunner 1992). Harrison's best-known composition is *Mass to Saint Anthony* (1954) for double unison chorus, trumpet, harp, and strings. Each movement is composed in a different mode, the vocal lines created from what the composer called "rhythmitized chant" with "just a tiny bit of Indian folk flavor" (Brunner 1992). Other works include *Four Strict Songs* (1951–55) for male chorus (preferably eight baritones), two trombones, piano, harp, strings, and percussion; *Nova odo* (1961–62) for male chorus, speech chorus, and orchestra, on text by the composer in English and Esperanto; *Easter Cantata* (1966) for alto soloist, mixed chorus, two trumpets, two trombones, glockenspiel, chimes, harp, and strings; and *La koro sutro* (1997) for mixed chorus and gamelan.

Leonard Bernstein (1918–1990) was among the most important musicians of the century, respected and admired for multiple talents as composer, conductor, pianist, and author. His influence extended from musical theater, to the championing of American works abroad, to probing and insightful performances of history's great masterworks. Hampered by a frenetic conducting schedule and constantly frustrated by negative critical response to his serious compositions, Bernstein nevertheless produced some wonderful choral music. The early *Hashkivenu* (1945) for tenor, mixed chorus, and organ already contained the operative elements of his mature style: warm, inviting harmonies with a slightly modern edge, dramatic sweep, arching lyricism, and jazzy rhythms.

In 1955 Bernstein composed incidental music for Jean Anouilh's play about Joan of Arc, *The Lark*, which included a set of three French choruses with drum and a set of five Latin choruses with bells. Years later the composer took Robert Shaw's suggestions, omitting two French choruses, expanding the Latin choruses, and placing the movements in a different order, thereby creating *Missa brevis* (1984). Still, Bernstein's collection of choruses for *The Lark* is a better piece. The writing, by turns charming and forceful, is spontaneous in the earlier work. The more rustic musical idioms of the French choruses also contrast effectively with the purposefully learned and arcane sound of the Latin. This contrast, however, does not make sense in *Missa brevis*. Further, Bernstein's reworking of Claude Le Jeune's *Revecy venir du printemps* (the opening French chorus) seems incongruous when fitted out with liturgical words and tagged on to the end of the Mass.

Bernstein's Symphony No. 3 (*Kaddish*, 1962; revised 1977) for speaker, soprano, boys' and mixed choruses, and orchestra is a problematic masterpiece. The work's success in performance relies to a great extent on the restraint of the narrator, who takes up several issues with God. This lengthy monologue—in reality the composer coming to grips with his own father—is occasionally way over the top, even by Bernstein's standards. The narrator's daunting task is to lift this text from the cellar of bad soap opera and infuse it with the same genuine emotion and dignity found in the music. The specters that haunted Bernstein's musical personality are everywhere in this piece: jazz, Bulgarian rhythms, an anguished homage to Mahler (which in itself may represent a child's efforts to please a stern and rigid father). Among numerous delights are clearly defined and subtly realized forms, exceptionally complex contrapuntal elements, application of various serial procedures, and a couple of memorable tunes. But there is never relief from the strain of misunderstanding and separation: even in the final exultant chorus of reconciliation one feels that the struggle for understanding has exacted a heavy toll. Incidentally, the primary melodic interval of this chorus, a descending fourth followed by a descending second, is also found in *Chichester Psalms* (1965) for boy soprano, mixed chorus, and orchestra (strings, brass, and percussion; later arranged for organ, harp, and percussion), and certain other religiously inspired compositions. Jack Gottlieb (1980, 287) referred to the frequent recurrence of this motive in Bernstein's music as a "symbol of Faith," pointing out that the motive plays a prominent role in the liturgical chant for the High Holidays.

Chichester Psalms was the result of a sabbatical leave Bernstein took following a New York Philharmonic season that included an extremely intense and somewhat controversial festival of avant-garde music. Afterward, Bernstein wrote a report of his sabbatical for *The New York Times* in which he attempted to describe, in verse, his pondering of avant-garde procedures and his thought process before and during composition of the psalms. He obviously thought well of his poem, reprinting it in two of his books, *The Infinite Variety of Music* and *Findings*. A charming, clever collection of rhymed couplets, it not only coined a remarkable, and exasperated, word for unbridled musical expression ("Physicomathematomusicology") but also left no doubt as to Bernstein's musical allegiance: toward the end, he acknowledged that his new piece was "Certain to sicken a stout John Cager / With its tonics and triads in B-flat major" (Bernstein 1966, 144–145). A reaffirmation of Bernstein's belief in the undying power of tonality, *Chichester Psalms* was destined to become one of the century's most popular pieces. Critics may have gone after its marriage of grating dissonance with saccharine sweetness, reliance on Bulgarian rhythms, and especially the quasi-pop feel of the last movement; but since these are all vital, if unfortunately obvious, aspects of Bernstein's personality, such observations are like pointing out a leopard's spots. The criticisms, therefore, have the same hollow ring as complaints about the formal structure of Gershwin's *Rhapsody in Blue*, or the naïve presence of *Ländlers* in Bruckner's symphonies. It is perhaps more profitable to observe the mastery with which Bernstein resolves his dissonant introductions, first into exuberant dance, lastly into serene gratefulness; the telescoping structure of the second movement, which juxtaposes assurance with tribulation; and the relationship and evolution of thematic ideas.

Bernstein's other works include arrangements of the Hebrew folk songs *Simchu na* (1947) for chorus and piano, and *Reena* (1947) for chorus and orchestra; *Yigdal* (1950) for mixed chorus and piano; *Two Harvard Choruses* (1957), "Dedication" and "Lonely Men of Harvard"; *Warm-Up* (1971) for unaccompanied mixed chorus, later incorporated into the theatrical Mass; the original unpublished version of *A Little Norton Lecture* (1973) for male chorus, later rewritten for soloists and incorporated into *Songfest*; and *Olympic Hymn* (1981) for mixed chorus and orchestra.

Others born prior to 1920 include Wallingford Riegger (1885–1961), whose few choral works include the invigorating and satisfying *Who Can Revoke?* (1948) for mixed chorus and piano, as well as *A Shakespeare Sonnet* (1956) for baritone, mixed chorus (without tenors), and chamber orchestra (or piano); Leroy Robertson (1896–1971), who composed *Oratorio from the Book of Mormon* (1955) for soloists, mixed chorus, and orchestra, as well as other choral pieces; George Gershwin (1898–1937), who contributed two charming madrigals, *The Jolly Tar and the Milkmaid* (1937) for soprano and tenor soloists, mixed chorus, and piano, and *Sing of Spring* (1937) for mixed chorus, both written for the film *A Damsel in Distress*; George Antheil (1900–1959), another musical experimenter, who is remembered for *Eight Fragments from Shelley* (1951) for mixed chorus and piano, and the cantata *Cabeza de Vaca* (1955–56) for mixed chorus and piano, orchestrated by Ernest Gold in 1959; Elinor Remick Warren (1900–1991), who wrote many anthems and partsongs in a neoromantic style, as well as several larger works, including *The Harp Weaver* (1933) for baritone, harp, female chorus, and orchestra; Ruth Crawford Seeger (1901–1953), a pioneering female composer who contributed *Three Chants* (1930) for soprano and alto soloists, female chorus (No. 1 and No. 3), and mixed chorus (No. 2); the individualistic theatrical composer Marc Blitzstein (1905–1964), who wrote *Cantatina* (1930) for female chorus and piano, *The Airborne Symphony* (1946) for narrator, tenor and bass soloists, male chorus, and orchestra, and *This Is a Garden* (1957) for chorus and orchestra, in a style heavily influenced by American popular song forms; Paul Creston (1906–1985), born Giuseppe Guttoveggio, who composed a significant amount of functional music for the Roman Catholic liturgy, as well as the Christmas oratorio *Isaiah's Vision* (1962) for chorus and orchestra, and the cantata *Calamus* (1972) for male chorus, brass, and percussion, on text by Walt Whitman; Radie Britain (1908–1994), whose love of her native Texas is obvious in her atmospheric partsongs, the larger *Brothers in the Clouds* (1964) for male chorus and orchestra (later arranged for mixed chorus and piano), and *Nisan* (1961) for female chorus, piano, and strings (later arranged for mixed chorus and piano); Jean Berger (b. 1909), an emigrant choral conductor from Alsace-Lorraine, whose large catalogue contains two works which have remained standard repertoire, the exquisite little psalm setting *The Eyes of All Wait upon Thee* (1959) and the larger *Brazilian Psalm* (1941), both for mixed chorus; Edwin Gerschefski (1909–1992), who was fond of composing choral settings of newspaper articles and letters, such as *Border Raid* (1966) for mixed chorus and piano and *Letter from BMI* (1981) for mixed chorus and chamber orchestra; Vladimir Ussachevsky (1911–1990), whose "Creation Prologue" (1960–61), the opening movement of his unfinished oratorio, *Creation*, is probably the earliest work written for chorus and electronic tape; Vivian Fine (b. 1913), who composed several choral pieces for women's voices, including *The Passionate Shepherd to His Love and Her Reply* (1938) for unaccompanied women's chorus, *Psalm 13* (1953) for baritone, treble chorus, and piano (or organ), *Sounds of the Nightingale* (1971) for soprano, women's chorus, and nine instruments, and *Oda a las ranas* (1980) for women's chorus, flute, oboe, cello, and percussion, on text by Pablo Neruda; Gordon Binkerd (b. 1916), who composed approximately one hundred small choral pieces, mostly on secular texts, in a tonal style colored by vivid chromaticisms and contrapuntal textures; and Jacob Avshalomov (b. 1919), who made significant contributions to the repertoire with, in addition to a number of unaccompanied pieces, several works for chorus and concertante instruments, such as *Tom O'Bedlam* (1951) for mixed chorus, oboe, tabor, and jingles, *I Saw a Stranger Yestre'en* (1968) for mixed chorus and violin, and *Songs of the Goliards* (1992–98) for mixed chorus and cello.

John La Montaine (b. 1920) studied with Howard Hanson and Nadia Boulanger. An avowed neoromantic, like Hanson, La Montaine possessed a natural lyricism and melodic gifts which found a natural outlet in choral music. Works include *Mass of Nature* (1966) for mixed chorus and orchestra, *The Nine Lessons of Christmas* (1975) for narrator, soloists, mixed chorus, and orchestra, *The Lessons of Advent* (1983) for double chorus, narrator, trumpet, handbells, harp, oboe, guitar, percussion, and organ, *The Marshes of Glynn* (1984) for baritone, mixed chorus, and orchestra, and several small pieces.

Born in Berlin, Lukas Foss (b. 1922) came to the United States in 1937. Although he studied in Paris, the bulk of his training took place at the Curtis Institute of Music, the Berkshire Music Institute, and Yale (with Hindemith). His music falls into two broad stylistic categories: the unabashed tonality of the early neoclassic works written before 1956 and the frank experimentalism of the music composed after 1960. Foss wrote no choral music in the intervening transitional period. His early pieces are characterized by many bold contrapuntal devices, occasional jazz influences, and an almost Brahmsian harmonic luxuriance. The best examples include *Behold I Build an House* (1950) for mixed chorus and piano (or organ); the cantata *A Parable of Death* (1952) for narrator, tenor soloist, mixed chorus, and orchestra, originally for strings and organ but later revised for full orchestra, on text by Rainer Maria Rilke; and *Psalms* (1955–56) for mixed chorus and two pianos or orchestra (the orchestration retains two pianos for the more soloistic passages). Later works, including *Fragments of Archilochos* (1965) for countertenor, two speakers (male and female), four chamber choirs, mixed chorus (ad lib), mandolin, guitar, and percussion (three players), are experimental in notation as well as musical syntax. Other works include the large cantata *The Prairie* (1944) for four soloists, mixed chorus, and orchestra, on text by Carl Sandburg, *Adon olom* (1951) for cantor, mixed chorus, and organ, *American Cantata* (1976) for tenor, chorus, and orchestra, and *De profundis* (1982) for unaccompanied mixed chorus.

Peter Mennin (1923–1983) developed a highly contrapuntal neoclassic style characterized by a rather international outlook and an almost incessant nervous energy. One of several important American symphonists, he composed his best choral works in large symphonic forms, namely *The Christmas*

Story (1949) for soprano and tenor soloists, mixed chorus, strings, brass quartet, and timpani, and Symphony No. 4 (*The Cycle*, 1949) for mixed chorus and orchestra. Two of his later works require children's voices: the large descriptive cantata *Cantata de virtute* ("The Pied Piper of Hamelin," 1969) for narrator, tenor, and bass soloists, children's and mixed choruses, and orchestra, and *Reflections of Emily* (1978) for boys' chorus, harp, piano, and percussion, on texts by Emily Dickinson. As in Bernstein's *Chichester Psalms* (which requests boy trebles) and *Kaddish*, the children must be professional-level singers.

Daniel Pinkham (b. 1923), a student of Copland and Boulanger, among others, demonstrated an affinity for choral writing very early in his career with his *Wedding Cantata* (1956) for mixed chorus and instruments; the perennially popular *Christmas Cantata* (*Sinfonia sacra*, 1957) for mixed chorus and brass; and the particularly original and innovative *Easter Cantata* (1957) for mixed chorus, brass, and percussion. His style, marked by highly concentrated means of expression, active rhythms, occasional antique influences, and vibrant, usually tonal, harmonies, is recognizable even in his more austerely dissonant works such as the poignantly brief *Requiem* (1963) for mixed chorus, brass, and doublebass (or organ). However, Pinkham's works with electronic tape, of which the mixed chorus *In the Beginning of Creation* (1970) is an example, do not always bear the same personal stamp. Among his numerous other works are *Three Motets* (1947, revised 1975) for treble chorus and organ or piano, *Festival Magnificat and Nunc dimittis* for mixed chorus with optional organ or brass, *Daniel in the Lion's Den* (1973) for tenor, baritone, and bass soloists, narrator, mixed chorus, two pianos, percussion, and tape, and several psalm motets for unaccompanied mixed chorus.

Ned Rorem (b. 1923), the country's foremost composer of art songs, also produced a sizeable quantity of choral music. His acuity in writing for a single voice is apparent in two large works: *A Sermon on Miracles* (1947) for soloist, unison chorus, and strings, and *Proper for the Votive Mass of the Holy Spirit* (1966) for unison chorus and organ. He composed a number of unaccompanied pieces on secular and sacred texts, of which the most popular, and perhaps the best, is a cycle of seven partsongs for mixed chorus called *From an Unknown Past* (1951). Written in Rorem's most pleasant diatonic style, these partsongs are by turns cheerful, rueful, and wizened. His works for mixed chorus and organ, of which the large anthem *Truth in the Night Season* (1966) is representative, tend to be more harmonically adventuresome. On nineteenth-century American texts, *An American Oratorio* (1983) for tenor, mixed chorus, and orchestra is thought by some to be among the best American works of the century's second half.

Duke Ellington (1899–1974) belonged to the older generation but did not produce any choral music until 1965, when he startled the country with his

Sacred Concert: In the Beginning God for two vocal soloists, mixed chorus, jazz orchestra, and dancer, which was premiered in San Francisco's Grace Episcopal Cathedral. After performing it in churches and synagogues throughout the United States and Europe, Ellington composed two additional concerts (1968, 1973). In notes written for the *Second Sacred Concert* (and published as liner notes for the subsequent recording), Ellington (1974) stated, "These concerts are not the traditional Mass jazzed up. . . . I think of myself as a messenger boy, one who tries to bring messages to people, not people who have never heard of God, but those who were more or less raised with the guidance of the Church." For these concerts Ellington used his band, professional jazz vocalists for soloists, and local church or school choirs. Having limited rehearsal time, no experience in choral writing, and no knowledge of the quality of the local choirs, he relegated the choral involvement to brief, mostly unison statements. Soloists were required not only to sing but also to recite texts over the band's rhythmic pulse—a rather unsettling precursor to late-twentieth-century rap style. In the best jazz tradition, performance order of the movements could be changed, and portions originally written for one Sacred Concert could be inserted into the others. No definitive score was published during Ellington's lifetime. In 1993 the Danish choral composer and conductor John Høybye collaborated with the jazz composer Peder Pedersen in producing a composite Sacred Concert comprised of selected material from all three. The Høybye-Pedersen version, published in 1997, makes the chorus an equal partner with the band by rewriting the choral parts altogether, creating real mixed-choir textures and substantially increasing the chorus's involvement. In 2001 G. Schirmer published virtually all the music of the three Sacred Concerts, in Ellington's original versions, as *The Best of the Sacred Concerts*.

Dave Brubeck (b. 1920), another jazz legend, did not begin composing for chorus until after Ellington's successful experiment. For the premiere of his first oratorio, *The Light in the Wilderness* (1967) for baritone, mixed chorus, optional jazz combo, organ, and orchestra, he provided program notes that were published in advance (Brubeck 1968, 31). In response to questions he faced regarding his motivations for writing an oratorio, he wrote, "I am a product of Judaic-Christian thinking. Without the complications of theological doctrine I wanted to understand what I had inherited in this world—both problems and answers—from that cultural heritage. This composition is, I suppose, one man's attempt to distill in his own thought and to express in his own way the essence of Jesus's teaching." In an interview about the same time (Coleman 1968, 28), Brubeck added that "some people might say that most jazz musicians are not equipped to write serious music. They said it about George Gershwin; and yet when *Porgy and Bess*, written thirty years ago, opened in Italy last season, it was hailed as a triumph. . . . Communication is communication. When music has something to say, and it is said honestly, people will listen." *The Light in the Wilderness* features improvisation and other jazz techniques, and juxtaposes polyrhythms, aleatoric passages, and twelve-tone melodies with sections in a more traditional church style. When it premiered it provided a stylistic breakthrough in American music. While some had considered Ellington's Sacred Concerts a publicity gimmick, most found them to be expressions of spiritual convictions too personal to be widely performed. *The Light in the Wilderness*, however, which is much more accessible to amateur performers, was published immediately after its premiere. This made it available for wide dissemination and relieved Brubeck of any continuing supervisorial role in subsequent performances.

Brubeck followed it with a steady stream of choral pieces, including the cantata *The Gates of Justice* (1970) for tenor and baritone soloists, mixed chorus, optional jazz combo, and organ (or brass); the Christmas pageant *La fiesta de la posada* (1976) for soprano, tenor, baritone, and bass soloists, mixed chorus, unison children's chorus, two guitars, two trumpets, double-bass, and percussion (ensemble can be extended with two violins and additional percussion); the Mass *To Hope! A Celebration* (1980) for priest (tenor), female and male cantors, mixed chorus, congregation (or unison chorus), handbells, celesta, and organ; the oratorio *Voice of the Holy Spirit* (1985) for baritone, mixed chorus, and orchestra; the large *Pange Lingua Variations* (1989) for mixed chorus, strings, brass, and percussion; and several smaller works.

Gunther Schuller (b. 1925) combined jazz and various other composition techniques, much as Ervín Schulhoff did, to create an amalgamated style called "Third Stream." His choral works include *Sacred Cantata* (1966) for mixed chorus and chamber orchestra, on text from Psalm 98; the positively unsettling oratorio about Cabeza de Vaca's adventures in the New World, *The Power within Us* (1971) for baritone, speaker, mixed chorus, and orchestra; and *Poems of Time and Eternity* (1972) for mixed chorus and nine instruments, on text by Emily Dickinson. The text of *The Power within Us* is a letter to the King of Spain, in which Cabeza de Vaca relates his shipwreck, rescue, and kindly treatment by the Indians, and the subsequent treachery of the Spanish in ruthlessly subjugating them.

Kirke Mechem (b. 1925) composed more than 150 choral works for all ensemble configurations, including children. His music is diatonic and has been praised for its "singing lines [and] imaginative and varied use of rhythm and texture for expressive ends" (Guelker-Cone 1987). It is further characterized by attention to detail, awareness of practical matters, and a flexibility that easily accommodates occasional fleeting dissonance. Representative works include *Make a Joyful Noise unto the Lord* (1951) for unaccompanied mixed chorus; the popular *The Seven Joys of Christmas* (1964) for unaccompanied mixed chorus, or with piano or harp (orchestra version 1974); the powerful cantata *Songs of the Slave* (1985–93) for soprano, bass-baritone, mixed chorus, and orchestra; and *Barter* (1994) for treble chorus, trumpet (or oboe), and piano four-hands.

Viennese-born Robert Starer (1924–2001) and Karl Kohn (b. 1926) escaped the Holocaust as teenagers and eventually settled in the United States. Both have produced formidable choral works.

Starer studied in Jerusalem for some time before coming to New York, and his essentially diatonic musical vocabulary—harmonically direct and melodically expressive—is seasoned with an occasional hint of Jewish modality. Works include the choral-orchestral cantatas *Ariel, Visions of Isaiah* (1959) and *Joseph and His Brothers* (1966); *Two Songs from Honey and Salt* (1964) for mixed chorus and brass quartet; Sabbath Evening Service (1967) for four soloists, mixed choir, and organ; the unaccompanied partsong cycle *On the Nature of Things* (1968); and the cantata *Images of Man* (1973) for four soloists, mixed choir, flute, horn, cello, harp, and percussion.

Kohn served in the United States Army during the war, returning to study at Harvard with Edward Ballentine, Irving Fine, Walter Piston, and Randall Thompson. His music is particularly notable for its broad variety of aural colors and uncompromising virtuosity. Usually chromatic and harmonically complex, its innate lyricism is accented by an almost unrelenting kinetic energy. Still, there is obvious concern to avoid unnecessary vocal difficulties, and in some works, such as the impressive and beautiful anthem *Also the Sons* (1973) for four soloists, mixed chorus, and organ, the vocal writing is downright easy. Other works include *Three Descants from Ecclesiastes* (1957) for mixed chorus and brass (or piano), *Three Golliard Songs* (1958) for male chorus, *Madrigal* (1966) for mixed chorus and piano concertante, and *What Heaven Confers* (1981) for mixed chorus and vibraphone (two players).

Earle Brown (b. 1926), an established leader of the American avant-garde, contributed *Small Pieces for Large Chorus* (1973), which requires two conductors. Gregg Smith (1980), for whom the work was composed, noted that "[Brown] has been especially instrumental in the development of graphic notation, open forms, and performer choice structures. *Small Pieces* utilizes these principles and as such is an important work in new choral music."

Dominick Argento (b. 1927) was inspired by the human voice. Like other successful opera composers, he developed a tonal style that is eclectic enough to incorporate diverse elements as needed for expressive effect without diluting his own forceful personality. He is particularly adept at large forms. Important choral works include the oratorio *Jonah and the Whale* (1973) for tenor, baritone, narrator, mixed chorus, and chamber ensemble, the song cycle *I Hate and I Love* (1981) for mixed chorus and percussion, and *Te*

Deum (*Verba Domini cum verbis populi*, 1990) for mixed chorus and orchestra, on various texts.

Richard Willis (1929–1997) composed music driven by neobaroque contrapuntal impulses, enriched tonal harmonies, and neoclassic formal concepts. He served as composer-in-residence at Baylor University for many years and was widely admired for his distinguished instrumental music. Several of his choral works, while relatively obscure, are also excellent. *This Day* (1995) for chorus and wind orchestra is particularly impressive. Emotional exuberance, idiomatic writing, warm and inviting harmonies, handsome proportions, and masterful instrumentation combine to make it one of the century's most attractive pieces for this ensemble combination. Other works include his evocative *The Parched Land* (1964) for unaccompanied mixed chorus, which won the Sigma Alpha Iota American Music Award; *Five Elizabethan Songs* (1966) for mixed chorus, flute, clarinet, violin, cello, and harp, which incorporates serial techniques; the effective, miniature *Two Madrigals* (1967) for unaccompanied mixed chorus; and the little psalm cantata *Give unto the Lord* (1968) for mixed chorus and piano, which balances its dramatic opening and dancelike midsection with a rapturously quiet ending.

In addition to several small choral works, Ron Nelson (b. 1929) composed the popular cantata *The Christmas Story* (1958) for narrator, baritone soloist, mixed chorus, organ, brass, and percussion. Written in a bright pandiatonic style, it is somewhat unusual in that it ends by relating the Slaughter of the Innocents. Nelson also collaborated with Harvard theologian Samuel Miller to create the impressive oratorio *What Is Man?* (1964) for narrator, soprano, and baritone soloists, mixed chorus, and orchestra (or organ, brass, and percussion; or piano and organ), and the uncommonly powerful anthem *God Bring Thy Sword* (1967) for mixed chorus, organ, and optional percussion.

Marvin David Levy (b. 1932) was best known as an opera composer, so it is only natural that his best choral music is dramatic and somewhat theatrical in nature. His major works, expressively atonal, are the Christmas oratorio *For the Time Being* (1959) for soloists, chorus, and orchestra, on text by W. H. Auden, and the oratorio *Masada* (1973) for narrator, tenor soloist, chorus, and orchestra. He also composed a Sacred Service (1964) for New York's Park Avenue Synagogue, and several smaller choral works.

Dale Jergenson (b. 1935), a pupil of Roy Harris, contributed numerous works for a variety of vocal and instrumental configurations. His style is broadly eclectic, often veering from the open, tonal sonorities of his teacher into the realms of pop and jazz. While his catalogue is full of functional compositions for church and school, his most successful pieces are larger concert works, notably the brilliant *Gloria* (1993) for double mixed chorus and *The Lament of Job* (1993) for unaccompanied mixed chorus. The latter effectively explores a number of avant-garde techniques with an eye to performance by good high school choirs as well as more advanced ensembles.

Frederick Lesemann (b. 1936) was virtually unknown among choral conductors. His large cantatas *The Garden of Proserpine* (1969) for mixed chorus and orchestra, and *Water in the Boat* (1987–89) for mixed chorus and chamber ensemble were well received by audiences and critics but did not generate the kind of collateral excitement necessary to ensure repeated performances. However, *Two Motets* (1996) for unaccompanied mixed chorus, on texts by Rabindranath Tagore and from the *Isha Upanishad*, carried the potential for widespread recognition. These pieces are not liturgical or even religious in a strict sense, but the title is appropriate considering the profoundly sacred nature of the texts. Like the rest of Lesemann's music, they are carefully constructed and delight in contrapuntal devices (for instance, the first motet begins with a canon at the fifth, in inversion). Conceptually, they hearken back to Johannes Ockeghem, Josquin Des Prez, Bach (the two motets constitute a Prelude and Double Fugue), and Stravinsky. But unlike Stravinsky and other composers of "objective" sacred music (Zoltán Jeney, for example—see chapter 5), Lesemann, aligning himself more with Des Prez, was not afraid of emotional impact. Further, the individual vocal lines are so well considered that resulting complex harmonic structures are not particularly difficult for singers to manage. Masterfully crafted and serene, *Two Motets* is a worthy successor to William Schuman's *Carols of Death*.

Phillip Glass (b. 1937), the world's best-known minimalist and a prodigious composer of operas, showed little interest in choral music as such. Nearing the close of the century his only choral work remained *Itaipu* (1989) for chorus and orchestra. In 1999, however, he produced Symphony No. 5 (*Requiem, Bardo, and Nirmanakaya*) for five soloists, children's and mixed choruses, and orchestra, for the Salzburg Festival. It was an immediate hit with audience, performers, and critics alike. The imposing twelve-movement structure is conceived as a bridge between past and future. The texts, compiled from Christian, Buddhist, Hindu, and various native sources, somehow create a feeling of unity. Mark Swed, who was present at the premiere, noted that Glass's style "functions less through the dialectic of contrasts, development, and reconciliation (as is the standard Western symphonic form) than through a powerful accumulation of ideas" (*Los Angeles Times*, 31 August 1999).

John Harbison (b. 1938) gained valuable experience while serving as music director of Boston's Cantata Singers from 1969 to 1973. He is a leader in the generation of composers for whom serialism is but one of several available techniques, and his music is noted for structural and contrapuntal clarity. Representative choral works include *Five Songs of Experience* (1974) for four soloists, mixed chorus, string quartet, and percussion, on text by William Blake, and the Pulitzer Prize–winning *The Flight into Egypt* (1986) for soprano and baritone soloists, mixed chorus, and chamber orchestra (two oboes, English horn, three trombones, strings, and chamber organ). Both works are highly evocative and quite effective. *Five Songs of Experience* calls for two percussionists and requires chorus members to play various African and Caribbean percussion instruments. Though Harbison had always wanted to set the poetry of William Blake, it wasn't until after conducting the Cantata Singers and Ensemble that he realized his idea would benefit most from a choral approach. In his own words, from the score's introductory note, "The calls for regeneration and reconciliation in the poems required a welcome effort to get back to beginnings and to be as inclusive, as little time-bound, as possible. The apparent simplicity, transparency, and subdued rhetoric of the poems suggested the creation of apparently-simple rhythms and harmonies." Harbison's hyphenated description, "apparently-simple," is correct. While the rhythms are indeed direct and essentially uncomplicated, the harmonies are another matter, since empty fourths and fifths occur with simultaneous half-step transpositions. A feeling of incantation is definitely achieved in the last movement, in which four different rhythmic motives are simultaneously and incessantly repeated under the rather static, homophonic chanting of chorus and soloists. *The Flight into Egypt* begins with an instrumental fugue and is, throughout, more consistently contrapuntal than the earlier work. There are three large choral sections. The first is a fugue based on the opening subject's inversion. The second is based on the first four notes of the choral fugue subject, and while more declamatory, it is still quite contrapuntal. The final chorus is a fugato derived from the opening subject. Although the tonal language is similarly modern, the choral writing in this piece is easier than in *Five Songs of Experience*, perhaps because singers can grasp the logical horizontal lines more quickly than single notes within a dissonant chord.

John Harbison: beginning of the second movement of *Five Songs of Experience*.

Paul Chihara (b. 1938) studied with Nadia Boulanger and Ernst Pepping, and composed extensively for film, theater, and ballet. While the influence of Pepping is present in the structures and tonal centers of his early *Magnificat* (1965) for female chorus and *Psalm 90* (1965) for mixed chorus, the harmonic and textural coloration also reflect his interest in Japanese music. Works from the seventies, such as *Ave Maria—Scarborough Fair* (1971) for male chorus and *Missa Carminum* (1975) for mixed chorus, combine liturgical elements with traditional folk songs. A more recent work is *Minidoka [Reveries of . . .]* (1995) for mixed chorus and two percussionists, in which Chihara uses Japanese folk songs and portions of the Japanese and American national anthems to evoke memories of his family's forced relocation in 1942 to Minidoka, Idaho, a United States government internment camp for Japanese Americans.

John Corigliano (b. 1938) composed several pieces for unaccompanied mixed chorus, and *What I Expected Was* (1962) for mixed chorus, brass, and percussion (later arranged for mixed chorus and piano), on text by Stephan Spender, in an appealing eclectic style. His earliest choral composition, the sensitive and well-crafted *Fern Hill* (1961) for mixed chorus, strings, harp, and piano (later arranged for mezzo, mixed chorus, and piano), on text by Dylan Thomas, remains his most popular work.

During the twentieth century virtually all compositional trends found proponents in the United States, including important experimenters, the first minimalists, a few neoromantics, several serialists, composers influenced by folk music, jazz, or electronic sounds, and many neoclassicists. However, with the possible exception of Alan Hovhaness, Morten Lauridsen (b. 1943) remains the only American composer in history who can be called a mystic. While it is impossible to predict the lasting impact of music that speaks with such immediacy, it is still fair to say that Lauridsen's probing, serene work contains an illusive and indefinable ingredient which leaves the impression that all the questions have been answered. In his earliest anthems and chamber works Lauridsen's language was often quite dissonant and occasionally atonal. Later he became profoundly influenced by Gregorian chant, not only in the primacy of pure melody but also in details of melodic contour and the way chant is married to the text. Neoclassic ideas inherited from his teacher, Halsey Stevens, are found in his contrapuntal procedures, formal schemes, and orchestration. In Lauridsen's later works, melodies have two easily identifiable characteristics: they are built from motives that can be isolated for contrapuntal development, and the inherent harmonic implications are limited to only two or three chords. Of these, at least one will be a pure triad and one will include the interval of a second or fourth. The contrapuntal interplay of melodic elements combined with the constant realignment of a few vertical sonorities—a Renaissance technique—results in the undulating and glistening textures for which Lauridsen's music is justly famous. The earlier works, *Mid-*

winter Songs (1980, orchestrated 1990) and *Madrigali: Six "Firesongs" on Italian Renaissance Poems* (1987) for unaccompanied mixed chorus, project a more complex and somewhat sharper harmonic edge than the later *Les chansons des roses* (1993), on French texts by Rainer Maria Rilke; the Requiem-like cantata *Lux aeterna* (1997) for mixed chorus and orchestra (or organ); or the Latin motets *O magnum mysterium* (1994), *Ave Maria* (1997), and *Ubi caritas* (1999), all for unaccompanied mixed chorus. Four of the five pieces that make up *Les chansons des roses* are for unaccompanied mixed chorus, but the set's finale, the incredibly popular "Dirait on," includes piano. This was composed sometime before the rest of the cycle as a loving, albeit intricately contrapuntal, tribute to the French *chanson populaire*. From 1993 Lauridsen's music rapidly increased in international popularity, and by century's end he had eclipsed Randall Thompson as the most frequently performed American choral composer.

Judith Lang Zaimont (b. 1945) gained wide recognition with her delightful madrigal set, *Sunny Airs and Sober* (1977) for unaccompanied mixed chorus, and with *The Chase* (1972), a breathtaking tour de force for solo piano set against mostly homophonic or unison choral writing. As her style evolved, the essential harmonic language—tonal, relying on triads with added notes, often in first or second inversion—absorbed additional chromatic coloration, rhythms became freer, and the innate lyricism grew more expressively angular. Later pieces include *Parable: A Tale of Abram and Isaac* (1986) for soprano, tenor, and baritone soloists, mixed chorus, and organ (or strings and harpsichord), the large cantata *Voices* (1996) for soprano and alto soloists, mixed chorus, brass, percussion, and synthesizers, and the atmospheric *Meditations at the Time of the New Year* (1997) for mixed chorus, glockenspiel, and tubular bells. Her largest and perhaps most significant work is the relatively early Sacred Service (1976, revised 1980) for baritone soloist, mixed chorus, and orchestra. Harmonically warm and rhythmically vital, Sacred Service is an example of direct expression at its best. It manages to maintain an overall stylistic consistency even as individual movements pay conceptual tribute to previous composers and styles: Mendelssohn, Handel, late-nineteenth-century oratorio choruses, jazz, and so on. More substantive than Milhaud's *Service sacré*, or any service by other Israeli or Jewish American composers, Zaimont's Sacred Service may be the most important since those of Ernest Bloch and Paul Ben-Haim.

Steven Stucky (b. 1949) studied with Richard Willis and Karel Husa, and in 1981 he published an award-winning biography of Witold Lutoslawski. From these men he learned the importance of atmospheric tonal coloration and supple formal structures. His music is always subtly refined, even in climactic moments of grand gesture. Good examples include the very early anthem *Ah, Holy Jesus* (1970) for mixed chorus and organ, and *Drop, Drop*

Slow Tears (1979) for unaccompanied mixed chorus. *Ah, Holy Jesus*, one of several anthems composed while Stucky was still an undergraduate, clearly demonstrates the kind of church music that can be created by talented composers who are not, in Roy Harris's words, "ashamed or afraid to try to capture the larger emotions of mankind in tonal beauty" (Strimple 1982). A setting of a Sarum plainchant, the smooth-as-silk modulations are particularly impressive. *Drop, Drop Slow Tears* is based on the famous anthem by Orlando Gibbons. It begins with free rhythmic repetitions of the word "drop" and rich modern sonorities created by intervals gradually expanding outward from a unison. The original tune eventually materializes, and Gibbons's harmonized version is given in full, punctuated by poignant interjections at cadences. Other works include the little madrigal *Spring and Fall* (1973) and *Cradle Songs* (1997), both for unaccompanied mixed chorus.

Frank Ferko (b. 1950), William Hawley (b. 1950), Libby Larson (b. 1950), Robert Kyr (b. 1952), Matthew Harris (b. 1956), Brent Michael Davids (b. 1959), and Eric Whitacre (b. 1970) are typical of the diversity found among the younger generation of American composers.

Frank Ferko's *Hildegard Motets* (1996) for unaccompanied mixed chorus and large *Stabat mater* (1997–98) for soprano and mixed chorus follow William Schuman's lead to extend and refine the concepts of bold harmony and lyric-dramatic presentation of text. The juxtaposition of the liturgical text, biblical passages, and other widely varied sources in *Stabat mater* is particularly intriguing.

William Hawley's retro style seems to be based on rules for the preparation and release of dissonance as found in the old Allen Irvine McHose theory book, *The Contrapuntal Harmonic Technique of the Eighteenth Century*, a perfect example being Hawley's popular Italian madrigal *Vita de la mia vita* (1995), which was written for Chanticleer. At times he achieves an impressionistic effect by leaving suspensions unresolved, as in *Two Motets* (1993) for double mixed chorus, on secular Latin texts. He also occasionally constructs seventh, ninth, or eleventh chords in such a way as to create faux clusters, as in *Alleluia, Dies santificatus* (1996) for mixed chorus and harp.

Libby Larson emerged during the twentieth century as an articulate spokesperson for the arts and a composer whose accessible style exudes charm, wit, and grace. Furthermore, she paid some attention to children, contributing the substantial *Song-Dances to the Light* (1994) for speaker, children's chorus, Orff instruments, and orchestra, as well as other works. While Larson composed numerous works for unaccompanied chorus, she was most effective when writing for chorus and small groups of instruments as with *The Settling Years* (1988), a suite of three pioneer texts for mixed chorus, woodwind quintet, and piano; *Missa Gaia* (1992); *Seven Ghosts* (1995) for soprano, mixed chorus, brass quintet, piano, and percussion; the lengthy

Eleanor Roosevelt (1996) for speaker, mezzo soloist, mixed chorus, clarinet, cello, piano, and percussion (played by chorus members); and *So Blessedly It Sprung* (1996) for mixed chorus, viola, harp, and piano.

Robert Kyr is among the most prolific composers of his generation, having composed numerous symphonies and concertos in addition to vocal works. His choral music is distinguished by a warmly compelling lyricism, as well as by a contrapuntal mastery that arises from his love of early music, especially the work of Dufay, Josquin Des Prez, and above all, Bach. In particular, Kyr's substantial *The Passion According to Four Evangelists* (1995) for four soloists, mixed chorus, and orchestra employs an extremely broad tonal pallette. In the composer's words (Seeley 1999, 17), the Passion makes "consistent use of variation and transformation techniques as opposed to the limited use of materials by Arvo Pärt. . . . It is a radical work since it runs counter to most of the tonal music of our day which is hardly concerned with contrapuntal refinement, or with modulatory paths that are any more complex than the tonic-dominant duality of functional tonality." Kyr also envisioned choral music as an intrinsic part of international peacemaking. At the end of the century he wrote that "by performing and hearing music from around the world, [one is] taking an active part in promoting understanding—and, ultimately, peace—[among] the diverse peoples of humankind. As a communal art, choral music is an especially moving way to experience the unity of all people; it has the power to bring us together as peoples of all races, ethnicities, and nationalities" (Kyr 2001). In addition to *The Passion According to Four Evangelists*, Kyr's choral works include *Magnificat* (1986) for soprano solo and mixed chorus (with optional instrumental doubling); the cantata-like *Unseen Rain* (1990, revised for chamber orchestra 1993) for soloists, mixed chorus, and five instruments; *The Inner Dawning* (1996) for two soloists, mixed chorus, and orchestra; *Watersongs* (1996) for mixed chorus and piano; *Three Italian Motets* (1998) and *On the Nature of Creation* (1999), both for unaccompanied mixed chorus; and Symphony No. 9 (*The Spirit of Time*, 2000) for four soloists, mixed chorus, and orchestra.

Matthew Harris impressed with his four suites for unaccompanied mixed chorus collectively entitled *Shakespeare Songs* (1989–95). His style is neoclassic with exceptionally direct tonalities. Thematic material is often created from small motives, unique to each part, which evolve into ostinatos. The constant interaction of different rhythmically charged voices creates an alluring energy as well as an occasional passing dissonance.

Brent Michael Davids utilized American Indian materials in several works, including the ceremonial *Night Chant* (1997) for mixed chorus and nose flutes.

Eric Whitacre, potentially the most significant of this group, freely applied a variety of late-twentieth-century techniques—clusters, aleatoric devices, mixed rhythms, harmonically enriched tonalities, canonic ostinatos—to choral settings of eclectically chosen poetry (Octavio Paz, James Joyce, e. e. cummings) and biblical texts. Particularly outstanding works include the brilliantly conceived *Waternight* (1996) for unaccompanied mixed chorus, which was a finalist in the 1997 Barlow Competition, and the authentically anguished setting of David's lament for Absolom, *When David Heard* (1999) for unaccompanied eight-part mixed chorus.

In 1998 the Walt Disney Company commissioned Aaron Jay Kernis (b. 1960), a Pulitzer Prize winner whose previous choral experience consisted of some unaccompanied partsongs, and Michael Torke (b. 1961), who had previously composed a Mass (1990) for baritone, mixed chorus, and orchestra, to each compose a large "Millennial Symphony." Disney chairman Michael Eisner had devised the project after attending a New York performance of Mahler's Eighth conducted by Robert Shaw. What made this commission different from others, besides the very large amounts of money involved, was Disney's contention that the success of the music could be ensured if Disney produced it the same way it produces movies, by dictating the content and approving the finished product before performance. The resulting works, Kernis's *Garden of Light* (1999) and Torke's *Four Seasons* (1999), both for soloists, children's and mixed choruses, and large orchestra, were therefore subjected to private performances for Disney executives in Los Angeles, with subsequent rewrites, before the premieres in New York on 8 October 1999. Both works are large-scaled and full of gracious sentiments, catchy tunes, and lush, unthreatening harmonies. Even within this scheme the composers' styles are easily distinguishable: Kernis is much more lyrical, with longer tunes and full orchestrations, while Torke's music is obsessed with motivic development, unpredictable rhythmic jolts, and the accumulation of momentum. It remains to be seen, however, if the project met Disney's expectations of success.

Other American composers include Alfred Burt (1920–1954), whose charming and heartfelt Christmas carols for mixed chorus became standard holiday repertoire; Edwin Fissinger (1920–1990), who contributed many effective small pieces in a rhythmically vital style; Jack Beeson (b. 1921), an opera composer who wrote many partsongs in a lyrical, harmonically conservative style; William Bergsma (1921–1994), whose expressively dissonant tonal style was used with great effect in the cantatas *Confrontation* (from *Book of Job*, 1963, revised 1966) for chorus and orchestra (or piano) and *The Sun, the Soaring Eagle, the Turquoise Prince, the God* (1968) for mixed chorus, brass, and percussion; Mark Bucci (b. 1924), whose unaccompanied choral cycle *The Wondrous Kingdom* (1962), on texts by Blake, Emerson, George Herbert, and from the Bible, creates an effective choral representation of the jungle; Morton Feldman (b. 1926), a leading figure of the American avant-garde who contributed *Chorus and Instruments I* (1963) for mixed chorus and seven instruments, *Chorus and Instruments II* (1967) for mixed chorus, tuba, and tubular bells, the remarkable *Rothko Chapel* (1971) for soprano, alto, mixed chorus, percussion, celesta, and viola, and *Chorus and Orchestra I* (1972) for soprano, mixed chorus, and orchestra; Lee Hoiby (b. 1926), best known for his operas, who wrote *Magnificat and Nunc dimittis* (1983) for mixed chorus and organ, as well as several impressive anthems; Grant Beglarian (b. 1927), whose attractive little cantata *And All the Hills Echoed* (1968) for baritone, mixed chorus, organ, and timpani was written as a companion piece for a *Messiah* sing-a-long; Leon Levitch (b. 1927), whose cantata *Song of Dreams* (1993) for soprano, tenor, mixed chorus, and orchestra, on Serbo-Croat text by his father, reflects his family's experience in an Italian concentration camp; Joseph Kantor (b. 1930), who contributed numerous partsongs and anthems, as well as the impressive *Three Psalms* (1994) for mixed chorus and organ (or orchestra); Gregg Smith (b. 1931), a tireless champion of American and twentieth-century music who also composed a number of eclectic choral works; John Biggs (b. 1932), whose numerous works promoting the concept of a universal God include *Japanese Fables* (1984) for narrator, mixed chorus, and chamber orchestra, on texts taken from Zen Buddhist stories and various haiku poets, *Mass for Our Time* (1990) for mixed chorus, four woodwinds, and chimes, with a thought-provoking text by Terre Ouwehand ("I believe the Big Bang was the Great Sound of God calling himself into new forms of Being!"), and *The Web of Life* (1994) for narrator, children's and mixed chorus, and chamber orchestra, on American Indian texts; Pauline Oliveros (b. 1932), a leader of the American avant-garde, who produced *In Memoriam Mr. Whitney* (1991) and other pieces for chorus and accordion; Robert J. Powell (b. 1932), whose church works are complemented by the attractive concert motet for unaccompanied double mixed chorus, *All They from Saba Shall Come* (published 1965), which pays homage to Jacob Handl; Maia Aprahamian (b. 1935), who gave the children's chorus a prominent role in her choral-orchestral cantatas *Prayers from the Ark* (1970), *Prologue to "John"* (1987), and *From the Beginning* (1996); Conrad Susa (b. 1935), who contributed the popular *A Christmas Garland* for mixed chorus, audience, and orchestra (or keyboard or brass), *Magnificat and Nunc dimittis* for mixed chorus and organ, *Carols and Lullabies (Christmas in the Southwest)* for mixed or male chorus, harp, guitar, and marimba, and numerous other works; Steve Reich (b. 1936), a founding father of minimalism, whose cantata *Desert Music* (1984) for chorus and orchestra, on text by William Carlos Williams, was enthusiastically received by audiences and critics; David Del Tredici (b. 1937), who combined the Bach chorale "Es ist Genug" with texts by Lewis Carroll in *Pop-pourri* (1968) for mixed chorus, rock band, and orchestra; William Thomas McKinley (b. 1938), best known as a prolific symphonist with entrepreneurial skills, who also contributed a few small pieces for unaccompanied mixed chorus and the oratorio *Deliverance, Amen* (1983) for mezzo, tenor, and baritone soloists, chorus, and orchestra; James Hopkins (b. 1939), who wrote a significant number of attractive, challenging, and award-winning anthems, as well as the larger choral-orchestral *Songs of Eternity* (1993), *Five American Folk Hymns* (1996), *From the Realm of the Sea* (1996), and *The Rossetti Songs* (1997); Steven Albert (1941–1992), whose tragic early death cut short the promise inherent in *Bacchae* (1970) for soloists, narrator, mixed chorus, electric guitars, saxophones, and orchestra; Sondra Clark (b. 1941), who contributed the well-received *Requiem for Lost Children* (1996) for soloists, children's and mixed chorus, and orchestra, as well as the impressionistic *Feline* (1999) for women's chorus and the more directly tonal *Crystal Palace* (1999) for unaccompanied mixed chorus; Jackson Berkey (b. 1942), whose *Arma Lucis* (1988, revised 1990) for unaccompanied mixed chorus gained an appreciative audience; Paul Reale (b. 1943), whose several choral works are crowned by the exquisite *Two Madrigals* (1979, 1985) for unaccompanied mixed chorus; Thomas Pasatieri (b. 1945), an accomplished opera composer who contributed the cantata *Permit Me Voyage* (1976) for soprano, chorus, and orchestra, and Mass (1983) for four soloists, mixed chorus, and orchestra; Maggie Payne (b. 1945), whose interest in the relationship of sound and space is apparent in her lovely, atmospheric *Desertscapes* (1991) for unaccompanied female voices; Janice Hammer (b. 1946), who impressed with her large-scale messianic legend, *On Paper Bridges* (1994) for unaccompanied mixed chorus; Robert Xavier Rodríguez (b. 1946), whose miniature *Lyrics for Autumn* (1976) for chamber chorus and cello, and little cantata *Tranfigurationis mysteria* (1980) for soprano, alto, and tenor soloists, narrator, mixed chorus, children's chorus, and orchestra reveal romantic inclinations within a modern tonal framework; Nick Strimple (b. 1946), who composed anthems, partsongs, and cantatas, as well as film and television scores utilizing chorus; John Adams (b. 1947), whose *Harmonium* (1980) for mixed chorus and orchestra, on texts by John Donne and Emily Dickinson, is widely admired and whose century-ending oratorio *El niño* (2000) for actors, dancers, soloists, mixed chorus, orchestra, and film successfully promoted the possibilities of mixed media; Donald Grantham (b. 1947), whose anthems for mixed chorus with organ, and tonally sophisticated settings of William Butler Yeats and Emily Dickinson for unaccompanied chorus, merit attention; Paul Schoenfield (b. 1947), whose neo-Renaissance *Four Motets* (1996) for unaccompanied mixed chorus, on Hebrew text from Psalm 86, is particularly beautiful and sensitive; Gwyneth Walker (b. 1947), whose works include the charming suite *Love—by the Water* (1996) for mixed chorus and piano; Mary Jane Leach (b. 1949), who contributed the adult-oriented treble choruses, *Ariadne's Lament* (1993), *Tricky Pan* (1995), *Windjammer* (1995), *Call of the Dance* (1997), and *O Magna Vasti Creta* (1997); Stephen Paulus (b. 1949), who became well known for large works such as *Voices* (1988) for chorus and orchestra, on texts by Rainer Maria Rilke, and numerous smaller partsongs and carol settings written in a conservative but sharp-edged neo-classic style; Joseph Jennings (b. 1951), who contributed several folk song settings and the large, impressionistic *Mater dolorosa* (1997) for Chanticleer; Larry Lipkis (b. 1951), who composed a variety of works, among them *Songs from a Cookbook* (1975) for mixed chorus and piano, *Rise up My Love* (1979) for mezzo, baritone, and unaccompanied mixed chorus, *Prophesies* (1984) for chorus and tape, *The Seeker* for chorus and brass quartet, and *Giunse alfin il momento* (1993) for mixed chorus and strings; Roger Bourland (b. 1952), whose partsongs, ambitious oratorio in memory of AIDS victims, and large "choral drama" *Rosarium* (1999) for soprano, tenor, and baritone soloists, mixed chorus, and orchestra, merit attention; Byron Adams (b. 1955), who composed for most ensemble configurations but became especially well known for his unaccompanied *Missa brevis* (1984) and other finely wrought male chorus pieces; David Conte (b. 1955), who developed an attractive lyric style in which the melodic application of major-minor cross relations facilitates rapid shifts in tonal centers; Mack Wilberg (b. 1955), whose greatest contributions were virile settings of folk songs accompanied by four-hand piano, percussion, and other instruments; Daron Aric Hagen (b. 1961), who contributed *Taliesin: Choruses from the Shining Brow* (1992) for mixed chorus and orchestra; Peter Salzman (b. 1961), who freely incorporated jazz elements into his impressive large suite, *Birth of Soul* (1996) for unaccompanied mixed chorus; Augusta Read Thomas (b. 1964), whose madrigal *The Rub of Love* (1995) and other works gained wide acceptance; Michael Karmon (b. 1969), who impressed with the sensitively understated three-movement suite, *Reflections* (1993) for unaccompanied mixed chorus, on Hebrew text; and David Cutler (b. 1971), who contributed the hauntingly theatrical *Chestnut Branches in the Court: A Cycle of the Holocaust* (1999) for four children, soprano, alto, tenor, and bass soloists, two narrators, cantor, mixed chorus, and percussion.

African American Composers and the Spiritual

The spiritual is similar to jazz in several ways, as one of America's greatest gifts to the world, and as an expression of the most profound longings of a people, often couched in utterances that seem joyful, playful, or even whimsical. The ultimate stature and significance of the spiritual has not always been clearly understood, either, as exemplified by Michael Kennedy's comments on Michael Tippett's *A Child of Our Time* (Blyth 1991, 242–243):

Tippett's use of five Negro spirituals as the equivalents of Lutheran chorales in Bach's Passions is often cited as the prime reason for the work's popularity and success. It is a marvelous dramatic coup, but it is by no means the sole cause of success. The spirituals are effective precisely because they fit naturally into the framework of Tippett's own music as its inevitable outcome. It is not the spirituals which "make" *A Child of Our Time*, it is *A Child of Our Time* which lifts the spirituals to a higher plane.

It is true that the spirituals "fit naturally into the framework of Tippett's own music as its inevitable outcome," but otherwise Kennedy could not be more wrong. The spirituals in question had, have, and will continue to have a substantial life of their own, quite apart from Tippett's oratorio. On the other hand, it is impossible to conceive of *A Child of Our Time* without them. Kennedy's view is simply typical of the condescension that commonly relegates the spiritual—and other folk music—to the "dessert" portion of otherwise "serious" choral concerts, refusing to believe that music of humble origins can, of itself, occupy a so-called higher plane.

The original intent and impact of the spiritual was movingly articulated before the Civil War by the ex-slave Frederick Douglass (1994, 23–25) in his first autobiography, written in 1845. In it he described slaves who, while walking to the plantation's main house ("the Great House Farm"),

> would make the dense old woods, for miles around, reverberate with their wild songs, revealing at once the highest joy and the deepest sadness. They would compose and sing as they went along, consulting neither time nor tune. . . . They would sometimes sing the most pathetic sentiment in the most rapturous tone, and the most rapturous sentiment in the most pathetic tone. Into all of their songs they would manage to weave something of the Great House Farm. Especially would they do this, when leaving home. They would then sing most exultingly the following words:—
>
> > "I am going away to the Great House Farm!
> > O, yea! O, yea! O!"
>
> This they would sing, as a chorus, to words which to many would seem unmeaning jargon, but which, nevertheless, were full of meaning to themselves. I have sometimes thought that the mere hearing of those songs would do more to impress some minds with the horrible character of slavery, than the reading of whole volumes of philosophy on the subject could do.
>
> I did not, when a slave, understand the deep meaning of those rude and apparently incoherent songs. I was myself within the circle; so that I never saw nor heard as those without might see and hear. They told a tale of woe which was then altogether beyond my feeble comprehen-

sion; they were tones loud, long, and deep; they breathed the prayer and complaint of souls boiling over with the bitterest anguish. Every tone was a testimony against slavery, and a prayer to God for deliverance from chains. The hearing of those wild notes always depressed my spirit, and filled me with ineffable sadness. . . .

I have often been utterly astonished, since I came to the north, to find persons who could speak of the singing, among slaves, as evidence of their contentment and happiness. It is impossible to conceive of a greater mistake. Slaves sing most when they are most unhappy. The songs of the slave represent the sorrows of his heart; and he is relieved by them, only as an aching heart is relieved by its tears.

After the Civil War these songs inspired several generations of composers. The first widely heard choral versions, created by the Fisk Jubilee Singers, were simple hymnlike arrangements for four-part mixed chorus. Just after the turn of the century Henry Thacker Burleigh (1866–1949), who had been a student of Antonín Dvořák at the National Conservatory in New York, made a number of more complex arrangements with more polished harmonies and occasionally with sophisticated piano accompaniments, after the manner of the European partsong. Notable examples still in use include *Deep River* (1917) for chorus and piano, and *Were You There* (1926) for unaccompanied mixed chorus. Thereafter, the spiritual was developed as a popular choral form by Hall Johnson (1888–1970), William Levi Dawson (1899–1989), Jester Hairston (1901–2000), and John W. Work (1901–1967). Their arrangements, which accentuated the spiritual's unique rhythmic characteristics while successfully blurring the line between newly composed and preexisting material, remain among the most often performed twentieth-century choral works. Outstanding examples include Dawson's *Balm in Gilead* (c. 1939) for mixed chorus and soprano soloist, and Hairston's *Hold On* (c. 1955) for mixed chorus and incidental tenor soloist. These and other arrangements were brought to an eager public throughout the century by choirs that specialized in spirituals and other African American music. In addition to the Fisk Jubilee Singers, the most outstanding were the Hall Johnson Choir, the Albert McNeil Jubilee Singers, and the Moses Hogan Chorale.

The culmination of the spiritual as partsong occurred during the 1990s in the work of Larry Farrow (b. 1950) and Moses Hogan (b. 1957), whose occasionally virtuosic arrangements set new standards for compositional sophistication and unadulterated vitality. Further, their work helped crystallize the idea that all folk idioms spring from related sources. For instance, the polyphonic layers in Hogan's brilliant *Elijah Rock* (published 1994) for unaccompanied mixed chorus are similar in concept to the tectonic montage of Janáček's works, while Farrow's work clearly demonstrates the kinship of American slave songs with various Caribbean folk forms.

The Albert McNeil Jubilee Singers, Osaka, Japan, 1999. Photo by Hajime Namura. Courtesy of Albert McNeil.

Important African American composers also created significant works which, while often influenced by the spiritual, were original in concept and content. Included among them are Robert Nathaniel Dett (1882–1943), William Grant Still (1885–1978), Florence Price (1888–1953), Margaret Bonds (1913–1972), Hale Smith (b. 1925), Thomas Jefferson Anderson (b. 1928), and Olly Wilson (b. 1937)

Robert Nathaniel Dett was a respected composer, pianist, educator, and essayist. The Hampton Institute Choir rose to national prominence under his direction (1913–31), and he cofounded the National Association of Negro Musicians. Dett composed in a neoromantic style. His oratorio *The Ordering of Moses* (1937) for soloists, mixed chorus, and orchestra was the first widely recognized large choral work by an African American composer. His unaccompanied partsongs and motets, of which the exquisite *Ave Maria* (c. 1930) and *Listen to the Lambs* are representative, deserve frequent performance. Among his other choral pieces are numerous arrangements of spirituals and other African American folk songs.

William Grant Still, like Dett, was educated at Oberlin College Conservatory. He studied composition with George Chadwick and Edgard Varèse, and orchestration with jazz greats W. C. Handy, Artie Shaw, and Paul White-man. Still settled into a very conservative musical language, although the rather conventional harmonies and rhythms often seem quite fresh in his hands, and eventually became the most famous African American composer of the twentieth century, internationally celebrated for his *Afro-American Symphony* (1931), several operas, and other instrumental works. His contributions to the choral repertoire include *Song of a City* (1938) for mixed chorus and orchestra, the powerful *And They Lynched Him on a Tree* (1940) for alto soloist, narrator, double mixed chorus (white singers as the lynch mob, black chorus as commentators), and orchestra, *From a Lost Continent* (1948) for mixed chorus and orchestra, *Plain Chant for America* (1968) for mixed chorus and organ (revised from an earlier work for baritone and organ), and partsongs.

The first female African American composer of international stature was Florence Price, who was known for several orchestra works, her piano concerto, and *Songs to a Dark Virgin*, made famous by Marian Anderson. Price's choral works consist of several partsongs for women's and mixed choruses. Her love of musical description, obvious in her partsongs, is well served by her neoromantic style. Representative works include *Song for Snow* (1934) for mixed chorus and piano, and *Moon Bridge* (1950) for three-part treble chorus (arranged from an earlier solo song).

Margaret Bonds, a student of Price and William Dawson, worked closely with the composer Will Marion Cook, who had an influence on her style, as she herself discussed on one occasion (Mildred Denby Green 1983, 48): "Will Marion Cook had an opportunity to present a Negro choir on NBC [and] I was sent to extract all of his choral parts, which, incidentally, he changed daily. Even now, when I write something for choir and it's jazzy and bluesy and spiritual and Tchaikovsky all rolled up into one, I laugh to myself, 'That is Will Marion Cook.'" A representative work is the cantata *The Ballad of the Brown King* (1954) for soloists, chorus, and orchestra (or piano). The Epiphany text centering on the dark-skinned wise man Balthazar was written especially for Bonds by Langston Hughes. Elements of jazz, blues, Caribbean, and other folk styles are combined with European techniques to form an interesting synthesis. Other works include Mass in D Minor (1959) for mixed chorus and organ, the cycle *Fields of Wonder* (1964) for male chorus and piano, on text by Langston Hughes, *Credo* (1972) for mixed chorus and orchestra, and partsongs and spiritual arrangements.

Hale Smith assimilated jazz and elements of serial technique to create a style that is both direct and subtle. His choral works include *In Memoriam—Beryl Rubenstein* (1953) for chorus and chamber orchestra, the jazz cantata *Comes Tomorrow* (1972) for chorus and percussion, *Toussaint l'ouverture 1803* (1979) for mixed chorus and piano, and the partsongs *I'm Coming*

Home for mixed chorus and piano, and *Two Kids* for unaccompanied mixed chorus.

Thomas Jefferson Anderson composed in a rhythmically complex style influenced by both jazz and modern post-serial techniques. His cantata *The Suit* (1998), on text by Philip Levine, can be considered representative. Anderson was drawn to the text—a poem about Levine's attachment to a zoot suit—because its Detroit setting was similar to the industrial town in Pennsylvania where he himself had grown up: both were unattractive and insensitive places where people struggled to find meaning in existence. The music illumines the various textual themes by combining bi- and tritonalities, jazz rhythms and harmonies, and a doo-wa section. Anderson's other choral works include the cantata *Personals* (1966) for narrator, mixed chorus, and brass septet, *This House* (1971) for male chorus and four pitch pipes, *Spirituals* (1979) for tenor soloists, narrator, children's and mixed choruses, jazz quartet, and orchestra, *Jonestown* (1982) for children's chorus and piano, and *Thomas Jefferson's Minstrels* (1982) for baritone, male chorus, and jazz band.

Olly Wilson, among the leading American practitioners of electronic music, combined electronic media with avant-garde techniques and African American idioms in his choral music. Important works include *Gloria* (1961) for unaccompanied mixed chorus, *Biography* (1966) for soprano and mixed chorus, *In Memoriam Martin Luther King, Jr.* (1968) for mixed chorus and electronic tape, and *Spirit Song* (1973) for soprano soloist, double mixed chorus, and orchestra.

Other significant African American composers include Undine Smith Moore (1904–1989), whose works include the cantata *Sir Olaf and the Erl King's Daughter* (1925) for three-part treble chorus and piano, and the oratorio *Scenes from the Life of a Martyr* (1982) for narrator, mixed chorus, and orchestra, as well as partsongs and spiritual arrangements; David N. Baker (b. 1931), a talented jazz composer who impressed with his cycle *Images Shadows and Dreams* (1993) for mixed chorus and instruments; Wendell Whalum (1931–1987), who often collaborated with Robert Shaw; the prolific Leslie Adams (b. 1932); Robert A. Harris (b. 1938), who produced a large number of partsongs, psalm settings, and other service music for all ensemble configurations; Adolphus Hailstork (b. 1941), whose partsongs and other works gained in prominence at century's end; David Hurd (b. 1950), who made valuable contributions to the Episcopalian liturgical repertoire; William C. Banfield (b. 1961), an enormously promising younger American composer; and Rosephanye Powell (b. 1962), whose invigorating anthems for unaccompanied mixed chorus, *The Word Was God* (1995), *Wait on the Lord* (1996), and *Ascribe to the Lord* (1997), successfully combine motet-like polyphony and structures with rhythms derived from the spiritual.

The Educational Market

The twentieth-century educational choral market in the United States was largely begun by Fredrik Melius Christiansen (1871–1955), director of the School of Music at Saint Olaf College; John Finley Williamson (1887–1964), founder of Westminster Choir College; Fred Waring (1900–1984), founder and director of the professional chorus the Pennsylvanians; and Peter J. Wilhousky (1902–1978), supervisor of music in New York City schools. The only composer among the group was Christiansen, who created a large number of choral pieces designed for use either at the collegiate level or with good church choirs. Williamson commissioned Roy Harris and other composers to craft pieces for his choir. Waring employed Roy Ringwald and Harry Simeone to compose and arrange for his publishing firm, Shawnee Press, and developed a system of phonetic spelling in which words are placed under the text in the score to teach students correct pronunciation while singing. Wilhousky encouraged arrangers to write for schools and made many choral arrangements himself, two of which became standard repertoire: *The Battle Hymn of the Republic* for mixed chorus and orchestra (or piano), and the ubiquitous Ukrainian *Carol of the Bells* for unaccompanied mixed chorus. While Williamson and Christiansen were not really concerned with making music for performance below college level, Wilhousky and Waring focused on high schools.

Composers to whom these men turned included Noble Cain (1896–1977), Will James (1896–1977), and Houston Bright (1916–1968). Cain and James were both enamoured of Russian style and wrote numerous, predominantly homophonic choral pieces. Their works, mostly set on religious texts, are characterized by the use of massive block chords that duplicate parts between women's and men's voices. James's *Almighty God of Our Fathers* (1941) for unaccompanied mixed chorus is perhaps the outstanding example of this style. Cain was also a talented and experienced choral conductor, and he wrote a basic text of the day entitled *Choral Music and Its Practice*. Bright composed many partsongs on a variety of secular texts in a melodious tonal style that occasionally provides a delightful harmonic shock. These pieces usually adhere to a clear four-voice (SATB) scheme: additional parts are added only for specific effects, and homophony and polyphony freely intermingle. An outstanding example is *When I Am Dead, My Dearest*, arguably among the best American settings of this text. Bright also celebrated the African American spiritual with *I Hear a Voice A-Prayin'* (c. 1955) for mixed chorus, and paid homage to Bach with the big double-choir motet *Hodie nobis coelorum rex* (c. 1965), which successfully maintains a thick contrapuntal texture over its relatively extended length. Although he made some excellent folk song arrangements, most of his work is completely original. Like composers in the Baltics, Great Britain, and Israel who were also concerned with providing high-quality repertoire for young singers and other amateurs, Bright created several little pieces that have stood the test of time, the musical content making them still appropriate for university and community choruses as well as high schools.

Around the middle of the century, publishers recognized the value of American musical theater by commissioning Clay Warnick and others to arrange choral medleys of virtually every successful Broadway musical. These medleys occupied the culminating position of most high school choral concerts and were exceedingly popular with collegiate and community choruses as well. This trend aided the development, later in the century, of vocal jazz ensembles and show choirs, for which Kirby Shaw, Ed Lojeski, and others provided challenging and idiomatic choral arrangements.

The repertoire dilemma in children's music was addressed by Ruth Krehbiel Jacobs when she founded the Choristers Guild in 1949. Thereafter, the Choristers Guild published attractive and functional music for children's choruses. Designed mostly to promote children's music in churches, it unfortunately never managed to attract the interest of major composers, relying instead on the creative abilities of children's conductors and other well-meaning amateurs. This is a primary reason why Chorister's Guild publications always adhere to basic song forms in easy keys, quite apart from a perceived need to keep the music simple.

A few composers who actively produced symphonies, chamber works, and other pieces for advanced performers aimed their choral efforts primarily at high schools, producing excellent pieces that took into account the vocal ranges and technical prowess of younger adult singers. Foremost among these was Emma Lou Diemer (b. 1927), whose edgy tonalities and clever rhythmic twists enliven her numerous choral works. Representative examples of her work include *Fragments of the Mass* (1960) for female chorus, *Three Madrigals* (1960) for mixed chorus and piano, on texts by Shakespeare, *Sing a Glory* (1964) for mixed chorus and orchestra (or band), *Madrigals Three* (1972) for mixed chorus and piano, and *Wild Nights! Wild Nights!* (1978) for mixed chorus and piano, on text by Emily Dickinson.

Prominent educational composers at century's end included Williametta Spencer (b. 1932), whose little masterpiece *At the Round Earth's Imagined Corners* (1965), *Four Madrigals on Texts by James Joyce* (1970), and *Missa brevis* (1974), all for unaccompanied mixed chorus, gave hope to high school conductors starved for good twentieth-century repertoire; James Mulholland (b. 1935), who wrote overtly sentimental partsongs often extended by grandiose piano parts; Mary Goetze (b. 1943) and Natalie Porter, whose considerable talents set them apart from others writing for young voices; René Clausen (b. 1953), who mastered a lush impressionistic style; Z. Randall Stroop (b. 1953) and Randol Alan Bass (b. 1955), who composed partsongs and cantata-like pieces in energetic and somewhat daring tonal styles; and Carl Strommen, whose pop-inspired partsongs are harmonically interesting and rich in melodic detail.

THE CHURCH MARKET

The leading Roman Catholic composers of the early twentieth century included John Baptist Singenberger (1848–1924), Nicola Aloysius Montani (1880–1948), J. Alfred Schehl (b. 1882), Mary Cherubim Schaefer (b. 1886), Pietro A. Yon (1886–1943), and Carlo Rossini (b. 1890), all of whom wrote in a conventionally direct style, occasionally utilizing Gregorian melodies.

Born in Switzerland, Singenberger studied in Austria and Germany before becoming a music instructor at Catholic schools in Saint Francis, Wisconsin. A devoted pupil of Cecilian Movement leader Franz Xavier Witt, he soon organized the American Society of Saint Cecilia, thereafter editing its monthly magazine. In Leonard Ellinwood's words (1970), Singenberger was a "pioneer in the development of liturgical music in the American Roman Catholic Church," and composed a significant amount of functional service music.

Nicola Montani was born in Utica, New York. He edited the *Saint Gregory Hymnal and Catholic Choir Book* (1920) as well as a great deal of Catholic liturgical music, wrote *The Art of A Cappella Singing*, and composed eight Masses and other service music. A most interesting instruction, which may in fact reflect common performance practice of Catholic music at that time, occurs in Montani's *Ave Maria* (1909) for three-part treble (or male) chorus and organ, in which the indications "Adagio, sotto voce" are cancelled two measures later with "Vibrato."

Alfred Schehl was born in Cincinnati and spent his life there, working as a violinist in the Cincinnati Symphony, organist-choirmaster in various Catholic churches, and choral director of the May Music Festival. Schehl was instrumental in the inclusion of old German Catholic hymns and congregationally sung Masses in the 1929 edition of the *Saint Gregory Hymnal*. Like his colleagues, Schehl composed several Masses.

Mary Cherubim Schaefer served as director of music at Saint Joseph's Convent in Milwaukee until 1938. Thereafter, she devoted her time to the composition of functional service music, including many Masses and motets.

Born in Italy, Pietro A. Yon immigrated to New York in 1907, becoming organist-choirmaster first at Saint Francis Xavier's Church and then at Saint Patrick's Cathedral. In addition to Masses, motets for the church year, and an oratorio, he composed the perennial Christmas favorite *Jesu Bambino* (1917) for mixed chorus and organ.

Carlo Rossini was also born in Italy, immigrating to the United States after service as a chaplain in the Italian Army during World War I. In addition to his church-related duties, he organized the Pittsburgh Polyphonic Choir. Rossini harmonized the Gregorian *Proper of the Mass for the Entire Ecclesiastical Year* (1933) and composed over fifteen Masses and numerous motets.

Paul Creston, widely admired outside the church for his symphonic and other concert music, composed *Requiem* (1938) for two-part male chorus and organ, *Missa solemnis* (1949) for male or mixed chorus and organ, and *Missa "Adoro te"* (1952) for female or mixed chorus and organ.

Masses in the newly approved English text began to appear very quickly after Vatican II. Most were strictly for liturgical use, such as those by composers Carroll Thomas Andrews (b. 1918) and John Lee. Others, such as Norman Dello Joio's first Mass and Paul Creston's *Missa "Cum jubilo"* (1968) for unaccompanied mixed chorus, were primarily intended for concerts or large church festivals. Joseph Roff (1910–1993), continuing the tradition of Carlo Rossini, provided English settings of the Gregorian *Propers of Sundays and Major Feasts* (1964) for unison, treble, male, or mixed chorus and organ. At the same time, Robert Moevs (b. 1920) composed *A Brief Mass* (1969) for mixed chorus, organ, vibraphone, guitar, and double bass in an attempt to demonstrate the feasibility of avant-garde procedures within the liturgy, and Richard Felciano (b. 1930) contributed motets for voices and electronic tape, most notably the male chorus *Double Alleluia for Pentecost* (1968), although these experiments were as short lived as similar Protestant efforts.

Afterward, choral music in the Roman Catholic Church generally ceased to be of interest. As the Ordinary of the Mass was gradually taken over by the congregation, the idea of providing motet cycles for the propers of important feasts (as some Europeans were doing) did not occur to important composers who might otherwise have been inclined to write for the church. Furthermore, as the American people began their journey into multiculturalism, the steadily increasing popularity of mariachi and other folk Masses performed and led by small ensembles replaced the choral Mass in many parishes. At the end of the century Norman Dello Joio, Alan Hovhaness, Gian Carlo Menotti, and Richard Proulx (b. 1937) were the only older composers of stature to have contributed to the new congregation-oriented rite. Among the few promising younger composers writing for the Roman liturgy were Leo Nestor (b. 1948) and Mark Carlson (b. 1952).

Leo Nestor, music director at the National Shrine of the Immaculate Conception in Washington, D.C., established a reputation as a skillful composer of partsongs. He also composed numerous liturgical works specifically for his accomplished church choir.

Mark Carlson's church music is exemplified by the colorful and majestic *Mass: Christ in Majesty* (1987) for mixed chorus and chamber orchestra (or organ), a practical and emotionally satisfying setting of the Kyrie, Gloria, and Agnus Dei texts.

Twentieth-century Protestant choral music generally developed in two distinct directions, the resulting styles being used interchangeably by various denominations. The first, primarily influenced by the late-nineteenth-century English Cathedral tradition and to a lesser extent by Bach and the Lutheran tradition, may be called the neo-European style. The second was a product of late-nineteenth-century revivalist music and can be called the evangelistic or revivalist style.

The neo-European style was encouraged by Peter C. Lutkin (1858–1931), founder of the department of church music at Northwestern University's School of Music, who is still remembered for his famous parting anthem, *The Lord Bless You and Keep You* (published 1900) for unaccompanied mixed chorus; and Clarence Dickinson (1873–1969), founder of Union Seminary School of Sacred Music in New York and composer of the popular Christmas anthem *The Shepherd's Story* (1913). While obviously based on late-nineteenth-century examples of the English anthem, such as *I Am Alpha and Omega* by Sir John Stainer (1840–1901) and the cantata-like *Hear My Words, Ye People* (1894) by Sir Charles Hubert Hastings Parry (1848–1918), neo-Europeanism represented both an outgrowth of and a reaction to the rather pretentious anthems for organ and solo quartet that were then popular in America's large urban churches. It boasted unique characteristics, notably a more compact structure with fewer solos and eventually a more typically American harmonic vocabulary. The development of the neo-European style can be traced not only to composers such as Horatio Parker and Amy Beach but also to Harry Rowe Shelley (1858–1947), whose works retained some lengthy solo passages and exhibited a particular fondness for augmented sixth chords (often appearing in conjunction with an ascending melody line); Seth Bingham (1882–1972), whose lyricism is exemplified in the cantata *Wilderness Stone* (1933) for soloists, mixed chorus, and orchestra, and the large anthem *Perfect through Suffering* (1971) for chorus and organ; H. Everett Titcomb (1884–1968), whose *Victory Te Deum* (1944), *O Love, How Deep*, and other anthems for mixed chorus and organ are still familiar to many congregations; David McKinley Williams (1887–1978), whose *In the Year That King Uzziah Died* (1935) for soprano, baritone, mixed chorus, and organ is still occasionally performed; and Carl F. Mueller (1892–1982), whose exquisite little anthem, *Create in Me* (published 1941) for mixed chorus and organ, remains a quintessential representative of the mature neo-European style.

Perhaps the greatest exponent of neo-Europeanism was Leo Sowerby (1895–1968), the only American church composer to win a Pulitzer Prize. His music is marked by frequent use of baroque contrapuntal forms and occasionally dissonant harmonies that are sometimes influenced by jazz or folk sources. Sowerby wrote well over a hundred anthems, numerous Communion services and canticles, and several cantatas, including *Forsaken of Man* (1939) for mixed chorus and organ, the Pulitzer Prize–winning *Canticle of the Sun* (1944) for mixed chorus and orchestra, *Christ Reborn* (1950) for mixed chorus and organ, and *Solomon's Garden* (1964) for mixed chorus and orchestra.

Others who extended the neo-European style well beyond the century's midpoint include Harold Friedell (1905–58), whose style reflects neo-Renaissance influences, Roberta Bitgood (b. 1908), Richard Purvis (1915–1994), Austin Lovelace (b. 1919), Gordon Young (1919–1998), Jane Marshall (b. 1924), and Dale Wood (b. 1934), whose style was influenced by Vaughan Williams and American folk hymnody.

The revivalist style began during the last quarter of the nineteenth century, when gospel songwriters such as George F. Root (1820–1895) and E. O. Excell (1851–1921) began publishing collections of gospel songs and newly composed anthems designed for volunteer choirs. In 1894 Edmund S. Lorenz (1854–1942) launched a magazine called *The Choir Leader*, which included several new anthems in each issue. In the first edition, Lorenz wrote, "As the music in this number and the list of authors indicate, the 'Choir Leader' will furnish music of a simple or only moderately difficult character. Our purpose is to help the mass of voluntary choirs, who desire music none the less valuable for being easy and unpretentious" (Wienandt and Young 1970, 314). Lorenz himself contributed anthems, as did Emma L. Ashford (1850–1930), Charles H. Gabriel (1856–1932), and Van Denman Thompson (1890–1969). Thompson was particularly facile. The sophisticated modulations and extended contrapuntal writing found in his large hymn anthems—for example, *Hymn to the Trinity* (1942) for mixed chorus and organ (or piano), based on "Come Thou Almighty King"—blurred the lines of separation between neo-European and revivalist styles.

The lines were redrawn during the 1950s, however, with the advent of John W. Peterson (b. 1921). Peterson expanded the revivalist tradition with chromatically saturated harmonies taken directly from Tin Pan Alley, barbershop, and other pop sources. Utilizing his own gospel songs as source material, he created a new type of evangelical church cantata for narrator, soloists, mixed choir, and organ or piano (or both), often combining his new music with older beloved hymns and gospel songs. These cantatas were unsophisticated except for frequently lush harmonic episodes, and spoke in direct and unthreatening terms to many evangelical congregations. Good examples include the somewhat early Easter cantata *Hallelujah! What a Savior*, which was also issued in SA, SAB, and Spanish-language editions, and the Christmas cantata *Night of Miracles* (1958). A fair appraisal was provided by Donald P. Hustad (1981, 225), who noted that "his works were criticized by 'serious' musicians, but they brought extended choral forms into churches which had never before sung a cantata."

It should be pointed out here that evangelicals and "serious" musicians will probably never agree on proper criteria for religious art. Music tends to be a kind of propaganda for evangelicals, since their worship—indeed, their collective world view—is based on the need to proselytize. Therefore textual content is everything. Music is simply a vehicle for the text, with the style chosen according to what is deemed most suitable for reaching the largest audience at a given time. For others, however, religious art means something quite different, as Gustav Mahler pointed out in 1905:

> Permit me to stress briefly that in matters of art only the *form* and never the *content* is relevant, or at least should be relevant, from a serious viewpoint. How the subject matter is treated and carried out, not what the subject matter consists of to begin with—that is the only thing that matters. A work of art is to be considered as serious if the artist's dominant objective is to master the subject matter exclusively by artistic means and resolve it perfectly into the "form" [gestalt] (you can interpret this word in the Aristotelian sense).—According to this principle *Don Giovanni*, for example (in which a rake does battle with God and the world), or, for example, the *Nibelung* tetralogy, in which incest, etc. etc. is not only the source of tragedy but is also made understandable, are serious works of art. That works like this do not desecrate even the highest religious festival is my unshakable conviction, whereas for example works like *Der Evangelimann* [a popular late-nineteenth-century musical by Wilhelm Kienzl] (in which Christ and all the saints are stock characters), or for example no end of Mary Magdalene or John the Baptist tragedies, in which the subject matter is selected simply for the purpose of tear-jerking—are in my opinion unserious works of art and in consequence not only unsuitable for any religious festival, but unsuitable for any purpose. (Blaukopf 1976, 242–243)

It is obvious that superficial similarities exist between the American evangelical cantata and those of Bach: duration, use of commonly known tunes, instrumentation based on ready availability, and so on. But the issue of form, as defined by Mahler, quite apart from the composers' respective talents, is the primary reason that Peterson's cantatas and the thousands of others like them bear no actual comparison to Bach's work.

Coincidental with the publication of Peterson's first cantatas, a further and more profound transformation of the revivalist style was taking place in African American churches where the combination of spirituals and gospel songs by white composers such as Philip P. Bliss (1818–1876) and Ira Sankey (1840–1908) evolved into a completely new genre through the assimilation of African American rhythms, vocal improvisation, and enriched harmonization. This new gospel style would become an extremely popular American choral form late in the century, producing numerous attractive compositions such as

Gospel Magnificat (1995) by Robert Ray (b. 1946), and *Worthy to Be Praised* (1993) for mixed chorus and piano by Byron J. Smith. Other gospel composers include Richard Smallwood (b. 1948), who combines elements of more classic church anthems with jazz and unique counterpoint, and Glenn Burleigh (b. 1958), whose music is very popular within the evangelistic communities.

The works of John Ness Beck (1930–1987) can be viewed as a continuation of Van Denman Thompson's efforts to synthesize the neo-European and revivalist styles. Beck successfully combined lush harmonies similar to those favored by John W. Peterson with expansive formal structures. Often utilizing hymn tunes and including brass with the normal organ accompaniment, Beck created several large anthems that became standard repertoire in churches of all denominations. The best-known are *Song of Exultation* (c. 1967) and *Upon This Rock* (c. 1967). Also worthy of mention is the large unaccompanied motet for six-part mixed chorus, *Osanna* (c. 1964).

The profound implications of Vatican II generated reexamination within mainstream Protestant denominations as well, resulting in a brief period of musical experimentation. Paul Fetler (b. 1920) and Daniel Moe (b. 1926) composed anthems, cantatas, and other Lutheran service music in a diatonic but dissonant harmonic style often based on fourths and added-note chords. Normand Lockwood, also composing for the Lutheran church, wrote choral music to accompany liturgical dance. Daniel Pinkham and others wrote sacred choral music accompanied by electronic tape. While several of these pieces are quite interesting and still occasionally performed, they initially met with stiff resistance from congregations who found no religious comfort in the austere nature of quartal harmony or clever electronic noises. Further, the musical establishment itself raised its eyebrows at the electronic pieces, since the composers in question had only recently turned to the idiom. In a lecture at Baylor University in 1969, Ross Lee Finney, commenting on the technically complicated nature of electronic composition and the years of committed study and practice required to master it, likened these composers and their works to sophomore theory students publishing their harmony exercises.

Up to this time the most significant musical contribution of the American Lutheran church had been the publication of many German baroque cantatas in English-language editions. Now there emerged a number of composers in addition to Daniel Moe and Paul Fetler who continued the work of Fredrik Melius Christiansen, producing music that made full use of the rich Lutheran traditions of chorale and instrumental accompaniment. Representative are Ludwig Lenel (b. 1914), who used chorale tunes in a manner similar to Hugo Distler, most notably in the brilliant unaccompanied mixed chorus motet *Christ Is Arisen* (1961); Walter Pelz (b. 1926), who frequently incorporated guitar and woodwinds into his sensitively wrought anthems; and Carl Schalk (b. 1929), who used chorale tunes and set several texts by the important Slovak poet-theologian Jaroslav Vajda, among them the highly evocative entrance hymn *Now* (1969) for unaccompanied mixed chorus. Others include Jan Bender (1909–1994), Leland Sateren (b. 1913), Paul O. Manz (b. 1919), David N. Johnson (b. 1922), and Ronald A. Nelson (b. 1927).

Another group of talented composers, who also happened to be outstanding organist-choirmasters in metropolitan (often Episcopal) churches, managed to build on the traditions of Seth Bingham, Leo Sowerby, and David McKinley Williams. This group, including Richard Dirksen (b. 1921), Gerre Hancock (b. 1934), Calvin Hampton (1938–1984), and McNeil Robinson (b. 1943), utilized the normal mixed chorus and organ configuration, sometimes in combination with other instruments. Successfully expanding the harmonic palette while retaining an essentially diatonic melodic vocabulary, and tightening the more expansive formal aspects of their mentors' music, they continued to produce challenging, lofty, and beautiful liturgical music for the duration of the century.

However, in many churches of all denominations—especially Methodist, Baptist, Presbyterian, and other more evangelical groups—music based on the most obvious and least thought-provoking aspects of American popular music was introduced into worship during the late sixties in an effort to retain or recapture the interest of youth otherwise interested in secular pursuits. This music was easily accepted by many teenagers, who welcomed the capitulation of leadership on the part of church officials. Many functional pieces for children and youth were produced in this style, and at length—as the baby boomers grew older—it was not only accepted as the lingua franca of children's and youth choirs but of many adult choirs as well.

This was quite different from what was happening in Europe, where the best composers continued to create music for the young, not only meeting their immediate functional and emotional needs but also broadening their awareness (as with Petr Eben and his *Trouvere Mass*, see chapter 5). These circumstances helped European adolescents to develop critical facilities necessary to mature into thinking adults and encouraged an interest in their great cultural treasures.

But this kind of solution was apparently unworkable in the United States for at least four reasons. First, the same great American composers who were not interested in composing for children were also not interested in composing for the church. Second, the Vietnam War fractured American society so deeply that cultural treasures embraceable by the entire, diverse citizenry were difficult to identify. It seemed that composers who continued to churn out music in either the neo-European style or the revivalist style would reach smaller and smaller audiences as congregations came to grips with their own multiculturalism. Third, across the spectrum of cultures comprising late-twentieth-century American society, perhaps the greatest common denominator was an infatuation with youth. It was much more important to appear trim, trendy, and youthful than to be wise, experienced, and cultured. The past was irrelevant—youth was "happening." The emphasis on youth, combined with an almost militant desire to replace worship services that challenged with services that made people feel good, naturally led to an emphasis on the entertainment potential of worship. Style became at least as important as content. While some churches managed to blend styles, others separated services entirely. Traditional services were maintained in churches where older members refused to submit entirely to the apparent secularization of worship, while contemporary services—sometimes meeting at the same time—were devised for the young (or young at heart), effectively cutting them off from their cultural roots and excluding everyone else from their collective future. (Late in the century this trend was also apparent in secular society, as exemplified by the advent of radio stations dedicated to music from a particular decade.) Fourth, the desire for worship to be entertaining created huge markets for publishers who further devalued the contributions of previous generations by aggressively marketing vast quantities of disposable music, which was driven by every whim of pop culture and calculated to remain well within the average listener's comfort zone. Because of this the great bulk of church music written in the United States during the last third of the century can be charitably characterized as adolescent easy-listening.

Textbook examples of this style are found in the works of Natalie Sleeth (1930–1992), whose success as a composer of children's music compelled her to write for mixed choir as well. Her music is strictly diatonic and always in bright, unadorned major keys (or minor keys for Lenten pieces), usually with no more than three sharps or flats. Phrases divide neatly into four-measure segments. Harmonies emphasize tonic and dominant. Tonal variety is often achieved by secondary phrases that pass through the dominant or concluding cadences that are modal or harmonically enriched. Occasionally, final sections (or verses) modulate up. The prevailing syncopation in common time is achieved by "pushing" the third beat, so that the rhythm of each measure is 3 + 3 + 2. Sleeth differs from hundreds of similar composers in the freshness of her melodies, a generally high-minded approach to selection of texts, a genuine contrapuntal skill that goes well beyond the ability to craft a two-voice canon, and an uncanny ability to make a simplistic and completely derivative style seem vital.

After Sleeth's death, adherents of this generic style—often referred to as "contemporary"—absorbed various lyrical and harmonic characteristics from the old revivalist style and the evangelical cantatas of John W. Peterson to produce music with more natural syncopation and a renewed harmonic reliance on seventh, ninth, and augmented sixth chords. The widespread, uncritical admiration of this music brings to mind Edward Gibbon's observation that during the last days of the Roman Empire the people's love for the insipid and derivative poetry of Ausonius "condemned the taste of his age" (Cahill 1995, 21).

Even in an environment in which commercialism took easy precedence over artistic integrity, a few composers still wrote almost exclusively for the church, their honest musical inclinations resulting in well-crafted, informed, and moving music written in a variety of styles (though usually based on traditional models), which also occasionally became quite popular. Chief among them are Lloyd Pfautsch (b. 1921), Robert H. Young (b. 1923), and K. Lee Scott (b. 1950), who share certain compositional attributes such as an avoidance of rhythmic gimmicks and saturated harmonies, an inclination toward profound and literate texts, an obvious understanding and appreciation of ancient church traditions and their continued relevance and application, and an acute awareness of technical limitations. Pfautsch and Young also contributed to the secular partsong repertoire. Pfautsch's greatest contributions, however, are found in innovative and boldly understated anthems such as *Reconciliation* (1964) for mixed chorus and trumpet, which utilizes unpitched rhythmic canons, *i thank you God* (1967) for unaccompanied mixed chorus, on text by e. e. cummings, and *Prayer* (c. 1975) for two-part mixed chorus and organ, on text by Dag Hammarskjöld. Young composed in a style openly indebted to Vaughan Williams, Healey Willan, and various practitioners of the English Cathedral tradition. His best works, such as the Christmas motet *Of the Father's Love Begotten* (1968) and the Lenten motet *The Christ-Child* (1997), are for unaccompanied mixed chorus. Scott often used preexisting tunes, but so thoroughly owned them that the resulting anthems can hardly be called arrangements. His organ accompaniments are particularly ingratiating without being difficult. Good examples include *Gracious Spirit Dwell in Me* (published 1984) and *Hilariter* (published 1991), both for mixed chorus and organ.

These composers, together with the Episcopalians, Lutherans, and those connected with concert and educational music, did not save the neo-European anthem. Instead they created from it something new: an accessible, purely American style, characterized by direct expression, sturdy construction, attractive melodies, warm harmonies, vibrant rhythms, broad sources of inspiration, and most of all a refusal to pander to easy trends or celebrate ignorance.

JEWISH COMPOSERS IN THE UNITED STATES

Throughout the twentieth century talented composers endeavored to complement and reflect the vital culture of American Jews. They were aided by appreciative community support, often manifested in the form of commissioning projects organized by major synagogues. The most famous of these, perhaps, was San Francisco's Temple Emanuel, which commissioned the famous services of Ernest Bloch and Darius Milhaud. Others also commissioned important works, including Central Synagogue and Park Avenue Synagogue in New York, and University Synagogue, Valley Beth Shalom, and Stephen S. Wise Temple in Los Angeles. In the final decade of the century these various commissioning projects were enhanced by the Milken Archive of American Jewish Music, which embarked on a recording project that would eventually comprise some sixty compact discs.

Perhaps the most prominent Jewish liturgical musicians at the beginning of the century were Sigmund Schlessinger (1835–1906), Max Spicker (1858–1912), and William Sparger, all organist-choirmasters who arranged and composed for their respective synagogues. In 1863 Schlessinger emigrated from Germany to Mobile, Alabama, where he served as organist and choirmaster at a Reform synagogue for forty years. He was also an opera fan, and found inspiration in the reforming works of Austrian composer Salomon Sulzer (1804–1890) and Polish-German composer Louis Lewandowski (1821–1894). He created synagogue music in the style of German Protestant church music, with occasional Verdian touches. Spicker, as an editor at G. Schirmer, also influenced the publication of numerous octavos that would become standard repertoire for choruses throughout the United States. In 1901 Spicker and Sparger jointly published a Sabbath Evening and Morning Service, which included pieces by non-Jewish composers, such as a setting of "S'u Sheorim" adapted from Charles Gounod's *Faust*.

Other important early figures were Gershon Ephros (1890–1978), A. W. Binder (1895–1966), and Heinrich Schalit (b. 1896).

The Polish-born Ephros served for many years as a cantor in New Jersey, enriching the synagogue repertoire with his collections of cantorial music and editions of liturgical choral works. His own style, of which *Biblical Suite* for soloist, mixed chorus, and piano is representative, is characterized by "sincere and beautiful melodic fancy, with very neat harmonization, and clean, strict counterpoint" (Rothmuller 1960).

A. W. Binder was born in New York City, becoming music director at the Free Synagogue there in 1923. He contributed many liturgical pieces and folk song arrangements for chorus, in addition to the cantata-like *Yiskor* (1949) for baritone, mixed chorus, and organ, and the "choral ballet" *Praise and Dance* (1961) for mixed chorus and dancers.

A native of Vienna, Heinrich Schalit first visited the United States in 1930, finally immigrating to New York in 1940. Although he immersed himself in the study of Sephardic chant, and although he apparently viewed the work of Salomon Sulzer and Louis Lewandowski with disdain, much of his music is free of orientalisms, instead exuding the feel of western European art music, as exemplified by the lovely *Psalm 23* for mixed chorus with optional organ. Schalit's major work was *Freitagabend Liturgie* (1932) for cantor, mixed chorus, and organ, which did include traditional tunes as found in Abraham Zevi Idelsohn's collection, and which was later revised and published in the United States as *Sabbath Eve Liturgy*.

Several composers of this generation concentrated on setting Yiddish texts. The Russian-born Lazar Weiner (1897–1982), justly famous for his art songs, composed the cantata *Legend of Toil* (1934) for soloists, mixed chorus, and piano, on text by I. Goichberg, *To Thee, America* (1942) for soloist, mixed chorus, and piano, on text by A. Leyeless, *The Golem* (1950) for tenor, bass, mixed chorus, and orchestra, on text by Halper Leivick, and *Biblical Suite* for soloist, mixed chorus, and piano. In Los Angeles, Morris Browda (1908–1965) wrote many small pieces, including the lovely lullaby *Viglid* (1961) for unison chorus and piano (or unaccompanied two-part treble chorus), on text by Isaac Leib Peretz. Maurice Rauch (1910–1994) contributed the inspiring cantata *Oib Nit Noch Hecher* for bass, mixed chorus, and piano, on a famous Chassidic tale, as well as other works.

Max Helfman (1901–1963) was born in Poland, coming to America in 1909. The technical difficulty and harmonic boldness of his early large work, *Aron ha-qodesh* (The Holy Ark), somewhat shocked New York synagogue audiences. Moving to Los Angeles, he devoted himself, with relentless energy, to work with amateur choral groups at the Brandeis Camp and produced a steady stream of choral works. Many, such as his famous *Sh'ma Koleinu*, became standard liturgical repertoire. He also composed a very impressive large cantata about the Warsaw ghetto uprising, *Di Naye Hagode* (1948) for mixed chorus and orchestra, written in Yiddish, and arranged several movements of Handel's oratorio *Judas Maccabaeus* for performance with Yiddish text.

Herbert Fromm (1905–1993) emigrated from Germany and eventually became an organist in Boston. In addition to choral compositions and important organ works for synagogue worship, he wrote numerous concert works, many on Jewish themes, such as *Psalm 23* for treble chorus and organ, *Six Madrigals* for unaccompanied mixed chorus, and *The Song of Miriam* for contralto, baritone, female chorus, and piano. Aron Marko Rothmuller (1960) described Fromm's music as "distinguished by a solid, progressive technique, not excessively modernistic or exploiting dissonance, yet of our time and colorful. His melodic invention often has affinities with the pentatonic scale of the *Neginot*, and this gives his compositions an attractive Jewish colouring."

Born in Berlin, Max Janowsky (1912–1991) relocated in Tokyo, New York, Chicago, and finally Milwaukee. Among his many influential works for Jewish worship is the service *Avodath Hakodesh* (1947) for cantor, chorus, and organ.

William Sharlin (b. 1918) contributed many liturgical compositions in a style characterized by canonic writing and rich tonal harmonies derived naturally from Jewish modes. The four-movement *Shabbat Suite* for mixed chorus and woodwind quintet (or piano), which can be considered representative, is equally effective as a concert work.

Aminadav Aloni (1927–1999) came to the United States as a student from Israel. He became music director at Valley Beth Shalom in Encino, California, and thereafter devoted himself to composition for the synagogue, film, and television. Aloni's works typically combine traditional Israeli and American popular elements in a rhythmically exuberant yet lyrical, though often angular, style. He also created liturgical works inspired by Ladino, Yiddish, and jazz. His highly original melodic gifts are exemplified in the poignant High Holiday piece, *Ahavat Olam* for baritone, mixed chorus, and organ (or piano), in which the traditional Rosh Hashanah *niggun* is combined with a new cantorial tune. Other works include *S'fatai Tiftach* (Open Thou My Lips, 1993), a collection of thirteen pieces for unaccompanied mixed chorus which contains Aloni's most advanced choral writing; *Hallelujah* for mixed chorus and keyboard; the popular Torah Service for cantor, mixed chorus, and organ; and *Uv'chein Tein Kavod* for mixed chorus and organ.

Samuel Adler (b. 1928) was born in Germany, son of the prominent cantor and liturgical composer Hugo Chaim Adler, who moved his family to the United States in 1939. Unlike other major American composers who happened to be Jewish, Samuel Adler devoted considerable energy to the composition of liturgical music. His mature style retained elements of his early diatonic and pandiatonic inclinations, as well as increased use of serial technique and occasional use of more common avant-garde devices. He is an outstanding symphonic and choral conductor as well, composing music that exhibits an understanding of technical problems without sacrificing artistic vision. In addition to a significantly large catalogue of liturgical pieces, Adler contributed the cantatas *The Vision of Isaiah* (1962) for bass, mixed chorus, and orchestra; *From out of Bondage* (1968) for four soloists, mixed chorus, brass quintet, percussion, and organ; *A Whole Bunch of Fun* (1969) for mixed chorus and orchestra, on texts by Gaius Valerius Catullus, Ogden Nash, Dr. Seuss, and others; *We Believe* (1974) for mixed chorus and eight instruments; other large works; and many secular partsongs.

Yehudi Wyner (b. 1929), son of Lazar Weiner, broke away from the Jewish musical heritage exemplified by his father's music, incorporating jazz and neoclassic elements into his style. His several choral works include the significant Friday Evening Service (1963) for tenor, mixed chorus, and organ, Torah Service (1966) for mixed chorus and instruments, and *Liturgical Fragments for the High Holidays* (1970) for unaccompanied mixed chorus.

Born in Brooklyn, Michael Isaacson (b. 1946) studied with Robert Starer at Brooklyn College and with Samuel Adler at Eastman School of Music. He became a tremendously important post–World War II Jewish composer, producing a large quantity of choral music notable for its subtle lyricism, warmly attractive harmonies, and well-balanced structures. Isaacson's liturgical works also explore a purposeful expansion of instrumental resources for use in Sabbath services. Typical works include *Hegyon libi* (1968) for mixed chorus and string quartet, *Nishmat Chayim* (1980) for mixed chorus and woodwinds, *Shir Ari* (1990) for mixed chorus and chamber orchestra, and the popular Chanukah cantata, *Aspects of a Great Miracle* (1997) for mixed chorus, brass, percussion, harp, and piano (or piano alone). Impressive smaller pieces include the secular *One More Spring* (1974) for mixed chorus, *Avinu Malkeinu* (1976) for cantor and unaccompanied mixed chorus, and *Sim Shalom* (1983) for cantor, mixed chorus, and keyboard. Of particular interest is the millennium service *L'Maaseih V'reisheet—to Recreate the World* (1999) for mixed chorus and prerecorded synthesizer, jointly commissioned and simultaneously premiered by over forty congregations throughout the United States.

Other Jewish composers include Joseph Achron (1886–1943), most famous as a violinist, who contributed *Salome's Dance* (1925) for mixed chorus, piano, and percussion, and a Sabbath Evening Service (1932) for baritone, mixed chorus, and organ; Isadore Freed (1900–1960), whose music became standard repertoire during the first half of the century; Robert Strassburg (b. 1915), whose many liturgical compositions are balanced by his settings of Walt Whitman, most notably the choral symphony *Leaves of Grass* (1989) for tenor, narrator, mixed chorus, and orchestra; Gershon Kingsley (b. 1925), who composed many scores for television and the stage, as well as the first Jewish liturgical service in rock style, *Sabbath for Today* (1968), and other synagogue music; Charles Davidson (b. 1929), whose cantata for children's choir and piano, *I Never Saw Another Butterfly* (1968), was among the earliest settings of poetry by children from Terezín; Meir Finkelstein (b. 1951), whose liturgical works are influenced both by his British musical training and American musical theater; Joseph Leonard, a blind organist whose *Hayom T'amtzenu* (published 1998) and *May the Words of My Mouth* (published 1998), both for unaccompanied mixed chorus, are typical of his several charming compositions for worship; and Charles D. Osborne, whose liturgical works were augmented by compositions designed for concert use, such as *Sephardic Havdallah* (1994) for tenor, mixed chorus, and piano (or chamber orchestra).

✎ 13

CANADA

Émigré composers formed an important ingredient in the music of Canada, as they did in the United States. Whereas several past Canadian composers were French, the early twentieth century witnessed a significant influx from Great Britain. Later in the century talented composers from Latvia and the United States would also settle there.

Guillaume Couture (1851–1915) was a leading proponent of the French musical tradition in Canada at the beginning of the century and an important teacher and choral conductor in Montreal. His *Requiem* (1906) and oratorio *Jean le Précurseur* (1907–1911) can be considered the culmination of the nineteenth-century French-Canadian aesthetic. Couture's style is traditional, exhibiting a sensitivity to dramatic aspects and an accomplished contrapuntal technique.

Anglo-Canadian heritage is best represented by the somewhat younger Healey Willan, (1880–1968), William Henry Anderson (1882–1955), and Alfred Whitehead (1887–1974).

Though born in England, Healey Willan spent his entire creative life in Canada, and he is certainly the best-known Canadian choral composer. Harmonically conservative but very much of the twentieth century, his music is steeped in the English cathedral tradition. His style reflects an obvious love of Gregorian chant, with a resulting free approach to rhythm and frequent melismas, tempered somewhat by a tightly controlled romanticism. Willan wrote numerous large works—*Te Deum* in B flat (1935–37) for chorus and orchestra, *Coronation Suite* (1952) for chorus and orchestra, Masses, Communion services, and canticles for the Roman, Anglican, and Lutheran rites—but his masterpieces are found among the smaller anthems and motets. Foremost is the religious partsong for Epiphany, *The Three Kings* for five-part mixed chorus. The three-part representation of the kings (TBB) is completely natural, the presentation of text perfect, the brief structure wonderfully conceived, the climax well timed, and the denouement sublime. Other noteworthy works include the popular "Hodie" and the particularly lovely "I Beheld Her Beautiful as a Dove," two of ten pieces included in *Liturgical Motets* (1928–37) for unaccompanied mixed chorus, as well as the hymn anthem *O quanta qualia* for mixed chorus and organ. Less successful is the grandly conceived *Apostrophe to the Heavenly Host* (1921) for two unaccompanied mixed choruses. The structure, which builds to a fine concluding rendition of "Lasst uns Erfreuen," is well considered, but the antiphonal effects are consistently commonplace and for once Willan's modally inspired melodic muse fails him. The lasting impression is one of empty effects partially salvaged by a great old hymn tune.

William Henry Anderson was a composer, choral conductor, and tenor in Winnipeg. His compositions are almost exclusively choral and reveal a decided affinity for the medium. His partsongs and arrangements, though not profound, were instrumental in developing a choral tradition in what was then a provincial, if not to say frontier, city. Works include *In the Morning* (published 1948) for tenor soloist and mixed chorus, and a substantial number of works for children's chorus.

Healey Willan: conclusion of *The Three Kings.*

Alfred Whitehead was born in England but moved to Canada in 1912. He held several important organist-choirmaster positions, was president of the Royal Canadian College of Organists for several years, and was head of music at Mount Allison University in New Brunswick. His sacred works impress by virtue of their solid craftsmanship and durability. Among his approximately four hundred choral works are the motets *Almighty God, Whose Glory* (published 1933) and *Come Holy Ghost in Love* (published 1967), both for unaccompanied mixed chorus; the anthems *Christ the Lord Is Risen* (1932) for mixed chorus and organ, and *Challenge to Free Men* (1951) for unison chorus and organ; numerous pieces for treble and male choruses; and carol arrangements and anthems based on tunes by Handel, Purcell, and other composers.

Leaders of the next generation included Lionel Daunais (1902–1982), Bernard Naylor (1907–1986), Jean Coulthard (1908–2000), Keith Bissell (1912–1992), Graham George (1912–1992), Violet Archer (1913–2000), Godfrey Ridout (1918–1984), and Talivaldis Kenins (b. 1919).

The impact of Lionel Daunais was particularly strong in Quebec, where his many settings of unaccompanied French partsongs, mostly for mixed chorus, became standard repertoire.

Bernard Naylor was born in England. Moving to Canada in 1932, he returned to England for extended stays twice before finally settling permanently in Canada in 1959. He was a student of Gustav Holst, John Ireland, and Ralph Vaughan Williams, and his art derived completely from the English choral tradition. Harmonically conservative, with melodies often moving by steps, Naylor's music achieves brief, though biting, points of dissonance after the manner of Bartók, Distler, and Randall Thompson, by refusing to make harmonic concessions to the linear integrity of individual parts. Important works include *The Annunciation According to Saint Luke* (1949) for soprano and tenor soloists, mixed chorus, and orchestra, *Nine Motets* (1952) for mixed chorus, *Stabat mater* (1961) for mixed chorus, strings, and woodwinds, *Three Sacred Pieces* (1973) for mixed chorus and orchestra, and numerous other unaccompanied pieces.

Jean Coulthard studied with a wide variety of teachers, including Copland, Milhaud, Schoenberg, and Vaughan Williams. Her lyrical style is tonal, with dissonance occurring as the natural result of linear interplay. She excelled in larger forms, such as *Choral Symphony* (1966–67) for chorus and orchestra; the cantata for the centennial of Vancouver, British Columbia, *This Land* (1967) for chorus and orchestra; and *Hymn of Creation* (1975–76) for mixed chorus and percussion.

Keith Bissell was not particularly famous outside Canada, but he exerted a singular influence on the choral community within the country by virtue of his large catalogue of works for virtually every choral configuration. Examples include *The Dark Hills* (1958) and *O Holy Spirit* (1962), both for un-accompanied mixed chorus; *Requiem* (1967) for treble chorus, on text by Robert Louis Stevenson; *The Passion According to Saint Luke* (1970) for narrator, children's and mixed choruses, organ, and orchestra; and *Theme, Variation and Epilogue* (1975) for soprano and viola soloists, mixed chorus, and strings.

Graham George created one of the great hymn tunes of the century, "The King's Majesty." His resulting hymn anthem, *Ride on! Ride on in Majesty!* (1939) for mixed chorus and organ, is a classic of its type. Understated and noble, it is laid out in an arch form: first and fifth verses in unison, second and fourth in unison with descant, third in four unaccompanied parts. Other works include several other anthems, both unaccompanied and with organ, *The Apocalypse of Saint John* for six soloists (SSATBB) and unaccompanied mixed chorus, and numerous works for treble chorus.

Violet Archer was influenced both harmonically and in terms of "practical" music by Paul Hindemith, her teacher. She therefore composed a substantial number of anthems and partsongs that are interesting but not difficult, as well as several larger works such as *Choruses from "The Bacchae"* (1938) for female chorus and orchestra, *Apocalypse* (1958) for soprano soloist, mixed chorus, brass, and timpani, and *Paul Bunyan* (1966) for mixed chorus and piano.

Godfrey Ridout studied with Willan but was also inspired by the older English composers Sir Edward Elgar and Sir Arthur Sullivan. His music is thoroughly tonal, and the occasionally rugged rhythms lend it a peculiarly North American character. Although he contributed excellent small pieces for a variety of vocal configurations, Ridout is at his best in larger works with orchestra. Among them are the dramatic symphony *Esther* (1952) for soprano and baritone soloists, mixed chorus, and orchestra, and *Pange lingua* (1960) for mixed chorus and orchestra.

Talivaldis Kenins emigrated from Latvia. Primarily a composer of important instrumental works, he nevertheless made a vital contribution to choral music. Particularly noteworthy are his several works for male voices, including arrangements of Canadian folk songs and settings of Latvian texts.

Composers who reached maturity after mid-century include Gabriel Charpentier (b. 1925), Charles M. Wilson (b. 1931), R. Murray Schafer (b. 1933), and André Prévost (b. 1934).

Gabriel Charpentier studied with Nadia Boulanger, developing a style that is melodically direct and harmonically rather conservative, though completely open to new ideas. Though particularly adept at writing music for the stage, including incidental scores, he did not neglect the choral idiom. Among his choral works are three Masses for unaccompanied chorus, the earliest dating from 1952, and *Permutation 1234* (1962) for unaccompanied mixed chorus.

Charles M. Wilson was a student of Lukas Foss and Carlos Chávez. His small but significant choral catalogue includes the cantata *On the Morning of Christ's Nativity* (1965) for soprano, tenor, and bass soloists, mixed chorus, and orchestra, the oratorio *The Angels of the Earth* (1966) for soprano and bass soloists, two narrators, mixed chorus, and orchestra, *Phrases from Orpheus* (1971) for mixed chorus and dancers, *Image out of Season* (1973) for mixed chorus and brass quintet, *Missa brevis* (1975) for mixed chorus and organ, and *Nocturnal-Paudash* (1983) for five-part mixed chorus (SSATB), piano, and tape.

R. Murray Schafer's style is perhaps best described as the free and intuitive use of virtually every technique to come in vogue during the middle third of the century. His profound interest in the nature of sound and the effect of sound on humans is easily seen in the spatial elements of his compositions as well as in the purely phonetic quality of his text settings. As an educator primarily interested in introducing new modes of expression and unlocking creativity, he has written numerous pieces for young performers which utilize advanced techniques but with an appropriately gauged difficulty factor. For example, *Epitaph for Moonlight* (1968) for youth choir (SATB, divisi) and various types of bells (optional) uses a graphic notation that does not specify pitches or rhythms; and yet if the composer's directions are followed, major triads and clusters built from half steps and whole steps miraculously appear. Other works include *Threnody* (1966) for five youth speakers, youth chorus, and youth orchestra, on texts by children who survived the bombing of Nagasaki, *Gita* (1967) for mixed chorus, brass, and tape, *Apocalypsis Part One: John's Vision* (1977) for soloists, choirs, wind, percussion, and organ, and *Apocalypsis Part Two: Credo* (1977) for twelve mixed choirs and tape.

After graduation from Montreal Conservatory, André Prévost studied in Paris with Messiaen, who taught him to use bold harmonies as colors on a large canvas. His first important choral piece, the cantata *Terre des hommes* (1967) for soloists, three choruses, and two orchestras, was chosen to open Expo '67 in Montreal. Other works include *Soleils couchants* (1953) for mixed chorus, on text by Paul Verlaine, *Psalm 148* (1971) for mixed chorus (two hundred voices!), four trumpets, four trombones, and organ, *Missa pro defunctis* (1973) for SATB soloists and mixed chorus, and *Ahimsa* (1983) for mezzo-soprano, mixed chorus, flute, piccolo, and string quartet.

Others from this generation include John Beckwith (b. 1927), Alfred Kunz (b. 1929), Michael R. Miller (b. 1932) and Donald Patriquin (b. 1938), who wrote many unaccompanied pieces; Ruth Watson Henderson (b. 1932), who composed a stimulating *Missa brevis* (1974) for mixed chorus and made significant contributions to the treble choir repertoire; Barrie Cabena (b. 1933), who composed much church music of very high quality; and Derek Healey (b. 1936), who wrote several anthems and accompanied partsongs.

Younger composers include José Evangelista (b. 1943), a 1997 Barlow Award finalist who had earlier impressed with *Coros tejiendo, voces alternando* (1975) for twelve-part mixed chorus and *O quam suavis* (1987) for mixed chorus; Anne Lauber (b. 1943), whose oratorio *Jesus Christus* (1985) and *Requiem* (1989), both for soloists, mixed chorus, and orchestra, clearly indicate a predilection for large forms; the Latvian emigrant Imant Raminsh (b. 1943), whose many justifiably popular partsongs for mixed chorus and treble chorus reveal unique melodic gifts couched in quasi-impressionistic harmonies; Stephen Chatman (b. 1950), an émigré from the United States whose accessible style, as exhibited in the suites *There Is Sweet Music Here* (1984) for mixed chorus and oboe, and *Due North* (1986) for unaccompanied mixed chorus, is eclectic in the best sense, full of clever modern twists and warm revelations; the prolific Nancy Telfer (b. 1950), who produced sacred and secular pieces for all vocal configurations, including the substantive *Missa brevis* (published 1985) for unaccompanied treble chorus; Jacques Desjardins (b. 1962), whose unaccompanied partsongs show great promise; and Stephen Hatfield (b. 1964), whose multicultural interests have resulted in stunning folk song arrangements and other works.

The Canadian Jewish community is also very strong and has produced several composers of international stature, including Ben Steinberg (b. 1930), Milton Barnes (b. 1931), Srul Irving Glick (b. 1934), and Sid Robinovitch (b. 1942). Each contributed a significant number of compositions for concert and synagogue worship, noteworthy for a high level of craftsmanship and attention to expressive detail. An exemplary work is Glick's *Sheeru Ladonye sheer chadash* (Sing unto the Lord a New Song, 1986) for mixed chorus, harp, and piano (or two flutes, two clarinets, French horn, harp, and strings). In this four-movement suite of psalm settings, the instrumental writing is colorful and idiomatic, the choral writing masterful. Prevailing contrapuntal textures are balanced by well-timed homophonic passages; delightful dance rhythms are further invigorated by occasional changing meters; tonal harmonies are spiced with added notes.

ꙮ 14

PACIFIC RIM

CHINA

Vocal music in China, as in other Asian countries, traditionally emphasized the solo voice. At the beginning of the twentieth century, however, many Chinese leaders viewed European culture as superior to their own, encouraging the adaptation of Western musical styles while inhibiting the continued development of traditional forms. Many composers, unwilling to completely abandon Chinese aesthetics, sought to create a hybrid art, often adapting Chinese scales for use with European instruments and procedures. Huang Tsu (1904–1938) and other composers successfully synthesized European and Chinese elements, especially in choral music, creating partsongs uniquely suited to the inflections of Chinese speech.

After the Communists gained power, traditional music remained suppressed and Western music was viewed with ambivalence. Composers such as Richard Strauss and Claude Debussy were not allowed, while Beethoven and Dvořák were officially approved. Russian works found favor, especially those written under the spell of socialist realism.

During this time Mao Tse-Tung collectivized all creative activity so that individual composers' names did not usually appear on scores. An exception was Hsien Hsing-hai (1905–1945), who was considered a national treasure. He composed a cantata and many partsongs, all of a political nature, in addition to the best-known Chinese work of the century: *Yellow River Cantata* (1939, revised 1941) for soloists, chorus, and orchestra. A student of d'Indy and Dukas, Hsien combined the simplest Chinese scales with Western instruments orchestrated in a primitively powerful way. His direct, intellectually shallow but emotionally potent style reflected the ideals of socialist realism exactly, and became the favored mode of expression during the Maoist period. If any subtlety existed in Hsien's music, it was surely ironed out in the numberless copycat works produced by the composer collectives.

Until the century's last decade, Chou Wen-Chung (b. 1923) was the best-known Chinese composer in the West. He came to the United States in 1946, never returning to China. His music fuses traditional Chinese elements with techniques learned from his teachers Otto Luening, Nicolas Slonimsky, and Edgard Varèse. Though he is primarily an instrumental composer, his *Poems of White Stone* (1958–59) for mixed chorus and instruments combines a confident vocal technique with the same subtle harmonies and colorful orchestration typical of his other works.

Tsang-houei Hsu (b. 1929) studied in France with André Jolivet and Olivier Messiaen. While he was the first Taiwanese composer to use avant-garde techniques, Hsu's style is more influenced by a profound knowledge of Taiwanese folk music, coupled with devices learned from earlier twentieth-century masters. Some of his greatest works are choral, including the twelve-tone cantata *Ping chi hsing*, Opus 8 (1958), the modal *Chu-kuo sung*, Opus 11 (1963–65) for children's chorus and orchestra, and the marvelous *Tsang hua yin*, Opus 13 (Burial Flowers, 1962) for mixed chorus and traditional instruments.

Chen Yi (b. 1953), Bright Sheng (b. 1955), and Tan Dun (b. 1957) attempted to create an evocative world music that combined Chinese and Western instruments, scales, structures, and texts. All three eventually settled in the United States.

Chen Yi graduated from the Central Conservatory in Beijing before immigrating to the United States in 1986, where she studied at Columbia University. She became well known through her position as composer-in-residence with Chanticleer and as a professor at the Peabody Conservatory in Baltimore. In 1998 Chen accepted an endowed professorship at the University of Missouri, Kansas City. Among Chen's choral works are *Three Poems from the Song Dynasty* (1985) for mixed chorus, on texts by Li Qing-zhao, Su Shi, and Xin Qi-ji; the delightful madrigal *Written on a Rainy Night* (1995) for mixed chorus; and the large *Chinese Myths Cantata* (1996) for male chorus, dancers, orchestra, and four traditional instruments: erhu (fiddle), yangqin (dulcimer), pipa (lute), and zheng (zither).

Bright Sheng studied at the Shanghai Conservatory before coming to New York in 1982, where he studied at Queens College and Columbia University. His early experience as a dance company accompanist in the province of Chinhai, near the Tibetan border, provided the raw material for his best-known choral piece, the riveting *Two Folk Songs from Chinhai* (1990) for mixed chorus and orchestra, which includes "Morningstar Lily" and "A Pair of Mules." Sheng pointed out, while reflecting on the origin and musical characteristic of these songs, that

> Chinese songs derive from local dialects and have a close connection
> with the geographical situations and natural surroundings of each
> specific region. Since the [Chinhai] region is noted for its mountains
> and steep cliffs, the folk songs there are known for their big intervallic

leaps in melody—the fourths, fifths, sevenths, eighths, and often even elevenths or twelfths. (Ledbetter 1994)

Commissioned by the American conductor John Oliver, *Two Folk Songs* mesmerizes by blending Chinese scales and oriental percussion effects with orchestral techniques, propulsive rhythms, and harmonic textures reminiscent of Stravinsky and Copland.

Tan Dun composed *Symphony 1997 Heaven Earth Mankind* (1997) for solo cello, children's chorus, bianzhong (large bronze bells), and orchestra in honor of the reunification of Hong Kong and China. Inspired by cellist Yo-Yo Ma and the 2400-year-old bianzhong discovered in Hubei Province in 1978, Tan (1997, 8) was also passionate about his inclusion of a children's chorus: "As a composer, when I hear these innocent children's voices, I feel they are chanting the past. When I listen to the sound of the bianzhong, I sense it is singing the song of the future. Maybe there really is no distinction between the past and future—everything is a circle." Tan also wrote the impressive *Water Passion after Saint Matthew* (2000) for soloists, chorus, and orchestra (see chapter 15).

Chuan-Sheng Lu and Fu-Yu Lin each contributed outstanding arrangements of Taiwanese folk songs. Particularly impressive is Chuan-Sheng Lu's *The Train* for treble chorus, which effectively introduces high-pitched chord clusters to evoke a train whistle.

Another composer of Chinese descent, Dai-Keong Lee (b. 1915) was born in Hawaii and studied at the Juilliard School and Columbia University. His music synthesizes academic training received from Aaron Copland and Otto Luening with a decidedly Hawaiian outlook. Choral works include *Canticle of the Pacific* (1943, revised 1968) for mixed chorus and orchestra, originally titled *Pacific Prayer*, and *Mele olili* (Joyful Songs, 1960) for soloists, mixed chorus, and orchestra.

JAPAN

Japan also had an extensive solo vocal tradition. But Japanese composers, eager to develop new modes of expression, quickly assimilated European musical ideas after the Meiji Restoration opened Japan to Western influences in 1868. The populace was receptive, and school choruses based on European models were established as early as 1872. By 1900 Japanese composers, led by Rentaro Taki (1879–1903), were composing songs and choral pieces utilizing European techniques, and as the century progressed composers inevitably experimented with combinations of various Western and Japanese elements. Still, late-nineteenth-century German ideals, and to a much lesser extent French impressionism, remained the dominant influences even after the introduction of serial technique and electronic music in the sixties.

Kōsaku Yamada (1886–1965) studied composition in Berlin with Max Bruch. Returning to Japan in 1914, he quickly became known as an orchestral conductor. His breakthrough as a composer occurred at the time of the coronation of Emperor Taishō (Yoshihito), for which he composed his first important work for chorus and orchestra, *Kimigayo zensōkyoku* (Prelude on the Japanese National Anthem, 1915). Throughout his life Yamada sought to reconcile German principles with rhythms and inflections peculiar to Japanese speech. Some of the best pieces in his extremely large catalogue are for women's voices and piano, including *Nairu-gawa no uta* (Song of the Nile, 1911), *Hikari motomete* (Seeking Light, 1921), *Ai no megami* (Goddess of Love, 1928), and *Funaji* (Sea Route, 1931). He also composed several cantatas for chorus and orchestra, including *Chikai no hoshi* (Star of Promise, 1908) and *Tenrikyō sanshōfu* (Hymn for the Tenrikyō, 1956).

Kiyoshi Nobutoki (1887–1965) was another important composer prior to World War II. He studied at the Berlin Singacademie with the choral conductor and composer Georg Schumann, developing an accessible style steeped in German romantic techniques but thoroughly Japanese in outlook. Nobutoki willingly exploited these qualities in service of the expansionist Japanese government of the thirties, producing many patriotic-nationalistic pieces, which helped fan the flames of militarism. Most influential was the cantata *Kaidō tōsei* (Along the Coast, Conquer the East, 1940). Other works include the early *Omoide* (Remembrances, 1915), *Kora, o omou uta* (Songs Recalling Children, 1931), and *Nyonin waka renkyoku* (Waka Poems by Women Poets), published posthumously.

Masao Ōki (1901–1971) was an almost completely self-taught composer whose European musical outlook was colored somewhat by Japanese melodic and harmonic elements. His large choral-orchestral works, including *Shinano ji* (Shinano Way, 1933) and *Ningen o kaese* (Restore Humanity, 1960), reflect his socialist ideology.

Tomojirō Ikenouchi (1906–1991) was an influential composition teacher. His impressive *Koi no omoni* (Burden of Love, 1974) for baritone soloist, mixed chorus, and timpani reveals his preference for French traditions. Among his important students are Sadao Bekku (b. 1922), whose *Ō-otoko no niwa* (Giant's Garden, 1962) for speaker, mixed chorus, orchestra, and tape also contains French coloration, and Toshi Ichiyanagi (b. 1933), whose predilection for aleatoric and other advanced techniques is obvious in several works for mixed chorus, including *Music for Living Space* (1969), with computer, and the unaccompanied *Extended Voices* (1967) and *Voice Act* (1973).

Osamu Shimizu (1911–1986) is perhaps the best-known composer of choral music, his partsongs and cantatas being among the most frequently performed Japanese works. Influenced by Buddhism as well as by traditional European musical thought, he created works that are predominantly lyrical, the well-structured melodies exuding a popular appeal. Though Shimizu composed some unaccompanied pieces, such as *Bara no sansaku* (Promenade in the Roses, 1965) for male chorus, his compositions usually call for accompaniment by piano or other instruments. Typical works include *Nagaki sō no hanashi* (Priest with a Long Nose, 1960) for mixed chorus and piano, the cantata *Yama ni inoru* (Prayer to the Mountains, 1960) for speaker, male chorus, and orchestra, and *Shi no fuchi yori* (1975) for mixed chorus and string trio.

Saburō Takata (1913–2000) is typical of the generation of composers who matured just after World War II. Traces of traditional Japanese elements lend an occasional impressionistic feel to an otherwise German style. His substantial output of choral music includes the male chorus *Kisetsu to ashiato* (Seasons and Footprints, 1958), the cantata *Musei dōkoku* (Wordless Tears, 1956–64) for soloists, mixed chorus, and orchestra, and several Masses, psalm settings, and other works for the Roman Catholic liturgy.

Minao Shibata (1916–1996) was a leading Japanese authority on European music history. In his numerous choral works, beginning with the modal *Magnificat and Nunc dimittis* (1951) for mixed chorus and organ, many Western compositional trends are displayed. Avant-garde techniques dominate in *Kadensho* (1971) for six soloists and six mixed choruses, as well as in the choral variations on a well-known folk song, *Oiwake-bushi kō* (1973) for mixed chorus and instruments.

Yoshirō Irino (b. 1921) was the first Japanese composer to rely primarily on Schoenbergian dodecaphony, incorporating some native elements into his style around 1966. Among his choral works are *Iwa* (Rock, 1958) for male chorus, *Three Pieces* (1960) for female chorus, *Three Pieces* (1960) for male chorus, *Fuji san* (Mount Fuji, 1966) for male chorus, and *Oni no yomesan* (Devil's Bride, 1970) for mixed chorus.

Kan Ishii (b. 1921) studied in Munich with Carl Orff, whose primitivism provided a perfect balance to Ishii's otherwise rather nationalistic inclinations. Although primarily a composer of ballets (many for the company of his father, Bac Ishii), Kan Ishii also wrote many pieces for chorus, and served for a time as president of the All-Japan Choral League. Among his works are *Kareki to taiyō no uta* (Song of the Withered Tree and the Sun, 1955) and *Otokonoko ga umareta* (A Boy Is Born, 1964), both for unaccompanied mixed chorus; the cantata *Ōinaru Akita* (Great Akita, 1974) for soprano, mixed chorus, and orchestra; and numerous folk song settings.

Joji Yuasa (b. 1929) took up composition after abandoning studies in medicine. Essentially self-taught, he was among the first Japanese composers to become interested in electronic music. Yuasa's music, whether for electronic or traditional media, displays a lively interest in the relationship of sound and space. Notable works include *Toi* (Questions, 1971) and *Utterance* (1971), both for mixed chorus; and *Projection on Basho's Poems* (1974) for chorus and vibraphone.

Tōru Takemitsu (1930–1998), the most important Japanese composer of the twentieth century, unfortunately composed very little choral music. His compositions combine a love of the most advanced techniques of Stravinsky, Schoenberg, Messiaen, and other modern European masters, with an interest in traditional Japanese elements. *Kaze no uma* (Horse in the Wind, 1962) for women's chorus is representative.

Other Japanese choral composers include Akira Ifukube (b. 1914), who composed the ode *Okhotsk* (1958) for chorus and orchestra; Michio Mamiya (b. 1929), who contributed the oratorio *15 June 1960* (1961) in memory of a student killed during anti-American protests, and other choral works that attempted to create a modern national style; Teizo Matsumora (b. 1929), who composed several large choral works, including *Flute of Evil Passions* (1965) for baritone, male chorus, and orchestra, *Apsaras* (1969) for women's chorus and chamber orchestra, *Totem Ritual* (1969) for soprano, mixed chorus, and orchestra, and *Hymn to Aurora* (1978) for mixed chorus and chamber ensemble; Toshiitsu Tanaka (b. 1930), whose several choral works are based on Japanese folk rhythms; Hikaru Hayashi (b. 1931), who composed numerous partsongs and the oratorio *Beggar's Song* (1962); Yuji Takahashi (b. 1938), whose *Michi-Yuki* (1971) for mixed chorus, two percussionists, and electric cello reflects the influence of Iannis Xenakis; and Shin-Ichiro Ikebe (b. 1943), who impressed with *Kusabi* (1972) for female chorus, eleven players, and dance, the Spanish-language *Five Chansons by García Lorca* for male chorus, and other works.

KOREA

Missionaries introduced Western music into Korea during the nineteenth century; but, although it was accepted alongside traditional forms, it did not really begin to thrive until after World War II. The Contemporary Music Society was formed to promote new music utilizing traditional Korean elements, new music written in Western style, and new music that combined Korean and Western materials.

Isang Yun (1917–1995) studied music in Japan and was imprisoned there during World War II. Afterward, he returned to Korea, assisting with the reestablishment of cultural activities. In 1956 he journeyed to Paris for study, moving on to Berlin in 1958, where he studied with Boris Blacher. From that time on Yun lived in Germany, except for an unfortunate two-year period (1967–69) in which he was returned to Korea and imprisoned as a Communist (later receiving a pardon). His music developed from strict twelve-tone serialism to a style emphasizing Asian modes of expression transmitted through Western techniques and instruments. His vocal works also display a fondness for instrumentally derived ornamentation, combined with pitched and unpitched vocalization. Representative works include the Buddhist oratorio *Om mani padme hum* (1964) for soprano and baritone soloists, mixed chorus, and orchestra, *Ein Schmetterlingstraum* (1968) for chorus and percussion, *An der Schwelle* (1975) for baritone, female chorus, organ, and instruments, and *Der weise Mann* (1977) for baritone, chorus, and chamber orchestra.

Un-Yung La (1922–1993) was a prolific composer, theorist, teacher, choral conductor, and church musician. Greatly influenced by Bartók and Kodály, he advocated the marriage of Korean folk elements with Western techniques. Melodic and harmonic aspects of his music often rely on church modes. Among his approximately fifteen hundred compositions are nine cantatas (including those for Christmas and Easter) for various choral-instrumental combinations, many pieces for children's choir, and some eleven hundred hymns. La's ten-volume music theory text—a standard resource for Korean musicians—includes a volume on choral arranging.

Byong-kon Kim (b. 1929) studied at Indiana University and eventually settled in the United States. His choral works include *A Sunday Hymn* (1965) for mixed chorus, *i am a little church* (1970) for mixed chorus and organ, and the impressive treble-chorus anthem *My Heart is Steadfast*.

Jung-sun Park (b. 1945) is a very important younger composer and a professor at Dankook University in Seoul. He received his advanced musical training at Eastman School of Music, where he received the Howard Hanson Prize. While his orchestral works have been performed throughout the world, he is particularly esteemed in Korea for his choral music. His style seamlessly mixes modern Western tonal and structural sensibilities with Korean scales and vocal techniques. These characteristics are showcased in the impressive *Inchon Mass* (1996) for unaccompanied mixed chorus, on Latin text, as well as numerous smaller works and folk song arrangements.

Other Korean composers include Boo Ki Chung, whose works include the powerful *Resentment Five Hundred Years* for mixed chorus, as well as Dong Whan Kim and Hee Jo Kim, whose numerous arrangements of Korean folk songs are outstanding.

PHILIPPINES

Spanish colonization, followed by the American protectorate, created a potentially lively choral atmosphere in the Philippines, although native composers seemed uninterested until the early sixties. Until that time the choral repertoire consisted mainly of American and European pieces brought by missionaries and school teachers, folk song arrangements made by a few local composers,

University of the Philippines Madrigal Singers at the Cultural Center of the Philippines, 1998. Courtesy of the University of the Philippines Madrigal Singers.

and Catholic church music inherited from the Spanish or written by church musicians such as Marcelo Adonay (1848–1928), who contributed a considerable body of liturgical music. The leading composers early in the century—Francisco Santiago (1889–1947), Nicanor Abelardo (1893–1934), and Antonio Molino (1894–1979)—were simply not interested in choral music. According to Andrea Veneracion (personal communication, 1998), only a dozen or so original Filipino choral pieces (other than functional church music) existed when she founded the famed University of the Philippines Madrigal Singers in 1963.

Thereafter, the situation changed. Composers, interested in combining traditional elements with modern Western techniques, now turned their attention to choral music. José Maceda (b. 1917) wrote *Ugma-ugma* (Structures, 1963) for instruments and chorus, the "first piece by a Filipino to employ exclusively non-Western instruments and to use structures based on densities and sound masses rather than melodies or harmonic formations" (Ryker 1991). Lucrecia Kasilag (b. 1918), a former Eastman student, composed the choral dance piece *Filisiana* (1964), which combined musical elements from Japan, China, India,

Indonesia, and the Philippines with a traditional Filipino plucked-string ensemble and avant-garde choral procedures. Her later *Dularawan* (1969), written for the inauguration of the Cultural Center of the Philippines, went a step further, its large ensemble of soloists, chorus, actors, dancers, and orchestra of Asian instruments creating a spectacular multimedia event.

Rosalina Abejo (b. 1922) composed several Masses and other liturgical pieces, in addition to the cantatas *Advent* (1957), *The Conversion of King Humabon* (1967), and *Redemption Oratorio* (1969). The secret of her richly variegated music, according to Ramon Pagayon Santos (Ryker 1991), lies in the assignation of "specific style devices to different emotions . . . [resulting] in pieces woven out of modal harmonies, ethnic rhythms, Tchaikovskyan textures, and Spanish-type melodies."

Jerry Amper Dadap (b. 1935) contributed a significant number of large-scale works, including choral-symphonic odes (1963, 1965), cycles for chorus and instruments (1964, 1967), *Lam-Ang Epic* (1973) for chorus, Asian instruments, and orchestra, and the oratorio *The Redemption* (1974), noteworthy for its complex harmonic structure.

Note: Palms face each other and move with one brisk outward motion to make bell sounds. On last bell sound, men raise clappers at chest height, away from body.

Ladies make bell sounds with one quick outward motion, keeping palms facing each other above shoulder height during rest marks. Men make sounds with clapper by holding it with right hand and striking it on the left palm.

Ruben R. Federizon: from *Gabaq-An*.

Ruben R. Federizon's *Gabaq-An* (1991) is representative of the works written for the University of the Philippines Madrigal Singers. A wildly colorful fusion of avant-garde devices and traditional elements, it requires the singers to play finger bells and bamboo canes struck with the hand. It also uses the Madrigal Singers' unique performance configuration (seated in a half circle) as a point of departure for ceremonial movement.

Other composers include Eliseo Pajaro (1915–1984), who augmented his earlier successful choral arrangements of Filipino and Ilocano folk songs with *Himig pilipino* (1972), a series of thirty educational choruses; and Bayani Mendoza de Leon (b. 1942), who composed several works for chorus and orchestra, including the choral poem *Los penitentes* (1967), the choral drama *Legend of the Land* (1968), and the choral fantasy *Sisa* (1968).

AUSTRALIA

Surely the most famous Australian composer is Percy Grainger (1882–1961), who left Melbourne to study in Frankfurt, eventually settling in the United States. Coming under the influence of Frederick Delius, he rejected his German academic musical training to seek a more "democratic" approach in the study of folk music. His original works, even those of small dimensions, suffer from structural problems. But his folk song settings go far beyond the traditional concept of arrangements, as if the strictures inherent in preexisting tunes were the catalysts needed to free his imagination. Contrapuntally rich, harmonically vivid, and idiomatic, they constitute a rich treasury of choral song. Typical examples include *Ye Banks and Braes o' Bonnie Doon* (1901) for chorus and whistlers, *The Three Ravens* (1902, revised 1943–49) for baritone, chorus, and five clarinets, *Sir Eglamore* (1904, revised 1912–13) for double chorus, brass, percussion, and strings, and *Brigg Fair* (1906, revised 1911) for tenor and chorus. Grainger's original works favor texts by Rudyard Kipling, from *The Sea-Wife* (1898–1905, revised 1947) for mixed chorus and brass, to the smaller *Tiger, Tiger* (1905) for male chorus.

After studies with Boulanger, Vaughan Williams, and Wellesz, Peggy Glanville-Hicks (1912–1990) settled first in the United States (1942–59) and eventually in Greece. However, she retained strong ties to her homeland, representing Australia at international music festivals and acting as advisor to the Australian Ministry of Information in New York. Her first work to gain international recognition was her *Choral Suite* (1937) for female chorus, oboe, and strings.

Malcolm Williamson (b. 1931) went to Europe after graduating from the Sydney Conservatory in 1950, settled in London in 1953, and became Master of the Queen's Music in 1975. He impressed with his early *Symphony for Voices* (1960), written in a modified serial style influenced by Messiaen and

Stravinsky, and *The Icy Mirror* (Symphony No. 3, 1972), on a libretto by Ursula Vaughan Williams, before churning out a series of pop-inspired works. Williamson's occasional attempts at a synthesis of pop and serial techniques have met with only mixed success, and he has been justifiably criticized for a willingness to settle for less than his best effort. *Symphony for Voices*, with its brilliant contrapuntal writing and well-balanced structure, remains his best work. Other choral pieces include the "concert-opera" *The Brilliant and the Dark* (1966), *Canticle of Fire* (1973) for mixed chorus and organ, *Ode to Music* (1973) for children's choir and orchestra, and *Mass of Christ the King* (1977).

Of those who remained in Australia, the most important are Margaret Sutherland (1897–1984), John Antill (1904–1986), Don Banks (1923–1980), George Dreyfus (b. 1928), Peter Sculthorpe (b. 1929), Colin Brumby (b. 1933), and Barry Conyngham (b. 1944).

Margaret Sutherland was born in Adelaide and studied at Melbourne University before journeying to London in 1923, where she studied composition with Arnold Bax, who greatly influenced her style. Her cantata *The Passing* (1939) for mixed chorus and orchestra, the smaller *A Company of Carols* (1966) for mixed chorus and piano, and several other small pieces are definitely tinged with English coloration and hint of French neoclassicism and other European trends in vogue between the world wars.

John Antill trained as a chorister at Sydney's Saint Andrew's Cathedral and conducted extensive research in aboriginal music, which he incorporated into his own style, recognized internationally as uniquely Australian. In addition to the oratorio *Song of Hagar* (1958) and the smaller *Cantate Domino* (1970) for unaccompanied mixed chorus, Antill composed the brilliant choral ballet *Black Opal* (1961) for mixed chorus and timpani, which explores nationalistic and aboriginal themes.

Don Banks was influenced by jazz, twelve-tone technique, and various native Australian elements, which he combined with a natural lyricism. His choral works, *Findings, Keepings* (1968) for mixed chorus, drums, and doublebass, and *Walkabout* (1972) for children's chorus and instruments, exemplify these tendencies.

George Dreyfus emigrated from Germany with his parents in 1939. Throughout his career he actively promoted Australian music, forming a chamber orchestra in 1970 devoted exclusively to its performance. An accomplished composer for film and television, Dreyfus developed a style that effortlessly fuses avant-garde techniques with popular elements. Among his choral works are *Homage to Stravinsky* (1968) for ten-voice mixed chorus, *Under the Gumtrees at Sunrise* (1968) for four soloists and double five-voice mixed chorus, and *Reflections in a Glass-House: An Image of Captain James Cook* (1970) for speaker, children's chorus, and orchestra.

Peter Sculthorpe was influenced early by Varèse, later by aboriginal music, and finally by Penderecki. The composite produced boldly colorful music constantly in search of new timbres and rhythms. The example of Penderecki dominates *Sun Music for Voices* (1965–66) for mixed chorus and percussion. Other examples of Sculthorpe's highly pictorial style include *Night Piece* (1966) for mixed chorus and piano, and *Sea Chant* (1968) for unaccompanied mixed chorus.

Colin Brumby studied in Melbourne and London before joining the faculty at the University of Queensland. His choral works include *Gilgamesh* (1967) for speaker, mixed chorus, brass, and percussion, *Charlie Bubbles' Book of Hours* (1969) for soloists, chorus, tape, and orchestra, *Celebrations and Lamentations* (1971) for speakers, soloists, chorus, and orchestra, and several Christmas cantatas and other large-scale works.

Barry Conyngham's early interest in jazz was enhanced by study with Peter Sculthorpe, resulting in his first choral work, *Farben* (1968) for mixed chorus. Conyngham's developing style was further stretched by study with Tōru Takemitsu in Japan and by his introduction to electronically generated sounds at Princeton. Other choral works include *Voss* (1972) for soprano, mixed chorus, piano, and orchestra, and the impressive *Imaginary Letters* (1980) for mixed choir.

NEW ZEALAND

Though well established at the beginning of the century, choral singing in New Zealand was profoundly influenced by England's Sheffield Musical Union, which gave concerts in Christchurch in 1911 under the direction of Sir Henry Coward. These reportedly superlative performances provided inspiration for local choral societies, churches, and composers alike. At the time, the main body of New Zealand's homegrown repertoire was produced by Robert Parker (1846–1937), Maughan Barnett (1867–1978), and the enterprising Australian Alfred Hill (1870–1960). The works of Parker and Barnett were firmly rooted in the English choral tradition, Parker writing many occasional pieces and Barnett much church music, as well as the large *Ode* (1900) for the Canterbury Jubilee Industrial Exhibition. Hill moved to New Zealand in 1892, living there until 1908. His cantata *Hinemoa* (1896) for soloists, chorus, and orchestra made a lasting international impression. Based on a Maori legend, it succeeded admirably in bringing native and European cultures together. Of it, a Maori teacher remarked, "I could not have believed that any European music could have so well interpreted the genius of Maori feeling" (Thomson 1991, 218). Hill's other works, which influenced the Australian composers John Antill and Roy Agnew, include another Maori-inspired cantata, *Tawhaki* (1897), as well as a Mass (1931) for unaccompanied mixed chorus.

Indigenous Maori works, such as the partsongs of Richard Puanaki (b. 1934) and Ngapo Wehi (b. 1934), exerted considerable influence on succeeding composers. Largely improvised, they are ceremonial and deeply spiritual in nature. Non-Maori choirs are not allowed to perform them without the special permission and blessing of the Maori people.

Perhaps New Zealand's best composer, Douglas Lilburn (b. 1915) developed an identifiable style that evolved through the influences of Sibelius and Vaughan Williams, Bartók and Stravinsky, and electronic media. A representative choral work is *Song of the Antipodes* (1946) for mixed chorus.

Other representative composers of choral music include Ronald Tremain (b. 1923), whose love of sparse textures and intellectual astringency, as demonstrated in *Tenera juventa* (1964) for chorus and two pianos, reflects the influence of Webern; Edwin Carr (b. 1926), who contributed *Blake Cantata* (1952) for children and small orchestra; David Farquhar (b. 1928), whose choral symphony *Bells in Their Seasons* (1974) shows the influence of Bartók and Britten; John Rimmer (b. 1939), a student of Tremain, who composed the interesting *Visions I* (1975) for mixed chorus and tape; Gillian Whitehead (b. 1941), whose Maori heritage and studies with Peter Maxwell Davies inform her *Missa brevis* (1965) for mixed chorus and the larger cantata *Babel* (1969–70) for soloists, mixed chorus, and orchestra; Victor Galway, who wrote many practical pieces for church and schools; and Vernan Griffith, who wrote three Masses and several cantatas.

Younger composers include Dorothy Buchanan (b. 1945), the first woman appointed to the position of composer-in-schools (the Christchurch region especially benefited from this); Ross Harris (b. 1945), who impressed with his Maori translation of I Corinthians 13, *Kia mau te rongo* (Live in Peace, 1983) for twenty-four-part mixed chorus and synthesized drone; David Griffiths (b. 1950), whose comment about voices—"I love their richness, color, and intensity and their correctly ordered use" (Thomson 1991)—is reflected in his practically conceived church works; David Hamilton (b. 1955), whose *Te Deum* and many other excellent choral pieces occasionally reveal the influence of George Crumb and Steve Reich; David Childs (b. 1969), who gained international recognition with a variety of impressive choral works; and Anna Griffiths (b. 1981), whose partsongs display an unusual maturity and promise.

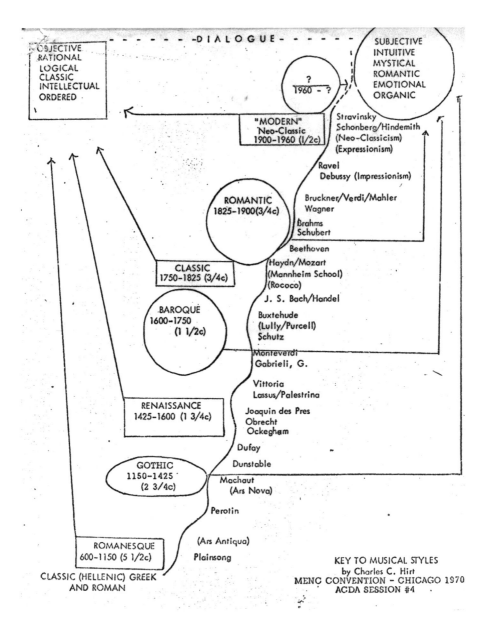

OBJECTIVE
RATIONAL
LOGICAL
CLASSIC
INTELLECTUAL
ORDERED

?
1960 - ?

SUBJECTIVE
INTUITIVE
MYSTICAL
ROMANTIC
EMOTIONAL
ORGANIC

"MODERN"
Neo-Classic
1900-1960 (1/2c)

Stravinsky
Schonberg/Hindemith
(Neo-Classicism)
(Expressionism)

Ravel
Debussy (Impressionism)

ROMANTIC
1825-1900 (3/4c)

Bruckner/Verdi/Mahler
Wagner

Brahms
Schubert

Beethoven

CLASSIC
1750-1825 (3/4c)

Haydn/Mozart
(Mannheim School)
(Rococo)

J. S. Bach/Handel

BAROQUE
1600-1750
(1 1/2c)

Buxtehude
(Lully/Purcell)
Schutz

Monteverdi
Gabrieli, G.

Vittoria
Lassus/Palestrina

RENAISSANCE
1425-1600 (1 3/4c)

Joaquin des Pres
Obrecht
Ockeghem

Dufay

Dunstable

GOTHIC
1150-1425
(2 3/4c)

Machaut
(Ars Nova)

Perotin

(Ars Antiqua)

ROMANESQUE
600-1150 (5 1/2c)

Plainsong

CLASSIC (HELLENIC) GREEK
AND ROMAN

KEY TO MUSICAL STYLES
by Charles C. Hirt
MENC CONVENTION - CHICAGO 1970
ACDA SESSION #4

Charles C. Hirt's chart of musical epochs. Courtesy of Charles C. Hirt.

ᥰ 15

AT CENTURY'S END

In 1970 Charles C. Hirt, founder of the Department of Church and Choral Music at the University of Southern California, made a presentation at the annual gathering of the Music Educators National Conference (MENC) in which he demonstrated the sequence of musical epochs by alternating circles and squares, swinging like a pendulum between romantic (subjective) and classical (objective) sensibilities. His chart, which became well known over the years, clearly showed that the duration of each stylistic period was approximately half the length of its predecessor. By the last third of the twentieth century the pendular swings had been reduced to a tremble, and it seemed no longer possible to distinguish the alternation of style in terms of romantic and classical impulses.

At century's end a rich variety of musical languages coexisted. Jazz, serialism, and minimalism were shown to be much more closely related than originally thought. Avant-garde procedures were commonplace. Impressionism reasserted itself as many composers became preoccupied with tone colors and vertical sonorities. Canon and neo-Renaissance points of imitation became the favored contrapuntal techniques as composers abandoned the tonal implications and discipline inherent in strict fugal writing. Attempts to incorporate popular music into otherwise esoteric styles were often successful, and folk music remained an almost constant inspiration.

Several regions of the world experienced politically motivated ethnic isolation during the 1990s, but in the arts multiculturalism asserted itself during the last decades of the century. Some emphasis was placed on the non-notated traditions of the South Pacific, South America, and Africa, although the predominant manifestation of multiculturalism consisted of countless folk song arrangements made to accommodate the standards of Eurocentric choral singing. While the cultures and traditions from which these songs sprang remained largely unknown to the performers, the arrangements still introduced conductors and choruses to scales, modes, and languages with which they were largely unfamiliar. During the same period, American and European choral

Charles C. Hirt, c. 1973. Courtesy of Lucy Alice Hirt.

musicians first heard the sub-bass tones produced by choirs of Tibetan Buddhist monks, learned of vital choral traditions in central Asia and the Indian subcontinent, and became acquainted with previously unknown composers such as Se Enkhbayar (b. 1956), a Mongolian whose works reached an international audience. In this unusually rich and varied environment composers seemed mostly interested in consolidating the vast melting pot of styles. While this consolidation often produced works whose tonal language seemed remarkably conservative, it was obvious that such profound cultural inter-mingling was also certain to provide many new opportunities for musical experimentation.

Besides the basic expansion of multicultural awareness, the most interesting new ideas in choral music during the twentieth century involved physical movement and other visual enhancements. Prokofiev's score for *Alexander Nevsky*, Ennio Morricone's score for *The Mission*, and subsequent works by Jerry Goldsmith, John Williams, and others made the chorus an integral part of many movie soundtracks; but beyond that, the pervasive influence of motion pictures created a steadily increasing interest in the mixing of choral music with visual and dramatic elements. During the late 1960s conductors experimented with rudimentary stage movement, for which the American conductor Frank Pooler coined the term "choralography," as well as with multimedia presentations that combined live performances with photos projected on an overhead screen. Meanwhile, using the choral ballets of Stravinsky, the oratorios of Honegger, and their own folk traditions as points of departure, composers such as Myriam Marbé and Ruben Federizon called for the chorus to perform highly stylized ceremonial movement, while other composers (mostly Scandinavian) created choral operas and other works that called for the chorus to accompany actors or dancers in some way. This trend culminated in John Adam's enormous *El niño*, a kind of New Age Christmas oratorio, written in collaboration with the stage director Peter Sellars, which superimposes multimedia effects on formal structures reminiscent of Handel. In a technical sense it also gazes backward at the less successful theatrical experiment of Debussy's *Le martyre de Saint-Sébastien*, thus bringing some of the century's artistic impulses full circle. During the last fifteen years of the century, as it became easier for people from around the world to meet directly, Western composers and conductors learned what Marbé and Federizon already knew: that many folk songs, from South Africa for example, actually require movement during performance. Further, the ever increasing popularity of show choirs presented an essentially untapped source of possibilities for serious composers, virtually assuring an expanded use of staged elements in twenty-first-century choral music.

A most exciting confluence of styles, cultures, and trends was achieved in the century-ending commissions awarded by the Stuttgart International Bach Academy to honor the coincidental juxtaposition of the year 2000 with the 250th anniversary of Bach's death. Four composers—Osvaldo Golijov, Sofia Gubaidulina, Wolfgang Rihm, and Tan Dun—composed new Passions for soloists, chorus, and orchestra. Widely separated from each other, as well as from Bach, in terms of culture, musical language, and artistic outlook, each composer produced significant and provocative works. Golijov, an Argentinean Jew of Romanian descent, vividly displayed his own multicultural heritage in *La pasión según San Marco*. Here, the vital traditions of South American street music (including improvisation and processional dance) meet the cantilena of eastern European Jewish liturgy (the final Kaddish even shifts from Spanish to Aramaic). Golijov's Jesus is a revolutionary, and the pulsing Latin rhythms create an atmosphere that celebrates the hope of a better future. Alex Ross commented in *The New Yorker* (5 March 2001) that it "drops like a bomb on the belief that classical music is an exclusively European art." Gubaidulina's *Johannes Passion* seems an extension of the Russian soul, with deep bass solos and terrific climaxes. The addition of passages from the Book of Revelations to the Russian-language gospel texts lends an apocalyptic vision to the music. Rihm's *Deus Passus* (Passion after Saint Luke) is couched in the language of German postmodernism and seems at first to be emotionally abstract. But by combining the gospel account of Jesus's persecution with texts by the Holocaust survivor Paul Celan, Rihm created a compelling reminder that all acts of inhumanity, even if two thousand years apart, are driven by the same evil impulses. Tan Dun, raised in Maoist China, was even further removed from the Christian tradition of Passion oratorio than Golijov. Still, Tan's *Water Passion after Saint Matthew* is remarkable in its presentation of the gospel narrative as ritual. Utilizing splashing water as a percussion instrument, thunder sheets played by the chorus (for the cataclysmic earthquake), and freely integrating Western techniques (including American country fiddling) with the vocal styles of Peking opera and Tuvan throat singers, *Water Passion after Saint Matthew*, in the words of Mark Swed (*Los Angeles Times*, 23 September 2000), "more effectively than anything I have ever heard, reveals music's underlying universality as it irresistibly combines seemingly unrelated musical worlds."

In a way, Josef Woodard was correct when referring to choral music as "an esoteric, if vital, tributary in the music world" (*Los Angeles Times*, 26 January 1999). Most great composers still concentrate their major efforts on large instrumental works and operas, and audiences often prefer to hear such music. But Janáček's "music of Truth" (Střelcova 1994) is still very much alive and can even be, as in the Passions described above, overpowering. It continues as an indispensable ingredient in Earth's cultural fabric. In a larger sense the tributary is at least as important as the great rivers of symphonic, operatic, and chamber music, because when people wish to express their innermost thoughts and dreams, they sing—and when they sing together, it is called choral music.

WORKS LISTS

The following lists include choral music by twentieth-century composers mentioned in the text. Lists are organized alphabetically by composer according to type of choral ensemble (mixed, boys' or children's, female or treble, male) and accompaniment (unaccompanied, piano, organ, other instruments, wind orchestra or band, chamber orchestra, full orchestra).

COMPOSITIONS FOR MIXED CHORUS

UNACCOMPANIED

Absil, Jean
  Three Choruses, Opus 14
Aguiar, Ernani
  Salmo 150
Aldema, Gil
  Ai, di, di, di, dai
  Jerusalem of Gold
Alfvén, Hugo
  Aftonen
  Sveriges flagga
Aloni, Aminadav
  S'fatai Tiftach (Open Thou My Lips)
Anderson, William Henry
  In the Morning
Andriessen, Hendrik
  Missa diatonica
  Omaggio a Marenzio
  Sonnet de Pierre de Ronsard

Antill, John
  Cantate Domino
Antoniou, Theodore
  Greichische Volkslieder
  Three Choruses
Ardévol, José
  Tres romances antiguos
Arrigo, Girolamo
  Due epigrami
  Tre madrigali
Augustinas, Vaclovas
  Hymn to Saint Martin
Auric, Georges
  Quatre chansons françaises
Avni, Tzvi
  On Mercy
  Song of Degrees
  Three Madrigals
Bacewicz, Grażyna
  Fugue for Double Chorus

Creston, Paul
Missa "Cum jubilo"
Cucu, Gheorghe
I Cannot Understand, Curata
Dallapiccola, Luigi
*Sei cori di Michelangelo
Buonarroti* (first pair)
David, Johann Nepomuk
Evangelienmotteten
Mass
Victimae pascali laudes
Davies, Peter Maxwell
Ecce manus tradentis
Five Carols
Dawson, William Levi
Balm in Gilead
Debussy, Claude
*Trois chansons de Charles
d'Orléans*
Dessau, Paul
Psalm 13
Psalm 15
Dett, Robert Nathaniel
Ave Maria
Listen to the Lambs
Diamond, David
Prayer for Peace
Two Anthems
Diepenbrock, Alphons
Carmen saeculare
Dimas, Blas Galindo
Dos corazones
Dimitrov, Georgi
Selected Choral Songs
Distler, Hugo
Choral-Passion
Geistliche Chormusik, Opus 12
Mörike-Chorliederbuch
Die Weihnachtsgeschichte
Doppelbauer, Josef Friedrich
*Cantate Domino canticum
novum*

Dreyfus, George
Homage to Stravinsky
Under the Gumtrees at Sunrise
Dubra, Rihards
Ave Maria
Duruflé, Maurice
*Four Motets on Gregorian
Themes*
Dvarionas, Balis
Raigardo Saltinelis
Eben, Petr
The Lover's Magic Spell
Ubi caritas et amor
Edlund, Lars
Choir Studies I–III
Elegy
Gloria
Mea culpa
Eespere, René
Glorificatio
Two Jubilations
Egk, Werner
Drei Chansons
Einem, Gottfried von
Unterwegs
Elgar, Sir Edward
Death on the Hills, Opus 72
Two Choral Songs, Opus 71
Two Choral Songs, Opus 73
Encinar, José Ramon
Por gracia y galania
Enescu, George
Silence
Erbse, Heimo
Drei Chöre
Eine Kleine Heine-Kantate
Eröd, Ivan
*Drei Gedichte aus Goethes
"West-Oestlicher Divan"*
Escher, Rudolf
Ciel, air et vents
Songs of Love and Eternity

[Harlap, Aharon]
   Three Songs
Harris, Matthew
   Shakespeare Songs
Harris, Roy
   Freedom's Land
   Psalm 150
   Symphony for Voices
   Three Songs of Democracy
Hartzell, Eugene
   Psalm 23
Hawley, William
   Two Motets
   Vita de la mia vita
Heiller, Anton
   Drei kleine geistliche Chöre
   Kleine Messe über
      Zwölftonmodelle
   Mixolydian Mass
Heininen, Paavo
   The Autumns
Hemberg, Eskil
   Eighteen Movements
   Love
   Messa d'oggi
   Signposts
Henderson, Ruth Watson
   Missa brevis
Henze, Hans Werner
   Orpheus behind the Wire
Heppener, Robert
   Canti carnascialeschi
Hill, Alfred
   Mass
Hillborg, Anders
   mua:aa:yiy::oum
Hilsley, William
   Vervehendes und Bleibendes
      (Sounds Fading and Sounds
      Lingering)
Hindemith, Paul
   Mass

Six Chansons
Twelve German Madrigals
Hogan, Moses
   Elijah Rock
Holmboe, Vagn
   Benedic Domino
   Dedique cor meum
   Expectavimus pacem
   Hominis dies
   Laudate Dominum
   Liber canticorum
Holst, Gustav
   Five Partsongs
   Nunc dimittis
   Six Choral Folk Songs
Howells, Herbert
   A Spotless Rose
Hristić, Stevan
   Dubrovaki Rekvijem
   Jesen (Autumn)
   Opello (Orthodox Memorial
      Service, several settings)
Husa, Karel
   Every Day
   Three Moravian Songs
Ichiyanagi, Toshi
   Extended Voices
   Voice Act
Iglesias Villoud, Hector
   Estampas corales
d'Indy, Vincent
   Les trois fileuses, Opus 97
Ippolitov-Ivanov, Mikhail
   "Bless the Lord, O My Soul,"
      from All-Night Vigil
   Liturgy
Irino, Yoshirō
   Oni no yomesan (Devil's
      Bride)
Isaacson, Michael
   Avinu Malkeinu
   One More Spring

Lajtha, László
  *Four Madrigals on Poems of
    Charles d'Orléans*, Opus
    29
  *Two Choruses on Poems of
    Charles d'Orléans*, Opus
    23
Larsson, Lars-Eric
  Missa brevis
Lauridsen, Morten
  Ave Maria
  Les chansons des roses (except
    "Dirait on")
  *Madrigali: Six "Firesongs" on
    Italian Renaissance Poems*
  O magnum mysterium
  Ubi caritas
Lazarof, Henri
  Canti
  The First Day
Leeuw, Ton de
  The Magic of Music
Leighton, Kenneth
  A Hymn of the Nativity
  Mass
Lendvay, Kamilló
  Winter Morning
Lenel, Ludwig
  Christ Is Arisen
León, Tania
  De-Orishas
Leonard, Joseph
  Hayom T'amtzenu
  May the Words of My Mouth
Leroux, Philippe
  Anima Christi
Lesemann, Frederick
  Two Motets
Lewkowitch, Bernhard
  Apollo's Art
  Five Danish Madrigals, Opus
    12

  Improperia
  Stabat mater
  Three Motets, Opus 11
  Three Psalms, Opus 9
Lidholm, Ingvar
  . . . a riveder le stelle
  Laudi
Ligeti, György
  Lux aeterna
  Morning
  Night
  *Three Fantasies after Friedrich
    Hölderlin*
Lilburn, Douglas
  Song of the Antipodes
Lindberg, Oskar
  Stjarntandning
Lipkis, Larry
  Rise up My Love
Lockwood, Normand
  *Out of the Cradle Endlessly
    Rocking*
Lorentzen, Bent
  New Choral Dramatics
    (Dimensions in choral speech
    and movement)
  *Two Choral Songs to
    Ensensberger*
Lukáš, Zdeněk
  Requiem
Luna, Margarita
  Alleluya
  Amor secreta
Lutkin, Peter C.
  *The Lord Bless You and Keep
    You*
Maderna, Bruno
  All the World's a Stage
Maiguashca, Mesías
  A Mouth-Piece
Malawski, Artur
  Little Choral Suite

Malec, Ivo
  Dodecameron
Martin, Frank
  Five Songs of Ariel
  Mass
Martinů, Bohuslav
  Dandelion Romance, from *Songs
    of the Uplands*
  Five Czech Madrigals
Marx, Karl
  Drei gemischten Chöre, Opus 1
Matthews, David
  Bones
  Green
  Sky
Mechem, Kirke
  *Make a Joyful Noise unto the
    Lord*
  The Seven Joys of Christmas (or
    piano, harp, or orchestra)
Mediņš, Jānis
  To Our Lady of Aglona
Melngailis, Emīlis
  Doomsday
  Gently, Slowly
  Midsummer Eve
  Move Gently and Quietly
  Nature and the Soul
  Skylark's Wedding
  The Sun Is Setting
Mendelssohn, Arnold
  Deutsche Messe
  Geistliche Chormusik
Mendes, Gilberto
  Beba Coca-Cola
Menotti, Gian Carlo
  Moans, Groans, Cries and Sighs
Messiaen, Olivier
  Chœurs pour une Jeanne d'Arc
  Cinq rechants
  O sacrum convivium! (optional
    organ)

Mignone, Francisco
  Cataretê
Migot, Georges
  Requiem
Milhaud, Darius
  Cantate de la guerre
  Cantate de la paix
  Cantique du Rhône
  Les deux cités
  Les momies d'Égypte
Milojević, Miloje
  Pir iluzije (The Feast of Illusion)
Mindel, Meir
  A Maya Prophecy
Moeran, E. J.
  Phyllida and Corydon
  Songs of Springtime
Mokranjac, Stevan
  *Divine Liturgy of Saint John
    Crysostom*
  The Glorification of Saint Sava
    (1906 version)
  "Zimski dani" (Winter Days),
    from *Rukoveti*
Moyzes, Alexander
  Instead of a Wreath
  Santa Helena
  Whose Organ Is Playing, Opus
    37
Mul, Jan
  Pater noster
Musgrave, Thea
  Four Madrigals
  Memento creatoris
  Rorate coeli
Naylor, Bernard
  Nine Motets
Nees, Vic
  Five Sacred Motets
  Stabat mater
Negrea, Marţian
  Album for Mixed Choir, Opus 10

Nielsen, Carl
  Three Motets, Opus 55
Nin-Culmell, Joaquín
  Three Traditional Cuban Songs
Noble, Ramón
  La Misa en México
Nobutoki, Kiyoshi
  Kora, o omou uta (Songs
    Recalling Children)
  Nyonin waka renkyoku (Waka
    Poems by Women Poets)
  Omoide (Remembrances)
Nørgård, Per
  Og der skal ikke mere gives tid
    (And Time Shall Be No More)
  Three Motets
  Wie ein Kind
Nørholm, Ib
  Songs, Opus 59
Nunes, Emanuel
  Minnesang
Nystedt, Knut
  De profundis, Opus 54
  The Path of the Just
Obradović, Aleksandar
  Little Choral Suite
Ohana, Maurice
  Swan Song
Okelo, Anthony
  Missa Mayot
Olsson, Otto
  Six Latin Hymns, Opus 40
Orbán, György
  Daemon irrepit callidus
Orbón, Julián
  Crucifixus
Orff, Carl
  Nänie und Dithyrambe
  Die Sänger der Vorwelt
  Stücke
Pablo, Luis de
  Yo lo vi

Pajaro, Eliseo
  Himig pilipino
Panchenko, Semyon
  Liturgy
  Panikhida (Funeral Service)
  Vigil
  Wedding Service
Papaioannou, Yannis
  Trihelikton
Park, Jung-sun
  Inchon Mass
Parker, Horatio
  Hymnos Andron
  School Songs
Pärt, Arvo
  And One of the Pharisees
  De profundis
  I Am the True Vine
  Magnificat
  Tribute to Caesar
  *The Woman with the Alabaster
    Box*
Partos, Oedoen
  Rabat tsraruni (Many Times
    They Have Afflicted Me)
  Six Songs
Penderecki, Krzysztof
  Agnus Dei
  Izhe zeruvimy (Song of
    Cherubim)
  Stabat mater
Pepping, Ernst
  Drei Evangelien-Motetten
  Deutsche Choralmesse
  *Deutsche Messe "Kyrie Gott
    Vater in Ewigkeit"*
  Missa dona nobis pacem
  Passionsbericht des Matthäus
Persichetti, Vincent
  *Hymns and Responses for the
    Church Year*
  Mass

Reiner, Karel
Peace Madrigal
Rodrigo, Joaquín
Triste estaba el Rey David
Ropek, Jiří
Pange lingua (1944, 1956)
Rorem, Ned
From an Unknown Past
Roussel, Albert
Le bardit des francs
Evocations, Opus 15
Madrigal aux muses, Opus 25
Psalm 80, Opus 37
Rózsa, Miklós
Psalm 23
To Everything There Is a Season
(optional organ)
The Vanities of Life
Rubbra, Edmund
Missa cantuariensis
Ruyneman, Daniel
De roep
Sonata
Rydman, Kari
Dona nobis pacem
Sancta Maria ora pro nobis
Saar, Mart
Mixed Choruses
Sakač, Branimir
Seven Movements
Umbrana
Salzman, Peter
Birth of Soul
Scelsi, Giacinto
Tre canti sacri
Schalk, Carl
Now
Schidlowsky, Leon
Missa dona nobis pacem
Three Pieces
Schmitt, Florent
Par le tempête

Schoenberg, Arnold
Dreimal tausand Jahre
Friede auf Erden, Opus 13
(Peace on Earth)
Moderner Psalm
Psalm 130
Three Folk Songs, Opus 49
Three German Folk Songs
Three Satires, Opus 28
Schoenfield, Paul
Four Motets
Schuman, William
Carols of Death
Five Rounds on Famous Words
Mail Order Madrigals
Perceptions
Prelude (or female chorus)
Schumann, Georg
How Great Are Thy Wonders
Three Chorale Motets, Opus 75
Schultz, Svend S.
Four Latin Madrigals
Quattuor fragmenta ex Ovidii
"Ars amandi"
Shvedov, Konstantin
Divine Liturgy
Sculthorpe, Peter
Sea Chant
Seeger, Ruth Crawford
Three Chants (No. 2)
Serebrier, José
Vocalise
Seter, Mordecai
Dithyramb
Jerusalem
Mo'adim
Motets
Sharett, Yehuda
Kumu to'ei midbar (Rise Ye,
Who Err in the Desert)
Shibata, Minao
Kadensho

Shostakovich, Dmitri
  Ten Poems
Sibelius, Jean
  Two Italian Songs
Singer, Malcolm
  Two Psalms
Sisask, Urmas
  Estonian Mass
Smith, Hale
  Two Kids
Sommerfeldt, Øistein
  Three Blake Songs, Opus 13
Spencer, Williametta
  *At the Round Earth's Imagined
    Corners*
  *Four Madrigals on Texts by
    James Joyce*
Spies, Claudio
  In paradisum
Staar, René
  Kyrie III "Notre Dame de Paris"
Stanford, Sir Charles Villiers
  Partsongs, Opus 110, 119, and
    127
  Three Latin Motets, Opus 51
Starer, Robert
  On the Nature of Things
Stenhammer, Wilhelm
  Three Choral Ballads
Sternberg, Erich Walter
  Praise Ye
Stevens, Halsey
  Campion Suite
  *An Epitaph for Sara and Roland
    Cotton*
  Go, Lovely Rose
  Lady As Thy Fair Swan
  Like As the Culver
Strategier, Herman
  Don Ramiro
Strauss, Richard
  An den Baum Daphne

Deutsche Motette
Stravinsky, Igor
  Anthem ("The dove descending
    breaks the air")
  Ave Maria (Slavonic)
  Credo (Slavonic: 1932,
    1964)
  Pater noster (Slavonic)
Stucky, Steven
  Cradle Songs
  Drop, Drop Slow Tears
  Spring and Fall
Suchoň, Eugen
  Aka si mi krasna (How
    Beautiful You Are)
  Of Man
Surinach, Carlos
  Songs of the Soul
Swider, Jozef
  Cantate Domino
Tajčević, Marko
  Cetiri duhovna stiha (Four
    Spiritual Verses)
  *Dvadeset srpskih narodnih
    pesama* (Twenty Serbian
    Folk Songs)
  Liturgija (Liturgy of Saint
    John Chrysostom)
  Three Madrigals
Taneyev, Sergey I.
  Hori (Choruses)
Tavener, John
  *Magnificat and Nunc dimittis
    Collegium Regale*
  Song for Athene
  Today the Virgin
  The Uncreated Eros
Tcherepnin, Nikolai
  Divine Liturgy (2)
  All-Night Vigil
Thomas, Augusta Read
  The Rub of Love

Thomas, Kurt
  Mass in A
  Psalm 137
Thompson, Randall
  Alleluia
  The Best of Rooms
  The Peaceable Kingdom
Thomson, Virgil
  Four Southern Folk Hymns
  *The Nativity As Sung by the
    Shepherds*
Tippett, Michael
  Plebs angelica
  Two Madrigals
Tobias, Rudolf
  Twelve German Motets
Toch, Ernst
  The Geographical Fugue
  Valse
Tomás, Guillermo
  Canto de guerra
Tormis, Velio
  Eesti kalendrilaulud (Estonian
    Calendar Songs)
Track, Gerhard
  Ex Sion species (From Zion's
    Beauty)
Traversari, Pedro
  *Himno pentatónico de la raza
    indígena de la América*
    (Pentatonic Hymn of the
    Indian Race)
Tučapsky, Antonín
  In honorem vitae
  The Year of Grace
Vaughan Williams, Ralph
  Five English Folk Songs
  Mass in G Minor
  O Taste and See
  *Psalm 48: O Praise the Lord of
    Heaven*
  Three Shakespeare Songs

Victory, Gerard
  Quartetto
Viderø, Finn
  Three Choral Songs
Villa-Lobos, Heitor
  Mass of Saint Sebastion
Vītols, Jāzeps
  The Castle of Light
  David before Saul
Vujic, Aleksandar
  Ave Maria
Walton, William
  All This Time
  A Litany
  Make We Joy Now in This Fest
  *Set Me As a Seal upon Thine
    Heart*
  What Cheer?
  *Where Does the Uttered Music
    Go?*
Warlock, Peter
  The Full Heart
Webern, Anton
  Entflieht auf leichten Kähnen,
    Opus 2
Weill, Kurt
  Die Legende vom toten Soldaten
  Recordare, Opus 11 (with
    children's choir)
Wellesz, Egon
  To Sleep
Werle, Lars Johan
  *Canzone 126 di Francesco
    Petrarca*
Whitacre, Eric
  Waternight
  When David Heard
Whitehead, Alfred
  Almighty God, Whose Glory
  Come Holy Ghost in Love
Whitehead, Gillian
  Missa brevis

Widmer, Ernst
  Ceremony after a Fire Raid
Wilenski, Moshe
  Uri Tsiyon
Wilhousky, Peter J.
  Carol of the Bells
Willan, Healey
  *Apostrophe to the Heavenly
    Host*
  Liturgical Motets
  The Three Kings
Williamson, Malcolm
  Symphony for Voices
Willis, Richard
  The Parched Land
  Two Madrigals
Wilson, Charles M.
  Phrases from Orpheus
Wilson, Olly
  Biography
  Gloria
Wyner, Yehudi
  *Liturgical Fragments for the
    High Holidays*
Xenakis, Iannis
  Knephas
  Nuits
  Serment
Young, Robert H.
  The Christ-Child
  Of the Father's Love Begotten
Yuasa, Joji
  Toi (Questions)
  Utterance
Zaimont, Judith Lang
  Sunny Airs and Sober
Zimmermann, Bernd Alois
  Tantum ergo
Zimmermann, Heinz Werner
  Wachet auf!

WITH PIANO

Aloni, Aminadav
  Ahavat Olam (or organ)
  Hallelujah
  Uv'chein Tein Kavod (or organ)
Antheil, George
  Eight Fragments from Shelley
Archer, Violet
  Paul Bunyan
Bergman, Erik
  Vier Galgenlieder
Bergsma, William
  Confrontation, from *Book of
    Job* (or orchestra)
Bernstein, Leonard
  Simchu na
  Yigdal
Boulanger, Lili
  Soir sur la plaine
Britain, Radie
  Brothers in the Clouds (or male
    chorus)
  Nisan (or female chorus and
    instruments)
Browda, Morris
  Viglid (unison version)
Burleigh, Henry Thacker
  Deep River
Chávez, Carlos
  La paloma azul (or chamber
    orchestra)
Copland, Aaron
  Old American Songs (or
    orchestra)
Corigliano, John
  Fern Hill (or orchestra)
  What I Expected Was (or
    instruments)
Dello Joio, Norman
  A Jubilant Song (or female
    chorus)

Dessau, Paul
  Hawel Hawalim
Diemer, Emma Lou
  Madrigals Three
  Three Madrigals
  Wild Nights! Wild Nights!
Eben, Petr
  The Bitter Earth (or organ)
Ephros, Gershon
  Biblical Suite
Fine, Irving
  Alice in Wonderland (or orchestra)
  The Choral New Yorker
Foss, Lukas
  Behold I Build an House (or organ)
  Psalms (or orchestra)
Gerschefski, Edwin
  Border Raid
Gershwin, George
  The Jolly Tar and the Milkmaid
Hamilton, Iain
  Cantata
Harlap, Aharon
  Cain and Abel (or orchestra)
  For Dust You Are, and to Dust You Shall Return
Heiller, Anton
  Tentatio Jesu
Idelsohn, Abraham Zevi
  Jephtah
Isaacson, Michael
  Sim Shalom (or organ)
Ives, Charles
  The Circus Band (or orchestra)
  General William Booth Enters into Heaven (or chamber orchestra)
  Serenity
Janáček, Leoš
  The Lord's Prayer (or organ)

  Elegy on the Death of Daughter Olga
Kingsley, Gershon
  Sabbath for Today
Kohn, Karl
  Madrigal
Kyr, Robert
  Watersongs
Lauridsen, Morten
  "Dirait on," from *Les chansons des roses*
  Midwinter Songs (or orchestra)
Lipkis, Larry
  Songs from a Cookbook
Nathan, Hans, ed.
  Folk Songs of the New Palestine (unison)
Osborne, Charles D.
  Sephardic Havdallah
Persichetti, Vincent
  Two Cummings Choruses
  Four Cummings Choruses
Peterson, John W.
  Hallelujah! What a Savior (or organ)
  Night of Miracles (or organ)
Price, Florence
  Song for Snow
Rauch, Maurice
  Oib Nit Noch Hecher
Ray, Robert
  Gospel Magnificat (or instruments)
Riegger, Wallingford
  A Shakespeare Sonnet (or chamber orchestra)
  Who Can Revoke?
Sculthorpe, Peter
  Night Piece
Schuman, William
  A Free Song (Secular Cantata No. 2) (or orchestra)

Holiday Song (or female chorus)
The Lord Has a Child (or female chorus)
Sessions, Roger
Turn, O Libertad
Sharlin, William
Shabbat Suite (or instruments)
Shimizu, Osamu
Nagaki sō no hanashi (Priest with a Long Nose)
Sibelius, Jean
Three Songs for American Schools
Smith, Byron J.
Worthy to Be Praised
Smith, Hale
I'm Coming Home
Toussaint l'ouverture 1803
Sutherland, Margaret
A Company of Carols
Sveinbjörnsson, Sveinbjörn
Royal Cantata
Thompson, Randall
Frostiana (or orchestra)
The Last Words of David (or orchestra)
Thompson, Van Denman
Hymn to the Trinity (or organ)
Tremain, Ronald
Tenera juventa
Walker, Gwyneth
Love—by the Water
Warlock, Peter
Balulalow
Bethlehem Down
Weiner, Lazar
Biblical Suite
Legend of Toil
To Thee, America
Wilhousky, Peter J.
The Battle Hymn of the Republic (or orchestra or band)

Willis, Richard
Give unto the Lord
Zaimont, Judith Lang
The Chase
Zeisl, Eric
Harlem Nightsong

WITH ORGAN

Achron, Joseph
Sabbath Evening Service
Aloni, Aminadav
Ahavat Olam (or piano)
Torah Service
Uv'chein Tein Kavod (or piano)
Andriessen, Hendrik
Missa Christus Rex
Missa in honorem Ss cordis
Augustinas, Vaclovas
Gloria
Avni, Tzvi
Deep Calleth unto Deep
Barber, Samuel
Prayers of Kierkegaard (or orchestra)
Bartulis, Vidmantas
Missa brevis
Beach, Amy
Service in A, Opus 63
Beck, John Ness
Song of Exultation (or piano)
Ben-Haim, Paul
Liturgical Cantata (or orchestra)
Bernstein, Leonard
Hashkivenu
Bialas, Günter
Lobet den Herrn
Binder, A. W.
Yiskor
Bingham, Seth
Perfect through Suffering

Bonds, Margaret
  Mass in D Minor
Britten, Benjamin
  A Boy Was Born (revised version)
  Festival Te Deum
  Jubilate Deo
  Missa brevis in D
  Rejoice in the Lamb
  Te Deum in C
Burkhard, Willy
  Psalm 93
Busto, Javier
  Ave Maria
Carnevali, Vito
  Missa "Rosa Mystica" (or treble
    or male chorus)
Casals, Pablo
  Eucaristica (or treble chorus)
Castelnuovo-Tedesco, Mario
  Sacred Service
Creston, Paul
  Missa "Adoro te" (or female
    chorus)
  Missa solemnis (or male chorus)
Dello Joio, Norman
  Prayers of Cardinal Newman
Dessau, Paul
  Hawel Hawalim (or piano)
Diamond, David
  Mizmor L'David
Dickinson, Clarence
  The Shepherd's Story
Diepenbrock, Alphons
  Hymnus de Sanctu Spiritu
  Missa in die festo
Eben, Petr
  The Bitter Earth (original
    version)
  Suita Liturgica
Effinger, Cecil
  *The Christmas Story According
    to Saint Luke*

Eggen, Arne
  Ave maris stella
Fauré, Gabriel
  Ave Maria, Opus 93
  Tantum ergo
Finney, Ross Lee
  Pilgrim Psalms (or orchestra)
Finzi, Gerald
  God Is Gone Up
  Magnificat
Foss, Lukas
  Adon olom
  Behold I Build an House (or
    piano)
Françaix, Jean
  Two Motets (unison chorus)
Gaher, Jozef
  The Death of Saul
Garūta, Lūcija
  God, Your Earth Is Burning
George, Graham
  Ride on! Ride on in Majesty!
Halffter, Cristóbal
  Misa ducal
Hamilton, Iain
  *Epitaph for This World and
    Time*
Hanson, Howard
  How Excellent Thy Name (or
    female chorus)
Hanuš, Jan
  Mše Hlaholska, Opus 106
    (Glagolitic Mass) (with
    optional bells)
Harris, Roy
  Mi Chomocho
Helfman, Max
  Aron ha-qodesh (The Holy
    Ark)
  Sh'ma Koleinu
Hoddinott, Alun
  Puer natus

Hoiby, Lee
  Magnificat and Nunc dimittis
Hovhaness, Alan
  A Simple Mass
Hovland, Egil
  Missa vigilate, Opus 59
  Saul
Howells, Herbert
  My Eyes for Beauty Pine
d'Indy, Vincent
  Pentecosten, Opus 75
Ireland, John
  No Greater Love
Isaacson, Michael
  Sim Shalom (or piano)
Janáček, Leoš
  The Lord's Prayer (or piano)
Janowsky, Max
  Avodath Hakodesh
Jermaks, Romualds
  Missa solemnis
Joubert, John
  *O Lorde, the Maker of Al
    Thing*
Kelterborn, Rudolf
  Kleine Psalmenkantate
Kim, Byong-kon
  i am a little church
Kodály, Zoltán
  Laudes organi
  Magyar mise (unison)
  Missa brevis (or orchestra)
Kohn, Karl
  Also the Sons
Kox, Hans
  In Those Days
Kronsteiner, Hermann
  Stille Nacht Messe
Lajtha, László
  Missa, Opus 54
Langlais, Jean
  Mass in Ancient Style

Lauridsen, Morten
  Lux aeterna (or orchestra)
Levy, Marvin David
  Sacred Service
Lockwood, Normand
  Choreographic Cantata
  Donne's Last Sermon
Luna, Margarita
  Misa quisqueyana
Martin, Frank
  Cantate pour le 1er août
Mathias, William
  Let the People Praise Thee
  Make a Joyful Noise
Menotti, Gian Carlo
  *Mass for the Contemporary
    English Liturgy*
Miskinis, Vytautas
  Pater noster
Moreno, Segundo
  Stabat mater
Mueller, Carl F.
  Create in Me
Nelson, Ron
  God Bring Thy Sword
Nin-Culmell, Joaquín
  Dedication Mass
Nowakowsky, David
  Adonai Z'charanu
  Closing Service for Yom Kippur
    ("Ne'ilah")
  *Preliminary Service and Evening
    Prayer for Sabbath Eve*
  Psalm 115
Ohana, Maurice
  Dies solis
  Lux noctis
Parry, Sir Charles Hubert Hastings
  I Was Glad
Peeters, Flor
  Jubilate Deo
  Jubilee Mass

Peterson, John W.
  Hallelujah! What a Savior (or
    piano)
  Night of Miracles (or piano)
Pfautsch, Lloyd
  Prayer
Phillips, T. K. E.
  Samuel
Ponce, Manuel
  Six Motets
Roff, Joseph
  *Propers of Sundays and Major
    Feasts*
Ropek, Jiří
  Missa brevis
  Pange lingua (1965)
Rorem, Ned
  *Proper for the Votive Mass of
    the Holy Spirit*
  Truth in the Night Season
Rossini, Carlo
  *Proper of the Mass for the Entire
    Ecclesiastical Year*
Rózsa, Miklós
  To Everything There Is a Season
    (or unaccompanied)
Schalit, Heinrich
  Freitagabend Liturgie (*Sabbath
    Eve Liturgy*)
  Psalm 23
Schul, Zikmund
  Mogen Awaus (Shield to Our
    Fathers)
Scott, K. Lee
  Gracious Spirit Dwell in Me
  Hilariter
Sessions, Roger
  Mass
Shaw, Martin
  With a Voice of Singing
Shibata, Minao
  Magnificat and Nunc dimittis

Sowerby, Leo
  Christ Reborn
  Forsaken of Man
Starer, Robert
  Sabbath Evening Service
Stevens, Halsey
  In te, Domine, speravi
  The Way of Jehovah
Still, William Grant
  Plain Chant for America
Stucky, Steven
  Ah, Holy Jesus
Suchoň, Eugen
  The Slovak Mass
Szabó, Ferenc
  Ave Maria
Talma, Louise
  In principio erat verbum
Tavener, John
  God Is with Us
Thompson, Van Denman
  Hymn to the Trinity (or
    piano)
Tippett, Michael
  Magnificat and Nunc dimittis
Titcomb, H. Everett
  O Love, How Deep
  Victory Te Deum
Urbanner, Erich
  Missa Benedicite Gentes
Vasconcellos, Jorgé Croner de
  Erros meus
Vaughan Williams, Ralph
  All Hail the Power
Vierne, Louis
  Messe solennelle
Walton, William
  Jubilate
  Missa brevis
  The Twelve
Weill, Kurt
  Kiddush

Wellesz, Egon
  Mass in F Minor
Whitehead, Alfred
  Challenge to Free Men
  Christ the Lord Is Risen
Willan, Healey
  O quanta qualia
Williams, David McKinley
  *In the Year That King Uzziah
    Died*
Williamson, Malcolm
  Canticle of Fire
Wilson, Charles M.
  Missa brevis
Wyner, Yehudi
  Friday Evening Service
Yon, Pietro A.
  Jesu Bambino
Zaimont, Judith Lang
  *Parable: A Tale of Abram and
    Isaac* (or instruments)
Zeisl, Eric
  Requiem ebraico (or chamber
    orchestra)

WITH OTHER INSTRUMENTS

Achron, Joseph
  Salome's Dance
Adler, Samuel
  From out of Bondage
  We Believe
Allende-Blin, Juan
  Open Air and Water Music
Anderson, Thomas Jefferson
  Personals
Antill, John
  Black Opal
Antoniou, Theodore
  Kontakion
Archer, Violet
  Apocalypse

Argento, Dominick
  I Hate and I Love
Arrigo, Girolamo
  La cantata Hurbinek
Atehortúa, Blas Emelio
  Cántico delle creature
Avshalomov, Jacob
  I Saw a Stranger Yestre'en
  Songs of the Goliards
  Tom O'Bedlam
Azguime, Miguel
  Yuan Zhi Yuan
Baird, Tadeusz
  Etiuda
Baker, David N.
  Images Shadows and Dreams
Banks, Don
  Findings, Keepings
Bárdos, Lajos
  A nyúl éneke (Song of the
    Rabbit)
Bark, Jan, and Folke Rabe
  *Air-Power Supply for Voices and
    Trombones*
  Disturbances in the Atmosphere
Beck, John Ness
  Upon This Rock
Beglarian, Grant
  And All the Hills Echoed
Bergsma, William
  *The Sun, the Soaring Eagle, the
    Turquoise Prince, the God*
Berio, Luciano
  Magnificat
  Questo vuol dire che
Bernstein, Leonard
  Chichester Psalms (or orchestra)
  The Lark (choruses for play)
  Missa brevis
Bialas, Günter
  Eichendorf-Liederbuch
  Indianische Kantate

Bibalo, Antonio
 Elegia per un'era spaziale
Birtwistle, Harrison
 The Fields of Sorrow
Bissell, Keith
 Theme, Variation and Epilogue
Boulez, Pierre
 e. e. cummings ist der Dichter
 Séquence
Brubeck, Dave
 La fiesta de la posada
 The Gates of Justice
 Pange Lingua Variations
 To Hope! A Celebration
Burian, Emil
 Requiem
Castelnuovo-Tedesco, Mario
 Kol nidre
 Romancero gitano
Chatman, Stephen
 There Is Sweet Music Here
Chihara, Paul
 Minidoka [Reveries of . . .]
Chilcott, Bob
 The Making of the Drum
Chou Wen-Chung
 Poems of White Stone
Corigliano, John
 What I Expected Was (or piano)
Coulthard, Jean
 Hymn of Creation
Cutler, David
 Chestnut Branches in the Court:
 A Cycle of the Holocaust
Dallapiccola, Luigi
 Canti di prigionia
Davidovsky, Mario
 Synchronisms No. 4
Davids, Brent Michael
 Night Chant
Davies, Peter Maxwell
 Veni Sancte Spiritus

Debussy, Claude
 Noël
 Petite cantate
Dello Joio, Norman
 Mass
 Mass in Honor of the Blessed
 Virgin Mary
 Mass in Honor of the Eucharist
 The Mystic Trumpeter
 Proud Music of the Storm
 A Psalm of David
 Psalm of Peace
 Song of the Open Road
 Years of the Modern
Dessau, Paul
 Requiem für Lumumba
Durey, Louis
 Dix choeurs de métiers
Eben, Petr
 Missa cum Populo
 Prague Te Deum
 Trouvere Mass
Edlund, Lars
 The Beatitudes
 Triad
Effinger, Cecil
 Four Pastorales
 Paul of Tarsus: Three Episodes
 in the Life of Paul the Apostle
Einem, Gottfried von
 Die traumenden Knaben
Ellington, Duke
 Sacred Concert: In the Beginning
 God
Englund, Einar
 Chaconne
Fanshawe, David
 African Sanctus
Federizon, Ruben R.
 Gabaq-An
Felciano, Richard
 Double Alleluia for Pentecost

Feldman, Morton
  Chorus and Instruments I
  Chorus and Instruments II
  Rothko Chapel
Finney, Ross Lee
  Edge of Shadow
Foss, Lukas
  Fragments of Archilochos
Françaix, Jean
  Three Epigrammes
Gesseney-Rappo, Dominique
  Missa brevior
  Le Rondo de Cupidon
  Tibi Gloria Domine
Glick, Srul Irving
  Sheeru Ladonye sheer chadash
    (Sing unto the Lord a New
    Song)
Grainger, Percy
  The Sea-Wife
  The Three Ravens
Haazen, Guido
  Missa luba
Halffter, Cristóbal
  Gaudium et spes
  Oración a Platero
Halffter, Rodolfo
  Pregón para una Pascua pobre
Harbison, John
  Five Songs of Experience
Harris, Ross
  Kia mau te rongo (Live in Peace)
Harris, Roy
  Alleluia
  Symphony No. 10 (*Abraham
    Lincoln Symphony*)
Harrison, Lou
  Easter Cantata
  *A Joyous Procession and a
    Solemn Procession*
  La koro sutro
  Mass to Saint Anthony

Henze, Hans Werner
  Fünf Madrigäle
  Jephte
Hindemith, Paul
  Apparebit repentina dies
Høffding, Finn
  Das Eisenbahngleichnis
Holliger, Heinz
  Scardanelli Zyklus (Scardanelli
    Cycle)
Holst, Gustav
  Two Psalms
Hovhaness, Alan
  Missa brevis
  The Way of Jesus
Hsu, Tsang-houei
  Tsang hua yin, Opus 13 (Burial
    Flowers)
Huber, Klaus
  Job 14
Ichiyanagi, Toshi
  Music for Living Space
Iglesias Villoud, Hector
  Concierto universitario
Ikenouchi, Tomojirō
  Koi no omoni (Burden of Love)
d'Indy, Vincent
  Le forgeron, Opus 104
  La vengeance du mari, Opus
    105
Ippolitov-Ivanov, Mikhail
  *Hymn of the Pythagoreans to the
    Rising Sun*
Isaacson, Michael
  Aspects of a Great Miracle
Ives, Charles
  The Celestial Country
  Psalm 90
  Three Harvest Home Chorales
Janáček, Leoš
  Ave Maria (Zdrávas Maria)
  Hospodine!

[Janáček, Leoš]
  Nursery Rhymes (second version)
Janson, Alfred
  Nocturne
  Tema
  Voices in a Human Landscape
Kagel, Mauricio
  Anagrama
  Hallelujah
Kasilag, Lucrecia
  Dularawan
  Filisiana
Kastal'sky, Alexandr
  The Railway Train
Koechlin, Charles
  Quinze motets de style archaïque
Kohn, Karl
  Three Descants from Ecclesiastes
  What Heaven Confers
Kyr, Robert
  Unseen Rain
La Montaine, John
  The Lessons of Advent
Langlais, Jean
  Psalm 117
Larson, Libby
  Eleanor Roosevelt
  Seven Ghosts
  So Blessedly It Sprung
Lazarof, Henri
  Cantata
Leeuw, Ton de
  Psalm 68
Leibowitz, René
  The Grip of the Given
  The Renegade
León, Argeliers
  Creador del hombre nuevo
Lesemann, Frederick
  Water in the Boat
Leviev, Milcho
  The Green House

Lindberg, Nils
  Requiem
Lindberg, Oskar
  Skansenkantat
Lipkis, Larry
  Giunse alfin il momento
  Prophesies
  The Seeker
Loeffler, Charles Martin
  Poème mystique
Maceda, José
  Ugma-ugma (Structures)
Maconchy, Dame Elizabeth
  And Death Shall Have No Dominion
Maderna, Bruno
  Three Greek Lyrics
Marbé, Myriam
  Ritual for the Thirst of the Land
Markopoulos, Yannis
  The Liturgy of Orpheus
Martin, Frank
  Ode à la musique
  Le vin herbé
Martinů, Bohuslav
  Field Mass
  Songs of the Uplands
Marx, Karl
  Versöhnender
Mennin, Peter
  The Christmas Story
Menotti, Gian Carlo
  The Unicorn, the Gorgon, and the Manticore
Migot, Georges
  L'Annonciation
  Cantate de la vie meilleure
  Du ciel et de mer
  De Christo
  La mise au tombeau
  La Nativité de Notre Seigneur

La Passion
Psaume 118
Le sermon sur la montagne
La sulamite
Moevs, Robert
  A Brief Mass
Moreno, Segundo
  Ave Maria
Mortensen, Otto
  Det var en lordag uften
  Seven Choir Songs
Naylor, Bernard
  Stabat mater
Nelhybel, Václav
  Estampie natalis
Nelson, Ron
  The Christmas Story
  What Is Man? (or orchestra)
Nilsson, Bo
  Ayiasma
  Vi Kommer att Traffas i Morgan
Nono, Luigi
  Cori di Didone
  Epitaffio per Federico Lorca,
    part 1
  La terra e la compagna
  Y entonces comprendió
Nørgård, Per
  It Happened in Those Days
Nunes, Emanuel
  Voyage du corps
Ohana, Maurice
  Avoaha
  Cantigas
Okelo, Anthony
  Missa Maleng
Oliveros, Pauline
  In Memoriam Mr. Whitney
Olsson, Otto
  Te Deum, Opus 26
Orff, Carl
  Catulli carmina

Parsch, Arnošt, and Miloš Štědroň
  Red Sun Rose Once
Pärt, Arvo
  Saint John Passion
  Solfeggio
Patterson, Paul
  Kyrie
Peeters, Flor
  Intrada festiva
Penderecki, Krzysztof
  Psalmy Dawida
Petrassi, Goffredo
  Orationes Christi
  Psalm IX
Pfautsch, Lloyd
  Reconciliation
Pinkham, Daniel
  Christmas Cantata (Sinfonia
    sacra)
  Daniel in the Lion's Den
  Easter Cantata
  Festival Magnificat and Nunc
    dimittis
  In the Beginning of Creation
  Requiem
  Wedding Cantata
Piston, Walter
  A Psalm and Prayer of David
Pizzetti, Ildebrando
  Attollite portas
Pousseur, Henri
  Invitation a l'utopie
Prévost, André
  Ahimsa
  Psalm 148
Ramirez, Ariel
  Misa criolla
  Navidad nuestra
Rasiuk, Moshe
  Sodom Square
Rasmussen, Karl Aage
  Mass

Ray, Robert
Gospel Magnificat (or piano)
Reda, Siegfried
Te Deum
Respighi, Ottorino
Laud to the Nativity
Rihm, Wolfgang
Nietzche-fragmente
Rimmer, John
Visions I
Rodrigo, Joaquín
*Musica para un Codice
Salmantino sobre letra de
Miguel de Unamuno*
Rodríguez, Robert Xavier
Lyrics for Autumn
Roldán, Almadeo
Curujey
Rorem, Ned
A Sermon on Miracles
Rutter, John
Gloria (or orchestra)
Sakač, Branimir
Omaggio—canto della commedia
Santórsola, Guido
*Concerto for Chorus without
Words*
Schafer, R. Murray
*Apocalypsis Part One: John's
Vision
Apocalypsis Part Two: Credo
Epitaph for Moonlight
Gita*
Schidlowsky, Leon
Missa in nomine Bach
Schifrin, Lalo
*Jazz Suite on Mass Texts
Rock Requiem*
Schoenberg, Arnold
Four Partsongs, Opus 27
Schuller, Gunther
Poems of Time and Eternity

Sculthorpe, Peter
Sun Music for Voices
Sharlin, William
Shabbat Suite (or piano)
Shibata, Minao
Oiwake-bushi kō
Shimizu, Osamu
Shi no fuchi yori
Sicilianos, Yorgos
*Episodia II
Parable*
Smith, Hale
Comes Tomorrow
Starer, Robert
*Images of Man
Two Songs from Honey and Salt*
Štědroň, Miloš, and Arnošt Parsch
Red Sun Rose Once
Stevens, Halsey
*Magnificat
Songs from the Paiute*
Strategier, Herman
The Shadow out of Time
Stravinsky, Igor
Les noces (The Wedding)
Mass
Surinach, Carlos
*Cantata de San Juan
Via crucis*
Svilainis, Giedrius
O quam tristis
Szöllösy, András
In Phariseos
Takahashi, Yuji
Michi-Yuki
Talma, Louise
Let's Touch the Sky
Tavener, John
*Coplas
Nomine Jesu
Responsorium in Memory of
Annon Lee Silver*

Voices
Tučapsky, Antonín
  The Time of Christemas
Urbanner, Erich
  Three Movements for Cello and Choir
Ussachevsky, Vladimir
  "Creation Prologue"
Varèse, Edgard
  Étude pour Espace
Vaughan Williams, Ralph
  O Clap Your Hands
Victory, Gerard
  Kriegslieder
Webern, Anton
  Two Songs, Opus 19
Weill, Kurt
  Das Berliner Requiem
Willis, Richard
  Five Elizabethan Songs
Wilson, Charles M.
  Image out of Season
  Nocturnal-Paudash
Wilson, Olly
  In Memoriam Martin Luther King, Jr.
Wyner, Yehudi
  Torah Service
Yuasa, Joji
  Projection on Basho's Poems
Yun, Isang
  Ein Schmetterlingstraum
Zaimont, Judith Lang
  Meditations at the Time of the New Year
  Parable: A Tale of Abram and Isaac (or organ)
  Voices
Zimmermann, Heinz Werner
  Magnificat
  Psalmkonzert

WITH WIND ORCHESTRA
OR BAND

Badings, Henk
  Whitman Cantate
Diemer, Emma Lou
  Sing a Glory (or orchestra)
Einem, Gottfried von
  Missa Claravallensis
Henze, Hans Werner
  The Muses of Sicily
Lockwood, Normand
  The Closing Doxology
Lutoslawski, Witold
  Trè poèmes d'Henri Michaux
Martin, Frank
  Musique pour le fêtes du Rhône
Persichetti, Vincent
  Celebrations
Prokofiev, Sergei
  Cantata for the Twentieth Anniversary of the October Revolution
Reger, Max
  Weihegesang
Siegmeister, Elie
  Cantata for FDR
Tomás, Guillermo
  La oración del creyente
Willis, Richard
  This Day

WITH CHAMBER ORCHESTRA

Argento, Dominick
  Jonah and the Whale
Badings, Henk
  Kantate VII (Ballade van die bloeddorstige Jagter)
Blacher, Boris, et al.
  Jüdische Chronik

Britten, Benjamin
  Cantata Misericordium, Opus 69
Burkhard, Willy
  Cantate Domino
  Genug ist genug
Chávez, Carlos
  La paloma azul (or piano)
Diamond, David
  A Secular Cantata
Eisler, Hanns
  Die Massnahme
Escobar, Aylton
  Missa Breve on Brazilian Folk Rhythms
Gerschefski, Edwin
  Letter from BMI
Grainger, Percy
  Sir Eglamore
Guarnieri, Camargo
  Cantata trágica
  Sêca
Gubaidulina, Sofia
  Jetzt immer Schnee
Haas, Pavel
  Psalm 29
Harbison, John
  The Flight into Egypt
Henze, Hans Werner
  Moralities
Hovhaness, Alan
  Wind Drum
Ives, Charles
  General William Booth Enters into Heaven (or piano)
Joubert, John
  The Martyrdom of Saint Alban
Korngold, Erich Wolfgang
  Passover Psalm
Kubik, Gail
  A Christmas Set
  Magic, Magic, Magic!

Kurtág, György
  Songs of Despair and Sorrow, Opus 18
Martinů, Bohuslav
  The Nativity, from *The Miracles of Mary*
Matsumora, Teizo
  Hymn to Aurora
Milhaud, Darius
  Les amours de Ronsard
Pärt, Arvo
  Berliner Messe
  Te Deum
Penderecki, Krzysztof
  Canticum canticorum Salomonis
Persichetti, Vincent
  Flower Songs (Cantata No. 6)
Poulenc, Francis
  Un soir de neige
Riegger, Wallingford
  A Shakespeare Sonnet (or piano)
Schoenberg, Arnold
  Kol nidre, Opus 39
Schuller, Gunther
  Sacred Cantata
Smith, Hale
  In Memoriam—Beryl Rubenstein
Suter, Robert
  Ballade von des Cortez Leuten
Tavener, John
  We Shall See Him As He Is
Vaughan Williams, Ralph
  Flos campi
  An Oxford Elegy
  Serenade to Music
  The Shepherds of the Delectable Mountains
Wagner-Régeny, Rudolf
  Genesis
Webern, Anton
  Two Songs, Opus 19

Yun, Isang
  Der weise Mann
Zeisl, Eric
  Requiem ebraico (or organ)

WITH FULL ORCHESTRA

Abejo, Rosalina
  Advent
  *The Conversion of King
    Humabon*
  Redemption Oratorio
Adams, John
  Harmonium
  El niño
Adler, Samuel
  The Vision of Isaiah
  A Whole Bunch of Fun
Alain, Jehan
  Missa brevis
  Requiem
Albert, Steven
  Bacchae
Anderson, Thomas Jefferson
  Spirituals
  The Suit
Andriessen, Hendrik
  Carmen saeculare
Antheil, George
  Cabeza de Vaca
Antill, John
  Song of Hagar
Antoniou, Theodore
  Die weisse Rose
Aprahamian, Maia
  From the Beginning
  Prayers from the Ark
  Prologue to "John"
Ardévol, José
  *Burla de Don Pedro a
    Caballo*
  Forma-Ballet

Argento, Dominick
  *Te Deum (Verba Domini cum
    verbis populi)*
Arutyunian, Alexander
  Cantata on the Homeland
  Hymn to the Brotherhood
  Ode to Lenin
  The Tale of the Armenian People
Avni, Tzvi
  *The Destruction of the Temple
    in Jerusalem*
  The Heavenly Jerusalem
Bacewicz, Grażyna
  Acropolis
  De profundis
  Olympic Cantata
Badings, Henk
  Apocalypse
  *Kantate VII (Ballade van die
    bloeddorstige Jagter)*
  Psalm 147
Baird, Tadeusz
  Egzorta
Balakirev, Mily Alexeyevich
  *Cantata for the Unveiling of the
    Glinka Memorial in Saint
    Petersburg*
Ballif, Claude
  Requiem
Barber, Samuel
  Prayers of Kierkegaard (or
    organ)
  The Lovers
Barnett, Maughan
  Ode
Bartók, Béla
  Cantata profana
Bassols, Xavier Montsalvatge
  *Egloga del Tajo (Eclogue of the
    River Tagus)*
Bautista, Julián
  Cantar del Mío Cid

Beach, Amy
  The Canticle of the Sun, Opus
    123
  The Chambered Nautilus, Opus
    66
  Mass in E-flat
Bekku, Sadao
  Ō-otoko no niwa (Giant's
    Garden)
Ben-Haim, Paul
  Hymn from the Desert
  Joram
  Liturgical Cantata (or organ)
  Three Psalms
  The Vision of a Prophet
Bennett, Richard Rodney
  Epithalamion
  Spells
Bergamo, Petar
  Farewell and Sailors of Podgora
Bergman, Erik
  Aton
  Noah
Bergsma, William
  Confrontation, from *Book of
    Job* (or piano)
Berio, Luciano
  Coro
  Sinfonia
Berkeley, Lennox
  Domini est terra, Opus 10
  Magnificat, Opus 71
  Mass, Opus 64
Bernstein, Leonard
  Chichester Psalms (or
    instruments)
  Symphony No. 3 (*Kaddish*)
Bingham, Seth
  Wilderness Stone
Binički, Stanislav
  Marš na Drinu (March on the
    Drina)

Birtwistle, Harrison
  The Mark of the Goat
Bissell, Keith
  *The Passion According to Saint
    Luke*
Blacher, Boris
  *Die Gesänge des Seeräubers
    O'Rourke und seiner
    Geliebten Sally Brown*
  Der Grossinquisitor
  Requiem
Bliss, Arthur
  Morning Heroes
Blitzstein, Marc
  This Is a Garden
Bloch, Ernest
  America
  Sacred Service (*Avodath
    Hakodesh*)
Bonds, Margaret
  The Ballad of the Brown King
  Credo
Bonet, Narciso
  Canco de bressol de la Verge
  Missa in Epiphanie Domini
Boulanger, Lili
  Du fond de l'abîme (Psalm
    130)
  Vieille prière bouddhique
Bourland, Roger
  Rosarium
Brian, Havergal
  Gothic Symphony
Britten, Benjamin
  Cantata accademica
  The Company of Heaven
  Saint Nicolas
  Spring Symphony
  War Requiem
  The World of the Spirit
Broqua, Alfonso
  Tabaré

Brubeck, Dave
  The Light in the Wilderness
  Voice of the Holy Spirit
Bruch, Max
  Damajanti, Opus 78
  Moses
  Österkantate, Opus 81
  Trauerfeier für Mignon, Opus 93
Brumby, Colin
  Celebrations and Lamentations
  Charlie Bubbles' Book of Hours
  Gilgamesh
Burkhard, Willy
  Das Gesicht Jesajas
  Das Jahr
  Mass
Bury, Edward
  Saint Francis of Assisi
Cardoso, Lindembergue
  Procissão das carpideiras
Carmel, Dov
  Festival Cantata
Casals, Pablo
  Hymn to the United Nations
  El pessebre
Casella, Alfredo
  Missa solemnis
Castellanos, Evencio
  El tirano Aguirre
Castelnuovo-Tedesco, Mario
  Esther
  Jonah
  "Noah's Ark," from *Genesis Suite*, Shilkret et al.
  Ruth
Caturla, Alejandro García
  Yamba-ó
Chadwick, George Whitefield
  Noël

Chávez, Carlos
  Llamadas
  Prometheus Bound
  El sol
Christou, Jani
  Mysterion
Cikker, Ján
  Cantus filiorum, Opus 17
Čiurlionis, Mikolajus
  De profundis
Clark, Sondra
  Requiem for Lost Children
Coelho, Ruy
  Fátima
  Oratória da paz
Constantinescu, Paul
  The Birth of Our Lord
  The Passion and Resurrection of Our Lord
Conyngham, Barry
  Voss
Copland, Aaron
  Canticle of Freedom
  Old American Songs (or piano)
Corigliano, John
  Fern Hill (or piano)
Coulthard, Jean
  Choral Symphony
  This Land
Couture, Guillaume
  Jean le Précurseur
  Requiem
Cowell, Henry
  The Creator
  . . . if He please
Creston, Paul
  Isaiah's Vision
Cuclin, Dimitrie
  David and Goliath
  Symphony No. 5
  Symphony No. 10
  Symphony No. 12

Dadap, Jerry Amper
  Lam-Ang Epic
  The Redemption
Dallapiccola, Luigi
  Sei cori di Michelangelo
    Buonarroti (third pair)
David, Johann Nepomuk
  Komm, Heiliger Geist
Davies, Peter Maxwell
  Job
Debussy, Claude
  Le martyre de Saint-Sébastien
Delius, Frederick
  A Mass of Life
  Sea Drift
  A Song of the High Hills
Dello Joio, Norman
  As of a Dream
  Four Songs of Walt Whitman
Del Tredici, David
  Pop-pourri
Dessau, Paul
  Grabschrift für Rosa Luxemburg
Dett, Robert Nathaniel
  The Ordering of Moses
Diamond, David
  This Sacred Ground
  To Music
Diemer, Emma Lou
  Sing a Glory (or band)
Diepenbrock, Alphons
  Hymne aan Rembrandt
Dohnányi, Ernst von
  Missa in Dedicatione Ecclesiae
Donner, Henrik Otto
  XC
Dumitrescu, Gheorghe
  Tudor Vladimirescu
Durey, Louis
  Eloges
Duruflé, Maurice
  Requiem, Opus 9

Dvarionas, Balis
  Salute to Moscow
Dyson, George
  The Canterbury Pilgrims
Eben, Petr
  Apologia Sokrates
  Sacred Symbols
Edlund, Lars
  Maria
Egge, Klaus
  Noreg-songer, Opus 16
Eggen, Arne
  King Olav
Egk, Werner
  Fürchtlösigkeit und Wohlwollen
Einem, Gottfried von
  An die Nachgeborenen
  Hymnus
  Das Stundenlied
Eisler, Hanns
  Deutsche Sinfonie
  Die Mutter
Elgar, Sir Edward
  The Dream of Gerontius
  The Music Makers
Enescu, George
  Vox maris
Englund, Einar
  Symphony No. 6 (*Aphorisms*)
Estévez, Antonio
  *Florentino, el que cantó con el
    diablo*
Fabini, Eduardo
  Patria vieja
Falla, Manuel de
  Atlántida
Farkas, Ferenc
  Fountain of Saint John
Farquhar, David
  Bells in Their Seasons
Feldman, Morton
  Chorus and Orchestra I

Finney, Ross Lee
  Earthrise: A Trilogy Concerned with the Human Dilemma
  Pilgrim Psalms (or organ)
Finzi, Gerald
  For Saint Cecilia
Fišer, Luboš
  Requiem
  Sonata for Chorus, Piano, and Orchestra
Foerster, Joseph Bohuslav
  May, Opus 159
  Mortuis fratribus, Opus 108
  Saint Wenceslaus, Opus 140
Fortner, Wolfgang
  An die Nachgeborenen
  Gladbacher Te Deum
Foss, Lukas
  A Parable of Death
  The Prairie
  Psalms (or piano)
Freitas Branco, Frederico de
  Missa solene
Froidebise, Pierre
  La navigation d'Ulysse
García, Juan Alfonso
  Campanos para Federico
  Paraíso cerrado
Gardner, John
  Herrick Cantata
  Mass in D
Gemrot, Jiří
  Psalm 146
Gesseney-Rappo, Dominique
  Aujourd'hier Aujoird'hui
  Dei populus liberatus
Ginastera, Alberto
  Psalm 150 (or piano)
  Turbae ad passionem gregorianam
Glass, Phillip
  Itaipu

Symphony No. 5 (*Requiem, Bardo, and Nirmanakaya*)
Goldsmith, Jerry
  Christus Apollo
Golijov, Osvaldo
  La pasión según San Marco
Górecki, Henryk
  Symphony No. 2 (*Copernicus*)
Gotovac, Jakov
  Koleda
Grabovsky, Leonid
  Four Ukrainian Songs
Gretchaninoff, Alexander
  Liturgia domestica
  Missa oecumenica
  Strastnaya sedmitsa (Passion Week)
Gruenberg, Louis
  A Song of Faith
Guarnieri, Camargo
  Sinfonia No. 5
Gubaidulina, Sofia
  Allelujah
  Aus dem Stundenbuch
  Johannes Passion
Hagen, Daron Aric
  Taliesin: Choruses from the Shining Brow
Halffter, Cristóbal
  Antifona pascual a la virgen "Regina coeli"
Halffter, Ernesto
  Canticum in memoriam P. P. Johannem XXIII
  Gozos de Nuestra Señora
Halldórsson, Skúli
  Pourquoi pas?
Hamilton, David
  Te Deum
Hanson, Howard
  The Cherubic Hymn
  Drum Taps

[Hanson, Howard]
  The Lament for Beowulf
  The Mystic Trumpeter
  A Sea Symphony
  Song of Democracy
Hanuš, Jan
  The Earth Is Speaking, Opus 8
  Ecce homo, Opus 97
  Requiem, Opus 121
  Song of Hope, Opus 21
  Symphony No. 7, Opus 116
    (*The Keys of the Kingdom*)
Harlap, Aharon
  Cain and Abel (or piano)
  The Fire and the Mountains
Harris, Roy
  Freedom's Land (or
    unaccompanied)
  Symphony No. 4 (*Folk Song
    Symphony*)
Hayashi, Hikaru
  Beggar's Song
Heiller, Anton
  Stabat mater
Helfman, Max
  Judas Maccabaeus (Handel)
  Di Naye Hagode
Henze, Hans Werner
  Chor gefangener Trojer
  Das Floss der "Medusa"
  Moralities
  Symphony No. 9
Hill, Alfred
  Hinemoa
  Tawhaki
Hilsley, William
  Seasons
Hindemith, Paul
  Cantique de l'espérance
  Chant de triomphe du roi David
  Custos quid de nocte
  Ite, angeli veloces

Das Unaufhörliche (The One
  Perpetual)
*When Lilacs Last in the
  Dooryard Bloom'd: Requiem
  for Those We Love*
Hoddinott, Alun
  Dives and Lazarus
  Sinfonia fidei (Symphony of
    Faith)
Holst, Gustav
  Choral Symphony
  Christmas Day
  Hymn of Jesus
Honegger, Arthur
  Les battements du monde
  Une cantate de Noël
  Christophe Colomb
  Cris du monde
  La danse des morts
  Hamlet
  Jeanne d'Arc au bûcher
  Judith
  Les mille et une nuits
  Le roi David
  Saint François d'Assise
Hopkins, James
  Five American Folk Hymns
  From the Realm of the Sea
  The Rossetti Songs
  Songs of Eternity
Hovhaness, Alan
  *And God Created Great
    Whales*
  Magnificat
Hovhanesyan, Edgar Sergeyi
  Antuni
  Erebuni
  Erku ap'
Howells, Herbert
  Hymnus Paradisi
  Missa sabrinensis (Mass of the
    Severn)

Stabat mater
Hristić, Stevan
    Resurrection
Hsien Hsing-hai
    Yellow River Cantata
Hsu, Tsang-houei
    Ping chi hsing, Opus 8
Husa, Karel
    An American Te Deum
    Apotheosis of This Earth (second
      version)
Ifukube, Akira
    Okhotsk
Iliev, Konstantin
    Septemvri 1923
Ishii, Kan
    Ōinaru Akita (Great Akita)
Ísólfsson, Páll
    Althing Festival Cantata
Ives, Charles
    The Circus Band (or piano)
    Holidays Symphony
    Symphony No. 4
Janáček, Leoš
    Amarus
    The Eternal Gospel
    Glagolitic Mass
    Na Soláni Čarták
Johansson, Bengt
    Cantata humana
    Missa sacra
Jongen, Joseph
    Mass
Joubert, John
    The Choir Invisible
    The Raising of Lazarus
Kabalevsky, Dmitri
    Requiem
Kadosa, Pál
    De amore fatali, Opus 31
Kagel, Mauricio
    Sankt-Bach-Passion

Kalomiris, Manolis
    Symphony No. 1 (*Of Manliness*)
Kaminski, Heinrich
    Magnificat
Kancheli, Giya
    Light Sorrow
Kastal'sky, Alexandr
    Glory!
    Requiem to the Fallen Heroes
    Songs to the Motherland
    To Lenin: At His Graveside
    The Year 1905
Kelterborn, Rudolf
    Die Flut
Kernis, Aaron Jay
    Garden of Light
Khachaturian, Aram
    Song of Stalin
Khachaturian, Karen
    A Moment in History
Khaïrat, Abu-Bakr
    Lamma bada
Kodály, Zoltán
    Budavári Te Deum
    Psalmus hungaricus, Opus 13
Kokkonen, Joonas
    Requiem
Kopelent, Marek
    De passione Saint Adalberti
    Martyris
Kox, Hans
    Requiem for Europe
Kozlovsky, Alexey
    Two Suites
Kreek, Cyrillus
    Estonian Requiem
Krein, Alyexandr
    Kaddish
Krenek, Ernst
    Opus sine nomine, Opus 238
Kubik, Gail
    In Praise of Johnny Appleseed

[Kubik, Gail]
  A Record of Our Time
Kurtág, György
  Korean Cantata
Kyr, Robert
  The Inner Dawning
  The Passion According to Four
    Evangelists
  Symphony No. 9 (*The Spirit of*
    Time)
La Montaine, John
  The Marshes of Glynn
  Mass of Nature
  The Nine Lessons of Christmas
Laburda, Jiří
  Glagolitica
  Metamorphoses
Lajtha, László
  Missa in tono phrygio (*Missa in*
    diebus tribulationis)
Lambert, Constant
  The Rio Grande
Landré, Guillaume
  Piae memoriae pro patria
    mortuorum
Landré, Willem
  Requiem in memoriam uxoris
Lauber, Anne
  Jesus Christus
  Requiem
Lauridsen, Morten
  Lux aeterna (or organ)
  Midwinter Songs (or piano)
Lee, Dai-Keong
  Canticle of the Pacific
  Mele olili (Joyful Songs)
Leeuw, Ton de
  Job
Leighton, Kenneth
  Columba mea
  Symphony No. 2 (*Sinfonia*
    mistica)

Lendvay, Kamilló
  Orogenesis
  Pro libertate
Leon, Bayani Mendoza de
  Legend of the Land
  Los penitentes
  Sisa
Leoncavallo, Ruggero
  Inno alla Croce rossa
Leoni, Franco
  Golgotha
Lesemann, Frederick
  The Garden of Proserpine
Levitch, Leon
  Song of Dreams
Levy, Marvin David
  For the Time Being
  Masada
Lewkowitch, Bernhard
  De Lamentatione Jeremiae
    Prophetae
Ligeti, György
  Requiem
Lindberg, Oskar
  Requiem
Lloyd, George
  A Symphonic Mass
Lloyd Webber, Andrew
  Requiem
Lockwood, Normand
  Prairie
Loudová, Ivana
  Little Christmas Cantata
  Vocal Symphony
Lutyens, Elisabeth
  Essence of Our Happinesses
Machavariani, Alexei
  The Day of My Motherland
Macmillan, James
  Quickening
Mägi, Ester
  Kalevipoeg's Journey into Finland

Mahler, Gustav
  Symphony No. 2 (*Resurrection*)
  Symphony No. 3
  Symphony No. 8 ("Symphony of
    a Thousand")
Maklakiewicz, Jan Adam
  Symphony No. 2 (*O Holy Lord*)
Malawski, Artur
  Gorgon's Island
Malengreau, Paul
  The Legend of Saint Augustine
Malipiero, Gian Francesco
  Missa pro mortuis
Malipiero, Riccardo
  Cantata sacra
Mamiya, Michio
  15 June 1960
Marić, Ljubica
  Pesme prostora (Songs of Space)
Martin, Frank
  Cantate sur la Nativité
  Les dithyrambes
  Golgotha
  In terra pax
  Psaumes de Genève
  Requiem
Martinů, Bohuslav
  The Epic of Gilgamesh
  Špalíček
  The Spectre's Bride
Marx, Karl
  *Und endet doch alles mit
    Frieden*
Mathias, William
  Lux aeterna
  This Worlde's Joie
Matsumora, Teizo
  Totem Ritual
Matthews, David
  Vespers
Maw, Nicholas
  Hymnus

McCartney, Paul
  Liverpool Oratorio
  Standing Stone
Mechem, Kirke
  The Seven Joys of Christmas (or
    unaccompanied or
    instruments)
  Songs of the Slave
Mendelsohn, Alfred
  1907
Mennin, Peter
  Cantata de virtute ("The Pied
    Piper of Hamelin")
  Symphony No. 4 (*The Cycle*)
Menotti, Gian Carlo
  *The Death of the Bishop of
    Brindisi*
  For the Death of Orpheus
  Jacob's Prayer
  Landscapes and Remembrances
  Llama de amor viva
  *Missa O Pulchritudo in
    honorem Sacratissimi Cordis
    Jesu*
  Muero porque no muero
  A Song of Hope
Messiaen, Olivier
  *La Transfiguration de Notre
    Seigneur Jésus-Christ*
Milhaud, Darius
  Ani maamin
  "Cain and Abel," from *Genesis
    Suite*, Shilkret et al.
  Pacem in terris
  Service sacré
  Symphony No. 3 (*Te Deum*)
Moeran, E. J.
  Nocturne
Mokranjac, Stevan
  Ivkova slava
Moore, Undine Smith
  Scenes from the Life of a Martyr

Moreno, Segundo
  Cuatro marchas triunfales
  La emancipación
Mulder, Ernest Willem
  Requiem
  Stabat mater
Musgrave, Thea
  The Five Ages of Man
Naujalis, Juozas
  Mass in C Minor
Naylor, Bernard
  *The Annunciation According to
    Saint Luke*
  Three Sacred Pieces
Negrea, Marţian
  Requiem, Opus 25
Nelson, Ron
  What Is Man? (or instruments)
Nepomuceno, Alberto
  As Uyaras
  Nonetto
Nielsen, Carl
  Aladdin
  *Cantata for the Fiftieth
    Anniversary of the Danish
    Cremation Union*
  Hymnus amoris, Opus 12
  Saul and David
  Sleep, Opus 18
  Springtime in Funen, Opus 42
Nilsson, Bo
  Nazm
Nobutoki, Kiyoshi
  Kaidō tōsei (Along the Coast,
    Conquer the East)
Nono, Luigi
  Epitaffio per Federico Lorca,
    part 3
  Il canto sospeso
  Prometeo, tragedia dell'ascolto
Nordgren, Pehr Henrik
  Agnus Dei

Nordheim, Arne
  Éco
  Wirkliches Wald
Nørgård, Per
  Babel
  Dommen ("The Judgement")
Nørholm, Ib
  Kenotafium, Opus 23
  Light and Praise, Opus 55
Novák, Vitězslav
  The Spectre's Bride, Opus 48
  The Storm, Opus 42
Nystedt, Knut
  The Burnt Sacrifice, Opus 36
  Lucis creator optime, Opus
    58
Ōki, Masao
  Ningen o kaese (Restore
    Humanity)
  Shinano ji (Shinano Way)
Olah, Tiberiu
  The Galaxy of Man
Orbón, Julián
  Liturgia de tres días
Orff, Carl
  Carmina burana
  Trionfo di Afrodite
Orrego-Salas, Juan
  The Days of God
  Missa in tempore discordiae
Paliashvili, Zakhary
  Festival Cantata
Paniagua, Raul
  Misa
Papaioannou, Yannis
  Daphnis and Chloe
  The Funeral of Sarpedon
Parker, Horatio
  The Dream of Mary
  Hora novissima
  King Gorm the Grim
  Morven and the Grail

Parry, Sir Charles Hubert Hastings
   An Ode to the Nativity
   Songs of Farewell
Parsch, Arnošt
   Welcoming the Spring
Partos, Oedoen
   Cantata
Pasatieri, Thomas
   Mass
   Permit Me Voyage
Patterson, Paul
   Mass of the Sea
Penderecki, Krzysztof
   Credo
   Dies irae
   Kosmogonia
   Lacrymosa
   Magnificat
   Polish Requiem
   *Saint Luke Passion (Passio et
      mors Domini Nostri Jesu
      Christi secundum Lucam)*
   Seven Gates of Jerusalem
   Te Deum
   Utrenja
Pepping, Ernst
   Das Jahr
   Te Deum
Pergament, Moses
   Den judiska sången (The Jewish
      Song)
Persichetti, Vincent
   The Creation
   Te Deum
Petrassi, Goffredo
   Magnificat
   Noche oscura
Petridis, Petros
   La belle dame sans merci
   *Requiem for the Last Emperor
      of Byzantium*
   Saint Paul

Pfitzner, Hans
   Von deutscher Seele
Pineda-Duque, Roberto
   Cristo en el seno de Abraham
   Piecitos
Pipkov, Lyubomir
   Oratorio for Our Time
   Soldier's Cantata
   Wedding
Pizzetti, Ildebrando
   Epithalamium
Plaza, Juan Bautista
   Campanas de Pascua
Popov, Gavriil
   Heroic Intermezzo
Popov, Todor
   Bright Festival
   Song for the Great Day
Posada-Amador, Carlos
   Cantata al miedo
Potter, A. J.
   Stabat mater
Poulenc, Francis
   Gloria
   Sécheresses
   Sept répons des ténèbres
   Stabat mater
Pousseur, Henri
   Midi-minuit
Prado, Alcides
   Missa de requiem
Prévost, André
   Terre des hommes
Prokofiev, Sergei
   Alexander Nevsky
   Ballad of an Unknown Boy
   Flourish, Powerful Land
   Ivan the Terrible
   On Guard for Peace
   They Are Seven
Quintón, José Ignacio
   Misa de requiem

Rääts, Jaan
  Karl Marx
  School Cantata
Rachmaninoff, Sergei
  The Bells
  Spring
Račiūnas, Antanas
  Tarybu Lietuva
Raphael, Günter
  Eine deutsche Totenmesse
  Judica Kantate
Rautavaara, Einojuhani
  The True and False Unicorn
Ravel, Maurice
  Daphnis et Chloé
Rawsthorne, Alan
  Carmen vitale
Reda, Siegfried
  Requiem
Reger, Max
  Die Nonnen, Opus 112
  Four Chorale Cantatas
Reich, Steve
  Desert Music
Reiner, Karel
  They Were a Thousand Years
    Old
Ridout, Godfrey
  Esther
  Pange lingua
Rihm, Wolfgang
  Deus Passus (Passion after Saint
    Luke)
  Dies
Robertson, Leroy
  Oratorio from the Book of
    Mormon
Rodríguez, Robert Xavier
  Tranfigurationis mysteria
Roger-Ducasse, Jean
  Au jardín de Marguerite
  Sarabande

  Ulysse et les sirènes
Ropek, Jiří
  Christmas Fantasy
Rorem, Ned
  An American Oratorio
Rosenberg, Hilding
  Den Heliga natten
  Symphony No. 4 (*The*
    Revelation of Saint John)
  Symphony No. 5 (*The Keeper of*
    the Garden)
Rutter, John
  The Falcon
  Gloria (or instruments)
  Requiem
Saint-Saëns, Camille
  Hail, California
  The Promised Land
Santa Cruz Wilson, Domingo
  Cantata de los rios de Chile,
    Opus 19
  Te Deum, Opus 4
Saygun, Adnan
  Yunus Emre
Scelsi, Giacinto
  La naissance du Verbe
Schafer, R. Murray
  Threnody
Schifrin, Lalo
  Cantionas Argentinas
  Cantos Aztecas
  Madrigals for the Space Age
  The Rise and Fall of the Third
    Reich
Schmidt, Franz
  Das Buch mit sieben Siegeln
Schmidt, Gustavo Becerra
  La araucana
Schmitt, Florent
  Psalm 47
Schnittke, Alfred
  Requiem

Starer, Robert
Ariel, Visions of Isaiah
Joseph and His Brothers
Stenhammer, Wilhelm
The Song
Stevens, Halsey
The Ballad of William Sycamore
Stibilj, Milan
Apokatastasis
Still, William Grant
And They Lynched Him on a Tree
From a Lost Continent
Song of a City
Strassburg, Robert
Leaves of Grass
Strategier, Herman
Rembrandt Cantata
Strauss, Richard
Taillefer
Stravinsky, Igor
Canticum sacrum ad honorem Sancti Marci nominis
Chorale Variations on "Vom Himmel hoch" by J. S. Bach
Oedipus Rex
Persephone
Requiem Canticles
A Sermon, a Narrative, and a Prayer
Symphony of Psalms
Threni: id est Lamentationes Jeremiae prophetae
Suchoň, Eugen
Psalm of the Carpathians, Opus 12
Suk, Josef
Epilogue
Suter, Hermann
Le laudi di S Francesco d'Assisi
Sutherland, Margaret
The Passing

Sviridov, Georgy
Kursk Songs
Land of the Fathers
My Father the Peasant
Oratorio pathétique
Poema pamyati Sergeya Yesenina
Szymanowski, Karol
Stabat mater
Symphony No. 3 (*The Song of the Night*)
Veni Creator
Tailleferre, Germaine
Concerto for Two Pianos, Chorus, and Orchestra
Takata, Saburō
Musei dōkoku (Wordless Tears)
Tal, Josef
The Death of Moses
A Mother Rejoices
Talma, Louise
A Time to Remember
Tan Dun
Symphony 1997 Heaven Earth Mankind
Water Passion after Saint Matthew
Tanev, Alexander
Chronicle of Freedom
Taneyev, Sergey I.
At the Reading of a Psalm
Tansman, Alexandre
"Adam and Eve," from *Genesis Suite*, Shilkret et al.
In Memoriam
Isaïe, le prophète
Psaumes
Tavener, John
Celtic Requiem
Introit for March 27, the Feast of Saint John Damascene
Ultimos ritos
The Whale

Tcherepnin, Alexander
  Baptism Cantata
  Le jeu de la Nativité
  Pan kéou
Tcherepnin, Nikolai
  *La descente de la Sainte Vierge à
    l'enfer*
Theodorakis, Mikis
  Requiem
Thomas, Kurt
  Jerusalem, du hochgebaute Stadt
Thompson, Randall
  Frostiana (or piano)
  The Last Words of David (or
    piano or male chorus)
  *The Passion According to Saint
    Luke*
  The Testament of Freedom (or
    piano or male chorus)
Thomson, Virgil
  Missa pro defunctis
Tinel, Edgar
  *Missa in honorem Beatae Mariae
    Virginis de Lourdes*, Opus 41
  Te Deum
Tippett, Michael
  A Child of Our Time
  The Mask of Time
  The Vision of Saint Augustine
Tobias, Rudolf
  Johannes Damascenus
  Des Jona Sendung
Toch, Ernst
  Cantata of the Bitter Herbs,
    Opus 65
  "The Covenant," from *Genesis
    Suite*, Shilkret et al.
Torke, Michael
  Four Seasons
  Mass
Tormis, Velio
  Kalevipoeg

Sun, Sea, Earth
Torres-Santos, Raymond
  Requiem
Tosar Errecart, Héctor A.
  Te Deum
Tsintsadze, Sulkhan F.
  The Great Way
  Immortality
Tuur, Erkkisven
  Missa lumen et cantus
  Oratorio ante finem saeculi
  Symphony No. 2
Urbanner, Erich
  Lateinisches Requiem
Valencia, Antonio María
  Requiem
Vargas, Téofilo
  Niño Dios
Vasconcellos, Jorgé Croner de
  *Vilancico para a festa de Santa
    Cecilia*
Vaughan Williams, Ralph
  Dona nobis pacem
  *Fantasia on the Old 104th Psalm
    Tune*
  Five Mystical Songs
  Five Tudor Portraits
  Hodie
  Sancta civitas
  A Sea Symphony
Veress, Sándor
  *Sancti Augustini psalmus conta
    partem Donati*
Vianna da Motta, José
  Lusiads
Victory, Gerard
  Hymnus vespertinus
Vieru, Anatol
  Cantata anilor lumină
    (Cantata of the Luminous
    Years)
  Miorița

Villa-Lobos, Heitor
  Chôro No. 10
  Forest of the Amazon
  Suite No. 4 (*Descobrimento do Brasil*)
Vycpálek, Ladislav
  Blessed Is the Man
  Czech Requiem
  Of the Last Things of Man
Wagner-Régeny, Rudolf
  Prometheus
Walton, William
  Belshazzar's Feast
  Gloria
  In Honour of the City of London
  Te Deum
Waxman, Franz
  Song of Terezín
Webern, Anton
  Das Augenlicht, Opus 26
  Cantata No. 1, Opus 29
  Cantata No. 2
Weill, Kurt
  Die Burgschaft
  Der Jasager
  Der Lindberghflug
  Die sieben Todsünden der Kleinbürger
  Happy End
Weiner, Lazar
  The Golem
Whitehead, Gillian
  Babel
Widmer, Ernst
  Rumo Sol-Espirial (Direction to the Sun Spiral)
Wilhousky, Peter J.
  The Battle Hymn of the Republic (or piano or band)
Willan, Healey
  Coronation Suite

Te Deum in B-flat
Williamson, Malcolm
  The Brilliant and the Dark
  The Icy Mirror (Symphony No. 3)
  Mass of Christ the King
Wilson, Charles M.
  The Angels of the Earth
  On the Morning of Christ's Nativity
Wilson, Olly
  Spirit Song
Yamada, Kōsaku
  Chikai no hoshi (Star of Promise)
  Kimigayo zensōkyoku (Prelude on the Japanese National Anthem)
  Tenrikyō sanshōfu (Hymn for the Tenrikyō)
Yun, Isang
  Om mani padme hum
Zaimont, Judith Lang
  Sacred Service
Zeisl, Eric
  Spruchkantate (Cantata of Verses)
Zemlinsky, Alexander
  Psalm 13, Opus 24
  Psalm 23
  Psalm 83
Zhukovsky, German
  Hail, My Fatherland
  The Knieper Ripples
  Prayer of World Youth
Zimmermann, Bernd Alois
  Lob der Torheit
  Requiem für einen jungen Dichter
Zweers, Bernard
  Aan de schoonheid (To Beauty)

COMPOSITIONS FOR BOYS' OR CHILDREN'S CHORUS

UNACCOMPANIED

Avidom, Menahem
Jerusalem Songs
Psalm Cantata
Hába, Alois
Children's Choruses, Opus 42
and 43
Halffter, Rodolfo
La nuez
Harlap, Aharon
My Friend Tintan
Holmboe, Vagn
Psalm 62
Kodály, Zoltán
See the Gypsies
The Straw Guy
Krenek, Ernst
*Three Madrigals and Three
Motets*, Opus 174
Mellnäs, Arne
Aglepta
Negrea, Marţian
Album for Children's Choir,
Opus 11
Persichetti, Vincent
Glad and Very
Saar, Mart
Children's Choruses (two
volumes)
Schul, Zikmund
Ki tavo al-ha'Arez (When You
Go to the Land)
Szabó, Ferenc
Urchin Song
Tavener, John
Notre pere
Vasiliauskaite, Kristina
Missa brevis

Weill, Kurt
Recordare, Opus 11 (with mixed
choir)

WITH PIANO

Anderson, Thomas Jefferson
Jonestown
Bennett, Richard Rodney
The Aviary
The Insect World
Britten, Benjamin
Friday Afternoons
Cowell, Henry
Do, Do, Do, Is C, C, C
Davidson, Charles
I Never Saw Another Butterfly
Diamond, David
A Song for Shabuoth
Kurtág, György
Dance Song
Lockwood, Normand
A Child's Christmas in Wales
Menotti, Gian Carlo
The Trial of the Gypsy
Nathan, Hans, ed.
Folk Songs of the New Palestine
(unison)
Rachmaninoff, Sergei
Six Songs for Children's Voices
Reiner, Karel
The Flowered Horse

WITH ORGAN

Roff, Joseph
*Propers of Sundays and Major
Feasts*

Santa Cruz Wilson, Domingo
Alabanzas de adviento, Opus 30

Xenakis, Iannis
Polla ta dhina (Hymn to Man)

WITH OTHER INSTRUMENTS

Balsys, Eduardas
Don't Touch the Blue Globe
Banks, Don
Walkabout
Britten, Benjamin
A Ceremony of Carols
Castelnuovo-Tedesco, Mario
The Fiery Furnace
Hanuš, Jan
Opus spirituale pro juventute,
Opus 65
Iliev, Konstantin
Chudnoto choro (The
Miraculous Dance)
Mennin, Peter
Reflections of Emily
Profeta, Laurenţiu
Six Pieces

WITH WIND ORCHESTRA
OR BAND

(none)

WITH CHAMBER ORCHESTRA

Alexander, Leni
From Death to Morning
Carr, Edwin
Blake Cantata
Holmboe, Vagn
Requiem
Hindemith, Paul
*Admonition to Youth to Apply
Itself to Music* (*Advice to
Youth*)
Landowski, Marcel
Notes de nuit

WITH FULL ORCHESTRA

Absil, Jean
Three Choruses, Opus 15
Three Choruses, Opus 18
Blockx, Jan
Feeste in den Lande
Gloriae patriae
Britten, Benjamin
Welcome Ode
Dessau, Paul
Haggada
Dreyfus, George
*Reflections in a Glass-House: An
Image of Captain James Cook*
Françaix, Jean
Five Chansons
Hsu, Tsang-houei
Chu-kuo sung, Opus 11
Larson, Libby
Song-Dances to the Light
Lockwood, Normand
Mass for Children and Orchestra
Thought of Him I Love
Menotti, Gian Carlo
Miracles
Profeta, Laurenţiu
Adventures in the Garden
Prokofiev, Sergei
Winter Bonfire
Shostakovich, Dmitri
*The Sun Shines on Our
Motherland*
Szönyi, Erzsébet
The Shivering King
Tinodi's Song about Eger
Williamson, Malcolm
Ode to Music

Compositions for Female or Treble Chorus

UNACCOMPANIED

Absil, Jean
  Three Choruses, Opus 6
  Three Choruses, Opus 24
Aguiar, Ernani
  Salmo 150
Avni, Tzvi
  The City Plays Hide and Seek
Badings, Henk
  Six Christmas Songs
Bárdos, Lajos
  Twenty Choruses
Bartók, Béla
  Twenty-seven Choruses
Bissell, Keith
  Requiem
Burkhard, Willy
  Nine Folk Songs
Carneyro, Claudio
  Ave Maria
  Musa popular
  Oracoes populares
  Quatro romances populares
Chihara, Paul
  Magnificat
Clark, Sondra
  Feline
Cowell, Henry
  With Choirs Divine (optional
    piano)
Diemer, Emma Lou
  Fragments of the Mass
Dryburgh, Margaret
  The Captive's Hymn
Fine, Vivian
  *The Passionate Shepherd to His
    Love and Her Reply*
Freitas Branco, Frederico de
  Missa "Regina mundi"

Harlap, Aharon
  Still Remembering Names
Harris, Roy
  Freedom's Land (piano ad lib, or
    male or mixed)
  A Whitman Triptych
Heiller, Anton
  Missa super "Erhalt uns Herr"
d'Indy, Vincent
  Le bouquet du printemps, Opus
    93
Irino, Yoshirō
  Three Pieces
Janáček, Leoš
  Kašpar Rucky
  Songs of Hradčany
Kim, Byong-kon
  My Heart is Steadfast
Klein, Gideon
  Bachuri L'an Tisa
Knussen, Oliver
  Frammenti da "Chiara"
Landowski, Marcel
  Cinq chants d'innocence
Leach, Mary Jane
  Ariadne's Lament
  Call of the Dance
  O Magna Vasti Creta
  Tricky Pan
  Windjammer
MacDowell, Edward
  Summer Wind
  Two College Songs
Mignone, Francisco
  Cantiga de ninar
Ohana, Maurice
  Lys de Madrigaux
Papaioannou, Yannis
  Songs of the Night

Payne, Maggie
Desertscapes
Persichetti, Vincent
Two Cummings Choruses
Pinkham, Daniel
Three Motets
Poulenc, Francis
Ave verum corpus
Petite voix
Price, Florence
Moon Bridge
Scelsi, Giacinto
Litanie
Yliam
Schuman, William
Prelude (or mixed chorus)
Seeger, Ruth Crawford
Three Chants (No. 1, No. 3)
Sigurbjörnsson, Thorkell
Missa miniscule
Staar, René
Kyrie II "Cathedrale de Lausanne"
Stravinsky, Igor
Four Russian Peasant Songs (first version)
Szöllösy, András
Planctus Mariae
Szymanowski, Karol
Agave
Demeter
Litany to the Virgin Mary
Takemitsu, Tōru
Kaze no uma (Horse in the Wind)
Tcherepnin, Alexander
Mass
Wagenaar, Johan
Three Double Canons, Opus 12
Wellesz, Egon
Quant' è bella giovinessa

WITH PIANO

Bernier, René
Sortilèges ingénus
Blitzstein, Marc
Cantatina
Castelnuovo-Tedesco, Mario
Naomi and Ruth
The Queen of Sheba
Dello Joio, Norman
A Jubilant Song (or mixed chorus)
Doniach, Shula
Rhymes from Carmel
Fine, Irving
Alice in Wonderland
Fromm, Herbert
The Song of Miriam
Janáček, Leoš
The Diary of One Who Vanished
The Wolf's Track
Lu, Chuan-Sheng
The Train
Lutoslawski, Witold
Twenty Polish Christmas Carols
Moore, Undine Smith
Sir Olaf and the Erl King's Daughter
Nathan, Hans, ed.
Folk Songs of the New Palestine (unison)
Persichetti, Vincent
Spring Cantata
Pijper, Willem
Two Ballades of Paul Fort
Schuman, William
Holiday Song (or mixed chorus)
The Lord Has a Child (or mixed chorus)
Spies, Claudio
Verses from the Book of Ruth

Wagenaar, Johan
Prière au printemps, Opus 18
Yamada, Kōsaku
Ai no megami (Goddess of
Love)
Funaji (Sea Route)
Hikari motomete (Seeking Light)
Nairu-gawa no uta (Song of the
Nile)

WITH ORGAN

Carnevali, Vito
Missa "Rosa Mystica" (or male
or mixed chorus)
Casals, Pablo
Eucaristica (or mixed chorus)
Nigra sum (or male chorus)
Creston, Paul
Missa "Adoro te" (or mixed
chorus)
Einfelde, Maija
Ave Maria
Fine, Vivian
Psalm 13 (or instruments)
Freitas Branco, Frederico de
Stabat mater
Fromm, Herbert
Psalm 23
Hanson, Howard
How Excellent Thy Name (or
mixed chorus)
Heiller, Anton
Adventmusik
Missa in nocte
Passionsmusik
Kronsteiner, Hermann
Kleine Stille Nacht Messe
Lajtha, László
Magnificat, Opus 60
Poulenc, Francis
Litanies à la vierge noire

Roff, Joseph
*Propers of Sundays and Major
Feasts*

WITH OTHER INSTRUMENTS

Badings, Henk
Drie Lucebertliederen
Blum, Robert
Two Meditations
Britain, Radie
Nisan (or mixed chorus and
piano)
Britten, Benjamin
A Ceremony of Carols
Dallapiccola, Luigi
*Sei cori di Michelangelo
Buonarroti* (second pair)
Domažlicky, František
Czech Songs
Einfelde, Maija
Peo persona
Encinar, José Ramon
Canción
Fine, Vivian
Oda a las ranas
Psalm 13 (or organ)
Sounds of the Nightingale
Fleischer, Tsippi
Lamentations
Glanville-Hicks, Peggy
Choral Suite
Holst, Gustav
*Choral Hymns from the Rig
Veda*, third set
Ikebe, Shin-Ichiro
Kusabi
Janáček, Leoš
Nursery Rhymes (first
version)
Kagel, Mauricio
Die Frauen

Klerk, Albert de
Missa Mater Sanctae laetitiae
Letelier-Llona, Alfonso
Vitrales de la anunciación
Lindberg, Oskar
Sommar jag in med blicken fast
Lockwood, Normand
The Birth of Moses
Loeffler, Charles Martin
Psalm 137
Martin, Frank
Chansons
Martinů, Bohuslav
Opening the Wells, from *Songs of the Uplands*
The Primrose
Mechem, Kirke
Barter
Meltzer, Michael
Porke Yorash (Why Do You Weep, Girl?)
Messiaen, Olivier
Mass
Nystedt, Knut
Suoni, Opus 62
Parker, Horatio
Seven Greek Pastoral Scenes
Persichetti, Vincent
Winter Cantata
Stravinsky, Igor
Cantata
Four Russian Peasant Songs (second version)
Yun, Isang
An der Schwelle

WITH WIND ORCHESTRA OR BAND

(none)

WITH CHAMBER ORCHESTRA

Carter, Elliott
The Harmony of Morning
Goleminov, Marin
Five Christmas Songs
Talma, Louise
Celebration
Wagner-Régeny, Rudolf
Schir haschirim (Song of Songs)

WITH FULL ORCHESTRA

Archer, Violet
Choruses from "The Bacchae"
Badings, Henk
Hymnus ave maris stella
Bartók, Béla
Three Village Scenes
Bernier, René
Sortilèges ingénus (or piano)
Debussy, Claude
La damoiselle élue
Nocturnes
Dohnányi, Ernst von
Stabat mater
Freitas Branco, Frederico de
Don João e as sombras
Holst, Gustav
The Planets
Kox, Hans
Litania
Lutoslawski, Witold
Twenty Polish Christmas Carols
Matsumora, Teizo
Apsaras
Messiaen, Olivier
Trois petites liturgies de la Présence Divine

Pizzetti, Ildebrando
  Filiae Jerusalem, adjuro vos
Prokofiev, Sergei
  Two Poems
Radíc, Dušan
  Symphonic Picture No. 2
Schuman, William
  Concerto on Old English Rounds

Tailleferre, Germaine
  La cantate du Narcisse
Tansman, Alexandre
  Prologue et cantate
Vaughan Williams, Ralph
  Magnificat
Warren, Elinor Remick
  The Harp Weaver

COMPOSITIONS FOR MALE CHORUS

UNACCOMPANIED

Adams, Byron
  Missa brevis
Bartók, Béla
  Four Old Hungarian Folk Songs
Bernstein, Leonard
  Dedication
  A Little Norton Lecture
  Lonely Men of Harvard
  Two Harvard Choruses
Ben-Haim, Paul
  Zwei Lieder
Bibalo, Antonio
  Serenata
Burkhard, Willy
  Frühlingsglaube
Busoni, Ferruccio
  Piano Concerto
Chihara, Paul
  Ave Maria—Scarborough Fair
Domažlicky, František
  May Song
Egge, Klaus
  Lyric Suite, Opus 8
Gotovac, Jakov
  Three Choruses for Young Men
Grainger, Percy
  Tiger, Tiger
Haas, Pavel
  Al S'fod

Hába, Alois
  Constitution of 9 May, Opus
    64
  Meditation, Opus 66
  Peace, Opus 67
  Three Male Choruses, Opus 65
Harris, Roy
  Freedom's Land (piano ad lib, or
    band or mixed chorus)
Hilsley, William
  Missa in nativitatis
Ikebe, Shin-Ichiro
  Five Chansons by García Lorca
Irino, Yoshirō
  Fuji san (Mount Fuji)
  Iwa (Rock)
  Three Pieces
Janáček, Leoš
  Kantor Halfar
  Maryčka Magdónova
  The 70,000
  The Wandering Madman
Klein, Gideon
  The First Sin
Kohn, Karl
  Three Golliard Songs
Komitas
  Chants of the Sacred Liturgy
Kwiatkowski, Ryszard
  Prayer of a Blind Somnambulist

Leeuw, Ton de
  Cloudy Forms
Lendvay, Kamilló
  Three Male Choruses
Leopoldi, Hermann
  Buchenwald Lied
Lewkowitch, Bernhard
  Three Songs for Male Chorus
MacDowell, Edward
  *College Songs for Male
  Voices*
Martin, Frank
  Chansons
Mokranjac, Stevan
  The Glorification of Saint Sava
  (1893 version)
Papandopulo, Boris
  *The Passion of Our Lord Jesus
  Christ*
Penderecki, Krzysztof
  Ecloga VIII
Poot, Marcel
  Chanson bachique
Poulenc, Francis
  *Laudes de Saint Antoine de
  Padoue*
  *Quatre petites prières de Saint
  François d'Assise*
Saar, Mart
  Men's Choruses
Schul, Zikmund
  Cantata Judaica
Shimizu, Osamu
  Bara no sansaku (Promenade in
  the Roses)
Shostakovich, Dmitri
  Faithfulness
Shvedov, Konstantin
  Divine Liturgy
Sibelius, Jean
  The Bridge Guard
  Karelia's Fate

Sigurbjörnsson, Thorkell
  Ode
Spies, Claudio
  Proverbs on Wisdom
Staar, René
  Kyrie I "Durham Cathedral"
Strauss, Richard
  Cantata
  Die Göttin im Putzzimmer
  (The Goddess in the
  Boudoir)
  Six Folk Songs
Szöllösy, András
  Fabula Phaedri
  Miserere
Tajčević, Marko
  Pesme od kola
Takata, Saburō
  Kisetsu to ashiato (Seasons and
  Footprints)
Tanev, Alexander
  Old Bulgarian Dances
Tormis, Velio
  Meestelaulud (Men's Songs)
Wellesz, Egon
  Fünf kleine Männerchöre

WITH PIANO

Bonds, Margaret
  Fields of Wonder
Britten, Benjamin
  *The Ballad of Little Barnard and
  Lady Musgrave*
Carter, Elliott
  The Defense of Corinth
  Emblems
Kox, Hans
  De kantate van Sint Juttemis
Nathan, Hans, ed.
  Folk Songs of the New Palestine
  (unison)

Thompson, Randall
  The Last Words of David (or
    orchestra or mixed chorus)
  Tarantella
  The Testament of Freedom (or
    orchestra, band, or mixed
    chorus)
Zipper, Herbert
  Dachaulied

WITH ORGAN

Carnevali, Vito
  Missa "Rosa Mystica" (or treble
    or mixed chorus)
Casals, Pablo
  Nigra sum (or treble)
Eben, Petr
  Missa in adventus
Harris, Roy
  Mass
Creston, Paul
  Missa solemnis (or mixed
    chorus)
  Requiem
Roff, Joseph
  *Propers of Sundays and Major
    Feasts*

WITH OTHER INSTRUMENTS

Anderson, Thomas Jefferson
  This House
  Thomas Jefferson's Minstrels
Bergman, Erik
  The Birds
Creston, Paul
  Calamus
Harrison, Lou
  Four Strict Songs
Kubik, Gail
  Litany and Prayer

León, Tania
  Heart of Ours—A Piece
Martinů, Bohuslav
  The Prophecy of Isaiah
Menotti, Gian Carlo
  My Christmas
Petrassi, Goffredo
  Coro di morti
Piston, Walter
  Carnival Song
Rasmussen, Karl Aage
  Parade
Scelsi, Giacinto
  Tkrdg
Schoeck, Othmar
  Eichendorff Cantata
Stravinsky, Igor
  Introitus
Tavener, John
  Ma fin est mon commencement
Varèse, Edgard
  Ecuatorial
Xenakis, Iannis
  Medea (incidental music)

WITH WIND ORCHESTRA
OR BAND

Cowell, Henry
  Fire and Ice
Dessau, Paul
  Grabschrift für Gorki
Harris, Roy
  Freedom's Land (or piano ad lib)
Pijper, Willem
  Réveillez-vous, Piccars
Thompson, Randall
  The Testament of Freedom (or
    piano or orchestra)

WITH CHAMBER ORCHESTRA

Varèse, Edgard
  Nocturnal
Wagner-Régeny, Rudolf
  Cantica Davidi regis
Zeisl, Eric
  From the Book of Psalms

WITH FULL ORCHESTRA

Blitzstein, Marc
  The Airborne Symphony
Britain, Radie
  Brothers in the Clouds (or
    mixed chorus or piano)
Chen Yi
  Chinese Myths Cantata
Cowell, Henry
  *Lines from the Dead Sea
    Scrolls*
Duruflé, Maurice
  Missa "Cum jubilo"
Hába, Alois
  For Peace, Opus 68
Harrison, Lou
  Nova odo
Luna, Margarita
  Vigilia eterna
Matsumora, Teizo
  Flute of Evil Passions

Pizzetti, Ildebrando
  Vanitas vanitatum
Potter, A. J.
  Saint Patrick's Breastplate
Reger, Max
  Die Weihe der Nacht, Opus 119
Schoenberg, Arnold
  A Survivor from Warsaw, Opus
    46
Shimizu, Osamu
  Yama ni inoru (Prayer to the
    Mountains)
Sibelius, Jean
  The Origin of Fire
Shostakovich, Dmitri
  Symphony No. 13 (*Babiy Yar*)
Stravinsky, Igor
  "Babel," from *Genesis Suite*,
    Shilkret et al.
  Oedipus Rex
  Zvezdoliki (Starface)
Surinach, Carlos
  Missions of San Antonio
Thompson, Randall
  The Last Words of David (or
    piano or mixed chorus)
  The Testament of Freedom (or
    piano, band, or mixed
    chorus))
Tsvetanov, Tsvetan
  Stalbata (Ladder)

BIBLIOGRAPHY

Adler, Alfred, Josee Konig, and Hanneke van Schaik, eds. 1992. *Muziek uit Theresienstadt*. Amsterdam: Stichting Concertante.

Alwes, Chester L. 1985. Formal structure as a guide to rehearsal strategy in *Psalm 90* by Charles Ives. *The Choral Journal* (April).

———. 1995. Paul Hindemith's *Six Chansons*: genesis and analysis. *The Choral Journal* (September).

Anderson, E. Ruth. 1982. *Contemporary American Composers: A Biographical Dictionary*. Second edition. Boston: G. K. Hall.

Anderson, Martin. 2001a. Estonian identity, part 1. *Choir and Organ* (March–April).

———. 2001b. Estonian identity, part 2. *Choir and Organ* (May–June).

Anderson, Robert. 1993. *Elgar*. New York: Schirmer Books.

Antokoletz, Elliott. 1997. *Béla Bartók: A Guide to Research*. New York: Garland.

Antolini, Anthony. 1993. Rachmaninov's Choral Concerto in G Minor: a century-old icon in sound. *The Choral Journal* (August).

Armstrong, Anton. 1996. The musical legacy of F. Melius Christiansen. *The Choral Journal* (November).

Arom, Simha. 1991. *African Polyphony and Polyrhythm*. Cambridge: Cambridge University Press.

Aune, Gregory J. 1996. The choral methodology and philosophy of F. Melius Christiansen: the tradition continues. *The Choral Journal* (November).

Bagdanskis, Jonas. 1974. *The Lithuanian Musical Scene*. Vilnius, Lithuania: Mintis Publishers.

Bahat, Avner. 1995. Moshe Rasiuk, composer. *Israel Music Institute News* 95 (1).

Bailey, Walter B., and Nancy Gisbrecht Bailey. 1990. *Radie Britain: A Bio-Bibliography*. Westport, Connecticut: Greenwood Press.

Barham, Terry. 1984. A macroanalytic view of Vincent Persichetti's *The Creation*, Op. 111. *The Choral Journal* (March).

————. 1985. Unifying elements in the Mass and *Winter Cantata* by Vincent Persichetti. *The Choral Journal* (December).

Barrow, Lee G. 1987. Ottorino Respighi's *Laud to the Nativity*. *The Choral Journal* (August).

Beck, Joseph G. 1996. Westminster Choir: recordings as history. *The Choral Journal* (November).

Belaiev, Victor. 1928. *Igor Stravinsky's* Les noces: *An Outline*. Translated by S. W. Pring. London: Oxford University Press.

Berio, Luciano. 1969. *Sinfonia*. Record liner notes. New York: Columbia Masterworks.

————. 1980. *Coro für Stimmen und Instrumente*. Record liner notes. München: Polydor International.

Berkovec, Jiří. 1969. *Josef Suk*. Prague: Editio Supraphon.

Bernstein, Leonard. 1966. *The Infinite Variety of Music*. New York: Simon and Schuster.

————. 1982. *Findings*. New York: Simon and Schuster.

Beyer, Anders, ed. 1996. *The Music of Per Nørgård*. New York: Scolar Press.

Biezaisi, Eriks, and Margarita Biezaisi. 1992. *Skandarbu Katalogugs*. Latvian composers catalogue. Adelaide: Muzikas Kratuves Izdevums.

Biggs, E. Power et al. 1968. Leo Sowerby: a symposium of tribute. *Music: The A.G.O. Magazine* (October).

Blaukopf, Kurt. 1976. *Mahler: A Documentary Study*. New York: Oxford University Press.

Blessinger, Karl. 1939. *Mendelssohn, Meyerbeer, Mahler: Drei Kapital Judentum in der Musik als Schlussel zur Musikgeschichte des 19. Jahrhunderts*. Berlin: B. Hahnefeld.

Bloch, Ernest. 1985. *Essays on the Philosophy of Music*. Translated by P. Palmer. Cambridge: Cambridge University Press.

Bloesch, Richard J., and Weyburn Wasson. 1997. *Twentieth-Century Choral Music: An Annotated Bibliography of Music Appropriate for College and University Choirs*. Lawton, Oklahoma: American Choral Directors Association.

Blom, Eric, ed. 1954. *Grove's Dictionary of Music and Musicians*. Fifth edition. New York: Saint Martin's Press.

————. 1961. *Grove's Dictionary of Music and Musicians*. Supplementary volume. New York: Saint Martin's Press.

Blume, Friedrich. 1974. *Protestant Church Music*. In collaboration with Ludwig Finscher et al. New York: W. W. Norton.

Blyth, Alan, ed. 1991. *Choral Music on Record*. Cambridge: Cambridge University Press.

Boronkay, Antal. 1992. Music of our age. *Hungarian Music Quarterly*. 3 (1).

Borton, Allen L. 1994. Ralph Vaughan Williams's *Hodie* at forty. *The Choral Journal* (December).

Bowen, Meirion. 1989. Sir Michael Tippett. *Musical America* (November).

Branco, João de Freitas. 1995. *História da música portuguesa*. Portugal: Publicações Êuropa América, LDA.

Braun, William. 1991. Prokofiev's choral works. *The Choral Journal* (May).

———. 1995. Music to sing and play: the choral works of Paul Hindemith. *The Choral Journal* (September).

Britain, Radie. 1996. *Ridin' Herd to Writing Symphonies: An Autobiography*. Lanham, Maryland: Scarecrow Press.

Brockway, Wallace, and Herbert Weinstock. 1958. *Men of Music*. New York: Simon and Schuster.

Brooks, Gene. 1997. An interview with Gian Carlo Menotti. *The Choral Journal* (March).

———. 1998a. An interview with Adolphus Hailstork. *The Choral Journal* (February).

———. 1998b. An interview with Gwyneth Walker. *The Choral Journal* (February).

Browne, John. 1994. Petr Eben: a composer in isolation. *Choir and Organ* (November–December).

Brubeck, Dave. 1968. *The Light in the Wilderness*. Music: The A.G.O. Magazine (February).

Brunner, David L. 1992. Cultural diversity in the choral music of Lou Harrison. *The Choral Journal* (May).

Buenting, Ruth M. 1992. For Christmas with love: the Alfred Burt carols. *The Choral Journal* (December).

Burton, Humphrey. 1994. *Leonard Bernstein*. New York: Doubleday.

Cahill, Thomas. 1995. *How the Irish Saved Civilization*. New York: Anchor Books.

Cain, Noble. 1932. *Choral Music and Its Practice*. New York: M. Widmark and Sons.

Calloway, Frank, and David Tunley, eds. 1978. *Australian Composition in the Twentieth Century*. Melbourne: Oxford University Press.

Carley, Lionel. 1998. *Frederick Delius: Music, Art, and Literature*. Brookfield, Vermont: Ashgate.

Carlson, Corydon. 1988. A sense of mission: an interview with Daniel Moe. *The Choral Journal* (September).

Carlson, S. 1960–61. Mauricio Kagel: *Anagrama*. *Nutida musik* 4 (3).

Carlson, Tom. 1970. Witold Lutoslawski: *Three Poems by Henri Michaux*. Record liner notes. New York: Scepter Records.

Carpenter, Humphrey. 1992. *Benjamin Britten: A Biography*. New York: Charles Scribner's Sons.

Castleberry, David H. 1993. The lyric voice in Samuel Barber's *Reincarnations*. *The Choral Journal* (February).

Catalano, Peter. 1991. Homage to Lutoslawski. *Musical America* (March).

Chase, Gilbert. 1959. *The Music of Spain*. Second edition. New York: Dover.

————. 1966. *America's Music*. New York: McGraw-Hill.

Chlopicka, Regina. 1991. The theme of good and evil in Penderecki's works. *Music in Poland* (44).

Chylinska, Teresa. 1993. *Karol Szymanowski: His Life and Works*. Translated by John Glowacki. Stuyvesant, New York: Pendragon Press.

Clark, Kenneth. 1969. *Civilisation*. New York: Harper and Row.

Clausen, René. 1996. The compositional style of F. Melius Christiansen. *The Choral Journal* (November).

Cloud, Lee V. 1992. Choral works by African American composers. *The Choral Journal* (September).

Cole, Malcolm S. 1977. Afrika singt: Austro-German echoes of the Harlem Renaissance. *Journal of the American Musicological Society* 30 (1).

Cole, Malcolm S., and Barbara Barclay. 1984. *Armseelchen: The Life and Music of Eric Zeisl*. Westport, Connecticut: Greenwood Press.

Coleman, David. 1968. Dave Brubeck. *Music: The A.G.O. Magazine* (February).

————. 1967. Rorem: Romantic with a capital r. *Music: The A.G.O. Magazine* (October).

Colijn, Helen. 1995. *Song of Survival: Women Interned*. Ashland, Oregon: White Cloud Press.

Collins, Brian. 1996. *Peter Warlock: The Composer*. Brookfield, Vermont: Scolar Press.

Conrad, Peter. 2000. *Modern Times, Modern Places: How Life and Art Were Transformed in a Century of Revolution, Innovation, and Radical Change*. New York: Alfred A. Knopf.

Cook, Eugene. 1977. Penderecki: the Polish question . . . and others. *Music Journal* (February).

Cooke, Mervyn. 1996. *Britten:* War Requiem. Cambridge: Cambridge University Press.

Corle, Edward, ed. 1949. *Igor Stravinsky*. New York: Duell, Sloane, and Pearce.

Craggs, Stewart R. 1995. *Edward Elgar: A Source Book*. Brookfield, Vermont: Scolar Press.

Crutchfield, Jonathan Eric. 1994. *A Conductor's Analysis of Gerald Finzi's* Intimations of Immortality; Lo, the Full Final Sacrifice; *and* Magnificat. D.M.A. dissertation, Southern Baptist Seminary.

Csengery, Kristof. 1984. Vocal-orchestral works by Lendvay and Soprani. *Hungarian Music News* (1–2).

Cummins, Paul F. 1992. *Dachau Song: The Twentieth-Century Odyssey of Herbert Zipper*. New York: Peter Lang.

Curtis, Marvin V. 1996. The lyric of the African American spiritual: the meaning behind the words. *The Choral Journal* (August).

Curtis, Marvin, and Lee V. Cloud. 1991. The African American spiritual: traditions and performance practices. *The Choral Journal* (November).

Czigany, Gyula, ed. 1970. *Contemporary Hungarian Composers*. Budapest: Editio Musica.

Dahlhaus, Carl. 1989. *Schoenberg and the New Music*. Translated by Derrick Puffett. Cambridge: Cambridge University Press.

Dent, Edward J. 1981. Feruccio Busoni: Piano Concerto and pieces for piano solo. Record liner notes. Hayes, Middlesex, England: EMI Records.

DiMedio, Annette Maria. 1990. *Frances McCollin: Her Life and Music*. Lanham, Maryland: Scarecrow Press.

Doering, William T. 1993. *Elliott Carter: A Bio-Bibliography*. Westport, Connecticut: Greenwood Press.

Douglass, Frederick. 1994. *Narrative of the Life of Frederick Douglass, an American Slave*. Henry Louis Gates, Jr. New York: Library of America.

Dox, Thurston. 1986. *American Oratorios and Cantatas: A Catalog of Works Written in the United States from Colonial Times to 1985*. Metuchen, New Jersey: Scarecrow Press.

———. 1989. Henry Cowell's choral bombshell. *The Choral Journal* (May).

Dressler, John C. 1997. *Gerald Finzi: A Bio-Bibliography*. Westport, Connecticut: Greenwood Press.

Egbert, Lee. 1998. Norman Dello Joio's secular choral music: conversations with the composer. *The Choral Journal* (October).

Ellington, Duke. 1974. *Notes for the* Second Sacred Concert. New York: Prestige Records.

Ellinwood, Leonard. 1970. *The History of American Church Music*. New York: Da Capo Press.

Engle, Robert. 1993. The changing concept of desirable tone quality in Samoan choral singing. *The Choral Journal* (May).

Eosze, László. 1962. *Zoltán Kodály: His Life and Work*. London: Collet's Holdings.

Euba, Akin. 1988. Ayo Bankole: a view of modern African art music through the works of a Nigerian composer. *Essays on Music in Africa* 1.

Evans, Peter. 1996. *The Music of Benjamin Britten*. Oxford: Oxford University Press.

Fanning, David, ed. *Shostokovich Studies*. 1995. Cambridge: Cambridge University Press.

Feofanav, Dmitry, and Allan Ho. 1989. *Biographical Dictionary of Russian/Soviet Composers*. New York: Greenwood Press.

Fidetzis, Byron. 1995. Petros Petridis: brief biography and registration of works. Translated by Olia Petidou and Evangelos Tyroglou. CD sleeve notes. Athens: General Publishing Company.

Flam, Gila. 1992. *Singing for Survival: Songs of the Lodz Ghetto, 1940–45.* Chicago: University of Illinois Press.

Fleuret, Maurice. 1972. Xenakis—a music for the future. Translated by Tom Sutcliffe and Meredith Oakes. *Music and Musicians* (April).

Floros, Constantin. 1993. *Gustav Mahler: The Symphonies.* Translated by Vernon Wicker and Jutta Wicker. Portland, Oregon: Amadeus Press.

Floyd, Malcolm. 1998. Composing the Music of Africa. Brookfield, Vermont: Ashgate.

Forbes, Elliot. 1974. Americana. *American Choral Review* 16 (4).

———. 1974. List of works by Randall Thompson. *American Choral Review* 16 (4).

Gangemi, Marie. 1995. *The Oratorio Society of New York 1873–1995.* New York: Oratorio Society of New York.

Gardavsky, Čenek, ed. 1965. *Contemporary Czechoslavak Composers.* Prague: Panton.

Gartenberg, Egon. 1978. *Mahler: The Man and His Music.* New York: Schirmer Books.

Gibbon, Edward. n.d. *The Decline and Fall of the Roman Empire.* New York: Modern Library.

Gilliam, Bryan. 1994. *Music and Performance during the Weimar Republic.* Cambridge: Cambridge University Press.

Gillies, Malcolm, ed. 1994. *The Bartók Companion.* Portland, Oregon: Amadeus Press.

Gordon, Eric A. 1989. *Mark the Music: The Life and Work of Marc Blitzstein.* New York: Saint Martin's Press.

Gorog, Lisa de. 1989. *From Sibelius to Sallinen.* New York: Greenwood Press.

Goss, Glenda Dawn. 1998. *Sibelius: A Guide to Research.* New York: Garland.

Gosta, Predrag, and John Haberlin. 2000. The Hungarian school of choral composers, 1950–2000. *The Choral Journal* (August).

Gottlieb, Jack. 1980. Symbols of faith in the music of Leonard Bernstein. *The Musical Quarterly* (April).

Gottwald, Clytus. 1996. Bach, Kagel und die Theologie des Atheismus. *Musik-Koncepte* (September).

Gradenwitz, Peter. 1978. *Music and Musicians in Israel.* Tel Aviv: Israeli Music Publications.

———. 1996. *The Music of Israel: From the Biblical Era to Modern Times.* Second edition, revised and expanded. Portland, Oregon: Amadeus Press.

Green, Mildred Denby. 1983. *Black Women Composers: A Genesis*. Boston: Twayne Publishers.

Green, Richard. 1995. *Holst: The Planets*. Cambridge: Cambridge University Press.

Greenfield, Philip. 1995. Herbert Howells: *Stabat mater*. *American Record Guide* (May–June).

Griffiths, Paul. 1993. *Stravinsky*. New York: Schirmer Books.

Griggs-Janower, David. 1995. The choral works of William Grant Still. *The Choral Journal* (May).

Grinde, Nils. 1992. *A History of Norwegian Music*. Translated by William H. Halverson and Leland B. Sateren. Lincoln: University of Nebraska Press.

Grover, Ralph Scott. 1993. *The Music of Edmund Rubbra*. Brookfield, Vermont: Scolar Press.

Guelker-Cone, Leslie. 1987. Kirke Mechem—an interview. *The Choral Journal* (April).

Guest, George. 1992. Herbert Howells: a personal remembrance. *The Choral Journal* (October).

Gulke, Peter. 1987. Zemlinsky, *The Mermaid*: an introduction. Translated by Chris Wood. CD sleeve notes. London: Decca Record Company.

Haar, James. 1974. Randall Thompson and the music of the past. *American Choral Review* 16 (4).

Hackett, David A. 1995. *The Buchenwald Report*. Boulder: Westview Press.

Halász, Péter. 1996. Kurtág: *Fragments*. *Hungarian Music Quarterly*. 7 (1–2).

Halstead, Jill. 1997. *The Woman Composer*. Brookfield, Vermont: Ashgate.

Hall, Roger. 1985. Randall Thompson. *Journal of Church Music*. (December).

Hallbreich, Harry. 1999. *Arthur Honegger*. Portland, Oregon: Amadeus Press.

Hamm, Charles. 1983. *Music in the New World*. New York: W. W. Norton.

Hansler, George E. 1957. *Stylistic Characteristics and Trends in the Choral Music of Five Twentieth-Century British Composers: A Study of the Choral Works of Benjamin Britten, Gerald Finzi, Constant Lambert, Michael Tippett, and William Walton*. Ph.D. dissertation, New York University.

Hanuš, Jan. 1996. *Labyrint svět*. Prague: Odeon.

Harbison, John. 1989. The ritual of *Oedipus Rex*. *Upbeat* (December).

Hemberg, Eskil. 1973. Swedish choirs at home and abroad. *Tradition and Progress in Swedish Music*. Translated by Brian Willson. New York: Schirmer Books.

Henry, Stephanie. 1992. *Jeanne d'Arc au Bûcher*: a collaboration between Arthur Honegger and Paul Claudel. *The Choral Journal* (March).

Hickman, Jon. 1999. A new edition of Poulenc's *Gloria*: review and errata list. *The Choral Journal* (November).

Hill, Peter. 1995. *The Messiaen Companion.* Portland, Oregon: Amadeus Press.

Hillier, Paul. 1997a. *Arvo Pärt.* Oxford: Oxford University Press.

———. 1997b. Minimalism in music. *Schwann Opus* (summer).

Hilsley, William. 1999. *Musik hinterm Stacheldraht: Tagebuch eines internierten Musikers 1940–1945.* Utrecht: Stichting Kasteelconcerten Beverweerd.

———. n.d. *When Joy and Pain Entwine: Reminiscences.* Utrecht: Syzygy Music.

Hindemith, Paul. 1952. *A Composer's World: Horizons and Limitations.* Cambridge: Harvard University Press.

Hines, Robert Stephan, ed. 1963. *The Composer's Point of View: Essays on Twentieth-Century Choral Music by Those Who Wrote It.* Norman: University of Oklahoma Press.

Hirshberg, Jehoash. 1990. *Paul Ben-Haim: His Life and Works.* Translated by Nathan Friedgut. Jerusalem: Israeli Music Publications.

———. 1995. *Music in the Jewish Community of Palestine 1880–1948.* Oxford: Clarendon Press.

Hirt, Charles C. 1946. *Graeco-Slavonic Chant Traditions Evident in the Part-Writing of the Russian Orthodox Church.* Ph.D. dissertation, University of Southern California.

Hitchcock, H. Wiley, and Stanley Sadie, eds. 1986. *The New Grove Dictionary of American Music.* Four volumes. London: Macmillan.

Hodgson, Anthony. 1984. *Scandinavian Music: Finland and Sweden.* London: Associated University Presses.

Hodgson, Peter J. 1997. *Benjamin Britten: A Guide to Research.* New York: Garland.

Hogarth, A. David. n.d. Krzysztof Penderecki: *Passion and Death of Our Lord Jesus Christ According to Saint Luke.* Record liner notes. New York: Philips.

Hopkins, John. 1985. Menotti's medieval menagerie producing *The Unicorn, the Gorgon, and the Manticore. The Choral Journal* (December).

Horsbrugh, Ian. 1982. *Leoš Janáček.* New York: Charles Scribner's Sons.

Houlahan, Michael, and Philip Tacka. 1997. *Zoltán Kodály: A Guide to Research.* New York: Garland.

Hustad, Donald P. 1981. *Jubilate! Church Music in the Evangelical Tradition.* Carol Stream, Illinois: Hope Publishing.

Jacobs, Arthur, ed. 1963. *Choral Music.* Baltimore: Penguin Books.

Jacobson, Joshua R. 1993. East meets West: choral composers of the Eastern Mediterranean School. *The Choral Journal* (May).

———. 1995. Music in the Holocaust. *The Choral Journal* (December).

Jermihov, Peter. 1993. Georgy Sviridov's *Kursk Songs*: peasant music transformed. *The Choral Journal* (August).

———. 1996. Links between composer and poet in Georgy Sviridov's "Poema pamiati Sergeya Esenina." *The Choral Journal* (December).

Johnson, David. 1963. William Walton: *Belshazzar's Feast*. Record liner notes. New York: Columbia Records.

———. n.d. Charles Ives: Symphony No. 2. Record liner notes. New York: Columbia Masterworks.

Johnson, Marlowe W. 1968. Daniel Pinkham: a composer for our time. *Music: The A.G.O. Magazine* (June).

Johnson, Robert Sherlaw. 1975. *Messiaen*. Berkeley: University of California Press.

Jones, Robert. 1994. The eclectic style of John Gardner. *The Choral Journal* (May).

Kalisch, Shoshana, and Barbara Meister. 1985. *Yes, We Sang! Songs of the Ghettos and Concentration Camps*. New York: Harper and Row.

Kappel, Vagn. 1967. *Danish Composers*. Third edition. Copenhagen: Det Danske Selskab.

Karas, Joža. 1985. *Music in Terezín 1941–1945*. Stuyvesant, New York: Pendragon Press.

Kárpáti, János. 1989. The vocal works of András Szöllösy. *Hungarian Music Quarterly* 1 (3–4).

Kater, Michael H. 1997. *The Twisted Muse: Musicians and Their Music in the Third Reich*. Oxford: Oxford University Press.

Kazarow, Patricia A. 1993. Contemporary African choral art music: an intercultural perspective. *The Choral Journal* (May).

Kean, Ronald M. 1993. Multicultural and ethnically inspired choral music: an annotated list. *The Choral Journal* (May).

Kennedy, Mary A. 1999. Copland and the folk song: sources, analysis, choral arrangements. *The Choral Journal* (May).

Kennedy, Michael. 1980. *The Works of Ralph Vaughan Williams*. Second edition. Oxford: Oxford University Press.

———. 1986. War and eroticism. *Listener* (February).

———. 1991. *Mahler*. New York: Schirmer Books.

———. 1996. *Richard Strauss*. New York: Schirmer Books.

Kent, Christopher. 1993. *Edward Elgar: A Guide to Research*. New York: Garland.

Kenyon, Nicholas. 1982. Looking for limits. *The New Yorker* (28 June).

Keren, Zvi. 1980. *Contemporary Israeli Music*. Bar-Ilan: Bar-Ilan University Press.

Kiefer, Peter. 1996. Fred Waring: a master "blender." *The Choral Journal* (November).

Kingman, Daniel. 1990. *American Music: A Panorama*. New York: Schirmer Books.

Kitz, Mitchell, ed. 1993. *Canadian Choral Music Catalogue*. Toronto: Canadian Music Centre.

Kleszynski, Kenneth. 1997. George Lloyd's music for chorus and orchestra. *The Choral Journal* (May).

Krebs, Stanley Dale. 1970. *Soviet Composers*. New York: W. W. Norton.

Kyr, Robert. 2001. An invitation to create music for peace. *International Choral Bulletin* 20 (3).

Lafite, Peter, ed. 1990a. Musik in Österreich nach 1945 I. *Österreichische Musik Zeitschrift* (October).

———. 1990b. Musik in Österreich nach 1945 II. *Österreichische Musik Zeitschrift* (November).

———. 1991. Musik in Österreich nach 1945 III. *Österreichische Musik Zeitschrift* (March–April).

Lambert, Philip. 1997. *The Music of Charles Ives*. New Haven: Yale University Press.

Lancaster, Thomas. 1997. Praising life: the choral music of Kenneth Leighton. *The Choral Journal* (December).

Lang, Paul Henry, ed. 1960. *Problems of Modern Music*. New York: W. W. Norton.

———. 1963. *Stravinsky: A New Appraisal of His Work*. New York: W. W. Norton.

Lang, Paul Henry, and Nathan Broder, eds. 1965. *Contemporary Music in Europe: A Comprehensive Survey*. New York: W. W. Norton.

LaPage, Jane Weiner. 1980–1988. *Women Composers, Conductors, and Musicians of the Twentieth Century: Selected Biographies*. Three volumes. Lanham, Maryland: Scarecrow Press.

Layton, Robert. 1993. *Sibelius*. New York: Schirmer Books.

Laszlo Lajtha: Quelques Oeurves. 1954. Paris: Alphonse Leduc.

Lebl, Vladimir. 1968. *Vitězslav Novák*. Translated by Jean Layton-Eislerova. Prague: Editio Supraphon.

Ledbetter, Steven. 1994. Elliott Carter: *Emblems* and other works; Bright Sheng: *Two Folk Songs from Chinhai*. CD sleeve notes. Port Washington: Koch International Classics.

Lehman, Robert W. 1992. The choral idiom of Herbert Howells. *The Choral Journal* (October).

Lewis, Geraint. 1976. Alun Hoddinott: *Sinfonia fidei*. CD sleeve notes. London: Decca Record Company.

Ligeti, György. 1968. Ueber neue Wege im Kompositionsunterricht: Ein Bericht. *Three Aspects of New Music*. Stockholm: Nordiska Musikforlaget.

Lindholm, Steen. 1995. Danish choral music since 1900. *Nordic Sounds* 3.

Livermore, Ann. 1972. *A Short History of Spanish Music*. New York: Vienna House.

Lorentzen, Bent. 1973. *New Choral Dramatics*. Copenhagen: Wilhelm Hansen; New York: Walton Music.

Luhring, Alan A. 1984. Toward a periodization for choral history. *The Choral Journal* (April, May).

Lundergan, Edward J. 1998. Musical metaphor: cyclic-interval structures in Britten's *War Requiem*. *The Choral Journal* (February).

Lutoslawski, Witold. 1968. About the element of chance in music. *Three Aspects of New Music*. Stockholm: Nordiska Musikforlaget.

Lyne, Gregory K. 1987. Edmund Rubbra: a lifetime contribution to choral composition. *The Choral Journal* (November).

MacDowell, Malcolm. 1972. Havergal Brian—Perspective on the Music. London: Triad Press.

Malm, William P. 1996. *Music Cultures of the Pacific, the Near East, and Asia*. Third edition. Upper Saddle River, New Jersey: Prentice-Hall.

Malone, Mark Hugh. 1990. William Dawson and the Tuskegee Choir. *The Choral Journal* (March).

Mankin, Linda. 1982. Programming contemporary choral music by women composers. *The Choral Journal* (December).

Mann, Alfred. 1974. Randall Thompson: psalm and gospel settings editorials. *American Choral Review* 16 (4).

Marco, Tomás. 1993. *Spanish Music in the Twentieth Century*. Cambridge: Harvard University Press.

Marshall, Ingram. 1997. Steve Reich: thirty years on the record. *Schwann Opus* (summer).

Matossian, Nouritza. 1990. *Xenakis*. London: Kahn and Averill.

Mawer, Deborah. 1997. *Darius Milhaud: Modality and Structure in Music of the 1920s*. Brookfield, Vermont: Ashgate.

McCoy, Jerry. 1989. New choral music from Germany. *The Choral Journal* (November).

———. 1994. Choral poetry: the extended choral works of Morten Lauridsen. *The Choral Journal* (November).

McCray, James E. 1968. *The British* Magnificat *in the Twentieth Century*. Ph.D. dissertation, University of Iowa.

———. 1993. Collaboration: Ursula and Ralph Vaughan Williams. *The Choral Journal* (February).

———. 1995. Daniel Pinkham's music for treble voices. *The Choral Journal* (March).

———. 1996. Michael Hurd's choral cantatas for children. *The Choral Journal* (December).

McCutchan, Ann. 1999. *The Muse that Sings: Composers Speak about the Creative Process*. Oxford: Oxford University Press.

McIntyre, John. 1993. Twentieth-century Latin American choral music: an introductory survey. *The Choral Journal* (May).

Mecham, Mark L. 1988. The choral music of Vladimir Ussachevsky. *The Choral Journal* (August).

Medek, Ivo. 1997. A few questions for Peter Graham. *Czech Music 5*.

Mellers, Wilfred. 1993. *Francis Poulenc*. Oxford: Oxford University Press.

Meredith, Victoria. 1994. Zoltán Kodály's *Psalmus hungaricus*: its new relevance in the changing world order. *The Choral Journal* (October).

Messiaen, Olivier. n.d. *Trois petites liturgies de la Présence Divine*. Record liner notes. Paris: Editions Costallat (Erato).

Meyers, Michael. 1991. *The Politics of Music in the Third Reich*. New York: Peter Lang.

Micheels, Pauline. 1993. *Muziek in de schaduw van het Derde Rijk*. Amsterdam: Walberg Pers.

Mihule, Jaroslav. 1990. Martinů: *The Spectre's Bride, Nipponari, Magic Nights*. Translated by Zoja Joachimová et al. CD sleeve notes. Prague: Editio Supraphon.

Minturn, Neil. 1997. *The Music of Sergei Prokofiev*. New Haven: Yale University Press.

Moddel, Philip. 1966. *Joseph Achron*. Tel Aviv: Israeli Music Publications.

Morgan, Richard. 2000. Within a rainbow: the choral and organ music of Knut Nystedt. *Choir and Organ* (September–October).

Morosan, Vladimir. 1986. *Choral Performance in Pre-Revolutionary Russia*. Ann Arbor, Michigan: UMI Research Press.

Mountford, Fritz. 2000. Fred Waring's tone syllables: his legacy to American choral singing. *The Choral Journal* (August).

Munson, Mark. Ned Rorem's *An American Oratorio*: an introspective work for our nation. *The Choral Journal* (May).

Music, David W. 1986. The anthems and motets of Ralph Vaughan Williams. *Journal of Church Music* (November).

Mussulman, Joseph A. 1996. *Dear People . . . Robert Shaw*. Second edition. Chapel Hill, North Carolina: Hinshaw Music.

Nelhýbel, Václav. 1971. The talent is here! *They Talk about Music*. Second volume. Edited by Robert Cumming. Rockville Center, New York: Belwin Mills.

Nettl, Bruno. 1995. *Heartland Excursions: Ethnomusicological Reflections on Schools of Music*. Urbana: University of Illinois Press.

Neufeld, Gerald. 1996. Structure, symbolism, and thematic transformation in Edward Elgar's *The Dream of Gerontius*. *The Choral Journal* (March).

Nicholls, David. 1991. *American Experimental Music 1890–1940*. Cambridge: Cambridge University Press.

Nketia, Joseph Hanson Kwabena. 1974. *The Music of Africa*. New York: W. W. Norton.

Nono, Nuria Schoenberg, ed. 1988. *Arnold Schoenberg Self-Portrait: A Collection of Articles, Program Notes, and Letters by the Composer about His Own Works*. Pacific Palisades, California: Belmont Music Publishers.

Norris, Geoffrey. 1994. *Rachmaninoff*. New York: Schirmer Books.

Norton, Kay. 1991. Choral music during the 1930s. *American Music Research Center Journal* 1.

Nott, Michael. 1990. *Karel Husa*. New York: Schirmer Books.

Oertelt, Henry A. 2000. *An Unbroken Chain: My Journey through the Nazi Holocaust*. Minneapolis: Lerner.

Ohtake, Noriko. 1993. *Creative Sources for the Music of Tōru Takemitsu*. Brookfield, Vermont: Scolar Press.

Olsvay, Endré. 1993. "Originality means reaching back to the origins": an interview with the composer Zoltán Jeney. *Hungarian Music Quarterly* 4 (1).

———. 1994a. A conversation with András Szöllösy. *Hungarian Music Quarterly* 5 (1).

———. 1994b. A conversation with Sandor Szokolay. *Hungarian Music Quarterly* 5 (2).

Oncley, Lawrence Alan. 1975. *The Published Works of Alexander Zemlinsky*. Ph.D. dissertation, Indiana University.

Orga, Antes. 1973. Krzysztof Penderecki. *Music and Musicians* (October).

Osmond-Smith, David. 1991. *Berio*. Oxford: Oxford University Press.

Pahlen, Kurt. 1990. *The World of the Oratorio*. Portland, Oregon: Amadeus Press.

Palmer, Anthony J. 1994. Choral music in Japan: a hybrid art. *The Choral Journal* (December).

Palmer, Christopher. 1978. Rózsa: *To Everything There Is a Season, The Vanities of Life, Twenty-third Psalm*. Record liner notes. Chicago: Entr'acte Recording Society.

Palmer, Larry. 1967. *Hugo Distler and His Church Music*. St. Louis: Concordia Publishing House.

Parks, Richard S. 1990. *The Music of Claude Debussy*. New Haven: Yale University Press.

Peduzzi, Lubomir. 1993. *Pavel Haas*. Brno: Tisk.

Peppercorn, Lisa M. 1996. *The World of Villa-Lobos*. Brookfield, Vermont: Scolar Press.

Percy, Gösta. 1967. Leading Swedish composers of the twentieth century. *Swedish Music Past and Present*.

Perle, George. 1960. Current chronicle: Germany. *The Musical Quarterly* (October).

Petridis, Petros. 1995. The Greek music: what is the method? Translated by Olia Petidou and Evangelos Tyroglou. CD sleeve notes. Athens: General Publishing Company.

Pickar, Catherine J. 1985. An analytical process applied to Kodály's *Missa brevis*. *The Choral Journal* (October).

Polkow, Dennis. 1987. Andrew Lloyd Webber: from *Superstar* to *Requiem*. *The Christian Century* (18–25 March).

———. 1992. Paul McCartney: rock meets classical. *Musical America* (January).

Pollack, Howard. 1992. *Harvard Composers: Walter Piston and His Students, from Elliott Carter to Frederic Rzewski*. Metuchen, New Jersey: Scarecrow Press.

Pooler, Frank. 1990. Choral extracts from the Chadwick memoirs. *The Choral Journal* (August).

Porter, Andrew. 1981. Musical events: celebration. *The New Yorker* (9 November).

Pysh, Gregory M. 1997. The choral music of Henryk Górecki. *The Choral Journal* (December).

Raksin, David. 1989. Schoenberg as teacher, part 3. *Serial: Newsletter of the Friends of the Arnold Schoenberg Institute* 3 (spring).

Ratcliffe, Shirley. 1999. Macmillan 2. *Choir and Organ* (July–August).

———. 2000. Listening within: a conversation with Sir John Tavener. *Choir and Organ* (September–October).

Redlich, Hans. 1965. Benjamin Britten: *Rejoice in the Lamb*, *Missa brevis*, *A Ceremony of Carols*. Record liner notes. London: Argo Record Company.

Reich, Wieland. 1995. *Mauricio Kagel:* Sankt-Bach-Passion. Saarbrücken: Pfau Verlag.

Riddles, Mark. 1996. The instruments are by their rhimes: an examination of the text in Britten's *Rejoice in the Lamb*. *The Choral Journal* (February).

Robinson, Kathleen E. 1994. *A Critical Study of Word/Music Correspondences in the Choral Works of Gerald Finzi*. First and second volumes. Ph.D. dissertation, Northwestern University.

Robinson, Ray. 1978. *Choral Music: A Norton Historical Anthology*. New York: W. W. Norton.

———. 1985. The *Polish Requiem* by Krzysztof Penderecki. *The Choral Journal* (November).

———. 1998a. Krzysztof Penderecki's *Seven Gates of Jerusalem*. *The Choral Journal* (May).

————. 1998b. The choral works of Krzysztof Penderecki: an annotated listing. *The Choral Journal* (November).

Robinson, Ray, and Allen Winold. 1976. *The Choral Experience*. New York: W. W. Norton.

Rockwell, John. 1983. *All American Music: Composition in the Late Twentieth Century*. New York: Alfred A. Knopf.

Rodriguez, Carlos Xavier. 1992. The textual and musical functions of the chorus in Stravinsky's *Oedipus Rex. The Choral Journal* (August).

Rosen, Judith. 1984. *Grażyna Bacewicz: Her Life and Works*. Stuyvesant, New York: Pendragon Press.

Ross, Alex. 2001. The Passion according to Osvaldo Golijov. *The New Yorker* (March 5).

Rothmuller, Aron Marko. 1960. *The Music of the Jews*. New York: A. S. Barnes.

Rubin, David M. 1980. Vincent Persichetti. *ASCAP in Action* (spring).

Ruden, Jan Olof. 1987. *Swedish Choral Music: A Selective Catalogue*. Stockholm: Swedish Music Information Centre.

Ryker, Harrison. 1991. *New Music in the Orient*. Buren, Netherlands: Fritz Kauf Publications.

Sabaneyeff, Leonid. 1927. *Modern Russian Composers*. Translated by Judah A. Joffe. New York: International Publishers.

Sadie, Stanley, ed. 1980. *The New Grove Dictionary of Music and Musicians*. Twenty volumes. London: Macmillan.

Saladino, David. 1995. An interview with Gordon Binkerd. *The Choral Journal* (April).

Salzman, Eric. 1981. Arnold Schoenberg: Prelude, "The Genesis Suite." *The Los Angeles Philharmonic Festival of Music Made in Los Angeles*.

Samuel, Claude. 1994. *Olivier Messiaen: Music and Color Conversations with Claude Samuel*. Translated by E. Thomas Glasgow. Portland, Oregon: Amadeus Press.

Saxton, Robert. 1988. Elisabeth Lutyens. *New Music*.

Schebera, Jürgen. 1995. *Kurt Weill: An Illustrated Life*. Translated by Caroline Murphy. New Haven: Yale University Press.

Schenbeck, Lyn. 1993. Discovering the choral music of Estonian composer Arvo Pärt. *The Choral Journal* (August).

Schoenberg, Arnold. 1964. *Arnold Schoenberg Letters*. Translated and edited by Erwin Stein. London: Faber and Faber.

Schorr, Yitzak. 1995. Meir Mindel—a composer who does not write "for the shelf." *Israel Music Institute News* 95 (1).

Schwartz, Elliott, and Barney Childs. 1998. *Contemporary Composers on Contemporary Music*. New York: Da Capo Press.

Schwarz, Boris. 1972. *Music and Musical Life in Soviet Russia, 1917–1970.* New York: W. W. Norton.

Seeley, Gilbert. 1969. *German Protestant Choral Music Since 1925.* D.M.A. dissertation, University of Southern California.

———. 1999. Robert Kyr: *The Passion According to Four Evangelists. Sforzando* (September).

Sharp, Timothy W. 1995. The choral music of Leo Sowerby: a centennial perspective. *The Choral Journal* (March).

Shiloah, Amnon. 1993. *The Dimension of Music in Islamic and Jewish Culture.* Brookfield, Vermont: Ashgate.

Shore, Clare, ed. 1996. *David Diamond: A Musical Celebration.* Stuyvesant, New York: Pendragon Press.

Shull, Ronald K., and Joachim Lucchesi. 1996. *Brecht and Music.* Stuyvesant, New York: Pendragon Press.

Simms, Bryan R. 1986. *Music of the Twentieth Century: Style and Structure.* New York: Schirmer Books.

Simon, Allen H. 1996. Deterministic techniques in Arvo Pärt's *Magnificat. The Choral Journal* (October).

Sinclair, Frances T. 1999. Celebration of youth and innocence: Benjamin Britten's *Welcome Ode. The Choral Journal* (May).

Sitsky, Larry. 1994. *Music of the Repressed Russian Avant-Garde, 1900–1929.* Westport, Connecticut: Greenwood Press.

Skans, Per. 1995. Gretchaninoff: Liturgy No. 4. CD sleeve notes. London: Olympia Records.

Slavický, Milan. 1995. *Gideon Klein: A Fragment of Life and Work.* Translated by Dagmar Steinová. Prague: Helvetica-Tempora Publishers.

Slonimsky, Nicolas. 1992. *Baker's Biographical Dictionary of Musicians.* Eighth edition. New York: Schirmer Books.

———. 1994. *Music since 1900.* Fifth edition. New York: Schirmer Books.

———. 2000. *Lexicon of Musical Invective: Critical Assaults on Composers since Beethoven's Time.* New York: W. W. Norton.

Slotterback, Floyd. 1993. The choral music of Dave Brubeck. *The Choral Journal* (August).

Smith, Barry. 1994. The music of Peter Warlock: it weeps so gaily and smiles so sadly. *The Choral Journal* (May).

Smith, Gregg. 1980. America sings: American choral music after 1950—the nontraditionalists. Record liner notes. New York: Turnabout.

Smolka, Jaroslav. 1970. *Česka Kantata á Oratorium.* Prague: Editio Supraphon.

Starr, Larry. 1992. *A Union of Diversities: Style in the Music of Charles Ives.* New York: Schirmer Books.

Stein, Erwin. 1956. Igor Stravinsky: *Canticum sacrum ad honorem Sancti Marci nominis*. *Tempo* (summer).

———. 1987. *Arnold Schoenberg Letters*. Berkeley: University of California Press.

Stepanek, Vladimir. 1988. Honegger: *Jeanne d'Arc au bûcher*. Translated by Stanislava Vomackova. CD sleeve notes. Prague: Editio Supraphon.

Stevens, Halsey. 1964. *The Life and Music of Béla Bartók*. Revised edition. New York: Oxford University Press.

———. 1968. The choral music of Zoltán Kodály. *The Musical Quarterly* (April).

Stevenson, Robert. 1952. *Music in Mexico*. New York: Thomas Y. Crowell Company.

———. 1966. *Protestant Church Music in America*. New York: W. W. Norton.

Stone, Ruth M., ed. 1997. *Africa*. New York: Garland.

Straus, Joseph N. 1995. *The Music of Ruth Crawford Seeger*. Cambridge: Cambridge University Press.

Stravinsky, Igor. 1947. *Poetics of Music*. Translated by Arthur Knodel and Ingolf Dahl. Cambridge: Harvard University Press.

Stravinsky, Igor, and Robert Craft. 1959. *Conversations with Igor Stravinsky*. New York: Doubleday.

———. 1962. *Expositions and Developments*. New York: Doubleday.

———. 1963. *Dialogues and a Diary*. New York: Doubleday.

———. 1969. *Retrospectives and Conclusions*. New York: Alfred A. Knopf.

Střelcova, Stanislava. 1994. Janáček: the music of truth. Translated by Veronika Bendová and Harriet Macková. CD sleeve notes. Prague: Studio Matous.

Strimple, Nick. 1982. An introduction to the choral music of Roy Harris. *The Choral Journal* (May).

———. 1998. The choral music of Leoš Janáček: an annotated discography. *The Choral Journal* (April).

Stroope, Z. Randall. 1991. Pluralism in the works of Heinz Werner Zimmermann. *The Choral Journal* (November).

Stuckenschmidt, H. H. 1969. *Twentieth-Century Music*. Translated by Richard Deveson. New York: McGraw-Hill.

Stuckey, Steven. 1981. *Lutoslawski and His Music*. Cambridge: Cambridge University Press.

Studebaker, Donald. 1986. The sacred choral music of Norman Dello Joio. *Journal of Church Music* (October).

———. 1988. The choral cantatas of Daniel Pinkham: an overview. *The Choral Journal* (December).

Stuhr-Rommereim, John. 1992. An interview with Rodion Shchedrin. *The Choral Journal* (April).

Stulken, Marilyn Kay. 1987. Flor Peeters. *Journal of Church Music* (September).

Szitha, Tunde. 1992. A Conversation with György Ligeti. *Hungarian Music Quarterly* 3 (1).

Tan Dun. 1997. Dream circle and reunification: *Symphony 1997 Heaven Earth Mankind*. CD sleeve notes. New York: Sony Music Entertainment.

Tansman, Alexandre. 1949. *Igor Stravinsky: the Man and His Music*. Translated by Therese and Charles Bleefield. New York: Putnam.

Tavener, John. 1999. *The Music of Silence: a Composer's Testament*. London: Faber and Faber.

Taylor, Robert. 1995. An examination of Stravinsky's fugal writing in the second movement of *Symphony of Psalms*. *The Choral Journal* (October).

Thayer, Fred. 1985. The choral music of Béla Bartók. *The Choral Journal* (August).

Thomas, Adrian. 1997. *Górecki*. Oxford: Oxford University Press.

Thomas, André Jerome. 1986. A brief analysis of Masses by black composers: Baker, Bonds, Ray, and Walker. *The Choral Journal* (December).

Thompson, Jon. 1999. *Job*: an oratorio by Peter Maxwell Davies. *The Choral Journal* (November).

Thomson, John Mansfield. 1991. *The Oxford History of New Zealand Music*. Auckland: Oxford University Press.

Threlfall, Robert, and Geoffrey Norris. 1982. *Catalogue of the Compositions of S. Rachmaninoff*. Brookfield, Vermont: Scolar Press.

Tiemstra, Suzanne Spicer. 1992. *The Choral Music of Latin America: A Guide to Compositions and Research*. Westport, Connecticut: Greenwood Press.

Tippett, Michael. 1972. The vision of Saint Augustine. CD sleeve notes. London: RCA.

Tovey, Donald Francis. 1937a. Ethel Smyth: Mass in D. *Essays in Musical Analysis* 5.

———. 1937b. Debussy: *The Blessed Damozel*. *Essays in Musical Analysis* 5.

———. 1937c. Gustav Holst: the *Hymn of Jesus*, Op. 37. *Essays in Musical Analysis* 5.

Town, Stephen, and Dennis Shrock. 1991. An interview with Ernst Krenek on the occasion of his ninetieth birthday. *The Choral Journal* (May).

Trice, Patricia J. 1996. Choral arrangements of spirituals: birth and perpetuation of a genre. *The Choral Journal* (August).

Varga, Balint Andras. 1986. Kurtág at sixty. *Hungarian Music News* 3 (2).

Vlad, Roman. 1960. *Stravinsky*. Translated by Frederick Fuller and Ann Fuller. Oxford: Oxford University Press.

Vogel, Jaroslav. 1981. *Leoš Janáček*. First American edition, revised. Edited by Karel Janovicky. New York: W. W. Norton.

Wallner, Bo. 1982. Wilhelm Stenhammer: *The Song, Two Sentimental Romances, Ithaca*. CD sleeve notes. Translated by Alain Blair, Robert Carroll, and Roger G. Tanner. London: Caprice.

Walsh, Stephen. 1993. *Stravinsky:* Oedipus Rex. Cambridge: Cambridge University Press.

Ward, Robert J. 1999. Percy Grainger as choral composer. *The Choral Journal* (May).

Watkins, Glenn. 1987. *Soundings: Music in the Twentieth Century*. New York: Schirmer Books.

Weissmann, John S. 1960. Current chronicle: Hungary. *The Musical Quarterly* (October).

White, Eric Walter. 1979. *Stravinsky: The Composer and His Works*. Second edition. Berkeley: University of California Press.

Whitehead, William. 2000. Beyond complexity: Michael Finnissy communicates his faith. *Choir and Organ* (March–April).

Whittall, Arnold. 1990. *The Music of Britten and Tippett*. Cambridge: Cambridge University Press.

Wienandt, Elwyn. 1965. *Choral Music of the Church*. New York: Free Press.

Wienandt, Elwyn, and Robert H. Young. 1970. *The Anthem in England and America*. New York: Free Press.

Wilheim, Andras. 1996. György Kurtág: list of works. *Hungarian Music Quarterly* 7 (1–2).

Wilson, Paul. 1992. *The Music of Béla Bartók*. New Haven: Yale University Press.

Wingfield, Paul. 1992. *Janáček:* Glagolitic Mass. Cambridge: Cambridge University Press.

Winnick, William. 1984. Pivot analysis in Bernstein's *Chichester Psalms*: a guide for singers. *The Choral Journal* (March).

Woerner, Karl H. 1960. Current chronicle: Czechoslovakia. *The Musical Quarterly* (October).

Wohlgemuth, Paul W. 1986. What's on the American choral composer's mind? *The Choral Journal* (March).

Wolverton, Vance. 1998a. Breaking the silence: choral music of the Baltic republics, part 1—Estonia. *The Choral Journal* (February).

———. 1998b. Breaking the silence: choral music of the Baltic republics, part 2—Latvia. *The Choral Journal* (April).

———. 1998c. Breaking the silence: choral music of the Baltic republics, part 3—Lithuania. *The Choral Journal* (May).

———. 1999. Baltic portraits: Cyrillus Kreek—an Estonian original. *The Choral Journal* (September).

Wright, David. 1996. Music of Villa-Lobos. CD sleeve notes. New York: BMG Music.

———. 2000. "Presidential" composer: the career of William Schuman. *Choir and Organ* (March–April).

Wyers, Gisele Eleanor. 2000. *The Third Act: The Embodiment of Meaning through Texture in the Choral Works of Robert Kyr.* D.M.A. dissertation, University of Arizona.

Wyton, Alec. 1967. Reminiscences: Healey Willan in a conversation with Alec Wyton. *Music: The A.G.O. Magazine* (December).

———. 1968. Duke Ellington at Saint John the Divine . . . a sacred concert of jazz. *Music: The A.G.O. Magazine* (March).

Yoell, John H. 1974. *The Nordic Sound: Explorations into the Music of Denmark, Norway, Sweden.* Boston: Crescendo Publishing.

Young, Percy M. 1964. *Zoltán Kodály: A Hungarian Musician.* London: Ernest Benn.

———. 1971. *The Choral Tradition.* New York: W. W. Norton.

———. 1995. *Elgar, Newman, and* The Dream of Gerontius. London: Ashgate.

Zakanyi, Emoke. 1987. The Hungarian National Chorus. *Hungarian Music News* (1).

Zemanová, Mirka. 1989. *Janáček's Uncollected Essays on Music.* London: Marion Boyars Publishers.

Zouhar, Zdenek. 1995. Bohuslav Martinů—choral composer. *Czech Music* 4.

INDEX